The Athenian Adonia in Context

Publication of this volume has been made possible, in part, through the generous support and enduring vision of Warren G. Moon.

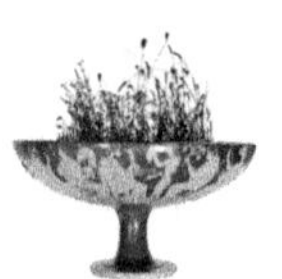

The Athenian Adonia in Context

The Adonis Festival as Cultural Practice

Laurialan Reitzammer

The University of Wisconsin Press

The University of Wisconsin Press
1930 Monroe Street, 3rd Floor
Madison, Wisconsin 53711-2059
uwpress.wisc.edu

3 Henrietta Street, Covent Garden
London WC2E 8LU, United Kingdom
eurospanbookstore.com

Printed in the United States of America

This book may be available in a digital edition

Library of Congress Cataloging-in-Publication Data

Names: Reitzammer, Laurialan, author.
Title: The Athenian Adonia in context: the Adonis festival as cultural practice / Laurialan Reitzammer.
Other titles: Wisconsin studies in classics.
Description: Madison, Wisconsin: The University of Wisconsin Press, [2016] | ©2016 | Series: Wisconsin studies in classics
Identifiers: LCCN 2015036817 | ISBN 9780299308209 (cloth: alk. paper)
Subjects: LCSH: Adonis (Greek deity)—Prayers and devotions. | Festivals—Greece—Athens. | Rites and ceremonies—Greece—Athens. | Athens (Greece)—Social life and customs.
Classification: LCC DF289 .R45 2016 | DDC 292.1/36—dc23
LC record available at http://lccn.loc.gov/2015036817

ISBN 9780299308247 (pbk.: alk. paper)

For
JOHN

Contents

Acknowledgments

I owe a tremendous debt to many friends and colleagues for support provided during the process of writing this book. In the early stages of this project I received honest criticism and guidance from Margaret Conkey, Mark Griffith, Donald Mastronarde, and especially Leslie Kurke, who has always provided me with a sense of direction at crucial moments.

Without the emotional as well as intellectual support of the "Lunch Circle" on the steps of Doe Library, this project would never have gotten off the ground. A number of people read drafts of all or part of the book, and to them I owe much gratitude: David Crane, Curtis Dozier, Gloria Ferrari Pinney, Jessica Gelber, David Jacobson, Deborah Kamen, John Oakley, Dimitri Nakassis, Ellen Oliensis, Kathryn Topper, and Elizabeth Young. My colleagues at the University of Colorado, Boulder have provided a welcoming and stimulating environment in which to work, and I am grateful especially to those who read chapters: Elspeth Dusinberre, Peter Hunt, and Sarah James. Special thanks are due to John Gibert, who read the entire work and saved me from many potentially embarrassing errors. My students in Boulder have continuously engaged me with many issues related to this book, and I thank, in particular, Sidney Christman, Elizabeth Deacon, Tyler Denton, James Faulkner, and Florencia Foxley, along with the entire Greek Mythology and Religion seminar of fall 2013. Laurie Glover, Sarah Olsen, and Milly Powell provided much needed help near the end of the project. I also thank Bernard Frischer, Robert Gurval, Michael Haslam, Kathryn Morgan, and Sarah Morris for getting me started in the field of classics.

Chapter 3 benefited from two anonymous *Classical Antiquity* reviewers, as well as audiences at Wellesley College and the 2005 meeting of the American Philological Association in Boston. Chapters 2 and 4 were improved thanks to audiences at the 2008 meeting of the American Philological Association in Chicago and at the University of Pennsylvania. A Loeb Classical Library Fellowship during fall of 2012 allowed me to work uninterrupted on the book. I am also grateful to the anonymous referees as well as the staff at the University of Wisconsin Press. Publication of this volume has been made possible, in part, through a Kayden Grant and a grant from the Center for the Humanities and the Arts from the University of Colorado, Boulder.

I owe a great deal to my family, in particular, my brother, Blake Reitzammer, and my aunt and uncle, Laura Powell and Bill Lewis. I thank my uncle, Alan Powell, for traveling through Greece with me, literally and metaphorically. My parents, John and Elizabeth Reitzammer, have provided tremendous support in every way possible during this journey. Finally, and most especially, I would like to express deep gratitude to John Ranucci, who along with our son, Lucas Ranucci, brings me great joy. This book is dedicated to him.

Abbreviations, Editions, and References

Addenda^{2}	T. H. Carpenter, T. Mannack, and M. Mendonça, eds. 1989. *Beazley Addenda.* 2nd edition. Oxford.
ARV^{2}	J. D. Beazley. 1963. *Attic Red-Figure Vase-Painters.* 2nd edition. Oxford.
BAD	Beazley Archive Database.
CPG	E. L. von Leutsch and F. G. Schneidewin, eds. 1958. *Corpus Paroemiographorum Graecorum.* Hildesheim.
CVA	*Corpus Vasorum Antiquorum.*
D-K	H. Diels and W. Kranz, eds. 1951–52. *Die Fragmente der Vorsokratiker.* 6th edition. Zurich.
FGrH	F. Jacoby. 1923–58. *Die Fragmente der griechischen Historiker.* Leiden.
FHG	K. Müller. 1841–70. *Fragmenta historicorum Graecorum.* Paris.
GP	A. S. F. Gow and D. L. Page, eds. 1965. *The Greek Anthology: Hellenistic Epigrams.* Cambridge.
IG	*Inscriptiones graecae.* 1873–. Berlin.
LIMC	*Lexicon iconographicum mythologiae classicae.* 1981–97. Zurich.
Merkelbach-West	R. Merkelbach and M. L. West, eds. 1967. *Fragmenta Hesiodea.* Oxford.
Paralipomena	J. D. Beazley. 1971. *Paralipomena: Additions to Attic Black-Figure Vase-Painters and to Attic Red-Figure Vase-Painters.* 2nd edition. Oxford.
PCG	R. Kassel and C. Austin, eds. 1983–. *Poetae Comici Graeci.* Berlin and New York.
PMG	D. L. Page, ed. 1962. *Poetae Melici Graeci.* Oxford.
P. Oxy.	*The Oxyrhynchus Papyri*, a series published under different editors.
SEG	*Supplementum epigraphicum Graecum.* 1923–. Amsterdam.
SIG^{3}	W. Dittenberger. 1915–24. *Sylloge Inscriptionum Graecarum.* Leipzig.
TrGF	B. Snell, R. Kannicht, and S. Radt, eds. *Tragicorum Graecorum fragmenta.* 1971–2004. Berlin.

Voigt E.-M. Voigt, ed. 1971. *Sappho et Alcaeus*. Amsterdam.

West M. L. West, ed. 1989–92. *Iambi et elegi Graeci ante Alexandrum cantati*. Oxford.

Abbreviations of journal titles are those used in *L'Année philologique*. All translations are my own unless otherwise noted.

Most proper names are in Latinized forms (e.g., Sophocles instead of Sophokles), but there are some exceptions when the Latinized form stood out to me as odd. When discussing Greek words, I prefer a direct transliteration and include long marks (e.g., *dêmos, Adôniazousai*; I do not, however, write Adônis). It has been impossible to maintain complete consistency.

Unless otherwise indicated, ancient authors are cited from the most recent Oxford Classical Text (OCT) series, or, where unavailable, from the most recent Teubner edition.

The Athenian Adonia in Context

Introduction

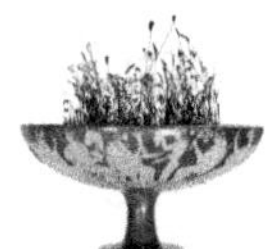

The citizen women of Classical Athens, while barred from the assembly and the council and unable to serve on juries in the law courts—the primary institutions of Athenian democracy—nevertheless had a place in the *polis*.[1] In their capacity as performers of ritual activity, their role was decidedly public and civic. Women participated in the workings of the *polis* as cultic agents, serving as priestesses, dedicators of statues, mourners at funerals, and basket bearers at important festivals. Women also took part in a number of female ritual activities, of which the Thesmophoria, in honor of Demeter and Korê (Persephone), is perhaps the best known. Classical Athenian women also engaged in a particularly audible and visible public performance when they participated in the Adonia, or Adonis festival, a ritual that featured lamentation on rooftops.

Once a year, to commemorate the death of Adonis, beloved of Aphrodite, Athenian women cultivated plants grown in pottery vessels, gardens of Adonis (Ἀδώνιδος κῆποι). They carried the gardens up to rooftops, where they then mourned the youth. The Adonia is often represented, both in our ancient sources and by modern scholars, as a marginal, private, exotic, even faintly ridiculous festival. By contrast, this book argues that the Classical Athenian Adonia is intimately bound up with such culturally and politically central events as the wedding (chapter 2), the civic funeral oration (chapter 3), and the creation of philosophy at Athens (chapter 4).

This is a book about the Classical Athenian Adonis festival, but it does not take a traditional approach to the study of this ancient cult. Typically, a study of an ancient Greek cult begins by extracting and collecting all the evidence for the cult and then proposing a reconstruction on that basis. In the case of the Adonia, several lines from Aristophanes's *Lysistrata* and Plato's *Phaedrus* can be discussed alongside a few fragments of Sappho, Theocritus's *Idyll* 15, Bion's *Epitaph on Adonis*, and remains from material culture—several inscriptions, a Hellenistic terracotta figurine, and a handful of Classical Athenian vase paintings. This dossier provides the basis for some widely diffused assumptions about the Adonia—for example (to take one of the most significant and enduring), the assumption that it is a private women's ritual with no substantive effect on the Athenian *polis*.[2] Yet this assumption, based as it is on decontextualized bits of information, is at best problematic. The crucial piece of evidence for the private, apolitical nature of the Adonia comes from the hostile "Official" in Aristophanes's *Lysistrata* (387–98). But surely the Official, a character who is an object of mockery within the comedy, does not grant us unmediated access to the Adonia. The fundamental methodological tenet of this book is that we have to read the surviving evidence about the Adonia *in context* in order to attain a more accurate and more complete view of how the festival functions both within its text and, more broadly, within Athenian culture. It is only by paying attention to the larger contexts (textual, visual, cultural) in which the evidence appears that we can gain access to the textured commentary (often counter-ideological) that this supposedly "peripheral" festival offers on mainstream practices.

The wresting of Adonis's myth and cult from their literary and performance context and artistic tradition has a long history. Apollodorus, who likely wrote during the first or second century CE, and who provides a narrative of the myth of Adonis, is an early representative of just such a habit. Apollodorus wrote a compendium of stories reduced to their skeletal elements. Although he attributes his narrative about Adonis to Panyassis of Halicarnassus (fr. 27 Bernabé), a fifth-century BCE epic poet and a near contemporary and relative of Herodotus, it is impossible to know how the epic poet made use of the myth since the mythographer has reworked and reduced Panyassis's verses to plot summary, and Apollodorus may have added details from other sources.[3]

In Apollodorus's account, Adonis was the son of Theias, king of Assyria, and his daughter Smyrna (*Bibl.* 3.14.4).[4] Smyrna developed an incestuous desire for her father, Theias, and, with the help of her nurse, managed to trick him into sleeping with her for twelve nights. When Theias was made aware of the incest, he came after Smyrna with his sword. She prayed to be made invisible, the gods took pity on her, and she metamorphosed into a smyrna (myrrh) tree.[5] Ten months later, Adonis was born from the tree. Aphrodite placed him in a chest and entrusted him to Persephone; Persephone took one look at him and refused to give him back to Aphrodite. Zeus intervened, and ultimately it was decided that Adonis would spend one-third of the year with Persephone and two-thirds with Aphrodite. Later, Apollodorus concludes, Adonis was killed by a boar.

Apollodorus makes no mention of the Adonis festival, the ritual performed annually in honor of Aphrodite and Adonis. In the lengthiest account of the Adonia to survive, Theocritus's *Idyll* 15, the Hellenistic poet portrays two married women, Praxinoa and Gorgo, attending the festival in Alexandria at the palace of

Queen Arsinoë II, wife of Ptolemy II Philadelphus. At the crowded palace, the women gaze upon a tableau depicting Aphrodite and Adonis, as well as offerings to the youth that include silver vessels containing gardens of Adonis. A hymnist sings in honor of Adonis, and she emphasizes that the present day marks the union of Aphrodite and Adonis and ritual mourning will take place on the following day.

The myth of Adonis sketched by Apollodorus and the account of the Adonia offered by Theocritus seem clear enough, but when we turn elsewhere for information about the youth and his cult, we are confronted with conflicting data. As with nearly all mythical tales, we run into trouble as soon as we attempt to trace genealogy.[6] Adonis is the son of Theias of Assyria and Smyrna in Panyassis's account.[7] But Apollodorus also gives Adonis's parents as Kinyras and Metharme, daughter of Pygmalion, king of Cyprus (3.14.3).[8] Meanwhile, [Hesiod] has Adonis as the son of Phoenix and Alphesiboea (Merkelbach-West fr. 139).[9]

Other aspects of Adonis's tale prove similarly intractable because it is impossible to know precisely when narrative details came to be attached to the youth. According to some accounts, after Adonis meets his death gored by a boar, an anemone flower is produced from his blood (Nicander fr. 65 Schneider = Σ Theocr. 5.92e Wendel).[10] This aspect of the narrative may be traced all the way back to a Near Eastern prototype of Adonis (Adonis's Eastern connections will be discussed in chapter 1), though it is not until the Hellenistic period that the flower metamorphosis is attested.[11]

On the ritual level, too, one is hard pressed to give a clear description of what transpired at an Adonis festival. The evidence for Adonis and his cult stretches from the Archaic period through Roman times; the myth and/or festival are attested in such disparate locales as mainland Greece (Athens, Sikyon, Argos), Egypt (Alexandria), Phoenicia (Byblos), Cyprus, Lesbos (Mytilene), and Asia Minor (Antioch, Myrina). Just how different was the Classical Athenian Adonia from the Hellenistic Adonia performed at Alexandria under the Ptolemies? This is a challenging question to answer, since the festival no doubt served different purposes within the context of a democracy at Athens, where, as we shall see, it had no official state backing, and within that of the Ptolemies in Egypt, where the festival is presented as a royal spectacle put on by the queen herself.[12] Although Athenian evidence suggests that the ritual took place on the rooftops, no such ritual space is mentioned in Theocritus's poem.[13] Athenian evidence also indicates that the gardens were planted in *ostraka*, broken terracotta vessels (Theophrastus, *Hist. plant.* 6.7.3).[14] The jagged edges of such planters may be seen in Classical Athenian vase painting on a lekythos from Karlsruhe (fig. 5) as well as on an acorn lekythos from Athens (fig. 21).[15] By contrast, the silver containers for the gardens of Adonis at Arsinoë's Alexandrian palace described in *Idyll* 15 (113–14) are far more lavish than Athenian vessels of terracotta. The festival may have spanned more days in Classical Athens than in Hellenistic Alexandria: while the Athenian evidence suggests the festival lasted eight days (Plato, *Phaedrus* 276b, where Socrates reports that eight days are needed for the cultivation of gardens of Adonis), Theocritus seems to indicate a two-day ritual when the hymnist asserts that ritual mourning will take place on the next morning.[16]

Not only must we exercise caution when confronted with evidence separated by time and space, but we must also consider the *medium* through which information concerning the Adonia is conveyed. Theocritus's *Idyll* 15, for example, positions itself deceptively as a poem that offers a rare glimpse of the daily life of two women, and the poem is terribly persuasive in its realism.[17] After all, Alexandria was a real place, and Arsinoë and Ptolemy were actual rulers. Our lengthiest surviving account of the Adonia is, however, hardly a historical document. Theocritus is drawing on a long literary tradition as he produces a new poetic genre, and Praxinoa and Gorgo, the two married women attending the festival, share characteristics with the stereotyped women who populate fifth- and fourth-century Athenian comedy as well as Hellenistic mime.[18] When Gorgo first sees the tableau of Aphrodite and Adonis at the palace, she exclaims, "How fine and lovely they are!" (λεπτὰ καὶ ὡς χαρίεντα, 79), employing a phrase that evokes λεπτότης, the new style of poetry that the Alexandrian poets Philitas and Callimachus advocate.[19] Attention is drawn to the women's Sicilian origins when a stranger interrupts them and ridicules their broad Doric accent (87–88). Although our information about Theocritus is limited, it seems likely that he, too, was from Sicily.[20] Praxinoa and Gorgo, then, are figures for the poet himself, and as one scholar has remarked, "like Gorgo and Praxinoa, Theocritus is bringing his Syracusan dialect to court, and with it the Sicilian mime as well."[21] Inasmuch as the tableau of Aphrodite and Adonis is described in words that resonate with a contemporary poetic program (rather than words that simply reflect reality), and inasmuch as the two women are figures for Theocritus (rather than actual women), Theocritus's poem cannot be taken to offer a straightforward depiction of an Adonia. Instead, the poem offers a *representation* of the festival for its own purposes; elements correspond to the festival, to be sure, but attention must be paid to the interference that distorts or obstructs our view.

To make further progress in our study of the Adonia, we need a methodological innovation. The Adonia does a kind of work within art and literature—our only evidence for the cult. While past studies have focused on what the Adonia *was* across time and space, I investigate how the Adonia *worked* in Classical Athens. My methodological contribution is to examine entire texts to see how the Adonia operates in a given textual context. Subsequent chapters will offer close readings of the most significant of these contexts, iconographic (chapter 2) and literary (chapters 3 and 4). The task of the first chapter, by contrast, is to provide a preliminary description of the larger context within which these visual and literary representations do their work. To that end, in chapter 1 I engage the same tangle of evidence that is frequently assembled by scholars in a traditional project of reconstruction. But because my goal is to get at the meaning (not the reconstruction) of the festival, my presentation is selective, not exhaustive, and organized around themes that are important to my project.[22] The first chapter introduces important notions and themes connected with the Adonia while discussing mythic data and cultic realia, as well as previous scholarship on the festival. This tour of the information available about the Adonia is also meant to illustrate the need for a textually and contextually specific approach to representations of the festival.

As we shall see, the framing of the Adonia in modern discussions has had an impact on scholars' conclusions. At the beginning of the twentieth century, Sir James Frazer emphasized the similarities between Attis, Adonis, and Osiris—a comparative approach that ranged widely across time and space.[23] He argued that the Adonia was a celebration of a dying god who is resurrected. By contrast, Marcel Detienne's 1972 examination of the opposition between the Adonia and the Thesmophoria produced an Adonia characterized by *death*, not life.[24] By making the Adonis festival the object of a single investigation, and by insisting on viewing the information we receive about the ritual within its textual, social, and cultural context, I move beyond the opposing views of Frazer and Detienne, where the Adonia is seen as representing *either* fertility *or* death, to argue that Athenian women actively employ metaphors of death—which are also metaphors of marital union from the perspective of the bride—in culturally, politically, and socially productive ways.

This book joins with other scholarly work that takes note of the role of women's ritual within the *polis*. The advances in the study of Greek religion made by Robert Parker and Walter Burkert have influenced my thinking about ancient ritual in general, as have more specific treatments of female ritual practices (Barbara Goff's *Citizen Bacchae*; Susan Cole's *Landscapes, Gender, and Ritual Space*; Matthew Dillon's *Girls and Women in Classical Greek Religion*; Joan Breton Connelly's *Portrait of a Priestess*) and works on ancient lamentation (Margaret Alexiou's *The Ritual Lament in Greek Tradition*; Helene Foley's *Female Acts in Greek Tragedy*).[25] Not one of these authors, however, examines the Adonia in any sustained way.[26] Attention to context—medium (vase painting or literary text), genre (comedy or philosophical dialogue), as well as larger textual, social, and cultural context—results in an adjustment of our views of the Adonia. Although my reading is very different from previous scholarship on the Adonia, I am situated within the interpretive tradition represented by certain scholars who have previously written on the festival, such as Detienne and John Winkler, and I will discuss their approaches in more detail in chapter 1.[27] Close readings of individual literary works were of little interest to past scholars writing on the Adonia, however, and this book makes every effort to examine carefully the mention of the festival within the literary work as a whole to see how the Adonia is connected with more general themes. As will become clear, this book also views the Adonia within an Athenian funerary framework, and much of the advance in our understanding of the festival that this book aims to accomplish is made possible by emphasizing the degree to which the Adonia involves collective performance of lament.

Comprehensive accounts of Greek religion tend to be Panhellenic discussions of festivals.[28] Such an approach tends to isolate the festivals "from the broader life of the society in which they are performed. The festivals of the various Greek states, torn from their place of origins, float in a sea outside time and space, occupied only by other festivals."[29] This book historicizes the Adonis festival by paying close attention to genre, time, space, and, above all, the larger literary or iconographic context.[30] Yet although I ground my discussion in Classical Athens, I inevitably draw on evidence from other regions and historical periods. In general, I take neither a severe positivist position—that until a detail is clearly attested it does not exist within the culture—nor an extreme structuralist position, marshaling evidence from radically different time periods with abandon.

Almost the only nonfragmentary Classical Athenian literary texts that survive in which the Adonia is mentioned are Aristophanes's *Lysistrata* and Plato's *Phaedrus*.[31] This book looks carefully at these texts *as a whole* by means of close reading and literary analysis to see the ways in which the festival functions within the comedy and the dialogue respectively. Before addressing these two literary texts in chronological order (in chapters 3 and 4), in chapter 2 I offer an analysis of a late fifth-century vase, a lekythos in Karlsruhe (fig. 5), that scholars agree is a visual depiction of the Adonis festival. I situate the images that appear on the vase within the context of wedding iconography and connect the Karlsruhe lekythos with a handful of vases associated with the Adonis festival, as well as objects that depict a female figure on a ladder.

Just as we must read literature with attention to conventions and genre, so too must we read iconography while addressing the encoded nature of the visual material. Iconographic representations of the Adonis festival will not reflect the ritual in any simple way. In my approach to the imagery on the vases associated with the Adonis festival, I am influenced by Gloria Ferrari and others, who pay particular attention to the conventional nature of scenes on Athenian vases.[32] This approach to iconography represents a dramatic break from previous approaches to vase painting in which the images are seen as reflections of reality. Instead, imagery is seen as analogous to language. Such a linguistic reading emphasizes that cultural concepts, rather than mirror images of daily life, are conveyed through iconography. As one scholar has recently remarked: "The imagery is accordingly taken as a formal system, a code, whose elements have conventional values. Reading the vase is a process of decoding, requiring of the reader familiarity with the senses that the various elements of the image conventionally convey. The ancient reader had this familiarity naturally; the modern reader acquires it by tracking imagery in as broad a range of occurrences as possible and working out its functions in different contexts."[33]

A debate concerning a plate of grapes that appears on a fragment of an Athenian red-figure lebes gamikos in Paris (fig. 6) demonstrates the kinds of problems that arise when a scene is taken to depict daily life.[34] In 1909, F. Hauser identified the image as a depiction of the Adonia because of the appearance of a ladder that he suggested led to a roof. Since grapes were available in Greece only in autumn, Hauser concluded that the Adonis festival was performed in the fall.[35] Two years later, Arthur Darby Nock argued that in fact in Greece grapes were available most of the year, certainly until March.[36] Nock also disassociated the vase from the Adonis festival since, as he pointed out, no ancient evidence mentions grapes in connection with the ritual. In 1966, Nicole Weill brought the vase back into the Adonis festival fold and used it to support the claim that the festival was celebrated during the summer.[37] The grapes, she suggested, were an early variety such as were grown at Corinth. Finally, in 1984, Charles Edwards insisted that the vase was a depiction of a wedding scene rather than an Adonis festival.[38] This scholarly discussion concerning the grapes is an example of problems that ensue when scenes are taken to depict daily life. Even if the image represents an Adonis festival, the scene is far from a straightforward depiction of Classical Athenian reality; instead, the images are conventional and need to be read within the context of similar visual language.

To better understand the visual imagery on the Karlsruhe lekythos (fig. 5), in chapter 2 I connect the visual elements that appear on the vase with similar imagery on other vases and objects in order to work out the function of the imagery. I also introduce a mythical story pattern important for the book as a whole, that of goddesses and mortals, and trace its appearance in literature as well as the visual arts. As in other manifestations of the goddess/mortal story, within the myth of Aphrodite and Adonis conventional gender roles are inverted. I survey structurally similar stories (Eos and Tithonus, Selene and Endymion, Aphrodite and Phaon, Aphrodite and Anchises) in which a powerful divine female takes a mortal for her paramour. The story pattern tends to resolve in a particularly problematic way for the chosen youth, who is killed or experiences impotence (literal or figurative). I suggest that the story of the goddess who desires a mortal youth reworks the normative trajectory of the wedding. Whereas the typical marital union results in a symbolic death for the bride, as she moves far from home, "dying" with regard to her former life, the goddess/mortal union results in a kind of death—literal or metaphoric—for the mortal male who is figured as a "bride." The inverted nuptial elements that appear in literary representations of Aphrodite and Adonis recur in iconographic representations of the pair.

In chapter 3, I address the earlier of two texts from the Classical period that mention the Adonia: Aristophanes's *Lysistrata*. In Aristophanes's comedy, as noted, an unnamed "Official" mentions the Adonia in a disparaging and dismissive manner (387–98). I suggest that the Official's characterization of the festival is not atypical. By examining descriptions of foreign cults in other texts, I locate the Adonia within Classical Athenian religious topography right alongside other non-established rituals—rites for Sabazius, nonmainstream Dionysiac cult, and rituals involving ecstatic dance and *tympana* playing. Although these various "marginal" rites are distinct in the eyes of their practitioners, to hostile outsiders they all look the same, and they are similarly described.

A scholion on line 389 of *Lysistrata* mentions that the play had an alternative title: *Adôniazousai*, "Women at the Adonis Festival." Reading the play with this title in mind, I show that Lysistrata and her allies metaphorically hold an Adonis festival atop the Acropolis. The public space of the Acropolis becomes notionally a private rooftop, and Adonia-like activity proliferates: boars, Aphrodite, gardens of Adonis, and lamentation all play important roles. A festival usually regarded as marginal by modern scholars thus becomes symbolically central to the play, as the sex strike conducted by the women notionally engaged in the ritual halts the Peloponnesian War.

The Official describes a lone wife lamenting Adonis atop her roof on the eve of the Sicilian expedition. In retrospect, she appears to be rehearsing the lamentation that will occur if the Athenians sail to Sicily, predicting the death and destruction the military venture will bring about. Inasmuch as Adonis is implicitly likened to the young sons who would be sent off to war and who would, like Adonis, die young, the Adonia of yore described by the Official—as well as the metaphorical Adonia held by Lysistrata and her allies—appear to be in dialogue with the rhetoric of funeral oration (*epitaphios logos*) that appears within the framework of the state funeral. Just as the Adonia enacts the wedding to offer a dissident message, so too, I suggest, the festival critiques the ideological message conveyed through *epitaphios logos*. Thucydides explains that once a year in the Kerameikos, Athenians mourned their war dead with a state-sanctioned funeral oration. Across town and at a different time of year—in the midst of the fighting season, during the summer—participants in the Adonis festival lamented the death of young plants that, like the young soldiers, died prematurely, too young to bear fruit. I argue that within the context of Aristophanes's play, the Adonia offers a challenge to the rhetoric of the war-ethic-affirming funeral oration. For example, Pericles's striking metaphorical use of the term *eranos*, "contribution," to describe the value of the fallen Athenians (Thucydides 2.43.1), is paralleled in *Lysistrata* (651) when the women claim a right to speak on behalf of the *polis* because of their *eranos*, "contribution": they supply the city with men.

Leaving behind weddings and funerals, chapter 4 takes a look at Plato's *Phaedrus* and the practice of philosophy. Plato, a keen cultural critic and observer of Athenian ritual, deploys the Adonia for his own purposes. Recognizing that the Adonia has the capability to enact important rituals and offer dissident meanings, Plato uses the Adonia as a metaphor as he constructs the new genre of philosophy. When Socrates mentions cultivation of gardens of Adonis near the end of *Phaedrus* in a discussion on writing, he explains that one would only engage in such a practice "for the sake of play and of festivity" (παιδιᾶς τε καὶ ἑορτῆς χάριν, 276b). I argue that it is precisely the characteristics of *paidia* (play) and *heortê* (festival) that attach themselves to the figure of the philosopher in Plato's works; in other words, the language used to describe the Adonia in *Phaedrus* is connected with the much larger issue of philosophical practice and the opposition between the playful and the serious that runs through Plato's dialogues. In the end, I suggest that Socrates's exploitation of the metaphor of the Adonis festival is part of his more general tendency to manipulate religious language.

In *Phaedrus*, Socrates paradoxically plays the role of one who cultivates gardens of Adonis as he tends to young Phaedrus, who begins to take on the characteristics of a delicate plant. As Socrates and Phaedrus take their walk along the banks of the Ilissus, through an area known as Kêpoi, "The Gardens," Socrates explicitly aligns gardens of Adonis with writing, which is characterized as less serious than engagement with a living interlocutor. But just as the supposedly fruitless written *logos* does have the potential to bear fruit, *Phaedrus* unexpectedly insists that cultivation of short-lived gardens of Adonis may prove to be a productive undertaking. The playful gardening becomes, in the end, an appropriate metaphor for Plato to employ for the practice of philosophy at Athens.

Ultimately, although a practice appears peripheral, it may, nevertheless, engage central activities. As we will see, the Adonia offers a commentary on mainstream cultural practices—the wedding and the civic funeral oration. This book traces the strains and the difficulties in marking the opposition between public and private, serious and trivial, central and peripheral with regard to the Adonia.

1 Adonis and the Adonia

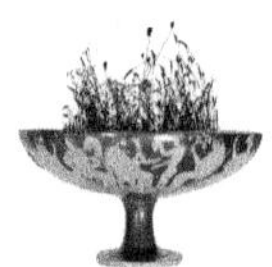

Trends in Representation, Ancient and Modern

There is scattered evidence for Adonis and his festival before the period and outside the place with which I am concerned, that is, fifth- and fourth-century Athens. Adonis is first attested in [Hesiod] (Merkelbach-West fr. 139), where he is the son of Phoenix and Alphesiboea. Although Adonis does not appear in Homeric epic, he seems to have furnished other epic poets with material. Panyassis of Halicarnassus made use of his story in a work now lost, as did Antimachus of Colophon, although both of these poets were also known as elegists, and the tale of Adonis may have appeared in Panyassis's *Ionika* or Antimachus's *Lyde*.[1] The archaic poet and seer Epimenides apparently mentioned Aphrodite's love for Adonis in a text that does not survive.[2]

That the youth was a concern in Sappho's poetry is clear from several fragments as well as attestations by later authors.[3] In fragment 140 (Voigt), a group of maidens (*korai*) report that Adonis is dead and ask Aphrodite what to do. She responds that they are to beat their breasts and rend their garments. This fragment emphasizes lament, making reference to the type of actions performed at funerals. Since the interaction between the chorus of *korai* and Aphrodite draws on the traditional call-and-response feature of lamentation, Sappho's fragment may have been intended for performance.[4] Additionally, two exclamations of woe over Adonis survive from Sappho's poetry (ὢ τὸν Ἀδώνιον, fr. 117B Voigt; ὢ τὸν Ἄδωνιν, fr. 168 Voigt). Here, the rare exclamatory accusative appears, a formula attested in ritual expressions of lament.[5] It is likely, then, that Sappho's fragments represent our earliest evidence for the cult of the Adonia.

But it is in fifth- and fourth-century Attic comedy that a sustained and vigorous, though quite evidently distorted, interest in Adonis and his ritual appears. Indeed, the bulk of our evidence for the Classical Athenian Adonia comes from this particular genre. Adonis appeared often enough in fifth- and fourth-century Athenian comedy that discussion developed years later over variants of his name (accusative Ἀδώνιον or Ἄδωνιν).[6] Although the works are no longer extant, a number of comic poets wrote plays with the title *Adonis*: Ararus, Antiphanes, Nicophon, Philiscus, and Plato.[7] As for the festival, it appears as a theme in a number of plays. Philippides wrote an *Adôniazousai* (*Women at the Adonis Festival*), and a scholion on line 389 of Aristophanes's *Lysistrata* suggests that the play may have been alternatively titled *Women at the Adonis Festival*, a detail that will be explored in chapter 3.[8]

Since my subject is the Adonia in Classical Athens, in what follows I isolate themes that appear in fifth- and fourth-century comedy, where we see a kind of explosion of interest in Adonis's myth and cult. In my thematic discussion, I draw on evidence from other times and periods, not to suggest unbroken continuity—the same Adonia repeated over hundreds of years—but to offer a holistic account of the youth and his cult to provide as full a picture as possible of what is known about the Adonia before embarking on a new approach in chapters 2, 3, and 4. I have selected five key topics: the marginalization of the cult; Adonis's death; gardens of Adonis and myrrh; lamentation, Aphrodite, and role-playing at the Adonia; and Adonis's Eastern origins. In what follows, I discuss the appearance of each theme both in ancient sources as well as in modern scholarship. All these themes reappear in subsequent chapters in various combinations. I mention iconographic evidence for Adonis and his cult in this chapter only in passing (to be discussed in detail in chapter 2).

That's Nothing Sacred!

One of the most important aspects of the representation of Adonis and his cult in Athenian comedy is a dismissive attitude.[9] Such an attitude is frequently smuggled into modern accounts of the Adonia. A speaker in a fragment of Cratinus from *Boukoloi* (*PCG* iv fr. 17) impugns the talent of Gnesippus, the son of Cleomachus, when the speaker exclaims that he would not deem the son of Cleomachus worthy to produce a choral performance for him, not even for the Adonia (ὃν οὐκ ἂν ἠξίουν ἐγὼ / ἐμοὶ διδάσκειν οὐδ' ἂν εἰς Ἀδώνια).[10] Although, as is often the case with comedy, it is a challenge to determine the precise nature of the joke (and I will return to this passage), the Adonia is clearly written off as an inferior, second-rate dramatic vehicle.[11] In Aristophanes's *Lysistrata* too, the Official belittles the Adonia as just one of a number of raucous foreign rituals destroying his *polis* (387–98). Such a view—ranging from benign disapproval to accusations of the ritual's harmful effects—becomes a topos with regard to the youth and his cult.

Similarly, the notion of foolishness and sterility is bound up with Adonis and the Adonia. Indeed, outside the genre of comedy, and slightly earlier, appears the proverb "sillier (ἠλιθιώτερος) than Praxilla's Adonis," which refers to the portrayal of Adonis in the poetry of the mid-fifth-century BCE Praxilla of Sikyon. In what remains of Praxilla's poem (fr. 1 Page = *PMG* 747), Adonis speaks, bemoaning the loss of the light of the sun and the moon, as well as "ripe cucumbers, apples, and pears." This statement led to the proverb being used of people without any sense (ἀνοήτων), "for someone who counts cucumbers and the rest with sun and moon is feeble minded" (εὐηθὴς γάρ τις ἴσως ὁ τῷ ἡλίῳ καὶ τῇ σελήνῃ τοὺς σικύους καὶ τὰ λοιπὰ συναριθμῶν).[12] Furthermore, although Adonis was marked by a special ability to return from the underworld each year to be with Aphrodite, he was certainly not strictly speaking divine, and Clearchus of Soloi, a near contemporary of Aristotle, reports that Heracles exclaimed, upon seeing an image of Adonis, "That's nothing sacred!" (οὐδὲν ἱερόν, fr. 66 Wehrli).[13] While Adonis was known for his questionable divinity and foolishness, gardens of Adonis (to be considered in detail below) were proverbial for sterility. "More fruitless than the gardens of Adonis" ran another proverb.[14] Beginning with Plato's *Phaedrus*, where Socrates opposes the cultivation of gardens of Adonis to proper farming that produces fruit (276b), an entire tradition associates the gardens with lack of productivity.[15]

This contemptuous view, which seems to originate in Attic comedy, is taken at face value by Marcel Detienne in the most recent book devoted to the Adonia, *Les jardins d'Adonis*, published in 1972 (translated in 1994 as *Gardens of Adonis*). Detienne's remains the most influential interpretation of the festival. In his discussion of the *Lysistrata* passage where the Official describes the Adonia in disdainful terms, Detienne explains that Aristophanes's account provides

> *a picture that was probably widely accepted by the Athenians* . . . a noisy festival of ill-repute in which the indecent behaviour of the women at their antics on the rooftops scandalises many citizens although the city does not allow the agitation of a handful of private individuals of the female sex who do not, after all, enjoy any political rights, to distract it from carrying on public life.[16]

Such a conception of the Adonis festival arises in large part from relying on the words of the Official as an accurate portrayal. Yet just as the Adonia is refracted through Theocritus's *Idyll* 15 (as discussed in the introduction), so too Athenian comedy, I suggest, offers a distorted version of the festival.

In 1990, John Winkler criticized Detienne's tendency to view the Adonia from the perspective of a male outsider to the festival, a perspective linked to Detienne's wholesale importation of the disparaging view of the Adonia from

Attic comedy.[17] Winkler attempted instead to consider the festival from the perspective of the participant. While Detienne had concluded that the festival underscored sterility and improper farming—the gardens of Adonis withered and died in the heat of the sun before producing any fruit—Winkler suggested that the festival's emphasis on improper farming was a joke on male sexuality. Far from viewing their own role as peripheral, the women involved in the Adonis festival emphasized the "marginal or subordinate role that men play in both agriculture (vis-à-vis the earth) and human generation (vis-à-vis wives and mothers)."[18] Yet, despite the critiques of Winkler and others, Detienne's general views on the Adonia have had staying power. Even current scholarship on the Adonia tends to ignore or dismiss the perspective of the women involved. For example, it has recently been suggested that in the cultivation of gardens of Adonis women "act out and thus confirm their inadequacies for an audience that implicitly comprises both themselves and their male-dominated polity."[19] In this book I heed Winkler's call to approach the Adonis festival from the perspective of the participants to suggest that the Adonia offered Athenian women an opportunity for public expression. In this light, it is no wonder that Classical Athenian comic responses to this festival tend to be negative. As we shall see, this is at least partly due to the festival's focus on lamentation, which makes it potentially troublesome within the Athenian *polis*.

Adonis's Double Experience of Death and the Trouble with Lettuce

Although Adonis is marked by a somewhat ambiguous relationship to mortality, nevertheless, his death is a major preoccupation of our sources in Athens and beyond.[20] Athenian comedy alludes to Adonis's double experience of death.[21] As we shall see, stories about Adonis's death are examples of etiological myth, myth that provides a reason (*aition*) for ritual performance.

In the myth first attested in Panyassis, by way of Apollodorus (*Bibl.* 3.14.4), Adonis dies twice—once in the underworld when possessed by Persephone, and also gored by a boar. The tale of the joint possession of the handsome youth by two powerful goddesses and Adonis's annual stay in the underworld became popular during the fifth century and held lasting appeal. After Panyassis, the first reference to the sharing of Adonis by two deities comes from Athenian comedy, in a fragment of Plato Comicus (*PCG* vii fr. 3).[22]

In a twist on Panyassis's narrative, a speaker explains that two divinities will lead to the youth's demise, not the goddesses Aphrodite and Persephone, but rather an unnamed female and *male* deity:

O Kinyras, king of the hairy-assed Cypriots,
Your child is by nature most beautiful and most marvelous
Of all humans, but two divinities will destroy him,
She being rowed by secret oars, and he rowing them. (fr. 3)[23]

The two divinities that will destroy the youth are modified by a passive and active participle (one "being rowed," ἐλαυνομένη, the other "rowing," ἐλαύνων) used in a sexual sense.[24] Athenaeus (*Deipn.* 456a–b) reports that the two divinities are none other than Aphrodite and Dionysus, who both desired Adonis, and the Hellenistic Phanocles (fr. 3 Powell) confirms that Dionysus is the male divinity to whom Plato Comicus alludes. The fragment highlights Adonis's ambiguous sexual status, as he is figured as both an active lover of a goddess and a passive beloved of a male god.[25]

While Plato alludes to Panyassis's narrative of the sharing of Adonis and his "death" in this way, a fragment of the comic poet Eubulus (*PCG* v fr. 13) refers obliquely to the alternative narrative concerning the death of Adonis involving the boar. This narrative, like others we will see shortly, involves lettuce: "Do not put lettuce (θριδακίνας) on the table for me, woman, or reproach yourself. For in this vegetable, the story goes, once Aphrodite laid Adonis, when he had died. So it came to be food for corpses." Here, a speaker from a play titled, significantly, *Astutoi* (*Impotent Men*) associates Adonis, corpses, and lettuce, explaining that he himself would prefer not to eat the vegetable. It seems that for the ancient Greeks, lettuce was associated with male sexual impotence, and Eubulus's joke turns on the pun for "dead" meaning "impotent" in Athenian comedy.[26]

Adonis appears elsewhere with lettuce as well.[27] While Eubulus does not explain what Adonis was doing in the lettuce, Nicander (second century BCE) reports that Adonis's fatal flight from the killer boar ended in lettuce (fr. 120 Schneider).[28] Callimachus (fr. 478 Pfeiffer, Athenaeus 2.69) explains that Aphrodite hid Adonis in lettuce, and apparently as early as Sappho, the story was told that Aphrodite placed Adonis in a bed of lettuce as he was dying, though this information comes late, by way of the fifteenth-century CE Comes Natalis (Test. 211c Voigt).[29]

It is impossible to know exactly when the boar detail became part of Adonis's story, but there is no reason to doubt that the myth was alive and well by the last quarter of the fifth century BCE. Not only does Eubulus in the early fourth century BCE likely refer to it, but so too does Euripides in the late fifth century.[30] At the end of Euripides's *Hippolytus* (1420–22), Artemis asserts that in revenge for the death of Hippolytus she will destroy the mortal beloved of Aphrodite with her arrows. Although Artemis mentions death by arrows instead of by boar, and Adonis is not explicitly named—Artemis uses an indefinite ὃς ἄν to refer to "whoever is especially dear" to Aphrodite (ὃς ἂν μάλιστα φίλτατος)—it is Artemis herself, according to Apollodorus (3.14.4), who sends the boar; and a scholion (1420) on the passage affirms that Artemis means Adonis.[31] Euripides certainly knew of and made use of Adonis's narrative and cult elsewhere, since gardens of Adonis are mentioned in one of his *Melanippe* plays (*TrGF* 5 fr. 514).

Adonis both dies (he is fatally gored by a boar) and does not die (he returns each year from his stay with Persephone in the underworld to be with Aphrodite). Modern scholarship has reconciled such mythical illogicality with difficulty. At the beginning of the twentieth century, Sir James Frazer argued that the Adonia functioned as a magic rite employed to promote the growth of crops.[32] Adonis was one of the dying and rising gods, like Osiris and Attis. In 1972, Marcel Detienne, by contrast, insisted that, far from a vegetation ritual emphasizing a dying god who was resurrected and returned to life, the main focus of the Adonis festival was on death. Detienne grounded his arguments in the contrasts between the Adonis festival and the Thesmophoria: structurally opposed to the Thesmophoria, which emphasized married women and procreation, the Adonia, according to Detienne, underscored seduction and sterility and was attended by courtesans. Yet Detienne's systematic opposition of the Thesmophoria to the Adonia resulted in some inaccurate claims, and a number of his assertions have since been discredited.[33] For example, scholars have taken issue with Detienne's insistence that courtesans were the sole attendees of the festival, noting that, while courtesans were likely involved in the festival, married women certainly took part as well. Aristophanes's *Lysistrata*, for example, has the wife of the Athenian citizen Demostratus mourning Adonis atop a roof (392, 395).[34]

Detienne's interpretation, however, offered a welcome corrective to the Frazerian dying/rising god and fertility ritual, a model that had ceased to explain the ancient evidence correctly.[35] Whereas Frazer had inadvertently imported Christian notions of a resurrection into his conception of Adonis as one of a number of dying and rising gods, Detienne's insistence that Adonis's *death*, not his life or resurrection, was the salient detail for the ancient Greeks remains a far more persuasive interpretation of the evidence.[36]

After all, the clearest passage to indicate that Adonis lives again after death comes from [Lucian]'s *de dea Syria* 6; yet it in no way refers to a resurrection in the Christian sense. [Lucian] is describing the Adonia that he witnessed at Byblos in the second century CE: "First they make offerings to Adonis as though to a corpse and on the next day they say that he lives and they send him to the air" (πρῶτα μὲν καταγίζουσι τῷ Ἀδώνιδι ὅκως ἐόντι νέκυϊ, μετὰ δὲ τῇ ἑτέρῃ ἡμέρῃ ζώειν τέ μιν μυθολογέουσι καὶ ἐς τὸν ἠέρα πέμπουσι). [Lucian]'s description, however, refers to the myth first attested in Panyassis in which Adonis "lives again" during his annual sojourn with Aphrodite.[37]

These stories about Adonis's death, as etiological myths, provide a reason (*aition*) for ritual performance. While an *aition* does not exist for every single ritual, etiological myth is an important subcategory within the larger category of myth.[38] To take just one example, a fragment of Pherecydes of Syros (fr. 68 Schibli) from his sixth-century BCE cosmogony describes the foundation legend for the ritual of the *anakalyptêria*.[39] During the Classical period, the ritual involved the unveiling of the bride, indicating her submission to her husband and her introduction into his house.[40] Pherecydes's fragment indicates that the *anakalyptêria* originated with the marriage of Zas and Kthonie and that this mythical marriage informs marriage in his own day, when he reports that "from this, the custom arose for both gods and humans" (ἐκ τούτου δ[ὲ] ὁ νόμος ἐγένε[το] καὶ θεοῖσι καὶ ἀνθρ[ώπ]οισιν). Also, as is well known, Euripides frequently ends his plays with an etiology for a cult.[41] The plays insist on the notion that a ritual is performed because of past mythical events. *Hippolytus*, for example, concludes with an explanation by Artemis that in Troezen brides will cut their hair on the eve of their wedding in honor of Hippolytus (1425–27).[42]

Ritual participants, then, may perform an action in the present because of past actions of mythical figures. Such a formulation provides an understanding of *one kind of relationship* between myth and ritual, and such a formulation describes the relationship between myth and ritual in the case of the Adonia.[43] In the Eubulus fragment discussed above, Aphrodite "laid Adonis out" (προὔθηκεν) in lettuce when he had died. The verb προὔθηκεν evokes the *prothesis*, the "laying out," an important part of the ancient Greek funeral that resembled the modern wake. Taken together, the passages that associate Adonis with lettuce suggest an etiology for the gardens of Adonis employed in the rite.[44] That is, Classical Athenian women cultivate gardens of Adonis at the Adonia, and this ritual action relates to stories told about the youth who was laid out for burial in lettuce.[45]

Gardens of Adonis and Myrrh

Evidence for gardens of Adonis comes from Classical Athenian comedy, which indicates that Athenian women carried the plants up to rooftops, where they lamented the death of Adonis. Aristophanes's *Lysistrata* has a married woman lamenting the death of Adonis on a roof, and Menander's *Samia* describes a boisterous all-night Adonia on the rooftops that included gardens of Adonis (45).[46] Information on the contents of gardens of Adonis comes late, but as we might expect they contained lettuce, as well as wheat, barley, and fennel.[47] In some descriptions of the Adonia, such as Plutarch's *Life of Nicias* (13.7) and *Life of Alcibiades* (18.3), women employ small images (εἴδωλα) of the youth in the ritual.[48]

It has been suggested that women placed the εἴδωλα in the gardens while the plants were still alive (it is not entirely clear *when* during the ritual the plants died, nor is it clear what causes their death, as will be discussed later), and that the gardens were used as funeral biers.[49] There is no fifth- or fourth-century Athenian evidence for the effigies nor for their placement in the gardens. Gardens alone sufficed as markers of the Adonis festival in Classical Athenian written and visual representations of the festival, and they sufficed, I suggest, because the gardens themselves, containing tender shoots that burgeon with life briefly but produce no fruit, represented Adonis.[50]

After all, it is well known that humans are described in agricultural terms in Greek literary texts, where a child is a young shoot (ἔρνος or θαλλός), the generations of humans are as leaves on trees, and a woman is a field to be plowed for the sowing of legitimate offspring.[51] Adonis himself is called "shoot" (ἔρνος) in a Hellenistic poem by Dioscorides (GP 1565–74 = *AP* 7.407). The poem's persona wonders where Sappho might be found and suggests she might appear "as mourner along with Aphrodite who laments the young shoot of Kinyras" (Κινύρεω νέον ἔρνος ὀδυρομένη Ἀφροδίτῃ/ σύνθρηνος, GP 1571). Here Aphrodite's lament for the youth blends into a lament for the tender plants in a garden of Adonis.[52] The Hellenistic poet Glycon also calls Adonis a "shoot" (Κύπριδος θάλος, *PMG* Adesp. 1029).[53] These texts thus mark a correlation between the plants cultivated in the gardens and the youth Adonis.[54]

It is highly likely that in ritual, too, the plants cultivated in the gardens of Adonis were thought to represent the youth—and so too myrrh. In stories told about Adonis, he is the fruit of the myrrh tree, born from Smyrna/Myrrha, whose name signifies "perfume" or "incense."[55] Adonis is metaphorically identified with myrrh in Bion's *Epitaph on Adonis* as the speaker exclaims, "Let all myrrh perish; Adonis, your myrrh, has perished," 78.[56] Material remains provide evidence for the use of myrrh in the Adonia. The gardens and myrrh are combined in a Hellenistic terracotta figurine (fig. 23) that depicts a young woman pouring a substance from an alabastron into a garden of Adonis.[57] Given that alabastra contained perfumed oils, she may be understood to be pouring myrrh into a garden of Adonis. A similar combination of gardens of Adonis and a poured substance appears on an acorn lekythos from Athens (fig. 21), where a female figure pours a liquid, likely myrrh, into her palm as she cultivates a garden of Adonis.[58] While stories about Adonis emphasize his death, the commemoration of his death in ritual includes multiple objects—gardens, as well as myrrh—that serve as stand-ins for the dead youth.[59]

In mythical accounts, the beautiful youth is shuttled between the underworld—where he spends part of the year with Persephone—and the heavens for his time with Aphrodite. So too, I suggest, at the Adonia women carry the ritual objects—the gardens and myrrh that represent the youth—up to the rooftops. Such a formulation represents a break from traditional interpretations of the transfer to the rooftops of the gardens of Adonis, since it is frequently said that women moved the gardens there so that the *Adônidos kêpoi* might wither in the heat of the sun during the summer.[60] Yet, although as we shall see there is evidence to suggest that the Adonia was performed during the summer, it is not clear how or when the gardens of Adonis died during the ritual, and it seems instead that the movement of the ritual objects (from low to high) relates to the movement between spheres (from the underworld to the heavens) described in myth.

The Season of the Adonia

There are good reasons to believe that the Classical Athenian Adonia was performed in the summer.[61] Indeed, both Plato (*Phaedrus* 276b) and Theophrastus (*Hist. plant.* 6.7.3) report that gardens of Adonis were grown "in summer" (θέρους). It is possible that Plato is employing *theros* in a loose sense, as, for example, Thucydides does when he uses *theros* to refer to the time of year that is suitable for military expeditions; in such cases the word may encompass our spring, summer, and fall.[62] Theophrastus, however, uses precise terms for the four seasons.[63] Because Adonis was imagined to be the fruit of the myrrh tree, and because myrrh is used in the ritual, the fact that myrrh is harvested during the Dog Days, according to Theophrastus (*Hist. plant.* 9.1.6), may have some bearing on the season in which it was performed. Later tradition and tradition outside Greece certainly associates the Adonis festival with summer.[64]

But while most of the evidence connects the Adonia with summer, a passage of Aristophanes about deliberations over the Sicilian expedition has suggested to some that the Adonia took place during the spring.[65] This controversy is worth considering because it underscores once again the need for attention to the medium through which the information about the Adonia is conveyed.

Thucydides indicates that the Sicilian expedition was discussed during the spring of 415 BCE. He mentions two meetings of the assembly. At the first (6.8.1–2), it was decided to send sixty ships to Sicily with Alcibiades, Nicias, and Lamachus in command. Thucydides places the famous speeches of Nicias and Alcibiades at the second meeting (6.8.3–26), held on the fifth day after the first meeting. According to Thucydides, the fleet set out during the summer (θέρους μεσοῦντος ἤδη, 6.30.1). In Plutarch's *Life of Nicias* 13.7 and *Life of Alcibiades* 18.3, the fleet ominously departs at the time of the Adonis festival, and the wailing of women fills the streets. Plutarch's description, then, accords with the other evidence for a summer date for the Adonia. Aristophanes's *Lysistrata*, however, portrays an

Adonia taking place at the time of a debate in the assembly (387–98), a debate that, as far as we can tell from Thucydides, seems to have occurred during the spring.[66]

Yet the Aristophanes passage is not meant to be a reference to the exact date of the Adonia. The comedy's audience—focusing on the dramatic exchange between Demostratus and his wife and its relevance within the context of the play—would not be in such a chronologically precise frame of mind that it would object that the Adonia actually took place after the assemblies but before the expedition set off. Aristophanes has collapsed time and events for an audience all too familiar with the disastrous undertaking in order to stress the antiphonal exchange between Demostratus and his wife. Demostratus's wife sings, "Alas for Adonis!" (αἰαῖ Ἄδωνιν, 393) and "Beat your breast for Adonis!" (κόπτεσθ' Ἄδωνιν, 396) in response to her husband's call to "Sail to Sicily!" (392) and "Levy Zakynthian troops!" (394). It is the foreboding nature of the mourning in connection with discussions about the failed military venture that is emphasized. In 411, when *Lysistrata* was performed, the audience knew in hindsight that the women lamenting Adonis on the eve of the Sicilian expedition were correct. The astute predictions of the women have implications for *Lysistrata*, since in the play the women attempt to stop the Peloponnesian War.[67]

The Death of the Plants

It is likely, then, that the Classical Athenian Adonia was performed during the summer. It is frequently claimed that the gardens died from exposure to the sun, since the ritual was performed during the hottest season. Yet while one searches in vain for an explicit assertion that the sun caused the death of the young shoots, there are some indications that the gardens died because they never took root properly.[68] Although his testimony is late, [Diogenianos] 1.14 (*CPG* 1.183) supports this notion clearly, when he remarks that gardens of Adonis "concern things untimely and not rooted. For since Adonis, the beloved of Aphrodite, as the story goes, died before he reached manhood, those who celebrated this—men and women—sowed gardens in vessels, and when the plants quickly withered because they had not taken root, they used to call them Adonis's [gardens]."[69] Here, it is worth emphasizing the correlation between the youth and the plants again, as Adonis dies before he reaches manhood just as the plants quickly wither.[70]

Plutarch also seems to stress the rootlessness of the gardens in a passage in which claims are made for the immortality of the soul (*de sera numinis vindicta* 560b–c).[71] Women who cultivate gardens of Adonis are likened to a hypothetical, "petty and frivolous" (μικρός . . . καὶ κενόσπουδος) divinity. In contrast to a serious divinity, who carefully implants divine souls in us, this hypothetical divinity is so unthinking as to put something he cares so much about in a bad vessel (i.e., bodies that cannot sustain life). Ephemeral souls in delicate flesh are likened to tender shoots that women who cultivate gardens of Adonis grow in *ostraka*. Plant imagery blends into a description of a human, as the flesh, like the shoots in a garden of Adonis, does not receive the "strong root of life" (βίου ῥίζαν ἰσχυράν).[72]

As we have seen, Frazer argued that the Adonia was a fertility ritual; in his view, gardens of Adonis represented Adonis and functioned as a magic ritual to promote crops. Detienne also argued for an equivalence between the gardens and the youth, but for him gardens of Adonis represented an anti-agricultural rite. Like Frazer and Detienne, I too suggest that the plants in the gardens represent Adonis, but not for Frazer's or Detienne's reasons. Instead, as I argue below, the plants represent Adonis *to be lamented*, since the women carry them up to the rooftops, where they play the role of the goddess Aphrodite, who laments the death of Adonis.

Lamentation, Aphrodite, and Role-Playing at the Adonia

A prominent feature of the Adonis festival was the lament for Adonis, and fifth- and fourth-century comedy emphasizes this component of the ritual. In Aristophanes's *Lysistrata* (387–98), the exchange between Demostratus and his wife includes call-and-response elements familiar to *thrênos*, "ritual lamentation," as Demostratus's wife wails "*aiai*" in response to her husband's demands for troops. *Thrênos* appears in connection with the Adonia outside Athenian comedy as well. The word appears in Plutarch's *Life of Alcibiades* (18.2–3) and *Life of Nicias* (13.7). Plutarch's *Alcibiades* explains that just before the fleet set sail for Sicily, an Adonia was held and women "were imitating a funeral, beating their breasts and they were singing *thrênoi*" (καὶ ταφὰς ἐμιμοῦντο κοπτόμεναι καὶ θρήνους ᾖδον, 18.3).[73] Sappho's fragment (fr. 140 Voigt) too features an amoebaean exchange between Aphrodite and a group of maidens. Choral lament elements predominate during the Hellenistic period as well. In Bion's *Epitaph on Adonis,* the Erotes, the Moirai, and the poem's narrator mourn the youth. While lamentation does not appear in Theocritus *Idyll* 15 (instead, the poem represents the union of Aphrodite and Adonis), the importance of mourning is emphasized when the hymnist explains that tomorrow Adonis will be lamented (132–35). This book argues that this emphasis on ritual lamentation at the Adonia is crucial to an answer to the question, "Why did women carry out the Adonia year after year?"

Scholars have expended a great deal of effort in the past fifty years grappling with questions about how ritual functions within a given culture and—more specifically within the field of classics—how ritual functions in ancient Greece.[74]

Does ritual provide a contrast to social life, offering opportunities to resist cultural norms? Or do ritual activities, rather, run parallel to social life, reinforcing constraints? Classicists in particular have tended to focus on the latter, on the community-building aspects of ritual.[75] Yet while ritual may act as a force of cohesion in society, it may also contain active and dynamic elements.[76]

When contesting, conflicting interests exist within a culture, as they certainly did in Classical Athens, ritual has the potential to become a means of resistance. Recently it has been suggested that "when gathered together for specific cult celebrations, particularly those that convene only women and exclude men, women may be plausibly seen as invited to think of themselves as a particular subculture. . . . Even while ritual may confirm the constraints on women's lives, then, it may also offer the most likely arena for the development of a dissident stance."[77] The Adonia is a particularly useful place to look for "dissident" messages, inasmuch as the performance of the festival places women in a central position in the *polis*, at the intersection between the public and the private—on the rooftops of homes, a place where they are still at home but can be seen and heard.[78]

The evidence for the Adonia overwhelmingly indicates that it was a women's festival and that married women as well as courtesans attended.[79] Although two inscriptions from Piraeus (discussed below) indicate male involvement, the inscriptions refer to a separate Adonis festival at Athens celebrated by Phoenicians and have little to do with the Adonia celebrated by Athenian women.[80] The Athenian Adonia, I suggest, offers a unique means of public female self-expression. Yet the public aspects of the Adonia have tended to be ignored because the festival has been consistently characterized as a private cult.

In past scholarship on Greek religion more generally, the public/private distinction was vastly overdrawn, and recent scholarship has insisted on the untenability of such a rigid distinction.[81] The Adonia in particular held a paradoxical position at Athens. Unlike regularly scheduled festivals with state backing, the Athenian Adonia had no month on the calendar devoted to it.[82] No Athenian temple to Adonis survives, since the ritual took place on the rooftops of homes.[83] Nevertheless, it was recognized alongside state festivals, even though aspects of its funding and scheduling justify labeling it an informal cult.[84] In Aristophanes's *Peace*, for example, the Athenians so desire to end the war that they are prepared to offer Hermes rites normally offered to other gods. The Mysteries, the Dipolieia, and the Adonia are to be held in honor of Hermes (418–20). The fact that the Adonis festival is juxtaposed with important cults of Demeter and Zeus, respectively, suggests that the ritual was a well-known component of the religious landscape even if the mention of the Adonia in connection with these other festivals is intended to be humorous.[85]

The failure to recognize the public role of the Adonia stems, in part, from the association of the cult with women, as well as the ambiguous status of the cult at Athens—Adonis is from the East and the Adonia is a foreign cult (to be discussed later). Yet the civic nature of lament also tends to be disregarded. Despite scholarly work emphasizing that lamentation was one of the few means of public self-expression open to ancient Greek women, little note has been paid to the public aspect of mourning at the Adonia.[86]

The Adonia imitates a funeral for Adonis, and as we have seen, the ritual action relates to stories told about a youth who was laid out for burial in lettuce. While we tend to think of funerals as private events, especially in the United States, where funerals usually do not have political force, funeral lamentation played such an important and troubling role within the Athenian *polis* that Plato felt the need to deal with it in his "political" dialogues, *Laws* and *Republic*.[87] Evidence from various parts of the Greek world from the sixth through the fourth centuries BCE indicates that legislation was passed to modify funerary practices, and in particular, it seems that attempts were made to restrict the roles of Attic women within the context of funerals.[88] Representations of funerals in Homer and on vase paintings suggest that archaic funerals included grandiose displays of wealth. Women's lamentation played a prominent role at the wake (*prothesis*), the procession to the grave site (*ekphora*), as well as the ceremony at the grave site. By contrast, in the early sixth century, laws attributed to Solon prohibited disorderly and excessive elements in women's festivals and funeral rites (Plutarch, *Solon* 21.4).[89] Although certainly the laws speak to a desire to curb aristocratic excess, they seem to have been aimed primarily at women.[90] After the legislation, the *prothesis* was to take place indoors (or in a courtyard), and it was to last only one day;[91] the *ekphora* was to occur before dawn and in silence. Hired mourners would not be permitted.[92] It has been suggested that "because the state did not extensively interfere with family life except where its own interests were at stake . . . we can assume that funerals were potentially a serious challenge to civic harmony."[93]

Although actual laments from funerals do not survive, our knowledge of the practice has been advanced through examinations of representations of lament, for example, in epic and tragedy.[94] Helene Foley has investigated the role of lamentation on the tragic stage to argue that mourning may be used as a force of resistance. Euripides's *Helen* showcases Helen herself hatching a plot to manipulate funeral ritual to escape the clutches of King Theoclymenus; she pretends to mourn Menelaus and manages to flee in the boat provided for her feigned funeral practices.[95] And in other tragedies, a character may express a form of political or social resistance by means of lamentation. In Aeschylus's *Libation Bearers*, the female chorus of slaves emphasizes its opposition to those in authority by means of its lamentations.[96] Foley concludes: "Funerals—especially at periods of social crisis—were very likely to be events at which tensions between public and private interests and emotions emerged in a particularly volatile form. I believe we can see political (and by political I mean issues relating to the *polis*) and social tensions of precisely this sort emerging in the way that death ritual and lamentation are represented on the tragic stage."[97]

Mourning, then, may have functioned as a means of resistance both on and off the tragic stage, and the Adonia, as an imitation of a funeral for Adonis, included *thrênos*. Lack of attention to the effects of the Adonia on the *polis* stems in part from a disregard for the importance of lament as a site for collective female resistance. But the Adonia was in honor of Aphrodite as well as Adonis;[98] and our vision of the Adonia as merely a private festival also arises from a flawed conception of Aphrodite, a goddess who has been consistently described in scholarship as the goddess of love and beauty.[99] Recent work, however, has underscored Aphrodite's civic import, highlighting, for example, connections between Aphrodite and warfare, as well as Aphrodite's place in the maritime sphere, and more specifically her links with the Athenian fleet. At Athens, Aphrodite was worshipped as Ourania, "Heavenly," as well as Pandêmos, "of all the people," and *en kêpois*, "in the gardens."[100] While it is not the scope of this project to provide a complete account of Classical Athenian Aphrodite, attention to the political import of cults of Aphrodite informs my approach to the Adonia.

A number of scholars have remarked in passing that women at the Adonia play the role of Aphrodite as they mourn Adonis, and indeed, implicit in the above discussion of etiological myth is the notion that ritual performers could identify with original actors as they carried out cult activities.[101] I would like to expand on this notion of participant identification at the Adonis festival. First, the performance of women at the Adonia should be seen within the larger context of recent scholarship concerning women as cultic agents.[102] Joan Breton Connelly, for example, has emphasized the performance of women in the public arena, specifically with regard to their position as priestesses.[103] Insofar as priestesses performed cult activities, they were seen as actors in the Athenian *polis* holding influential positions, a very different view from that of the passive and sequestered citizen wife. Of course, as we have seen, the Adonia was not a state-sanctioned cult, and no evidence for a priestess appears in connection with the cult; nevertheless, I suggest that women's role at the Adonia should be viewed against this broader background of female ritual activity. The Adonia, furthermore, is distinctive because women as cultic agents take on the persona of Aphrodite, whose male partner dies. The tale of

Aphrodite and Adonis is but one example of a narrative involving female divinities and their unfortunate mortal consorts (this narrative will be explored in chapter 2). Such an identification with Aphrodite "analogizes the woman to a goddess to support her claim to subjectivity and active desire."[104] The hierarchy in the myth, as we shall see, inverts typical gender hierarchy because the female deity is more powerful than the mortal male who dies.

Finally, the ritual of the Adonia involves a collectivity, a group of lamenting women, and at least in literary representations of the cult, choral lament elements appear, as seen in the antiphonal singing of Demostratus and his wife in Aristophanes's *Lysistrata*; the chorus of *korai* in Sappho (fr. 140 Voigt); and the chorus of Moirai who mourn Adonis in Bion's *Epitaph on Adonis*.[105] Indeed the speaker in the fragment of Cratinus (*PCG* iv fr. 17) may be remarking on the choral nature of the lamentations at the Adonia when he exclaims: "He did not grant a chorus to Sophocles when he asked but did grant one to Cleomachus, whom I would not deem worthy of producing a choral performance for me, not even for the Adonia." To most scholars, the joke is simply that state-sponsored choruses were not a feature of the Adonia, which was "just a private feast."[106] Occasionally, the public *spectacle* of the festival is invoked to explain Cratinus's comparison with the theater, but the lament that was such an important feature of the ritual tends not to be acknowledged; nor do scholars tend to mention the dancing.[107] While I do not claim that the Adonia included choral performance strictly speaking, the fact that literary texts include choruses of lamenting female figures, as well as dancing women, indicates that the festival may have drawn on this profoundly important feature of Athenian life.[108]

At Athens, we find no institutionalized dancing for women, even though in other places female *choroi* are typical.[109] Nevertheless, a recent examination of the evidence concerning female choruses in Classical Athens suggests that, although Athens did not have the sort of choral performances known from, for example, Sparta, female Athenians nevertheless danced in Athens in "alternative" choral performances.[110] Thus, even if the performances at the Adonis festival were not formal and state-funded, they should not be thought of as un-choral.

The chorus acting for and as the community has been well established.[111] In Greek texts, a chorus may function as a metaphor for civic accord or lack of union, as a group may "sing in harmony" or its members may disagree; the chorus models the civic community (or lack thereof).[112] Women at the Adonia, as a collectivity, occupy a particular space in which, as I will argue in chapters 2 and 3, they present a critique of dominant Athenian discourse surrounding the wedding and the funeral. The unique position of women atop roofs is a distinguishing feature of the cult. Rooftop space is a not uncommon place for characters in tragedies, especially divinities, to find themselves.[113] Women at the Adonia take on the role of Aphrodite and appear "on high"—in the space often reserved for gods and goddesses in drama.

Eastern Origins

The Official in Aristophanes's *Lysistrata* connects the ritual for Adonis with a ritual for Sabazius, another divinity from the East worshipped at Athens during the Classical period. Rituals for Adonis, Sabazius, and other divinities comprise a category of "foreign" cult, a problematic notion that will be discussed in chapter 3. At present, what is important is the fact that Adonis is known to Classical Athenians as one of a number of Eastern divinities.[114] Although competing accounts are given for Adonis's parentage and homeland, he is always from the East. As we have seen, [Hesiod] describes him as the son of Phoenix (Merkelbach-West fr. 139), an appellation that perhaps indicates his provenance as "the Phoenician."[115] Panyassis has Adonis hailing from Assyria, and the fragment from Plato Comicus (*Adonis PCG* vii fr. 3) examined above describes Adonis as son of Kinyras, king of the Cypriots.[116] While Kinyras himself is said to be from Cyprus as early as Homer's *Iliad* 11.20, this is the earliest reference that links Adonis to Cyprus.[117] Because the Classical Athenian Adonia is the focus of this book, it does not investigate the origins of the Adonia, nor does it trace Adonis's arrival from the East.[118] Adonis is one of many foreign gods taken over by the Athenians; my concern is what the Athenians do with him. Nevertheless, it is worth emphasizing that Adonis is decidedly Eastern in the minds of Classical Athenians, even as he does not correspond exactly to any Eastern divinity, and some mention of his Near Eastern counterparts is in order.[119]

Adonis's very name indicates his Eastern ties, since it is related to the Semitic title *adôn*, which means "lord" and which was often used for divinities.[120] The Greeks took the Semitic title for a proper name. Many parallels have been drawn between Adonis and prototypes like Tammuz, Dumuzi, Baal, and Ešmun. Although no scholar today would advocate a return to Frazer's free-associative comparativism, the resemblances are striking, especially between Adonis and the Mesopotamian Tammuz (Dumuzi), on the one hand, and Aphrodite and the Near Eastern goddess Ishtar (Inanna), on the other.[121] Just as Aphrodite mourns Adonis, Ishtar weeps for Tammuz, and both stories serve as etiologies for rituals. It is thought that worship of Tammuz moved west as Assyrian domination spread—from Mesopotamia, through Syria/Palestine, and on into Greece. Both the Adonia and the Tammuz cult share a summer date. Athenian women weeping for Adonis resemble Babylonian and Palestinian women weeping for Tammuz at the temple in Jerusalem (Ezekiel 8:14–15, dating from the sixth century BCE).[122]

The rooftop lament also seems to be a Near Eastern feature.[123] The myth of Adonis shared by Aphrodite and Persephone also relates to a Sumerian myth in which Dumuzi spends half the year with Ereshkigal, queen of the underworld, and half with Inanna.[124]

An account of an Adonia celebrated in the Phoenician city of Byblos from *On the Syrian Goddess*, attributed to Lucian, would appear to provide information about Adonis in his homeland (or at least one possible homeland), but the text is fraught with difficulties.[125] It is a late text (second century CE), and the author, whoever he is, offers a pastiche of Herodotus, imitating his style and dialect.[126] [Lucian] relates that Byblos contains the grave of Adonis as well as a river bearing his name (8), a river that each year turns red either because of the blood from Adonis's wound or from an influx of reddish mud.[127] The glimpse of the Adonia offered by *On the Syrian Goddess* tantalizes. Although no mention of gardens of Adonis appears, there is ritual prostitution (6) as well as a public building (μέγα ἱρὸν Ἀφροδίτης Βυβλίης) where mysteries (ὄργια, 6) for Adonis are performed.[128] Far from delivering information about the origins of Adonis, however, this text seems to describe an Adonia that has been reimported from Greece back to Syria.[129]

While [Lucian] locates Adonis's grave and tomb in the Phoenician city of Byblos and purports to describe an Adonia during Roman Imperial times, two inscriptions (*IG* II^2 1261 and *IG* II^2 1290) from Piraeus, the port city of Athens, suggest that during the fourth and third centuries BCE Phoenicians were celebrating the Adonia there. The first, *IG* II^2 1261, dates to the end of the fourth century BCE and records three decrees of the *thiasôtai*, "members of the *thiasos*—religious group," of Aphrodite who honor Stephanos, son of Mylothros.[130] The inscription mentions a sacrifice as well as a procession of the Adonia that is led by Stephanos "according to ancestral practice," κατὰ τὰ πάτρια (10).[131] The *polis* of origin of Stephanos and the *thiasôtai* is not mentioned, and they are likely non-Athenian men, because it is unlikely that Athenian men at the end of the fourth century BCE could claim to be worshipping Adonis in accordance with ancestral practice. Stephanos might be a metic; he is given no demotic, and he is a "maker of breastplates."[132] A second inscription, *IG* II^2 1290, dated a bit later (mid-third century BCE) and also from Piraeus, mentions Salaminioi, probably from Cyprus, who honor an *epimelêtês* in connection with an Adonia. We know that an expatriate Cypriot-Phoenician cult to Aphrodite was active in Athens at this time, as attested by another fourth-century inscription from Piraeus (*IG* II^2 337) that records a grant of *enktêsis* for a cult of Aphrodite to Kitian merchants (dated 333/332).[133] Kition was a town on the island of Cyprus that was ruled by a Phoenician dynasty during the fourth century, where a sanctuary of Aphrodite/Astarte and a shrine to Astarte have been excavated.[134]

Although cooperation between foreigners and Athenians is attested with regard to the worship of Bendis (whose cult was adopted as a state religion by the end of the fifth century), no evidence survives of such joint practice with regard to the Adonia.[135] The sacrifice and procession described in *IG* II^2 1261 and the formal organization indicated in *IG* II^2 1290 suggest that these inscriptions refer to an Adonia independent of the rooftop ritual performed by Athenian women.[136] Nevertheless, these inscriptions suggest that Phoenicians were expressing their own religious identity in a foreign land by means of the Adonia, alongside and separate from Athenian women, who adopted a foreign cult for their own purposes.

This discussion of themes related to the Adonia—a dismissive attitude toward the cult, as well as key notions about Adonis's death, the gardens of Adonis and myrrh, lamentation, and his Eastern origins—while useful as a sketch of the larger context in which Classical Athenian iconographic and literary representations of the festival operate, cannot get us very far in understanding what the festival meant in Classical Athens. This chapter suggests, rather, the need for a new approach. Chapter 2 contains the first of three analyses of the Adonis festival in context: an examination of the iconographic context for the Adonia.

2 Weddings

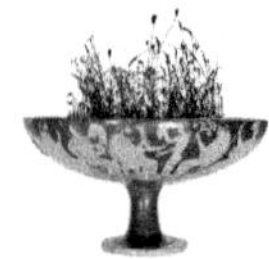

Stairway to Heaven

A late fifth-century Athenian lekythos from Karlsruhe (fig. 5) is a securely identified depiction of the Adonis festival.[1] It features a female figure on a ladder moving what has been convincingly shown to be a garden of Adonis.[2] The female figure, however, is not labeled, so it is unclear whether she is to be interpreted as Aphrodite or a participant in the festival.[3] The challenge of determining whether the figure on the Karlsruhe lekythos is Aphrodite or a ritual actor underscores the difficulties faced in separating myth from cult with regard to the Adonia. If we determine, on the one hand, that the female figure is Aphrodite and that we are in the realm of myth, we must contend, on the other hand, with what seems to be a realistic portrayal of the contemporary ritual practice of the cultivation of the gardens of Adonis. If, by contrast, we interpret the female figure as a ritual actor and assume that the vase realistically depicts the cult as practiced, we must come to terms with imagery indicating that we are in the realm of myth—the large nude winged male and the partial nudity of the female figure.[4]

A handful of other red-figure Athenian vases that date mostly from the late fifth and early fourth century depict female figures and Erotes moving objects up and down ladders (figs. 6–15).[5] They represent a variety of shapes: lekythos, hydria, skyphos, lebes gamikos.[6] Although the vases have been discussed for over 150 years, their interpretation remains controversial, and no consensus has emerged.[7] It has been argued that, like the Karlsruhe lekythos, the vases portray women involved in an Adonia and that the ladder is an identifying feature of the festival.[8] After all, Classical Athenian women carried gardens up to their rooftops during the ritual, and the women needed to gain access in some way. In this interpretation, the ladder is seen as a realistic detail related to contemporary ritual practice.

To make matters more complicated, a few of these vases (figs. 6, 11, 13, and 15) have been interpreted not as depictions of the Adonia but rather as marriage ceremonies, specifically the moment of the *epaulia*, which refers to a gathering held the day after the wedding, when the bride received gifts.[9] In this reading, the ladder leads to the second story of the house. It is suggested that in wealthy homes the bridal chamber (*thalamos*) was on the second floor; the day after a wedding the bride descended by means of a ladder to greet her gift-bearing friends. Lysias (1.9–10) provides evidence for the arrangement of women's quarters upstairs, accessible by a ladder or stairs (*klimax* may be translated either way).[10] In this interpretation, again, the ladders are seen as a realistic detail, referring to fifth- and fourth-century Athenian houses.

Because the scholarly discussion concerning the vases that depict female figures on or near ladders has continued for such a length of time and because there remains no agreement about what the vases signify, it is likely that the terms of the debate (Adonia versus wedding) are themselves problematic. Instead, we might begin by emphasizing that the destination beyond the upper rungs of the ladder remains mysterious. To argue that the female figures are headed either to the roof (Adonia) or to an upper story (*epaulia*) may be misguided.

More recently, the ladder that appears on these vases has been seen in metaphorical or symbolic terms.[11] On an Apulian red-figure volute krater in Naples, a seated Aphrodite holds a miniature ladder in her hand, and here the ladder functions as a kind of attribute of the goddess.[12] The "ladder" in question on the volute krater may be a xylophone, a mysterious object that appears on Apulian vases and is sometimes identified as a rattle, or sistrum.[13] The object tends to appear in erotic or funeral contexts with women. It is rarely being played. It has been suggested that the "instrument assumed at some point a symbolic value," and that in some cases it is an attribute of the bride; the instrument has also been connected with the Adonia.[14] Yet even as the symbolic force of the ladder is rightly recognized on vases like the volute krater in Naples and on the disputed scenes mentioned above, the disputed vases are said to depict *either* an Adonia *or* a wedding.[15]

The approach that I began emphasizing in the introduction and chapter 1 (and will continue to emphasize in chapters 3 and 4) with regard to literary texts applies equally to material culture: just as we must read literary texts carefully because they do not reflect the cult in any simple way, so too we must approach visual representations of the Adonis festival with care. An iconographical element that appears on the surface to be straightforward—a ladder—may in fact carry complex connotations. It is the symbolic and metaphorical force of the ladder that I wish to emphasize. To understand the symbolic force of the ladder on the

Karlsruhe lekythos, we need to read the vase in context, that is, within the context of similar visual language.

In general, ladders do not appear frequently in ancient Greek iconography and literature (though I discuss parallels in this chapter). Female figures on ladders appear still more rarely. What connects the images on the disputed vases and makes them distinctive and worth examining as a group is the woman on (or near) the ladder. The controversy concerning these vases points to *connections* between the Adonia and the ancient wedding.

The overarching claim of this chapter is that the depiction of the Adonia on the Karlsruhe lekythos includes conventional nuptial iconography, and that the vase, along with other images that feature ladders and female figures, serves as one class of evidence suggesting that women at the Adonia may have been commenting on wedding practices in the performance of the ritual for Adonis. These connections between Adonis, his cult, and the wedding are surprising. After all, the wedding, in terms of its centrality to Athenian life, would appear to be diametrically opposed to the culturally peripheral Adonia. Modern scholarship tends to characterize the union between Aphrodite and Adonis as the antithesis of marriage, a relationship defined by seduction, with Adonis as lover, rather than husband. Adonis dies young. The couple does not produce children. While agricultural metaphors are prominent in weddings, where the woman is handed over for the "plowing of legitimate children," by contrast, the short-lived gardens of Adonis seem to have very little to do with the production of Athenian citizens.[16]

Yet written and visual depictions of Aphrodite and Adonis, as I will show, draw on nuptial elements, and the relationship between the pair, while certainly concerned with erotic attraction and seduction, is simultaneously figured in terms of a marriage, albeit an inverted one, with Aphrodite in the dominant position. In Theocritus's *Idyll* 15, for example, Adonis is explicitly called γαμβρός, "bridegroom" (129). Of course, Adonis is a distinctive bridegroom, and the adjective "rosy-armed" (ῥοδόπαχυς), which modifies "bridegroom," is not used elsewhere of male figures.[17] Unlike typical grooms, who tend to be much older than the bride (Aristotle recommends the bride be eighteen and the groom about thirty-seven), in Theocritus's poem Adonis is very young ("eighteen or nineteen years old," 129; he has "kisses that do not prick," 130).[18] To be sure, the relationship between Aphrodite and Adonis is distinctive. Yet the marital aspect of their union is all but ignored by modern scholars.[19]

My aim in this chapter is to situate the Karlsruhe lekythos and other vases that draw on similar visual formulae within a nuptial context. The first step, however, is to examine literary and visual representations of Aphrodite and Adonis, where, I argue, Adonis is figured as a "bride."[20] The myth of Aphrodite and Adonis is but one of a series of stories the Greeks told about goddesses and their mortal paramours. I suggest that, like other mortal lovers of goddesses, in literary texts Adonis is figured as a bride, and the narrative pattern reworks the traditional trajectory of the wedding. Whereas the typical union results in a symbolic death for the bride, the goddess-mortal union results in a death—literal or metaphoric—for the mortal male involved. The narrative of the desiring goddess and her young lover inverts conventional Athenian gender roles, specifically with regard to marriage.[21] Although at times visual evidence from antiquity conflicts with written evidence, in the case of the goddess-mortal myth the written evidence and the material record confirm each other, and this inversion of roles is expressed in vase painting too, since pictorial depictions of the divine-mortal pair also draw on wedding imagery. Understanding how the myth of Aphrodite and Adonis inverts the wedding in both literary and iconographic portrayals will put us in a better position to tackle the visual images on the Karlsruhe lekythos as well as the disputed vases mentioned above.

Goddesses and Mortals

Aphrodite frequently makes an appearance when women mourn men in Homer. Given Aphrodite's connections with *aphrodisia*—one of the ways the Greeks could refer to "sex"—it seems (to us) most inappropriate to invoke this particular goddess at funerals.[22] Nevertheless, Briseis is "like golden Aphrodite" (ἰκέλη χρυσέῃ Ἀφροδίτῃ) when she mourns Patroclus (19.282). When Hector's body is brought back to Troy, Cassandra is compared to "golden Aphrodite" (24.699). "Golden Aphrodite" is again invoked when Andromache, the quintessential lamenter, first sees Hector's dead body being defiled by Achilles: in her grief, Andromache throws from her head the veil that "golden Aphrodite" had given her on her wedding day (22.468–72). Certainly, in the *Iliad* and the *Odyssey*, "desire" (*pothos, himeros, terpsis*) is frequently associated with lamentation.[23] Yet despite the fact that lamentation provides a release of emotion and thus can be seen as appropriate to mourners, this explanation for the references to Aphrodite does not quite satisfy. Helen, a figure closely linked to Aphrodite and *aphrodisia*, is permitted the last word of the *Iliad* as she laments the death of Hector, again bringing the goddess implicitly into a scene of mourning (24.762–75).[24] Aphrodite, then, looms large in the *Iliad* when women sing dirges over the bodies of deceased mortal men. How can this be explained?

The Greeks had access to a story pattern that included a powerful female mourning the death of her beloved, a youth who died in the prime of life: the tale of the goddess and her mortal lover. I suggest that when women lament in Homer, the narrative of goddesses and mortal men is activated.[25] In the *Iliad*, lamentation provides a rare opportunity for a woman to speak publicly; the mourner becomes a crafter of narrative. Although bereft of her loved one and powerless in the face of death, the woman in grief tells a story as she sings her dirge. Thus, Andromache, Hecuba, and Helen have the honor of being the first to shape Hector's *kleos* at the end of the *Iliad*.[26]

The relationship between Aphrodite and a deceased mortal man is a concern during the Classical period too, as Athenian tragedy summons figures like Hymenaeus and Hippolytus within a nuptial context. Both were mortal youths associated with Aphrodite, Hippolytus by his strident disavowal of the goddess's powers, Hymenaeus by his too-close connections with *aphrodisia* and Aphrodite—in some accounts Hymenaeus is the son of Aphrodite and hidden by the goddess in the ether (in a fragment of Euripides's *Phaethon*, 227–35 Diggle).[27] The notion that either Hymenaeus or Hippolytus might be invoked at weddings is peculiar given that both figures died before their own weddings.[28] Hymenaeus died on his wedding night, yet he is called upon in wedding refrains.[29] Hippolytus was destroyed as a result of his inattention to Aphrodite and *aphrodisia*, yet in *Hippolytus* Artemis explains that young women will dedicate their hair to him in mourning on the eve of their weddings (1425–27).[30] Elements of a funeral, then, are enacted within the context of a wedding, as cries ring out in honor of the deceased Hymenaeus, as hair is cut in mourning for Hippolytus, who never made it to his own wedding.

Behind these tales lies the narrative pattern of divine females desiring mortal youths. When an immortal goddess becomes smitten with a mortal man, an uncomfortable conflict of hierarchies—goddess/mortal and male/female—must be negotiated.[31] Typically in human relationships between men and women, the woman occupies the subordinate position. But in a relationship between a divinity and a mortal, the human participant—in this case the male—is subordinated: "Sexual intimacy between a human male and a goddess is therefore impossible to think in simple terms because the relative status of the two cannot be determined. The relationship must be adjusted somehow to make it conceivable."[32]

Relationships between figures such as Aphrodite and her lovers (Anchises, Adonis, Phaon, and Phaethon), as well as between a few lesser deities with theirs, such as Eos (with Tithonus) and Selene (with Endymion), partake of this structure. The pattern works as follows: the goddess desires a young, beautiful, mortal man;[33] she removes him far from civilization, hiding him away; ultimately, the youth dies or becomes sexually incapacitated (or both) and never returns to human society.[34] The relationships are structurally equivalent whether the goddess participant is Aphrodite or Eos, and whether the mortal involved is Adonis, Phaon, or Tithonus.[35]

In the *Odyssey* we can glimpse the workings of the relationship from the mortal perspective (Odysseus) as well as the divine (Calypso). First, the mortal: in book 10, Odysseus fears a loss of virility if he sleeps with Circe. After pointing out that she clearly has the upper hand since she has turned his companions into pigs, he exclaims, "While you have me here, you plot against me, ordering me to go into your bedroom and mount your bed so that you may make me weak and unmanned (ἀνήνορα) when I am naked" (339–41).[36]

It is a testament to Odysseus's superhuman heroic status that he escapes from the clutches not only of Circe but also of Calypso, who remarks on the problematic nature of the goddess-mortal relationship from an entirely different perspective in book 5.[37] Calypso rails against the gods, characterizing them as "jealous of goddesses when they have sex with mortal men publicly" (παρ' ἀνδράσιν εὐνάζεσθαι / ἀμφαδίην), "if one makes the man her own husband" (φίλον . . . ἀκοίτην) (119–20). Here, Calypso employs the adverb ἀμφαδίην (120) to describe the goddesses' relationships with the mortal men. Frequently translated as "publicly" or "openly," the word underscores the unconcealed nature of the relationship, as in the "public marriage," ἀμφάδιον γάμον, mentioned in the *Odyssey* (6.288). Calypso also characterizes the mortal male participant in these cases as "husband" (ἀκοίτην, 120).[38] The relationships between goddesses and mortals described by Calypso, then, are figured as quasi marriages. Calypso continues, providing examples of the negative effects of such relationships. In the past, Eos and Demeter were not permitted to continue their endeavors with their mortal lovers, Orion and Iasion, respectively. The men were killed, and Calypso suggests that the situation is no different now that she herself has taken up with the mortal Odysseus. As Calypso makes clear, the goddess-mortal narrative tends to resolve in a manner that thwarts the desiring goddess, leaving her bereft, and incapacitates the mortal man (though Odysseus, of course, is an exception).

Aphrodite's affairs also inevitably have troubling ramifications for the mortals involved. In the *Homeric Hymn to Aphrodite*, when Anchises discovers he has slept with Aphrodite, he is horrified. He exclaims: "Do not make me unmanned (ἀμενηνόν) living among mortals, but take mercy on me, since a man is not virile (οὐ βιοθάλμιος ἀνήρ) who sleeps with the immortal goddesses," 188–90. Just as in the *Odyssey* Odysseus worries that relations with Circe might affect his virility, so too Anchises expresses similar fears that he might become "unmanned," using a different adjective, ἀμενηνός.[39] The *Homeric Hymn to Aphrodite* further underscores Anchises's powerlessness in the face of the goddess, as Aphrodite narrates to him the harrowing tale of Eos and Tithonus, another goddess-mortal pairing that does not end well for the mortal involved. While Tithonus is granted immortality and thus never experiences a literal death, Eos neglects to request that he never grow old. As a result, Tithonus withers away leaving nothing but a voice. While Anchises is neither killed nor rendered (literally) impotent in the *Homeric Hymn to Aphrodite*, Aphrodite commands that Anchises not reveal the affair to a single soul, leaving him intact but depriving him of voice in the matter and threatening him with Zeus's thunderbolt. That threat, combined with the cautionary tale of Eos and Tithonus, underscores Anchises's metaphorical impotence, his deprivation of power. In other accounts of Aphrodite's relationship with Anchises, he *is* killed or enfeebled by lightning.[40]

Adonis faces similar difficulties, and his story resolves in a similarly problematic way. Adonis dies, gored by a boar; he is also associated with lettuce, which was believed by the Greeks to turn men impotent.[41] According to Nicander (fr. 120 Schneider), Adonis ran into a bed of lettuce to hide from the boar and died there, while Callimachus (fr. 478 Pf.) has Adonis hidden by Aphrodite in lettuce. When we find that the unfortunate Phaon, another lover of Aphrodite, is concealed in the same vegetable as Adonis (Cratinus *PCG* iv fr. 370), the youths are thus marked as equivalent within the structure of the story. For a mortal man, becoming erotically entangled with a goddess results in death or a loss of manhood or power. This brief survey of the narrative of the goddess who desires a mortal youth offers a starting point for what interests me here, namely, the particular ways that nuptial elements are incorporated into relationships between goddesses and mortal men.[42]

Adonis the Bride in Literary Texts

Greek literature is filled with macabre moments when weddings and funerals intersect. In tragedy, young women who die before marriage may be described as wedded to Hades.[43] Persephone serves as the mythic paradigm for such a "bride of death."[44] Abducted by Hades, Persephone dies with regard to her former existence, and she moves to her new home beneath the earth. Sophocles's Antigone takes the tragic topos to an extreme, becoming a "full-fledged bride of Hades," as she explains that Hades leads her away, alive, to Acheron (810–13), and as she addresses her tomb as bridal chamber (ὦ τύμβος, ὦ νυμφεῖον, 891).[45] To underscore the perverse nature of a death, Greek authors might evoke the arresting image of marriage torches lighting a funeral pyre or call to mind the change from wedding song to *thrênos*, along with the shift from hymeneal to funereal garb, a change Admetus makes in Euripides's *Alcestis* when he mourns the death of his wife (922–25).[46]

In an attempt to explain this preoccupation with the connections between weddings and funerals, scholars have emphasized the similarities between the two rituals.[47] At both weddings and funerals, ancient Greek women played a crucial role, performing the very same actions with different significations.[48] Brides at weddings, as well as mourners at funerals, offer locks of hair; both ceremonies involve ritual bathing.[49] Weddings and funerals include adornment, crowning, and a journey to a new location.[50] The two *rites de passage* are thus parallel; the individual undergoing either a wedding or a funeral must be separated from a former status and integrated into a new one.[51]

The myth and cult of Adonis also highlight the merging of a wedding and a funeral, the intersection between *aphrodisia* and death, but with a twist: Adonis is figured as a bride. As early as Sappho, the death and ritual mourning of the youth are emphasized in a passage that contains an implicit bridal element (fr. 140 Voigt). In this fragment, Adonis is described as *habros*, "delicate," an adjective that is used to describe the youth elsewhere.[52] Andromache is so described in another of Sappho's fragments detailing Andromache's marriage to Hector (fr. 44.7 Voigt), and in Sophocles's *Women of Trachis*, the chorus sings of Heracles and the river god Acheloüs battling over a bride-to-be described as *habros* (523). *Habros*, then, is an adjective that may evoke the sphere of weddings and characterize a bride.[53] But in Sappho's fragment "*habros* Adonis" has died. *Hymenaeus* turns to *thrênos* as Aphrodite directs the *korai* to perform typical funeral rites, the beating of breasts and rending of garments.

The wedding-to-*thrênos* movement in connection with Adonis appears also during the Hellenistic period in Theocritus's *Idyll* 15. When Praxinoa and Gorgo slip through the crowd into Arsinoë's palace, Praxinoa remarks, "All inside said the man locking up the bride" (ἔνδοι πᾶσαι, ὁ τὰν νυὸν εἶπ' ἀποκλᾴξας, 77).[54] This comment, along with the tableau the women have come to see depicting the union of Aphrodite and Adonis, emphasizes that the palace is imagined to represent the space of the wedding of Adonis and Aphrodite. While the poem underscores the union with Aphrodite and Adonis as bridegroom (γαμβρός, 129), the hymnist explains that mourning will take place on the next day. Bion's *Epitaph on Adonis*, too, is preoccupied with the intersection between weddings and funerals and includes the familiar topos of wedding song turned to lamentation. Upon the death of Adonis, Hymenaeus himself extinguishes the torches and scatters the marriage crown to the winds. He ceases singing his own song, "Hymen! Hymen!" and replaces it with "Alas, Adonis!"

Adonis is still more forcefully associated with being a bride when he is assimilated to the position of Persephone, the "bride of death" par excellence, in the story told by Panyassis by way of Apollodorus (3.14.4).[55] In this account, Persephone refuses to return Adonis to Aphrodite; Zeus intervenes; and all parties agree that Adonis will divide his time annually between Persephone and Aphrodite. The story calls to mind Persephone's own narrative—her abduction by Hades and the resulting annual arrangement by which she spends part of the year with Hades and part of the year with her mother, Demeter. This tale, however, has

Adonis in the position of possessed bride, shared between two powerful goddesses. As Hades refuses to release Persephone in the myth of her own abduction, so Persephone exerts her power over the captive Adonis in the Apollodorus passage ("when she saw him, she did not return him," ὡς ἐθεάσατο, οὐκ ἀπεδίδου, 3.14.4), refusing to give him back to Aphrodite.[56] Persephone fulfills a similar role in Bion's *Epitaph on Adonis*, when the Fates attempt to call Adonis back from the dead: he is unable to respond because Persephone will not release him (94–96).[57] Adonis's story is distinctive: it represents a significant adjustment to the "bride of death" topos.

While Calypso alludes to marriage in her characterization of the goddess-mortal relationship, the *Homeric Hymn to Aphrodite* contains the most profound engagement with elements drawn from the wedding in the narrative of Aphrodite's amorous relationship. In that poem, Aphrodite plays specifically on nuptial conventions as she seduces Anchises. When Zeus afflicts Aphrodite with desire, she goes to Paphos, where, after a bath, the Graces anoint her with ambrosial bridal oil (ἀμβροσίῳ ἑδανῷ, 63), and she is adorned with finery and gold.[58] Once she arrives at Anchises's hut, Aphrodite appears before him "like an unmarried *parthenos*" (παρθένῳ ἀδμήτῃ . . . ὁμοίη, 82).[59] This particular disguise is chosen "lest he be frightened" (83). Aphrodite-the-*parthenos* explains that she was dancing for Artemis (118) with many potential brides (119–20) when Hermes abducted her and informed her that she would become the wife of Anchises (κουριδίην ἄλοχον, 126–27). Aphrodite explains that she will make a good daughter-in-law, that a dowry will be sent directly, and that a wedding feast will be held. All the elements that Aphrodite masterfully employs evoke the expected wedding trajectory, including the chorus of maidens from which brides in myth tend to be abducted.[60]

Aphrodite plays the role of marriageable young girl and seductively offers Anchises the role of husband, suggesting that he lead her to his house and show her to his parents (133–35).[61] But just as Aphrodite only temporarily plays the part of the mortal bride, so too Anchises only temporarily is led to believe that he will play the part of the husband actively leading his bride to a new home. In phrasing that recalls the Circe episode in the *Odyssey*, Anchises responds, "I would choose, lady like a goddess, after mounting your bed to go down to the house of Hades" (βουλοίμην κεν ἔπειτα, γύναι εἰκυῖα θεῇσι,/ σῆς εὐνῆς ἐπιβὰς δῦναι δόμον Ἄϊδος εἴσω, 153–54).[62] These are ominous words for the mortal lover of a goddess. Of course, in the *Homeric Hymn to Aphrodite*, Anchises does not die—he becomes the father of Aeneas. But as we have seen, his powerlessness is underscored when she narrates the tale of Tithonus and Eos. *Aphrodisia* spells a kind of death for Anchises.

Upon Aphrodite's arrival at Anchises's hut, wild animals, including lions and bears, greet her. They delight her, and she casts desire into their hearts, causing them to couple (69–74). Later in the poem, just before Aphrodite and Anchises sleep together, those same wild animals reappear in a description of Anchises's bed, which is strewn with the skins of lions and bears (158–60). Anchises as virile hunter had killed those animals, and one scholar remarks that the skins are "a symbol of Anchises' power, just as Heracles' lion skin is a symbol of his strength."[63] Yet Anchises's power and strength lie decidedly in the past. The reappearance of the wild animals in the poem—this time as skins of now dead beasts—marks a movement from sex to death, from *aphrodisia* to *thanatos*. In case we had forgotten the structure of the relationship, the poet makes it explicit: "The mortal man lay by the immortal goddess, not knowing who she was" (166–67).

The narrative of the goddess and her mortal lover reworks traditional nuptial elements. As discussed above, Persephone functions quite literally as a "bride of death" since she marries the king of the underworld. In the *Homeric Hymn to Demeter*, Persephone is seized unwillingly (3, 19–20) from a meadow where she is picking flowers, and she shouts and screams as she is carried off in Hades's chariot to his home beneath the earth, where she is hidden from view (her mother is unable to locate her). The union of Persephone and Hades also functions as a paradigm for human marriage.[64] Ancient marriage operates as a kind of ritualized abduction, a symbolic death from the young girl's point of view.[65] Like Persephone, the bride dies with regard to her former life, leaving the company of her friends and frequently moving far from home.[66] Of course, she goes on to embark on a new life of fertility, if all goes according to plan, with the production of legitimate children for her new household—just as Persephone returns to the world above each year to reunite with her mother during a period that is tied to the fertility of the earth—but such events take place well after the wedding. Marriage is not presented in a particularly positive light in ancient texts, at least not from the perspective of the young bride. One thinks of Sophocles's *Tereus* or Euripides's *Medea*, where female characters express distress at having to move far from home and learn new customs. The young woman is described as a kind of immigrant to a foreign land, a resident alien in her new home. Ancient Greek wedding iconography frequently depicts chaste brides lifted by the groom into a chariot or led with a firm grip on the wrist (χεὶρ ἐπὶ καρπῷ) by their new husbands from *oikos* to *oikos*, a gesture that indicates the transfer of the bride to her husband's control.[67] Indeed, wedding iconography shares similarities with pursuit and abduction scenes and operates on a continuum with such imagery.[68]

Helene Foley explains, "In human culture, women are circulated among men in order to link one household, tribe, or city with another. Persephone's role in what has been called the 'traffic in women' creates a new relation between earth, Olympus (heaven), and Hades (the world of the dead below) by linking them for the first time in her own person."[69] Yet within the myth of the young male mortal Adonis, it is *Adonis* who circulates between the goddess of the underworld and the Olympian divinity.

Clearly, metaphors of commercial transaction underlie the practice of marriage. Technical terms such as ἔκδοσις, and ἐκδιδόναι—words that signal the transfer of the bride to the groom—also indicate a "giving out," a "leasing" of the bride.[70] The words ἐγγύη and ἐγγυᾶν, usually translated respectively as "betrothal" and "to hand over" or "to pledge," also operate within the schema of commercial metaphor. The words evoke an image, that of laying valuables in an underground vault. This metaphor "structures the sense of *engue* as 'deposit,' one that suits its use both as guarantee and betrothal."[71] Marriageable women are imagined to be stored away in an underground vault, "capital withdrawn from circulation," to be revealed and moved to their new home when the time is right.[72]

The word *thalamos*, which frequently means simply "inner room" or "resting place," may be employed to describe such a "chamber" where the bride is stored away.[73] For example, in accounts of Danaë's enclosure (Pherecydes fr. 26 *FGrH*, and Apollodorus 2.4.1), she is confined first in a *thalamos* and next in a *larnax* (in which her son is also enclosed). It has been suggested that "the *larnax* is thus a kind of second *thalamos*, another enclosure for the unmarried woman and, in this case, for her son as well. . . . Certain images of Danaë in vase painting represent her dressed as a bride in the *larnax*. Such a representation suggests that the chest in this story is a functional equivalent of the vault from which the woman would emerge for her wedding."[74]

The connections drawn between the unmarried woman and the *thalamos* or *larnax* suggest that the *larnax* in which Adonis is hidden in Apollodorus evokes the nuptial sphere.[75] Adonis, like the valuable bride, is hidden away (κρύφα, κρύψασα, 3.14.4) in a *larnax* on account of his beauty while he is young (διὰ κάλλος ἔτι νήπιον, 3.14.4); that is, he is entrusted to Persephone. When the bride is revealed, Persephone will not give him back.

Adonis is just one of a number of youths who are hidden away. Phaon too is concealed, as is Hymenaeus, in the ether, according to a fragment of Euripides's *Phaethon* (227–35 Diggle). In the *Odyssey*, Calypso's name evokes the verb καλύπτειν, "to cover" or "to conceal," which perhaps indicates the "hiding" she is only temporarily able to carry out with regard to Odysseus.[76] The relationship reworks nuptial elements since the mortal youth is concealed in the same way as the marriageable young woman.

Stories of unions of goddesses and mortals invert conventional ancient Greek gender roles, specifically with regard to the movement of the bride within the context of marriage. Like a vulnerable *korê* picking flowers in a meadow, Adonis just might be abducted by a goddess. As we will see, visual depictions of Adonis and Aphrodite also refer to wedding iconography. But as we might expect, Adonis hardly appears in the position of dominating husband leading the bride to her new home. Instead, he luxuriates in a garden setting or relaxes with his lyre, ready to receive fruits from Eros. Thus far, I have examined the theme of goddesses and mortals in literary texts and I have introduced evidence from times and places other than Classical Athens in order to emphasize the nuptial elements involved in such a narrative pattern. The remainder of this chapter focuses on Classical Athens and visual representations of Adonis and his cult dating for the most part to the end of the fifth and the beginning of the fourth century.

Adonis the Bride in Iconography

The story of the female divinity and her youthful consort held much appeal, in particular among playwrights during the Athenian Classical period.[77] Plato Comicus and Antiphanes each wrote a *Phaon*, and Plato's version involves an address by Aphrodite to a gaggle of Phaon's admirers.[78] Cratinus, too, was interested in the beautiful youth.[79] Alcaeus wrote an *Endymion*, and Euripides a *Phaethon*.[80] Of all the mortal lovers of goddesses, however, Adonis appears to have been the most popular, with a great many comedies devoted to him and to his festival.[81]

Visual artists also drew on the theme of the goddess who desires a mortal male, and the pursuit of Tithonus by Eos is depicted in Classical Athenian vase painting.[82] Hundreds of examples speak to the popularity of the theme. The iconography associated with Eos and Tithonus is eerily repetitive (as is the iconography of erotic pursuit in general). Tithonus runs off to the right in sheer terror, his right arm trailing behind him; or he seems poised to defend himself by clobbering Eos with his lyre or his spear. These images indicate the terrible and terrifying aspects (from the mortal's perspective) associated with being taken by a goddess.[83] Although divine pursuit scenes were popular subjects for vase painters during the Classical period, Aphrodite does not tend to chase Adonis across the visual field on vases that survive.[84] Instead, the aftermath of the abduction/marriage is portrayed—the serene union between Aphrodite and Adonis. These images of Aphrodite and Adonis are examined below to show that they draw on wedding iconography.

Beginning in the late fifth century, a large number of vases depict elaborately dressed female figures wearing jewelry and diadems in interior settings. A bride is frequently the focus of attention, and many of these images depict what appear to be wedding or *epaulia* scenes. Such scenes have been used to piece together the ancient wedding.[85] Often called *gunaikeiôn* scenes, these images feature women in attitudes of repose accompanied by objects such as chests, mirrors, spinning baskets, alabastra, and sashes. Erotes flutter about, and while inscriptions sometimes identify the females as mythological figures or personifications, often the figures are not inscribed.

A tremendous amount of scholarship has been devoted to the female figures in these scenes, because they appear with such regularity in red-figure interior scenes of adornment and weddings.[86] An example of this sort of iconography is a red-figure pyxis in New York, featuring Aphrodite and her attendants, who include Peitho, Hygieia, and Paidia.[87] Aphrodite sits on a chair, while well-coiffed, elaborately draped individuals from her retinue offer chests, sashes, and jewelry.

While such figures may be given names, as in the vase mentioned above, and thus may be marked to some extent as individuals, they also correspond to the paradigm of the "band of maidens" that appears frequently in poetry.[88] Many such narratives describe a group of young women, one of whom is marked as distinctive within a marital context. Frequently the maiden plays in a meadow, an externalization of her reproductive potential.[89] The maiden is separated from the group, and the group may express grief, underscoring the loss associated with the removal of the girl. Examples of figures in texts who represent all or part of this common motif include Persephone, who in the *Homeric Hymn to Demeter* plays in a meadow with her friends; the maidens described in Alcman's *Partheneion*; and a number of choruses of young women in tragedy.[90] On vases too the performance of the maiden's desirability often leads to abduction, and just as the companions express grief in poetry, so too they express fear in the images of abduction.[91]

The Horai adorning Aphrodite in the shorter *Homeric Hymn (6) to Aphrodite* (5–18) function as a literary paradigm for the maiden outstanding among peers.[92] In this passage, the Horai appear as the band of maidens attending Aphrodite, as they offer her clothing, a crown, and jewelry. The Horai are also described as participating in divine *choroi*, a public showcasing of valuable female attributes that tends to lead to marriage. The necklaces that the Horai place on Aphrodite's neck are the ones "with which the golden-filleted Horai themselves were adorned" (11–12) when participating in divine *choroi*. The necklaces thus provide a connection between the outstanding maiden (Aphrodite) and the group of her peers (the Horai), as is so often the case in red-figure scenes populated by jewelry-clad female figures (like the red-figure pyxis in New York mentioned above). In the *Hymn*, when the gods see Aphrodite, they are all so amazed at her beauty that every last one of them wants to take her home to be his wife (16–18). The Horai have admirably performed their job of adorning the "maiden."

A number of vases—all dating from the end of the fifth century to the beginning of the fourth—clearly identify Adonis by name and depict the youth accompanied by Aphrodite and other female figures. These images feature nuptial imagery and can be connected to the *gunaikeiôn* scenes described above by the reappearance of conventional iconographic elements. I limit my discussion below to vases that mark the youth as Adonis in an inscription, and I do not aim for a comprehensive account of Adonis in ancient Greek visual arts.[93] In particular, I examine a late fifth-century Athenian vase attributed to the Meidias Painter (fig. 1), a richly decorated hydria that incorporates the wedding-scene type described above to portray Aphrodite and Adonis.[94] The Meidias Painter's portrayal of the goddess and the youth offers a visual counterpart to the textual phenomenon I have described thus far in this chapter. The wedding scene between goddess and mortal is transferred to an outdoor garden where tendrils replace spinning baskets, chests, and furniture.[95]

On the Meidias Painter's hydria (fig. 1), Adonis, identified by inscription, lyre at his side, reclines comfortably in Aphrodite's lap, gazing up languidly at Himeros (also identified by inscription), who flutters above, spinning an *iunx*. Tendrils indicate a garden setting, and Adonis and Aphrodite are surrounded by female figures, whose names appear above or near their heads. To the left of Himeros, Eurynoê, seated on a rock, points at a bird perched on her left finger, Eutychia gazes into a mirror near Eudaimonia, and Chrysothemis engages another Eros figure. To the right of Aphrodite and Adonis, Paidia lolls in the lap of Hygieia near Pandaisia, and another Himeros dances to the *tympanon* played by Pannychis.

Inasmuch as the narrative of the relationship between Aphrodite and Adonis is structurally similar to other goddess-mortal pairings, it comes as no surprise to find that Phaon, another consort of Aphrodite, is portrayed almost identically in terms of visual vocabulary on a vase also attributed to the Meidias Painter and found in the same Etruscan tomb as the Adonis hydria (fig. 2).[96] Phaon plays a lyre beneath an arching tendril, glancing at Dêmonassa seated next to him. While it is not entirely certain how Dêmonassa, "mistress of the *dêmos*," is to be interpreted, at the very least, she has something to do with the *dêmos*, and, given that Aphrodite had the epithet *Pandêmos* at Athens, Dêmonassa likely evokes Aphrodite.[97] A great many female figures surround the lovers, three of whom are the same as those who also appear on the Adonis hydria, Eudaimonia, Hygieia, and Pannychis.

The same visual language, then, has been used to depict Adonis and Phaon, both mortal lovers of the goddess Aphrodite.[98] Adonis holds a lyre, so too Phaon; both have long, wavy curls; both are "rather soft and plump."[99] The structural similarities that make Adonis and Phaon interchangeable in literature may be glimpsed on the two vases; that is, Adonis and Phaon *look* the same.

The Meidias Painter's Adonis hydria (fig. 1), then, depicts the relationship between a goddess and a mortal, and just as written texts incorporate elements drawn from the nuptial sphere, so too the vase incorporates wedding iconography. Adonis is surrounded by personifications—more or less interchangeable, undifferentiated, glamorous females. Adonis also regularly appears with a band of maidens in literary texts. Sappho's fragment (fr. 140 Voigt) has a chorus of *korai* mourning Adonis's death. In Theocritus *Idyll* 15, as Adonis moves between earth and Acheron, the Horai, the same figures mentioned above who adorn Aphrodite in the *Homeric Hymn to Aphrodite*, accompany him (102–5).[100] In Bion's *Epitaph on Adonis,* Sappho's lamenting chorus of *korai* is replaced by three female groups—the Charites (the Graces, 91–93), the Moirai (the Fates, 94–95), and a group of mountain nymphs (19), who all mourn Adonis.

The Meidias Painter, then, in his portrayal of Aphrodite and Adonis, has depicted a band of maidens familiar from myth. But this band of maidens is atypical in one important respect: Adonis is one of their number. In mythical tales of abducted maidens, the group will lament the loss of one of its members. In the case of Adonis, he is the one who is mourned. Given the distinctive nature of the goddess-mortal relationship, the singled-out individual is Adonis, who finds himself in the position of bride. Indeed, elsewhere, on a lekythos from Berlin where Adonis appears with Eunomia, Eukleia, and Eros, it has been suggested that Adonis sits in a posture in which brides commonly sit, "indicating ambivalence, facing one way but turning back the other."[101]

Although I have emphasized the importance of the undifferentiated *group* of female figures because of the ways in which the band of maidens symbolizes the marriageability of the singled-out young girl, on the Meidias Painter's Adonis hydria (fig. 1), inscriptions are included that indicate that this band of maidens is distinctive. Pandaisia (Banquet-Feast) is one of the figures appearing with Aphrodite and Adonis, and she may evoke the wedding feast.[102] What is more, the myth of Aphrodite and Adonis differs from other such tales of female divinities and their lovers because an annual ritual is connected with the myth, and elements on the vase evoke the ritual.[103] The presence of Pannychis (All-Night-Revel), banging away on her *tympanon* for the entertainment of Himeros (Desire), evokes the celebrations overwhelmingly associated with women and attested for many Athenian festivals including the Adonia.[104] On the Meidias Painter's Adonis hydria, Paidia, "Play," relaxes in Hygieia's lap. In Classical Athenian texts, *heortê*, "festival," is conceived of as an enjoyable interlude, a rest from toil, a kind of "play" (*paidia*), and *paidia* is used specifically to describe the Adonia.[105] Paidia seems also to have a special iconographic relationship with Adonis, as she appears elsewhere with the youth and Aphrodite on a late fifth-century lekythos in Paris attributed to Aison (fig. 3), a kind of abridged version of the Meidias Painter's hydria.[106] The Meidias Painter's Adonis hydria, then, alludes to the cult as it includes female figures that call to mind the performance of the Adonis festival.

Like the maiden who belongs to the group of her peers, Adonis appears as an erotic object in a nuptial context on the Meidias Painter's hydria (fig. 1), and Adonis's desirability is further emphasized by the *iunx* that Himeros spins directly in front of Adonis's upturned face. The *iunx* makes rare iconographic appearances.[107] While an *iunx* is not a nuptial object strictly speaking but is rather an instrument of erotic magic, the *iunx* along with the related wryneck bird tend to appear in a nuptial context in iconography.[108] Pindar explains (*Pythian* 4.213–19) that Aphrodite brought the *iunx* down to humans from Olympus (Οὐλυμπόθεν, 214) in order to help Jason in his erotic dealings with Medea. According to various accounts, the *iunx*, or wryneck, was originally a nymph pursued by Zeus and subsequently turned into a bird. The bound bird on a wheel that Aphrodite offered to mortals was simplified over time, and the device eventually became a wheel or disc that was spun and made a whirring noise. The purpose of the *iunx* was to draw the beloved to the lover, and it becomes the object of choice for the spurned and the lovelorn.[109]

Pindar emphasizes the fact that the *iunx* is a bird (ὄρνιν, *Pythian* 4.215–16) yoked to a wheel, and it has been suggested that the bird Eurynoê holds on the Meidias Painter's Adonis hydria may be an *iunx*/wryneck as well.[110] The small bird appears with Adonis on at least one other vase, the lekythos in Berlin mentioned above in connection with Adonis's ambivalent "bridal" posture, where Eukleia has a lyre in her left hand and holds a bird on a finger of her right hand. A small bird perched on an outstretched finger is not an uncommon element of Classical Athenian red-figure and tends to appear in connection with female figures (often Aphrodite and her associates) in nuptial contexts.[111]

The bird appears on an object that is invariably mentioned in discussions of wedding iconography, the Eretria Painter's late fifth-century epinêtron (fig. 4).[112] On the panel that depicts Alcestis's *epaulia*, Hippolytê, Alcestis's sister-in-law, gestures at a bird in exactly the same way that Eurynoê does on the Adonis hydria (fig. 1), holding the bird on her left hand and pointing at it with her right.[113] Hippolytê and Eurynoê have similar, carefully arranged hairstyles and ribbons or bands in their hair, and both are seated. Just to the right of Hippolytê, Alcestis leans against the bridal bed. On the Meidias Painter's hydria (fig. 1), the curve of Adonis's right arm and the articulation of his index finger as he leans against Aphrodite echo the curve of Alcestis's right arm and the articulation of her index finger as she leans against the bridal bed.

Thus far, I have introduced the narrative of goddesses and mortals to argue that Adonis is figured as a bride in literary texts, and that images of Aphrodite and the youth also draw on nuptial themes. Since visual and literary representations of the myth of Adonis incorporate elements from the wedding, it is possible that women at the Adonis festival were commenting on the wedding. An examination of extant *epithalamia*, wedding songs, will suggest with a bit more precision the ways in which women at the Adonia may have had the potential to rewrite the wedding.

Wedding Songs and the Adonia

Although Sappho's poetry is removed in space and time from Classical Athens, her *epithalamia* fragments are our best-preserved examples of songs sung at weddings.[114] In general, the images and metaphors associated with Greek weddings remain relatively consistent over time. While Athenian tragedy and comedy refer to the genre of *epithalamia* and may be used to provide additional evidence, Sappho's poems offer a more secure reference point for this discussion, and Classical Athenians were certainly well acquainted with her poetry.[115]

The themes that have been a concern in this chapter—Aphrodite, Adonis, and weddings—are also themes in Sappho's poetry. Aphrodite appears as the most prominent divinity. She is called by four names (Cytherea, Cypris, Cyprogenea, and Aphrodite); she is invoked (e.g., fr. 1, fr. 2, fr. 5 Voigt); she speaks (fr. 1, fr. 140 Voigt); and she is said to be the cause of passion (fr. 102 Voigt).[116] Aphrodite's relationship with Adonis is also a subject of Sappho's poetry (fragment 140, fr. 117B, fr. 168 Voigt), and her fragments provide us with what appears to be our earliest evidence for the ritual of the Adonia.[117]

A great many of Sappho's fragments concern the wedding, and it is no surprise that the Hellenistic Dioscorides emphasizes the nuptial sphere when he characterizes Sappho's poetry (GP 1565–74 = *AP* 7.407).[118] Dioscorides's poem explores three Sapphic realms in an attempt to send greetings to the poet. Beginning with the Muses, with whom he first associates her, Dioscorides turns to a second Sapphic space: the wedding. He then shifts from weddings to funerals, from *hymenaios* to *thrênos*, and portrays Sappho alongside Aphrodite, lamenting Adonis. In the process, Discorides evokes the movement from wedding to funeral, the topos that I have argued stories about Adonis evoke.

At least from the point of view of the bride, the wedding represented a symbolic death, and what is known about *epithalamia* in general confirms this negative view of the experience. According to a scholion on Theocritus *Idyll* 18, *epithalamia* were sung to drown out the virgin's screams during her first sexual experience.[119] In some accounts, a guard, *thyrôros*, was posted outside the bridal chamber to prevent the bride's friends from coming to her assistance.[120] One of Sappho's fragments mentions just such a doorkeeper, emphasizing the enormity of his feet (fr. 110 Voigt). Another fragment indicates that the friends of the bride sang to her outside the door all night long (fr. 30 Voigt). Pindar, too, describes the companions of the bride singing comforting songs (*Pythian* 3.17–19 Maehler).[121] The wedding, then, clearly evoked negative associations from the bride's perspective.

Yet if we read Sappho's *epithalamia* fragments with attention to Adonis festival themes and metaphors, we will find that the Adonia reworks elements of the wedding, putting a different spin on nuptials. In wedding songs, bridegrooms are compared to figures worthy of praise, and Sappho's fragment 111 describes the imminent arrival of a γάμβρος, "bridegroom," one who is specifically like Ares:[122]

> Raise high the roof, carpenters, *hymenaios*!
> A bridegroom will come equal to Ares, *hymenaios*!
> Bigger by far than a big man. (fr. 111 Voigt)

The figure of Adonis the γάμβρος seen on the Meidias Painter's hydria, stretched out in Aphrodite's lap with his lyre, hardly shares similarities with a bridegroom who is like the god of war. Furthermore, Sappho's phrase describing the groom, "bigger by far than a big man" (ἄνδρος μεγάλω πόλυ μέσδων), carries sexual innuendo; the virility of the Sapphic γάμβρος presents a stark contrast to Adonis, given his associations with lettuce, and the connotations evoked by that particular vegetable.[123] Unlike Adonis, who never quite arrives at manhood, we are explicitly told in the Sapphic fragment that the Ares-like bridegroom is arriving.

The bridegroom described in Sappho's fragment is so large that he reaches the roof beams. And, indeed, gods and goddesses are described in Greek literature as being quite large, especially when they appear to mortals, sometimes even reaching to the roof. So it is with Aphrodite in the *Homeric Hymn to Aphrodite* when she finally reveals herself in all her glory to the startled and horrified Anchises: "She stood in the hut, and her head touched the well-made roof" (ἔστη ἄρα κλισίῃ, εὐποιήτοιο μελάθρου / κῦρε κάρη, 173–74). Aphrodite, as a larger-than-life bride, shares similarities with the enormous groom described in Sappho's wedding song. Within the context of the relationship between Aphrodite and Adonis, then, Aphrodite is more akin to a γάμβρος than Adonis is.

In Sappho's fragment 111 (Voigt), the bridegroom is so large that the carpenters (τέκτονες ἄνδρες) must be called in so that the entire *oikos*, for which the roof (μέλαθρον) stands, may be reconfigured.[124] Symbolically, of course, when a bridegroom arrives, the makeup of the *oikos* changes as the bride leaves one household and is led to another. Typically the Greek roof was metonymically associated with the husband.[125] Thus, Clytemnestra calls Agamemnon "the column supporting the high roof" (Aeschylus *Agamemnon* 897–98). In *Odyssey* 1.333, when Penelope appears for the first time, she stands beside the pillar that supports the roof, an appropriate position since Odysseus is away.[126] In marriage iconography women are led from one *oikos* to another by their husbands. The dangling feet and rigid posture of the woman being placed into a cart seen on a loutrophoros (ca. 430) in Berlin (fig. 22) is a representative example of this custom.[127] While typical wedding iconography frequently includes the gesture χεὶρ ἐπὶ καρπῷ, and while ancient Greek women are inevitably defined in relation to their husbands, Adonis does not appear alone in iconography and is entirely defined by his relationship to Aphrodite.[128] Although from Sappho to Euripides "the roof seems to have been much connected with the husband, whose tall stature it dominates and protects,"[129] in literary representations of the Adonis festival, women are associated with the roof, as they carry gardens of Adonis there to perform lamentations.

The bride who is led to her husband's house is also often associated with fruit in Greek literature and the visual arts. This notion is artfully expressed in Sappho's fragment that concerns the neglected apple reddening on the topmost branch:

> As the sweet apple turns red on the high branch
> high up on the highest branch, the apple pickers have forgotten it
> no, they haven't forgotten it but they were not able to reach it. (fr. 105a Voigt)[130]

The apple is commonly seen to represent the bride in this fragment.[131] Within the context of a wedding, men woo the *parthenos* and vie with one another in their attempt to pluck her. Here, the bride—the delectable piece of fruit—is out of reach.

Fruit was used during the wedding ceremony since custom held that the bride was to eat a piece of fruit in her new home as part of her process of assimilation to the new household. The custom was a long-standing one: according to tradition, Solon decreed that the bride eat a quince within the context of the wedding.[132] On red-figure vases, brides occasionally appear with fruit. For example, on an Attic red-figure loutrophoros in Toronto, a bride holds a piece of fruit, while she herself is held by the arm by the groom.[133]

Just as brides are offered fruit, so too Adonis is offered trays of fruit in vase painting. On the Paris lekythos (fig. 3), Eros offers Adonis a tray of fruit. And on a lekythos in Berlin mentioned above, Eunomia offers Adonis a fruit tray. At Arsinoë's palace in Alexandria, Theocritus's Adonis is surrounded by seasonal fruit (*Idyll* 15.112), precisely what he misses most in Praxilla's hymn, where he longs for cucumbers, pears, and quinces (fr. 1 Page = *PMG* 747). Like Persephone, who, in the *Homeric Hymn to Demeter,* ate a pomegranate seed in the underworld (an action that bound her to Hades forevermore), and like brides in Classical red-figure vase painting, then, Adonis is associated with fruit. Indeed, just as a bride is described as a "sweet apple" in the Sappho fragment, Theocritus describes Adonis as ὡραῖος (1.109), the sort of adjective one might employ to describe a delectable looking apple.[134]

A wedding included lamentation, given that in her transition from *parthenos* to *nymphê* the bride could be seen to mourn the loss of her status as *parthenos*:

> (νύμφη). παρθενία, παρθενία, ποῖ με λίποισ' ἀ‹π›οίχῃ;
> (παρθενία). †οὐκέτι ἤξω πρὸς σέ, οὐκέτι ἤξω.†
>
> Bride. Maidenhood, maidenhood, where are you going leaving me?
> Maidenhood. No longer will I come to you, no longer will I come. (fr. 114 Voigt)

In this fragment, the bride addresses her lost maidenhood upon her marriage, and in her address she incorporates typical elements drawn from ritual lament. Laments tend to include direct address of the deceased (here, maidenhood) and the accusation that the deceased "left" the speaker.[135] In Sappho's fragment, the *parthenia* takes the place of the deceased body at a funeral. While maidenhood is lamented at a wedding, Adonis is mourned at the Adonia. Just as maidenhood may be figured as a trampled flower, so Adonis in some accounts is metamorphosed into an anemone, a flower whose life is very brief.[136]

I have argued that literary and visual representations of Aphrodite and Adonis include nuptial elements, with Adonis in the position of bride. I have also suggested, by means of a close reading of Sappho's *epithalamia* fragments, that women at the Adonia may be reflecting upon the wedding. Weddings involve a reconfiguration of the *oikos* (as represented by the roof), lamentation (the *parthenos* for her lost maidenhood), the possession of the bride by the bridegroom, and a preponderance of plant and fruit imagery (bridegroom as tender shoot, bride/maidenhood as an apple or flower). The Adonis festival draws on all these components, modifying each element slightly. Rather than being led by their husbands to another *oikos* for the production of legitimate children, women cultivate gardens of Adonis and move them up ladders to rooftops. Instead of lamenting their lost status as *parthenoi*, the participants in the Adonis festival lament the death of Adonis. Now that we have established a nuptial framework for the myth and cult of Adonis, we can return to the Karlsruhe lekythos (fig. 5) and the disputed vases mentioned at the beginning of this chapter. Such a nuptial framework will allow us to better understand the imagery on these vases.

The Karlsruhe Lekythos and Nuptial Imagery

The late fifth-century lekythos in Karlsruhe (fig. 5), attributed to the circle of the Meidias Painter, depicts a female figure wearing only a himation and standing on the first rung of a ladder. She receives a vessel—a broken, upturned amphora, containing plants—from a winged male figure, probably Eros. A similar container sits between the two figures on the ground, and another vessel, of an entirely different shape, is behind Eros. All three vessels contain what appears to be vegetal matter sprouting from them, while the vessel behind Eros contains additional round objects. Two female figures with raised palms flank Eros and the woman on the ladder. All three female figures wear jewelry and have carefully styled hair with ornaments. The central female figure is usually identified as Aphrodite, but no inscription identifies her or any other figure on the vase. As mentoned at the start of this chapter, the two broken vessels have been convincingly identified as gardens of Adonis.

The central image on the Karlsruhe lekythos is a female figure on a ladder moving objects. This is curious, for women do not tend to appear on or near ladders in Greek texts or iconography. The ladder is invariably assumed to be the means by which the gardens are transported to the rooftop. Yet the destination of the female figure is unclear: no architectural indications of any kind appear. The female figure on or near a ladder (who moves objects) is the key to why we should treat *as a group* the vases mentioned at the beginning of this chapter (figs. 6–15) and interpreted as *either* an Adonia *or* a wedding.[137] In what follows, I offer a close reading of the Karlsruhe lekythos to connect iconographical elements with the other vases that have been connected to the Adonis festival. I treat first the ladder and the vessels that are depicted on the vase. Next, I examine the other elements (the partial nudity of the female figure, the depiction of potted plants, Eros, and the female figures who flank the central scene). I suggest that all these details resonate within the context of both the Adonia and the wedding.

Ladders

In Greek art and literature, it is overwhelmingly *men* who use ladders when going about their daily activities: getting on and off ships, engaging in siege warfare, or attempting to gain access to the roofs of houses.[138] In a metaphorical sense, one could "use the ladder," for example, in speech making, yet, as is the case with utilitarian ladders, it is men who "use the ladder," not women.[139] In Greek literature, one also finds references to another class of ladders that are more important for my purposes, namely, cosmic ladders, and examples of mortals who attempt to ascend—by means of these stairways to heaven—to the realm of the gods and goddesses.[140] Of course, these attempted ascents to the gods are largely unsuccessful.[141] Otus and Ephialtes wished to pile Pelion on Ossa on Olympus "so that the heavens might be approached" (ἵν' οὐρανὸς ἀμβατὸς εἴη, *Od.* 11.316), and Pindar reports that they "stretched a swift ladder to the steep sky" (πιτνάντες θοὰν κλίμακ' οὐρανὸν ἐς αἰπύν, fr. 162 Maehler).[142] The story of Otus and Ephialtes is a cautionary tale: they planned to fight the gods, and the hubristic mortals are seen as a menace. Otus and Ephialtes end up shooting each other, tricked by Artemis. The point of these stories, at least in part, is that humans can never hope to reach the heavens. Ladders and overreaching seem to go hand in hand, and these tales of mortals attempting to scale the heights all involve humans, specifically mortal men, failing in their attempts to reach the heavens.[143]

In literature and iconography, then, it is rare to see a female figure on a ladder. But Pindar offers a vision of Themis traveling along a celestial ladder to Olympus as she becomes the wife of Zeus: "First the fates led prudent Ouranian Themis . . . to a holy ladder of Olympus along the gleaming road to be the ancient wife of Zeus Soter" (πρῶτον μὲν εὔβουλον Θέμιν οὐρανίαν . . . Μοῖραι ποτὶ κλίμακα σεμνὰν / ἆγον Οὐλύμπου λιπαρὰν καθ' ὁδόν / σωτῆρος ἀρχαίαν ἄλοχον Διὸς ἔμμεν, fr. 30.1, 3–5 Maehler). Themis is described as "Ouranian," an epithet that is used of other divinities but that certainly evokes Aphrodite, who was worshipped as Ourania at Athens and elsewhere.[144] In the Pindar fragment, a ladder results in a successful and proper marriage, that is, a marriage that produces offspring, as Themis gives birth to the Horai. This ladder carries nuptial associations and not because it leads to the second story of a house.

Ladders carry a highly symbolic charge within a marital context elsewhere, as is apparent from the dedication of a terracotta ladder at the shrine of Nymphê on the south slope of the Acropolis.[145] Here, a boundary stone was discovered—marking Nymphê's shrine—along with many loutrophoroi and a votive ladder. The appearance of the votive ladder within the shrine of a nuptial divinity indicates a close relationship between the object and the wedding.[146]

A few other objects—medallions and votive reliefs dating from the fifth and fourth centuries BCE—depict a female figure on or near a ladder (figs. 16–19). On these objects, the female figure transports vessels, including some that are shaped like the vessels depicted on the vases associated with the Adonia.[147] In these other media, as on the Karlsruhe lekythos (fig. 5), the destination is not indicated. The female figure in these cases also tends to be identified by scholars as Aphrodite. Occasionally nuptial elements appear. Sometimes "Aphrodite" is seminude, and the space through which she moves may be marked as celestial by a crescent moon and stars. In these scenes—just as is the case in the scene on the Karlsruhe lekythos (fig. 5) and the scenes with a ladder interpreted as depictions of an *epaulia* (figs. 6, 11, 13, 15)—it is also unclear where the ladder leads; no scholar, however, argues that in these images of "Aphrodite" the ladder leads to a roof or to a second story.

A fragment of a late fifth-century votive relief depicts a female figure in profile, identified as Aphrodite, descending a ladder (fig. 16).[148] In her hand she holds a vessel with a flaring foot and a wide mouth with a handle, and she wears a short veil that has been connected with wedding iconography; for example, it has been compared to Alcestis's short veil on the Eretria Painter's epinêtron (fig. 4).[149] Very similar in appearance to the votive relief is another relief—once in the Museo Kircheriano, now unfortunately lost—that portrays a veiled Aphrodite descending a ladder (fig. 17), also holding a widemouthed vessel.[150] To the right, Eros hovers in the air, and a goat with a kid leaps beneath a crescent moon.[151] Aphrodite, the ladder, and celestial imagery appear again on a silver disk from Building Z in the Kerameikos that dates to ca. 370–60 BCE (fig. 18).[152] This time, however, instead of making use of the ladder, Aphrodite rides sidesaddle on a goat (with kids leaping below) through a landscape dotted with stars and a crescent moon.[153] To the right, Eros flies in with a crown for Aphrodite's head (a common iconographic element in wedding scenes), and a youth hovers just to the left of the ladder holding an incense burner.[154] So, too, on a late fourth-century relief from Sparta (fig. 19), Aphrodite rides on a goat (kids leaping below), while Erotes hover nearby, and a ladder appears in the background on the right.[155] Finally, on a late fourth-century circular marble disk from Athens, the goat-riding Aphrodite is depicted along with a widemouthed vessel (with flaring foot and handles) hovering in the air to the left of the goddess (fig. 20).[156] Although no ladder appears on the marble disk, it is clear from the Kerameikos amulet (fig. 18) and the Sparta relief (fig. 19) that the goat-rider Aphrodite may be connected iconographically with the ladder, and the vessel that seems to float in the sky on the marble disk is an element of a consistent visual vocabulary that appears on these objects.[157] Given the rarity of the appearance of a female figure carrying objects on or near a ladder, these images of "Aphrodite" on a ladder provide a set of comparanda for the Karlsruhe lekythos (fig. 5), the scenes identified as an Adonia (figs. 6–15), as well as the subset of images identified as depictions of an *epaulia* (figs. 6, 11, 13, 15).

Vessels and Myrrh

On the Karlsruhe lekythos (fig. 5), "Aphrodite" is receiving a garden of Adonis from Eros. Another garden appears on the ground, and a vessel is depicted behind Eros. On the objects discussed above, where "Aphrodite" and the heavenly ladder appear, a vessel with a wide mouth and flaring pedestal foot, usually with handles, frequently is indicated. To be sure, the vessels are not identical—they are more or less carefully executed; some are larger; some are smaller. It seems likely, however, that they allude to the same sort of object.[158]

Strikingly similar are the widemouthed vessels depicted on the agora relief and two of the vases associated with the Adonia—the hydria in the British Museum and the lekythos in Berlin (figs. 8 and 9).[159] On the vases, a woman in profile descending a ladder reaches down toward a vessel offered her by a standing female figure. The Berlin lekythos includes a large *thymiatêrion* (incense burner) between the two central figures (just beneath the vessel offered to Aphrodite), and a *thymiatêrion* also appears on another lekythos in St. Petersburg (fig. 7; the *thymiatêrion* appears just to the right of the ladder). On a lekythos in London, Eros is descending the ladder with a *thymiatêrion* in his hand (fig. 10).[160] These details make it likely that rituals involving incense are depicted, and that the widemouthed vessel is a "thurible," or incense burner.[161]

Incense—for example, frankincense (*libanos*) and myrrh (*muron*)—was used in many cults and was associated with divinities other than Aphrodite, but it is especially associated with rituals for Aphrodite and Eros.[162] In particular, incense plays a part in the ancient wedding, with incense burners appearing in red-figure nuptial scenes.[163] In Xenophon's *Symposium*, brides are anointed with myrrh (2.3). And in Sappho (fr. 44.30 Voigt), frankincense and myrrh are mentioned within the context of the marriage of Hector and Andromache.[164] So too Menander's *Samia* includes incense in a list of wedding preparations (673–74).

As seen in chapter 1, incense is also important to the myth and cult of Adonis. After all, Adonis's mother is Myrrha, or Smyrna—Greek words for myrrh—who is metamorphosed into the myrrh tree. Myrrh was used for perfumes, and it was burned as incense. In Theocritus *Idyll* 15, Adonis is offered golden alabastra of Syrian myrrh (Συρίω δὲ μύρω χρύσει' ἀλάβαστρα, 114). And Adonis is equated with myrrh in Bion's *Epitaph on Adonis*: "Sprinkle him with Syrian unguents, with myrrh. Let all myrrh die. Adonis, your myrrh, has died (τὸ σὸν μύρον ὤλετ' Ἄδωνις)" (77–78).

As I have argued in chapter 1, a correlation exists between the figure of Adonis from myth and the objects (the gardens of Adonis and the incense/myrrh) employed in the Adonis festival, inasmuch as the objects are the ritual accoutrements that represent the youth at the Adonia. On the Karlsruhe lekythos (fig. 5), the two gardens of Adonis function as stand-ins for the youth. The vessel behind Eros on the lekythos is of a decidedly peculiar shape;[165] however, a lekythos in New York (fig. 12) associated with the Adonia offers a parallel. Here, the odd container appears twice: to the left of Eros, immediately behind his bent foot (in the same position behind Eros as on the Karlsruhe lekythos), and in the field above. All three of these containers—the container depicted on the Karlsruhe lekythos and the two depicted on the New York lekythos—hold round objects, all have a wide mouth, and all have handles. It has been suggested that the vessel depicted on the New York lekythos (fig. 12) might be a kernos or kerchnos, a somewhat obscure ritual vessel, examples of which have been found in excavations at the Athenian agora and Eleusis.[166] On the New York lekythos, the two "kernoi," as well as the funnel shaped vessel held by the winged figure, all appear to be filled with earth.[167] Vegetal matter may be indicated (traces of green appear), and it is possible that the "kernos" is a depiction of another garden of Adonis.[168] For my purposes, a certain identification of the "kernos" depicted on the Karlsruhe lekythos is not necessary, though it seems likely that it represents either a garden of Adonis, a container for offerings such as incense, or some combination of the two ritual objects (garden and myrrh).[169]

The appearance of the curiously shaped vessel, a container that does not resemble anything from Athenian daily life (though as seen above it does resemble an obscure ritual object), suggests that the Karlsruhe lekythos could be participating in the sort of discourse on primitive life that Gloria Ferrari and others have argued appears in Athenian vase painting.[170] Some Athenian vases allude to a golden age, a time before the reign of Zeus and Cronus. A fragment of Empedocles (128 D-K) describes such a period when humans were under the sole rule of Aphrodite:

> For them there was no Ares as god, no Kydoimos, no Zeus as king or Cronus or Poseidon, but queen Aphrodite [some words missing]. They propitiated her with holy statues (εὐσεβέεσσιν ἀγάλμασιν), painted animal figures (γραπτοῖς τε ζώιοισι), perfumes of crafted fragrance (μύροισί τε δαιδαλεόδμοις), unmixed myrrh as sacrifices (σμύρνης τ' ἀκρήτου θυσίαις), and fragrant frankincense (λιβάνου τε θυώδους), pouring to the ground libations of golden honey. The altar was not drenched by the unmixed slaughter of bulls, but this was the greatest defilement among humankind—to bereave of life and to eat noble limbs.

The passage evokes a golden age, not a scene from contemporary daily life or a ritual as practiced. I suggest that it operates as a textual parallel for the scene described visually by the Karlsruhe lekythos, a scene that evokes not the here and now in Athens but a time long ago. In the Empedocles passage, the offerings to Aphrodite include a heavy emphasis on incense (perfumes, myrrh, and frankincense), which, as we have seen, is a feature of many of the vases associated with the Adonia, as well as a number of the objects that depict "Aphrodite" on a ladder. While the passage does not mention gardens of Adonis, and while I do not suggest that it describes an Adonis festival in any direct way, the scene shares many similarities with the Adonia described in Theocritus *Idyll* 15. In Theocritus's poem, a tableau of Aphrodite and Adonis evokes the "holy statues" (εὐσεβέεσσιν ἀγάλμασιν) described by Empedocles. Not only are the couple offered Syrian myrrh (114) and cakes made of honey, but the animal images described by Theocritus ("all things that fly and creep," πάντ' . . . πετεηνὰ καὶ ἑρπετά, 118) call to mind the "painted animal figures" (γραπτοῖς τε ζώιοισι) in the Empedocles passage.

The Karlsruhe lekythos (fig. 5), far from mechanically depicting the Adonis festival, offers a vision of "Aphrodite," who travels along a celestial ladder carrying objects that represent the youth Adonis. Archaism and foundation legends often appear in the iconography of cult, and we may see the Karlsruhe lekythos evoking a foundation myth for the Adonia.[171] Such an interpretation removes us from the world of daily life and into a mythical realm, bringing us back to the problem articulated at the beginning of this chapter, namely, the challenge of determining whether the figure on the Karlsruhe lekythos is Aphrodite or a ritual actor. An interpretation of this scene as a foundation myth helps explain the blending of the mythical and the real on the Karlsruhe lekythos.[172]

Nudity and Potted Plants

On the Karlsruhe lekythos (fig. 5), "Aphrodite" is nearly naked. Our discussion of the objects above indicates that occasionally "Aphrodite" on a ladder is also seminude. Female nudity is fairly unusual on Classical Athenian red-figure vases, and there is something still more unsettling about the exposure of a scantily clad female figure on a ladder.[173] It is a commonplace that in Greek sculpture and vase painting, women are depicted clothed and men naked.[174] When such "risqué" scenes occur (i.e., when a female figure is not part of a bathing scene or a sympotic scene where nudity might be expected), if the scene is determined to be mythological, the woman tends to be identified as Aphrodite; or if the scene is interpreted as a scene from daily life (a genre scene), she might be connected with the transition of a woman from *parthenos* to *gunê*. Thus, it is suggested that a red-figure lebes gamikos in Athens on which a seminude woman sits on a *klismos* flanked by Erotes and female figures bearing gifts, "indicates clearly that the bride has made the transition from Artemis to Aphrodite; her bare breasts suggest her sexuality now that she has become a married woman."[175] Likewise, the nude sculpted bust on the Eretria Painter's epinêtron (fig. 4) is taken by many scholars to be Aphrodite herself or a representation of a young girl's transition to mature woman.[176] A seminude female figure, then, may evoke Aphrodite or a married woman.

In Bion's *Epitaph on Adonis*, Aphrodite runs through the fields in her grief, her clothing falling down to her navel in a state of disarray, her breasts made bloody as she beats her chest (25–27).[177] Indeed, in Bion's poem, Aphrodite seems to act like female participants at the Adonia; she is more "human" than we would expect. After all, she bleeds in the poem (22) and not divine *ichor*.[178] At Theocritus's Adonia as portrayed in *Idyll* 15, breast baring will be an element of the celebration on the next day during the mourning ceremony, as the hymnist describes, "Having released our hair and letting drop our garments to our ankles, we will begin the clear song with breasts bared (στήθεσι φαινομένοις)," 134–35.[179] And in an epigram of Dioscorides, an onlooker comments on the sexual appeal of a certain Kleo's milky-white breasts during the ceremony in honor of Adonis, wishing he could be as lucky as the youth for whom women mourn (GP 1479–82 = *AP* 5.193).[180] Literary representations of the Adonia feature Aphrodite or ritual participants in the throes of lamentation, their clothing disheveled, breasts bared.[181]

Still another iconographic element on the Karlsruhe lekythos links weddings and the Adonia: potted plants. Potted plants do not tend to appear frequently in Classical Athenian red-figure iconography, but when they do appear, they may be associated with two contexts: the Adonia and the nuptial sphere. On the Eretria Painter's epinêtron (the panel that depicts Alcestis's *epaulia*, fig. 4), two female figures arrange plants in two lebetes gamikoi and a loutrophoros—vases typically associated with the wedding.[182] Multiple scholars have suggested that the Eretria Painter's epinêtron (fig. 4) depicts a performance of the Adonia and that the plants represent gardens of Adonis.[183] In fact, the particular plants and containers on the epinêtron do not at all resemble the gardens of Adonis that are depicted, for example, on the Karlsruhe lekythos (fig. 5), the acorn lekythos from Athens (fig. 21, discussed below), and the Hellenistic terracotta figurine (fig. 23). Nevertheless, given the rarity of potted plants in iconography, it is remarkable that they appear only in these two specific contexts—the wedding and the Adonia. On another vase, a red-figure pyxis in London by the Eretria Painter, the Nereids are depicted in a nuptial setting, and two black-figure lebetes gamikoi and a loutrophoros contain branches.[184] One of the Nereids spins an *iunx*, an object that we have already seen mesmerizing Adonis on the Meidias Painter's hydria (fig. 1). While the Eretria Painter's epinêtron (fig. 4) certainly does not depict a performance of an Adonis festival (the vessels depicted on the Eretria Painter's epinêtron and red-figure pyxis do not contain whole plants, like those grown in a garden of Adonis, but rather branches or sprigs), the fact that potted plants appear within a nuptial sphere as well as within the cultic context of an Adonia is just one further example to support the claim that the iconography associated with weddings resonates within the context of an Adonia.

Erotes and Bands of Maidens

On the Karlsruhe lekythos (fig. 5), a life-size winged creature hands "Aphrodite" a garden of Adonis. Although uninscribed, he tends to be identified as Eros. So, too, on figures 5–14, Erotes hover or stand in the background or foreground, frequently providing assistance by moving objects such as incense, gardens of Adonis, boxes, crowns, and jewelry.[185] Erotes appear in Theocritus *Idyll* 15, hovering about the bower setting at the Alexandrian Adonia in the palace of Queen Arsinoë (120–22). And in Bion's *Epitaph on Adonis*, Erotes prepare Adonis's body for a funeral while also serving as a chorus that mourns Adonis (79–85).

The appearance of small, winged Erotes during the second half of the fifth century marks a shift in the visual portrayal of Eros.[186] The diminutive creatures become quite popular in wedding iconography, where they offer crowns or jewelry to adorn the bride. When we are confronted with such benign creatures, it is easy for us to forget that during the Archaic and early Classical period, winged figures are frequently aggressive and often move *bodies*—either in rape/pursuit scenes or images that depict the transport of the deceased.[187] On the Karlsruhe lekythos, the life-size Eros calls to mind the Archaic Eros, as he hands "Aphrodite" a garden of Adonis, an object that represents the deceased youth.

The connection between Adonis and his ritual accoutrements (gardens of Adonis/incense as analogues for the youth) helps explain the rarely discussed inscriptions on the Karlsruhe lekythos (fig. 5). Although the figures on the lekythos are not identified by name, ΚΑΛΗ is printed to the right of the female figure on the left, while ΚΑΛΟΣ floats above the head of the life-size Eros. In Classical Athenian red-figure scenes, *kalos*/*kalê* inscriptions appear in a nuptial context where the groom and/or the bride is emphatically pronounced to be handsome or beautiful.[188] For example, a red-figure loutrophoros that depicts a wedding procession includes a groom who leads a bride by the wrist; the bride is identified as ΚΑΛΗ and the groom as ΚΑΛΟΣ.[189] A similarly inscribed fragmentary pyxis from the Acropolis by the Penthesilea Painter depicts a veiled and seated female figure described as *kalê* receiving adjustments from an attendant. To the left the groom is described as *kalos* (although it is hard to tell if he is, in fact, *kalos*, as only his feet survive).[190] In Bion's *Epitaph on Adonis*, *kalos* is employed so frequently to describe Adonis that it becomes a kind of epithet for the youth, often appearing at line endings along with his name, καλὸς Ἄδωνις.[191] On the Karlsruhe lekythos, in place of *kalos* Adonis, Eros, depicted as a beardless youth, holds a garden of Adonis, a "beautiful" representation of Adonis on the ritual level.

Earlier in this chapter, I discussed the "bands of maidens" from poetry—groups of young girls who play or dance together until one of their number is abducted or married off (as we have seen, frequently there is not much of a distinction between these fates). An acorn lekythos in Athens (fig. 21) attributed to Aison depicts a band of maidens familiar from poetry alongside a garden of Adonis.[192] No inscriptions identify the figures. On the far left of the lekythos, a woman with carefully styled hair and jewelry tends to three gardens of Adonis.[193] The containers sit atop a table and are of different shapes; however, the middle one is a smaller version of the broken and upturned amphora depicted on the Karlsruhe lekythos (fig. 5). To the right appears a group of three female figures that appear to be drawn straight from an interior *epaulia* scene, and, in fact, the scene on the acorn lekythos (fig. 21) has been interpreted as a wedding scene.[194] One young woman stands and gestures toward an Eros in the air, while a second woman sits holding a third woman on her lap. Such lap sitting occurs frequently in depictions of weddings.[195] The woman who sits comfortably on her companion's lap on the acorn lekythos at Athens resembles to a striking degree the central females on figures 6, 11, and 13, images that have been identified as *epaulia* scenes.

As we have seen, within the context of a wedding, a female figure amid a band of maidens is singled-out and transferred to a new household. Such a movement appears in the Pindar fragment (fr. 30 Maehler) that describes a mythical wedding, where the Moirai lead Themis along a ladder to the heavens, as she becomes the wife of Zeus. In literary accounts of Adonis, he too is singled-out and moved between two spheres by a band of maidens. The Horai lead Adonis up from Acheron, presumably to Aphrodite in Theocritus's *Idyll* 15 (102–3). The verb *agein,* which is frequently used in the middle voice to mean "to marry," is employed in Theocritus's poem to describe Adonis as well as in the Pindar fragment to describe Themis with only a difference in tense, as the Horai "led" (ἄγαγον) Adonis and the Moirai "were leading" (ἆγον) Themis.[196]

The Karlsruhe lekythos (fig. 5) draws on the conventions of red-figure wedding and adornment scenes that depict female figures and their attendants. The vase depicts female figures transferring a ritual object that represents Adonis the bride up a heavenly ladder. The ladder connects the viewer to a space through which the Horai and Aphrodite might move, leading Adonis—or an object that represents the youth (a garden or incense)—to the heavens.

This chapter has assembled elements of iconography generally associated with the Adonis festival to argue that these elements are also documented in nuptial imagery.[197] The nuptial connections on the Karlsruhe lekythos, along with the wedding elements in visual and iconographic representations of Adonis and his cult, suggest that Athenian women at the Adonia may have been reflecting upon the wedding. At the Adonia, Athenian women harness the narrative of goddesses and mortals through the medium of public lamentation. In so doing, they give voice to a distinctive way of conceptualizing gender roles. This offers them a different, albeit temporary, subject position—that of the powerful goddess Aphrodite. Athenian women at the Adonia identify with a goddess who, in the *Homeric Hymn to Aphrodite,* manipulates nuptial elements for her own ends. At the end of the Adonia, after the women come down from the rooftops, they return to their lives. But for that fragile moment, in the performance of the ritual, they play the role of the goddess Aphrodite.

A fragment of Sappho connects weddings and the path to Olympus. The speaker remarks, "For we are going to a wedding" (σ]τείχομεν γὰρ ἐς γάμον, fr. 27.8

Voigt) and, a few lines later, "the road to great Olympus" (ὄδος μ[έ]γαν εἰς Ὄλ[υμπον, fr. 27.12 Voigt), an image that evokes the cosmic ladder, the stairway to heaven discussed in this chapter. It is not clear from what remains of the fragment whether there is a road to great Olympus for mortals in connection with a wedding.[198] Perhaps, fleetingly, at an Adonis festival there is such a path, and the Adonis festival offers the women who perform the ritual a different perspective on the traditional wedding.[199]

3 Funerals

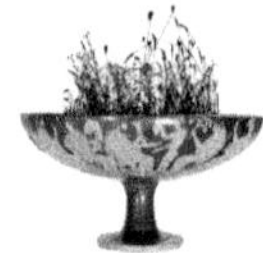

Aristophanes's Adôniazousai

Chapter 2 emphasized the importance of viewing images of Adonis and his cult within a nuptial frame and suggested that the Athenian Adonia draws on and critiques the wedding ceremony; the Adonis festival enacts elements of nuptial ritual with a twist. At the same time, the Adonia comments on another prominent ritual, the funeral, and in this chapter, I will return to the importance of the public role of lamentation (introduced in chapter 1) within the framework of the Adonis festival. For Aristophanes's *Lysistrata* preserves a description of an Adonis festival in the mouth of the Official character, and his portrayal of the cult foregrounds lamentation.

In *Lysistrata*, Lysistrata and her allies take over the Athenian Acropolis.[1] Their objective is to put a stop to the Peloponnesian War, and to this end they intend to hold a sex strike until their goal is achieved. Soon after Lysistrata's plan has been clearly articulated, and the women have sworn an oath indicating their commitment, the Official stumbles onstage and characterizes the actions of Lysistrata and her friends as an Adonis festival (387–98). The Official recalls overhearing a woman mourning Adonis while he and others were embroiled in discussions in the assembly over whether to undertake the Sicilian expedition. He connects the current actions of Lysistrata and her friends with this past performance, describing what he sees when he arrives as a group of boisterous, sexually depraved women—a threat to his *polis*—and associating their activities with foreign cult.

Many have accepted uncritically the Official's description of the Adonia and have drawn conclusions about the festival from his remarks. The Adonia is thus characterized as an apolitical women's festival and is invariably described as private.[2] But does the Official, a character with a specific role in Aristophanes's comedy, offer unmediated access to the festival? After all, the Official is mocked and metaphorically killed onstage, and the women whom he disparages triumph in the end.[3] Although some Athenians may have identified with the Official and echoed his disdain for the rowdy cult, he presents at best an incomplete or partially accurate representation of the festival.

The first part of this chapter examines descriptions of other "foreign" rituals—a problematic category explained below—specifically maenadic rituals and other nonmainstream Dionysiac rites, to suggest that the Official's characterization of the Adonia accords with other portrayals of such practices at Athens at the end of the fifth century. When the festival is contextualized within a much broader discourse concerning ritual in the *polis*, we may be less inclined to trust the Official's characterization of the festival. Instead, this chapter suggests that competing versions of the Adonis festival existed at Athens and that insiders and outsiders to the cult might convey conflicting notions of the Adonia's role in the *polis*.

In the second part of this chapter, I take as my starting point a scholion on line 389 that suggests *Lysistrata* may have been alternatively titled, *Adôniazousai*, "Women-at-the-Adonis-Festival." On the use of the word Ἀδωνιασμός by the Official (389), the note reads: "For the women used to celebrate a festival for Adonis and they used to carry garden-thingies up to their rooftops. And some, for this reason, call (or subtitle) the drama *Adôniazousai*" (ἑορτὴν γὰρ ἐπετέλουν τῷ Ἀδώνιδι αἱ γυναῖκες καὶ κήπους τινὰς εἰς τὰ δώματα ἀνέφερον. τινὲς δὲ ἐκ τούτου τὸ δρᾶμα Ἀδωνιαζούσας ἐπιγράφουσιν).[4] This title is rejected, with a dismissive οὐ καλῶς (not correctly), and most scholars have followed suit. A close reading of *Lysistrata* with attention to Adonis festival elements, however, suggests that Lysistrata and her allies hold a metaphorical Adonia atop the Acropolis, deploying foreign ritual in order to successfully stop the Peloponnesian War. Such a reading of *Lysistrata* insists on the public role of the Adonia (contrary to what the Official would have us believe), since, within the context of the play, an Adonis festival puts an end to the Peloponnesian War. My argument is slightly distanced from a suggestion of a real enactment of the Adonia. Instead, as I will argue, the play emphasizes elements of the festival that would have resonated with an Athenian audience familiar with the myth and cult of Adonis, such as the Acropolis as rooftop, the importance of Aphrodite, the boar, myrrh, and lamentation. The Adonis festival can thus be seen to provide a kind of template or cultural script for the play.

Polis Disordering

In *Lysistrata,* the Official who explicitly alludes to the Adonia is, specifically, a *proboulos*, a representative of a fairly new civic office in 411 BCE, the year when *Lysistrata* was produced.[5] The position of *proboulos* was created after the failed Sicilian expedition and represented a shift in the mechanics of Athenian democracy. The holder of the new office embodied broad powers, including the ability to allot funds and levy troops.[6] The Official recalls the doomed military venture in his very first remarks, as he marches onstage full of bluster, disgusted and disapproving:

Πρ. ἆρ' ἐξέλαμψε τῶν γυναικῶν ἡ τρυφὴ
χὠ τυμπανισμὸς χοἰ πυκνοὶ Σαβάζιοι,
ὅ τ' Ἀδωνιασμὸς οὗτος οὑπὶ τῶν τεγῶν,
οὗ 'γώ ποτ' ὢν ἤκουον ἐν τἠκκλησίᾳ;
ἔλεγεν ὁ μὴ ὥρασι μὲν Δημόστρατος
πλεῖν εἰς Σικελίαν, ἡ γυνὴ δ' ὀρχουμένη
"αἰαῖ Ἄδωνιν" φησίν, ὁ δὲ Δημόστρατος
ἔλεγεν ὁπλίτας καταλέγειν Ζακυνθίων
ἡ δ' ὑποπεπωκυῖ' ἡ γυνὴ 'πὶ τοῦ τέγους
"κόπτεσθ' Ἄδωνιν" φησίν· ὁ δ' ἐβιάζετο,
ὁ θεοῖσιν ἐχθρὸς καὶ μιαρὸς Χολοζύγης.
τοιαῦτ' ἀπ' αὐτῶν ἐστιν ἀκολαστάσματα. (*Lysistrata* 387–98)

Official: Has the depravity of the women caught fire for everyone to see, and all their *tympana* playing and cries of "Sabazius!" and this Adonis-festival-activity on the rooftops, which once I was hearing when I was in the assembly? Demostratus was saying—may he rot—"Sail to Sicily!" and meanwhile his wife was dancing away and saying, "Alas for Adonis!" And Demostratus was saying to levy Zakynthian hoplites, and she, rather tipsy, was up there on the roof saying, "Beat your breast for Adonis!" But he rammed it through, Demostratus did, that man hated by the gods, that polluted Cholozyges. Such are the unruly acts from these women.

The Official, unlike the spectators, is unaware of Lysistrata's plans. He quickly takes stock of the situation: *it* has flared up once again (ἐξέλαμψε, 387)—he has heard it all before, a few years back.[7] But what is *it* that has, once again, reared its head at the center of his city? He rattles off a kind of list, three elements that will be discussed in detail below: "the depravity of the women," (τῶν γυναικῶν ἡ τρυφή, 387); "their *tympana* playing" (χὠ τυμπανισμός, 388); and "cries of Sabazius" (χοἰ πυκνοὶ Σαβάζιοι, 388). The Official then reminisces about a time, not too long ago, when the debate over the Sicilian expedition was being held in the assembly. During the debate, the wife of Demostratus could be heard lamenting the death of Adonis on a nearby rooftop.[8] The remainder of the Official's monologue concerns his perception of the Adonis festival, and the elements mentioned earlier—the τρυφή, the τυμπανισμός, and the πυκνοί Σαβάζιοι—are subsumed under the larger rubric of Ἀδωνιασμός (Adonis festival activity).[9]

Although the Official begins by mentioning "depravity" (τρυφή), Sabazius (a foreign divinity from the East), and *tympana* playing—three elements that, as we shall see, are markers of foreign cult in the Athenian imagination—the Adonia takes over the moment it is mentioned. The demonstrative adjective (οὗτος, 389) links the activity of the women whom he currently sees atop the Acropolis with the Adonia he remembers from a few years back before the fleet set sail and acts as a kind of hinge linking past and present ("this Adonis-festival-activity on the rooftops which once I was hearing when I was in the assembly," ὅ τ' Ἀδωνιασμὸς οὗτος οὑπὶ τῶν τεγῶν,/ οὗ 'γώ ποτ' ὢν ἤκουον ἐν τἠκκλησίᾳ, 389–90). The Official then recounts a pivotal moment in Athenian history when debates over whether to sail to Sicily inauspiciously coincided with an Adonia. The Official names Demostratus as instigator of the failed Sicilian expedition and characterizes him as "hated by the gods" (ὁ θεοῖσιν ἐχθρός, 397) and "polluted" (μιαρός, 395). As the Official concludes his narrative, he returns to the present scene atop the Acropolis, directly linking Lysistrata and her allies with Demostratus ("such are the unruly acts from these women," τοιαῦτ' ἀπ' αὐτῶν ἐστιν ἀκολαστάσματα, 398). Lysistrata and her accomplices, then, are seen as a force of disorder for the *polis* and are connected with the individual who precipitated the disastrous military endeavor.[10]

I will return to the Sicilian expedition in the second half of this chapter, but first, I emphasize that it tends to go unnoticed that the Official's characterization of the Adonis festival operates within a more general conversation about non-mainstream cult. The Official's description of the activities of Lysistrata and her friends essentially serves as a definition of foreign cult as imagined at Athens, but his definition both applies and does not apply to the Adonia.

Foreign Cult at Athens

First and foremost, what the Official disapproves of involves τρυφή. Indeed, the Official returns to τρυφή soon after, emphasizing the wanton nature of the women: "For whenever we ourselves sink to the same level as the women and we teach them to luxuriate excessively (τρυφᾶν), such schemes bloom from them," 404–6). The word τρυφή, at the end of the fifth century, evokes a constellation of connotations—excess (specifically Eastern excess), luxury, a lack of restraint, as well as effeminacy.[11] By this period, τρυφή may be a characteristic of men or of women, but as far as the Official is concerned, it is specifically τρυφή connected with women—he emphasizes women both times he uses the word—that is at the heart of the trouble in the *polis*.

While the Official begins with τρυφή, he quickly moves on to τυμπανισμός, focusing on the kettledrums that were used in the worship of a variety of ecstatic cults. During the late fifth century, *tympana* were primarily connected in the minds of Athenians with maenadic worship of Dionysus.[12] In the opening speech of the *Bacchae*, for example, Dionysus orders his *thiasos* to take up their *tympana* and make a loud noise so that the city of Cadmus may see them (59).[13] Later in the play, Pentheus, speaking to the disguised Dionysus, says that he will either sell the women or make them slaves, "having put a stop to their racket and the din of their hide drums" (513–14). Much like the character Pentheus in the *Bacchae*, precisely what the swaggering Official finds so appalling is the loud noise that these women produce with their *tympana*, the rhythmic thumping of crowds of ecstatic women.[14]

In addition to τρυφή and τυμπανισμός, the Official mentions πυκνοί Σαβάζιοι, "lots of Sabazius cries"—*too much* Sabazius as far as he is concerned.[15] The πυκνοί Σαβάζιοι are connected with the preceding τυμπανισμός and not just in the mind of the Official character in *Lysistrata*. For it is not only Dionysus and his followers who are associated with *tympana*. Kettledrums were the instruments of choice in the worship of Sabazius, and Sabazius is a god whose ritual has been described as "Dionysiac experience under another name."[16]

Even though Sabazius is decidedly *not* Adonis, the Official is associating the two as he moves from πυκνοί Σαβάζιοι to Ἀδωνιασμός. To understand the Official's perspective on the Adonia, a consideration of descriptions of foreign cult at Athens during the Classical period is in order, since, as we will see, τρυφή, τυμπανισμός, and πυκνοί Σαβάζιοι are distinctive elements of Classical Athenian discourse concerning foreign cult.

Indeed, a similar connection between foreign deities that are in fact distinct occurs in Demosthenes's *On the Crown* (259–60), a speech written in 330 BCE, about eighty years after *Lysistrata* was produced. Demosthenes wishes to paint a particularly defamatory picture of his opponent. He brings all manner of charges against Aeschines in order to besmirch his character: his family is poor; his father is a slave; when he was growing up, he spent entirely too much time with his mother. Another way Demosthenes taints the name of his opponent is to connect him with the worship of certain deities from the East, specifically Sabazius and Attis. In a vivid and theatrical description, Demosthenes speaks of Aeschines racing through the streets with crowds of unbridled women, brandishing snakes, shouting Sabazius cries, and reveling in Attis devotion. Indeed, later in the speech, he returns to the subject of Aeschines's mother, calling her a *tympanistria* (18.284).[17] Demosthenes associates Aeschines quite explicitly with the worship of very particular marginal deities, treating Sabazius and Attis as nearly one and the same.[18]

Demosthenes deploys foreign religious practices in order to belittle his opponent, disparaging Aeschines by describing his involvement in certain unsavory activities—worship of Sabazius, Attis devotion, and practices that evoke certain kinds of Dionysiac rituals—all jumbled together, a hodgepodge of nonmainstream activity. Meanwhile, Demosthenes aligns himself with deities of quite another sort. Earlier in the speech, the orator had paused and lingered, quite dramatically, as he invoked Pythian Apollo along with other gods and goddesses connected with the native soil of Attica (18.141). For certain fifth- and fourth-century Athenians like Demosthenes, some divinities are simply more established, more mainstream. During the Classical period, orators do not stand up and proclaim publicly that they themselves are devotees of cults such as that of Sabazius or Attis or Adonis.[19] Rather, they choose to associate their opponents with such activity.[20]

Of course, Demosthenes's description likely does not refer to a ritual as it was actually practiced, given the hostile purpose of the passage. What is more, the foreign ritual is surprisingly Greek. The priestess who officiates is Aeschines's mother, a Greek woman; the activities call to mind Dionysiac and Orphic rites that were indigenous to Greece; and elements of the ritual seem drawn from the Athenian marriage ceremony.[21] The comments of Demosthenes regarding Aeschines's nonmainstream ritual conduct are important to keep in mind when attempting to come to terms with the remarks of the Official in *Lysistrata*, inasmuch as both passages indicate a hostility to foreign practices.

Scholars have categorized deities like Adonis, Attis, Cybele, Bendis, and Sabazius as "foreign" gods. Yet it has been suggested that "the 'foreign gods' . . . are not a group recognized as such by the Greeks. They are assembled by modern scholars, in the belief that they [the foreign gods] were in fact first worshipped outside of Greece."[22] And because of the negative valuation placed on foreign ritual, modern scholars have tended to describe such ritual as an aberration, essentially un-Greek, an infection from abroad.[23] Yet these so-called foreign cults were modified and adapted once they were imported to Athens, and we should not expect an Athenian description of a foreign cult to offer accurate information about the original rites for the deity in his or her homeland.[24] The category "foreign cult" is problematic because the distinction is not so much between Greek and non-Greek as between established and nonestablished religion.[25]

Nevertheless, foreignness did function as a metaphor for the ancient Greeks, and it is this notion that interests me. For example, ecstatic dancing and *tympana* playing are markers of foreign cult, and these actions (even if not *really* foreign) can underscore the strangeness of a ritual.[26] Such practices are very much associated with Dionysus, who is portrayed in literary texts as an Eastern divinity only just arrived, although the Greeks were worshipping Dionysus as early as Mycenaean times.

A certain kind of dancing and the sound of particular instruments, then, may indicate that a cult is metaphorically foreign even if the cult is decidedly Greek, and it is in this sense that I use the term foreign cult. Rituals in honor of gods such as Sabazius and Adonis, as well as certain nonmainstream rituals for Dionysus included such ecstatic elements. The notion that foreignness can function as a metaphor helps explain the ambiguous position in the *polis* that some cults inhabit, including the Adonia, which has been described as "paradoxical . . . both within and outside the canon."[27] The strangeness of such rituals is worth keeping in mind, since it is not only modern scholars who describe foreign cult in negative terms. Some ancients too—like the Official—were troubled by certain kinds of ritual in the *polis*.[28] The ancients criticized such cults specifically for frivolity (παιδιά) and luxuriousness (τρυφή).[29] Thus, τρυφή—what worries the Official in *Lysistrata*—is a defining characteristic of ecstatic foreign cult.

I suggest that a specific set of associations is attached to certain foreign cults in the minds of Athenians. Classical Athenian portrayals of maenadic rituals for Dionysus, as well as descriptions of informal Dionysiac rites, consistently characterize the participants as engaging in sexual activity, drinking, and playing *tympana*. Furthermore, the distinction between the participant and the spectator becomes blurred, as witnesses to the cult become involved in the ritual activity. Descriptions of the Adonia are surprisingly similar to such portrayals of Dionysiac experience. Fifth- and fourth-century Athenians, then, tend to class together foreign cults—certain Dionysiac rituals and the Adonia—that were in fact distinct. This suggests that the Official offers only a partial perspective on the Adonia, a perspective that needs to be examined within the context of stereotypes about such activities.

Of course, Classical Athenian texts do not characterize all foreign ritual in exactly the same way. For example, Bendis is a foreign god, yet rituals for Bendis do not carry the same associations that the Adonia carries. What is more, in what follows, I do not discuss state-sanctioned rites for Dionysus, like the Great Dionysia. Instead, descriptions of maenadic practices and nonmainstream Dionysiac practices will be my focus. I am not investigating maenadic ritual as practiced—no unambiguous evidence indicates that maenads actually performed rites at Athens during the Classical period—but rather the fact that Classical Athenians enjoyed thinking about maenadic ritual and that descriptions of such rituals bear striking resemblances to descriptions of the Adonia.

Sex, Drugs, and Kettledrums

Euripides's *Bacchae*, more than any other extant play, offers an extended meditation on nonestablished religious practice. After all, the play considers the place of foreign cult in the *polis*, as Dionysus, the "new" god, arrives.[30] Inasmuch as Dionysus is native *and* nonnative, established *and* nonestablished, civic *and* wild, he inhabits a paradoxical position, one that has been described as a "double identity."[31] Pentheus's characterization of maenadic activity in *Bacchae* warrants comparison with the Official's portrayal of the Adonia, since, like the Official, Pentheus is a representative of the state; like the Official, Pentheus is opposed to foreign ritual; and like the Official, Pentheus is similarly ineffective in his opposition to nonestablished religious activity.

Three elements of maenadic activity are consistently emphasized in *Bacchae*. The women who revere Dionysus are characterized as sex obsessed, drunk on wine, and associated with the clatter of *tympana*. In his opening lines, Pentheus explains that the women of Thebes have left their homes for what are in his view feigned Bacchic rituals. In reality, he says, they are each "slinking off to a deserted place to serve the beds of men" (222–23), and "they serve Aphrodite before Bacchus" (225).[32] Pentheus suggests that the rituals in honor of the new god are sexual in nature, and, to be sure, anxieties about uncontrolled sex and, more specifically, questions of paternity and illegitimate children loom large in this play.[33]

The utter inextricability of Aphrodite and Dionysus in *Bacchae* is underscored by still another character, the messenger who explains to Pentheus that "when wine is no longer present, there is no Aphrodite, and there is no longer any other pleasure for people" (773–74). Dionysus is of course associated with wine (we are told in the play that Dionysus introduced it to humans, 278–80), and he is closely identified with the liquid, when Teiresias remarks that Dionysus "is poured out to the gods" (284). Pentheus's vivid image of women on the slopes of Mount Kithairon with wine mixing bowls (221–22) is but the first of several instances when he characterizes the women as bibulous and associates Dionysiac worship with wine.

The king of Thebes, then, associates the women's ritual with sex and with drinking. But it is the kettledrums that really get to him. In the prologue to *Bacchae*, Dionysus orders his band of followers to strike their *tympana* so that the city of Cadmus may see (61). In this formulation the persistent thumping sound becomes a spectacle. The *tympana* are mentioned again in the *parodos*, and it is likely that the chorus carried the instruments with them given that they refer to "*this*" kettledrum (τόδε, 124). Pentheus is most disturbed by the kettledrums when he exclaims, thoroughly frustrated, that he will put a stop to the racket and threatens to make the women slaves at the looms (511–14).

Meanwhile, despite Pentheus's insistence that sex, wine, and kettledrums characterize the women's ritual, the messenger reports that the women are, rather, conducting themselves chastely and temperately (686). The messenger goes on to explain, "[They are] not as you say, drunk on wine and the sound of the pipe, slinking off to deserted spots and hunting Aphrodite through the forest" (686–88).

The messenger's remark is a succinct formulation of Pentheus's triadic characterization of maenadic activity, and, moreover, in the messenger's description *auloi* (pipes), rather than the percussion instrument, provide the orgiastic music (or, rather, do *not* provide the orgiastic music, since the messenger asserts it is not happening).

While the messenger manages to witness maenadic activity and return unscathed, Pentheus does not fare so well. Despite Pentheus's hostility to Dionysus and his followers, by the end of the play he becomes precisely what he despises, namely, a participant in maenadic practices. Ultimately, Pentheus finds the rites for Dionysus irresistible, and he too is drawn into the Dionysiac sphere.

It is frequently said that the interchange between spectator and participant that occurs in Euripides's *Bacchae* is characteristic of the Dionysiac experience, just one of many polarities that Dionysus tends to blur.[34] And indeed, Pentheus's description of the maenads and his experience with them is similar to Xuthus's description of his own maenadic experience in Euripides's *Ion* (550–54). In *Ion*, Xuthus has just realized that Ion is his son, and he and Ion attempt to determine who Ion's mother could be. To this end, Xuthus recalls his participation in a Dionysiac ritual, in which, as a result, an illegitimate child was produced (or rather *notionally* produced, since within the context of the play it turns out that this is, in fact, not how Ion came to be conceived). Nevertheless, at this moment in the play, the Dionysiac festival that Xuthus attended is understood to be the kind of event where this sort of thing could easily transpire—sex with a participant on the part of an overeager spectator, resulting in a child. Just as Pentheus's descriptions in *Bacchae* associate Dionysiac ritual, sex, and drinking, so too does Xuthus's portrayal of his experiences in *Ion*.

It is also revealed during the discussion that Xuthus was, to some degree, a participant in the ritual. Of course, Xuthus is a man, and maenadic worship of Dionysus is predominantly associated with women.[35] But just as in *Bacchae*, when Pentheus is overcome by the Dionysiac and becomes a maenad, so too for Xuthus the dividing line between spectator and participant becomes a bit difficult to perceive. Like Pentheus (but rather less disastrously), Xuthus is brought into the *thiasos*, the maenadic group, as he describes himself as "in the throes of Bacchic pleasures" (553).[36]

I emphasize the characterization of maenadic activity in *Bacchae* and *Ion*, along with the disintegration of the boundary between spectator and participant in both texts because the Adonis festival and maenadic worship of Dionysus look very similar in texts that imagine them. For example, Moschion, a character in Menander's *Samia*, also has a run-in with a group of women and their ritual practices (38–49), but this time the ritual is the Adonia.[37] As Moschion describes it, the ruckus was keeping him awake and seemed like fun to him, so he looked on for a while, becoming a spectator. A pregnancy results, and much of the rest of the play is concerned with the illegitimate child that resulted from the one-night stand at the all-night party.

Menander's *Samia* allows us to revisit the issues that were brought to the fore in *Bacchae* and *Ion*. Even though the Adonia is not the same as maenadic ritual, it is nevertheless described in ways that evoke descriptions of ecstatic Dionysiac worship. Pentheus's and Xuthus's tendency to associate certain kinds of ritual activities with sex is, once again, emphasized with Moschion's confession of the pregnancy. Again, for Moschion, the distinction between spectator and participant is blurred, inasmuch as he joins in the Adonis festival. The very same descriptive cluster, then, surrounds the Adonia, suggesting that the festival is part and parcel of a more general discourse surrounding a particular kind of religious experience at Athens.

If we return to *Lysistrata*, we find that the pattern recurs: sex, drugs, and kettledrums. The Official characterizes the women as oversexed and unruly (387).[38] Once again, the association between female ritual practice and drinking appears, as the Official describes the woman on the roof as "a little tipsy" (395) and references the cries of Sabazius, whose rites, as we have seen, resemble those of Dionysus. The thudding *tympana* continue to be a key component in the portrayal of the Adonia (388).

What is more, in *Lysistrata*, the spectator is drawn into the ritual, as was the case in representations of maenadic activities. By the time Lysistrata and her friends are finished with him, the Official is dressed as a woman and given a veil and a sewing basket (529–38). And right after this exchange, a mock funeral is held for the Official and he is dressed as a corpse (599–613). The Official, who had earlier been so opposed to the foreign ritual practices of the women in his *polis*, is then, metaphorically killed, as Pentheus is literally.

To summarize: I have suggested that a specific set of associations is attached to certain foreign practices—specifically maenadic practices—at Athens, and I have contextualized the Adonia within a much broader discourse surrounding such ritual. By examining the ways that Athenians conceived of a variety of nonmainstream rituals, and by looking closely at descriptions of what happens when groups of women get together to perform practices considered by many to be nonestablished and foreign, I have teased out a precise cluster of elements that appears again and again. Characters in male-authored texts describe women who get together in these groups as sex-obsessed, drunken revelers, accompanied by kettledrums. Just as Sabazius and Attis have unsavory associations for Demosthenes and are invoked by him as a strategic way of undermining his opponent, so it is with

Adonis for the Official, as he dismisses the ritual practice that unnerves him as foreign. The spectator—Pentheus, Xuthus, Moschion, the Official in *Lysistrata*—repeatedly becomes precisely what he is describing, and in the case of Pentheus and the Official in *Lysistrata,* the spectator becomes precisely what he despises.

The emphasis in all these texts on the collapse of the boundary between spectator and participant indicates a deep concern about the effects of certain ritual practices upon the *polis*. It is commonly observed that maenadic activity presents a civic threat—if only an imagined one. After all, maenadic practices are portrayed as antithetical to marriage and fundamentally destructive to the household.[39] Like such troubling maenadic practices, excessive lamentation may also be seen to pose a threat to the *polis*, and the Adonia, with its emphasis on female lamentation, shares another characteristic with the depiction of maenads in literary texts, inasmuch as intensely grieving women are likened to bacchants in Greek tragedy.[40]

In Aristophanes's *Lysistrata*, as we have seen, the actions of the women are fundamentally destructive to the *polis* as far as the Official is concerned. Lysistrata and her friends represent to him a civic threat. But the Official is a comic character embedded within *Lysistrata,* and his position within the context of the play must be taken into account. There is a contrary pull to the Official's version of what the women atop the Acropolis are doing.

Polis Ordering: Aristophanes's *Adôniazousai*

Ritual—of all sorts—is prominent in *Lysistrata*.[41] After all, this play contains the much-discussed roster of elite female ritual practice at different life stages (640–47). The first lines of *Lysistrata* signal the centrality of religious festival in the play as a whole, and they warrant careful scrutiny, not only because they are programmatic, but also because they set up an opposition between two kinds of ritual in the *polis*. An irritated Lysistrata appears onstage, muttering under her breath. The women she has convened are late: "But if someone had called them to a festival of Bacchus, or of Pan, or to Kolias or to a festival of Genetyllis, it wouldn't even be possible to get through because of the kettledrums (ὑπὸ τῶν τυμπάνων). But as it is, not one single woman is present here (1–4)." The play begins in the middle of Lysistrata's train of thought. Her first word is an adversative "but" (ἀλλά). Thus, from the very beginning, an opposition is established. The implication is that Lysistrata has summoned a group of women for some purpose that is diametrically opposed to whatever it is that connects the worship of Bacchus, Pan, Kolias, and Genetyllis.

Lysistrata herself provides a link between the four divinities, a certain musical instrument—the *tympanon*—precisely what the cranky Official rails against when he makes his entrance and what, as we have seen, rankles Pentheus. Kolias and Genetyllis are more obscure to us than Bacchus and Pan, but they evoke Aphrodite and τρυφή—that charge levied by the ancients against foreign cult.[42] As we have seen, Dionysiac practices are frequently associated with sex in the Greek imagination, and Pan is linked no less to the erotic sphere, appearing in literature and vase painting with his ever-present entourage of nymphs, playful creatures that are extremely sexually active and fertile; he is also the father of the satyrs.[43] Bacchus, Pan, Kolias, and Genetyllis, then, are a cluster of deities connected with *tympana* and erotic elements—the sort of activity that the Official considers detrimental to the health of the *polis*. Lysistrata's opening lines, then, evoke the notion of foreign cult that I have been discussing.[44]

The festival that Lysistrata is convening is antithetical to rites for such deities. Instead, she and her accomplices intend to carry out a plan that will save Greece: "The preservation (σωτηρία) of all Hellas is in the hands of women" (29–30). Lysistrata avows repeatedly that the security and well-being of Greece are at stake and underscores this with the repetition of the verb σώσειν (41, 46). Lysistrata and her allies are securing the state and acting as a force for order. What the women atop the Acropolis are doing would appear to be opposed to Ἀδωνιασμός—opposed, at least, to the Official's characterization of Adonis festival activity.[45]

Lysistrata indicates that she is a staunch supporter of traditional Athenian religion, and she is indeed closely linked with Athena, the patron deity of Athens. Lysistrata's name is connected with the similarly named priestess of Athena Polias, Lysimachê, who held office in 411 BCE, when *Lysistrata* was produced.[46] Lysistrata's name is important to the play. The instigator of the revolutionary plan to stop the Peloponnesian War is named very quickly, within the first lines (6), and the rapidity with which the audience learns her name is remarkable because in most of Aristophanes's plays, the naming of the hero or heroine is delayed, often until quite near the end.[47] Not only is Lysistrata given a name within the first ten lines; her name is repeated.[48] Its literal meaning is supposed to be noticed.

The priestess of Athena Polias, of course, had an established role in the Athenian *polis*. This was, perhaps, one of the most prominent positions that *anyone*—male or female—could hold during the Classical period at Athens.[49] Both names—Lysistrata and Lysimachê—mean essentially the same thing ("Army Releaser," "Battle Releaser"). At one point, Lysistrata even spells out for the audience the meaning of the name, as well as her connection with the priestess of Athena Polias, when she pronounces that if their plan works they will all be known all over Greece as Lysimachês (551–54).[50] In sum, as Lysistrata explains in her first words, she and her allies are up to something serious, something in line with mainstream Athenian religion.

Given what Lysistrata says in the opening lines of the play, as well as her connections with Athena and established religion, how can the Official see τρυφή and hear τυμπανισμός and cries of Sabazius? As we have seen, as far as the Official is concerned, these women are indulging in celebrations that are connected with Adonis.[51] From one perspective, that of the Official, what the women are doing carries the force of destruction. Their actions are linked with Ἀδωνιασμός, feminine excess, and all that is opposed to the good of the state. Lysistrata, by contrast, represents the women's actions as a force for order, denying their association with such unpalatable practices.

As seen above, Aristophanes's *Lysistrata* may have been alternatively titled *Adôniazousai*, "Women at the Adonis Festival." *Adôniazousai* was also the title of a play by Philippides, and the youth and his festival appear as a theme in a number of Classical Athenian comedies.[52] Indeed, much of our evidence for the myth and cult of Adonis comes from comedy (discussed in chapter 1). As I will suggest, Lysistrata and her friends metaphorically hold an Adonis festival atop the Acropolis. To be sure, Lysistrata and her friends never say, *we are holding an Adonia*, and I do not suggest that an Adonis festival actually takes place before the spectators' eyes. Nevertheless, specific elements associated with the Adonis festival are smuggled into the play. Yet this is not the Official's stereotyped version of an Adonia; instead the women convene an Adonia with civic import. Foreign ritual is thus deployed by Lysistrata and her allies to stop the Peloponnesian War—a notion that should encourage us to reconsider views of the Adonis festival as marginal. Calling the play *Adôniazousai* rather than *Lysistrata*, the name of the action-driving character who is onstage for most of the play, shifts our focus to a group activity that is to a large degree unspoken and unseen, but that is, nevertheless, always lurking in the background and given political import.

In what follows, first I consider Aphrodite's importance to the play, as well as the manipulation of space in *Lysistrata*, both the notional space of the play and the real space at the base of and atop the Acropolis. I suggest that the Acropolis becomes a sort of rooftop space and that boars and myrrh—two components of the myth of Adonis—make appearances in the play as women play the role of Aphrodite. In relation to the women, the men begin to take on characteristics of powerless Adonis figures, and the women can be seen to be cultivating metaphorical gardens of Adonis. Finally, I return to the Official's angry speech (387–98) and consider the role of lamentation at the Adonia. While the Official recalls lamentation by a woman at an Adonia just before the Sicilian expedition sets sail, Lysistrata and her allies successfully bring about a cease-fire by activating elements from the Adonia that would have resonated in the minds of spectators familiar with the cult.

Athena (Lysistrata) *versus Aphrodite* (Adôniazousai)

If we could dispense with the title *Lysistrata*—imagine it away for a moment—and pretend that we had no idea what the play was called, it would seem that the character Lysistrata is central to this play, and the group activity of the Adonia is not. Lysistrata is the instigator of the action; she is onstage for much of the play. The Adonia, by contrast, comes up explicitly only once in the passage I have examined above. To most who read (or see) *Lysistrata,* the religious heart of the play lies on the Acropolis, with Athena. The focus would seem to be public, official, state-sanctioned religion, centering on the patron deity of Athens. The play appears to have little to do with a peripheral, foreign ritual that took place on the roofs of houses, a festival bound up with the goddess Aphrodite. However, as a handful of scholars have pointed out, Aphrodite is as crucial to *Lysistrata* as Athena.[53] The action of *Lysistrata* involves a sex strike by women who take over the Acropolis in order to put an end to the Peloponnesian War. There is thus a denial or a displacement of Aphrodite during the course of the play, which results in a preoccupation with *aphrodisia,* as sexual jokes and innuendo abound. Such an argument suggests that we might want to take the scholion seriously, and this motivates my reading of the play.[54]

As we have seen, inasmuch as she is an "army disbander," Lysistrata is linked with Athena and the priestess of Athena Polias. But Lysistrata is also associated with Aphrodite. Indeed, in the passage mentioned above, in which Lysistrata explains that the women will be known as "Lysimachês," she emphasizes that this will come about if Eros and Aphrodite breathe desire into the men (551–54). In a misguided attempt to make *Lysistrata* obey a strict logic, many have made a distinction between Plan A (the sex strike) and Plan B (the takeover of the Acropolis); the former is associated with Aphrodite, the latter with Athena.[55] It is often suggested that the sex strike is then replaced by the Acropolis takeover or that the sex strike is simply forgotten. Yet the peace is, in the end, referred to as that "which the Cyprian goddess fashioned" (1289–90). In fact, *both* Aphrodite and Athena are crucial to the play's trajectory. As one scholar has suggested, "Lysistrata's plan actually involves putting each goddess in the service of the other."[56] The action of the play turns on the interpenetration of both plans. Also, the particularities of the threat posed by the women change depending on whom you ask. The chorus of old men is not overly concerned about the sex strike. Instead, what worries them most is the fact that the women have taken over the Acropolis (480–83). The young men, on the other hand, are most bothered by the sex strike and seem far less interested in the fact that the women's gathering takes place in a very particular civic space. Though the division throughout the play appears to be simply men versus women, there are two distinct age groups within that opposition—young and old—each with its own concerns.

It is significant that Lysistrata delays making her plan known. For more than the first hundred lines, neither the audience nor the women she has gathered together know precisely what Lysistrata has in mind. Instead, a pile-up of adjectives describes her scheme obliquely. Soon after she comes onstage, Calonice asks what it is that Lysistrata is devising. Instead of immediately revealing the plan for the sex strike and the Acropolis takeover, Lysistrata employs descriptive adjectives—πηλίκον, μέγα, and παχύ (23–24). These adjectives, which Lysistrata intends to use to describe her plan as "important," "weighty," and "significant" take on specifically sexual connotations in the opening banter with Calonice ("big," "meaty," "thick"). The adjectives insistently take on an *erotic* valence, a signification that squelches any other meaning they might have had. Even though there has been no explicit mention of the goddess Aphrodite yet, the goddess is saturating this play. As the play unfolds and the sex strike takes its toll on the men, Aphrodite takes up more and more space verbally as sexual innuendo and jokes multiply, even as the sex-strike plan is "forgotten" or "replaced" by the Acropolis takeover.

Acropolis as Rooftop

In the world of the play, the women take over the Acropolis, a space situated up high. Indeed, the notional space of the Acropolis becomes a crucial character, as important as a Lysistrata or an Official.[57] Reconstructing the staging of ancient plays is notoriously difficult, but it is reasonable to assume that for portions of *Lysistrata*, two stage levels were employed: a lower area as well as a higher level that indicated the Acropolis.[58] By the end of the fifth century, a single story *skênê* with a flat roof was in use in the Theater of Dionysus.[59] If there was a Lenaion theater, and if this play was performed at it, as seems to be the case, the scenic accoutrements would have most likely been similar. In many of Aristophanes's plays, this structure is referred to as τέγος, "rooftop."[60] The text of *Lysistrata* repeatedly indicates such a low/high spatial arrangement, especially in the seduction scene between Myrrhine and Cinesias, where the verb *katabainein,* "to descend," is used by both characters. Cinesias calls out to Myrrhine, "Come down here!" (873, 883); eventually she agrees to descend ("I must go down," 884).[61]

In terms of the real space of the Acropolis and the lower area surrounding it, during the fifth century Aphrodite had a place down low, and Athena had a place at the top.[62] On the north slope of the Acropolis, situated among a series of caves, was a precinct of Eros and Aphrodite.[63] Aphrodite's space at the base of the Acropolis is not a prominent space—at least not when compared to the vast area devoted to

Athena on the top.[64] The precinct of Eros and Aphrodite is a small grotto on the periphery, not a monumental and centrally located temple like the Parthenon.

Allusions to this real division of sacred space abound in the world of the play. The women move, symbolically, from low to high, from the marginalized space of Aphrodite—the area of the north slope, with its slippery rocks, caves, and grottoes—up to the central space of Athena, the religious heart or crown of the city, where the patron deity is worshipped, and where one can walk among the towering columns of the Parthenon. As the women take over the Acropolis, intent on a plan that involves a sex strike, there is a concomitant movement of *aphrodisia* from low to high, up into the space of Athena.[65]

As we saw above, *Lysistrata* insists on a denial of Aphrodite and *aphrodisia,* even as *aphrodisia* becomes the focus of the drama. Just before the seduction scene between Myrrhine and Cinesias begins, Lysistrata calls out to her comrades from her lookout spot and reports that she sees a man, maddened, in the grip of the *orgia* of Aphrodite (831–32).[66] Of course, what Lysistrata means is that Cinesias is in the grip of sexual desire. But she is also separating the activities of the women atop the Acropolis from his activities, saying in effect, "We aren't performing the rites of Aphrodite up here, but look, he *is* down there."[67] His location and spatial separation from the women is emphasized.[68] At the same time, while Lysistrata is up high in Athena's space, peering down on Cinesias, who is overcome down below by the *orgia* of Aphrodite, she invokes Aphrodite with great attention, naming the goddess elaborately by mentioning three places that the divinity frequents ("Mistress Aphrodite, of Cyprus and Cythera and Paphos," 833–34). Lysistrata disavows *aphrodisia,* τρυφή, female sexuality—those distinctive elements of certain kinds of foreign cult that I have explored above—from the beginning, as she announces the serious import of her plan to save Greece. Yet Lysistrata's plan depends on precisely what it excludes. In this case, her plan depends on the exclusion and arousal of Cinesias (as well as the exclusion and arousal of all the other men). Cinesias must be there, overcome by the *orgia* of Aphrodite, for the plan to have its effect. In fact, the men (as opposed to the women) are assimilated to the position of participants in nonmainstream, foreign cult when Lysistrata describes the warmongering men shopping in the agora as Corybantes (555–58). As Lysistrata evokes crowds of Corybantic, maddened men (μαινομένους, 556), she draws on connections between Dionysiac and Corybantic rites that Euripides also evokes in his *Bacchae* (123–29).[69] Lysistrata's description of the men as Corybantes is punctuated with a "by Paphian Aphrodite" as a kind of "amen." As she defines the men's actions, Lysistrata repeatedly proclaims: we are not *that.* Lysistrata never asserts *we are holding an Adonis festival.* Yet as she and her comrades occupy the Acropolis, the space is transformed. It has been suggested that "as the play proceeds the distinction between Acropolis and home collapses; the action in the public and private worlds becomes one. Myrrhine, as she tortures her aroused husband, turns the acropolis into a bedroom replete with blankets, pillows, and perfume."[70]

Looked at another way, the Acropolis becomes not an *oikos* or bedroom but rather a sort of rooftop, a τέγος. At Athens during the Classical period, a rooftop is neither an extremely likely place to be nor entirely out of the ordinary. Aeschylus's *Agamemnon* begins with the watchman on the roof, and Aristophanes's *Wasps* opens with Bdelycleon similarly positioned. A rooftop is, obviously, part of an *oikos*, "house," yet it is outside the *oikos*. As such it is neither wholly public nor wholly private. It is not a central space where most daily activities are performed, nor is it entirely peripheral, given the vantage (and the visibility to others) one has when one is up there.[71] If there is one thing that the Official emphasizes, it is that the Ἀδωνιασμός he remembers so vividly at the time of the Sicilian expedition took place on the *rooftop* (ἐπὶ τῶν τεγῶν, 389, 395).[72] His words mark the actions of the women he sees as an Adonia and the space atop the Acropolis as a rooftop, "*this* Adonia-activity on the roof" (ὅ τ' Ἀδωνιασμὸς οὗτος οὑπὶ τῶν τεγῶν, 389). In *Lysistrata*, the Acropolis has metamorphosed into a strange sort of in-between space associated with both Aphrodite and Athena. A group of women has taken it over and excluded men, and in this sense, it is not quite private and not quite public. The Acropolis is at the center of the *polis*, yet men have been excluded from it and individuals who are not fully enfranchised citizens and who are more strongly associated with the *oikos* occupy it. All of this is temporary, of course: the women never say they will stay there. They will descend and return to their homes, just as the watchman and Bdelycleon come down in *Agamemnon* and *Wasps* respectively.[73] As a kind of rooftop, the Acropolis provides a vantage point from which the women can look down upon the men—men like Myrrhine's husband, Cinesias.

The spatial movement of the women in the play and the transformation of the Acropolis into a rooftop space correspond to the action involved in an Adonis festival. Having planted the "seeds" of her plan, Lysistrata and the women, like women at an Adonis festival who ascend to the rooftops, climb atop the Acropolis. Indeed, as we shall see, the play contains still more parallels with the Adonia, beginning with the oath scene and ending with the cessation of hostilities at the close of the play.

Boars, Cosmetics, and Myrrh

In order to bring her revolutionary idea to fruition, Lysistrata stages an extended formal oath—the most elaborate of all those found in Aristophanes's plays.[74] After some discussion, Lysistrata recommends that they "sacrifice" a large jug of wine.[75] Just before the oath is taken, Lysistrata remarks: "Seize this *boar* (κάπρος) with me.

Mistress Persuasion and cup of friendship, kindly receive this sacrifice from the women," 202–4. Lysistrata calls the large jug of Thasian wine a κάπρος, a "boar," the very animal that killed Adonis.[76] It is appropriate that she do so, as she and her allies are staging an oath-taking ceremony that involves a sacrifice, and boars were certainly among possible sacrificial animals.[77] But many animals were used in such ceremonies—goats, bulls, and so on. It is significant that she grasps a κάπρος and not a goat or a bull or even a piglet.

In Greek literature, a κάπρος is, most often, a *wild* boar, a fierce and formidable animal, the likes of which left Odysseus with a scar and terrorized the Calydonians and Erymanthians.[78] The ability to vanquish a boar, to be a kind of Heracles, reveals one to be a force to be reckoned with. By "seizing the boar," the women of *Lysistrata* assert control over a force of potential destruction—they are, after all, trying to halt a war. As they lay hands upon the boar, they repeat the oath after Lysistrata, swearing off sexual relations with their husbands.

In fact, the play begins and ends with boars. In the closing lines of *Lysistrata*, the Spartan men compare themselves to boars during the battle of Thermopylae (1254–56). We are to understand that the Spartans were "like boars" because of their valor and courage in their opposition to the Persians. While the play begins with a group of women laying hands on and thus taking control of the "boar," by the end of *Lysistrata*, normative sexual relations are well on their way to being re-established, with the Spartan men's description of themselves as boars. At the same time, the end of the of play marks a return to more-typical sacrifice, with mention of domesticated, rather than wild, pigs.[79] Boars and sacrifice, then, bracket the play.

Not only does the symbolic movement from the "low" space of Aphrodite to the "high" space of the Acropolis as well as the appearance of the boar signal an Adonia, but just as women at an Adonia play the role of Aphrodite, so too the women of the play take on the characteristics of the goddess as they try to end the war. Stopping the war necessitates making use of certain stereotypes. At the beginning of the play, Calonice wonders how women could do anything "prudent" (φρόνιμον) or "brilliant" (λαμπρόν), since their main activity is to "sit idly, decked out with flowers, wearing saffron robes, and adorned with Cimberic gowns and fancy shoes" (42–45). Lysistrata responds that that is precisely how they will put a stop to the fighting, by means of these very things, their adornment, "saffron robes and myrrh and fancy shoes and red cosmetics and diaphanous chitons" (46–48). The mission is to save Greece, and in order to do so, Lysistrata and her cohorts will employ such accoutrements. How can these items save the city? These adornments are precisely the same weapons that Aphrodite herself uses to wield her power when she sets out to seduce Anchises in the *Homeric Hymn to Aphrodite*.

After Zeus casts desire for Anchises into Aphrodite's heart, she heads straight for her temple at Paphos on Cyprus, to get dressed up (κοσμηθεῖσα, 65). The *kosmos*—the perfume and jewelry and fine clothes that Aphrodite chooses to wear—recurs like a refrain throughout the *Hymn*. After she is adorned (58–67), she comes to Anchises, and he marvels at her shining garments, her bracelets, and her necklaces (84–90). Then, after a brief discussion, he removes the *kosmos* (161–66), and they have sex.

In the shorter *Homeric Hymn to Aphrodite*, the Horai adorn (ἐκόσμεον, 11) Aphrodite with fancy clothing and gleaming jewelry, the kind they themselves like to sport (κοσμείσθην, 12), and when they are finished showering her with adornment (κόσμον, 14), they lead her into a gathering of immortals. When Aphrodite arrives, the gods are wonder struck (θαυμάζοντες, 18) and find her extremely alluring. Every last one of them wants to take her home specifically to become his *wife* (κουριδίην ἄλοχον, 17).[80]

This is, more or less, the trajectory of *Lysistrata*, where the focus is similarly on adornment. The comedy plays on the manner in which women can use their trappings to bring war to an end. The words *krokôtophorousa* and *kekallôpismenê* ("wearing saffron gowns" and "all made up") appear not only in the opening exchange between Lysistrata and Calonice but again in the oath ceremony. As Lysistrata's allies dutifully swear after her, Calonice's line is repeated exactly as before, not once but twice (219–20). Lysistrata takes Calonice's words and, very shrewdly, employs them for her own purposes. The accoutrements of femininity are emphasized as a source of power. Just as Aphrodite makes use of her *kosmos* in the *Homeric Hymns* to attract Anchises and all the assembled immortals, the women of *Lysistrata* use their *kosmos* to arouse the desire of their husbands; the men are wonder struck, and every last one of them desperately wants to take his wife back home.[81] In the process, the men agree to stop a war. The women have employed *kosmos* in an attempt to set in order (*kosmein*) the *polis*—putting themselves and the city (indeed, all of Hellas) in order, by playing the role of the goddess Aphrodite. We may even imagine that the women "play Aphrodite" specifically in her guise as Aphrodite Pandêmos if we take Pandêmos to signify a force for civic harmony, as many scholars have argued.[82]

When Lysistrata seizes the "boar," she invokes Peitho, who is frequently linked with Aphrodite in literature.[83] Archaeologically, too, there are connections between the two deities: the sanctuary of Peitho and Aphrodite Pandêmos was situated on the southwest slope of the Acropolis.[84] Aphrodite also appears with Peitho in vase painting. Aphrodite's defining action is to persuade (*peithein*); however, the *Homeric Hymn to Aphrodite* notes the limits of Aphrodite's powers vis-à-vis three divinities: Artemis, Hestia, and Athena.[85] Although in the *Hymn*, Aphrodite cannot "persuade" Athena (πεπιθεῖν, 7), Lysistrata and her friends, who are closely associated with Aphrodite, take over the warrior goddess Athena's space and persuade the men of Greece to stop the Peloponnesian War.[86] Given that Aphrodite is, in some sense, invading the space of Athena, she can be seen to have some degree of power over the goddess who is normally immune to her persuasive abilities.[87]

In *Lysistrata*, in addition to making use of alluring garments, the women employ μύρον, "perfume," to persuade the men (42–48). The use of μύρον provides still another connection to Adonis and his festival, both in myth and ritual. As seen in chapter 1, in stories told about Adonis, his mother, Myrrha, while pregnant is turned into a myrrh tree—a tree that is essential for the production of certain perfumes and incense. It is from this tree that Adonis is later born.

In *Lysistrata*, Myrrhine, "Myrtle," who is at one point called Μυρρίον, "Little Myrrh" (906), plays a decisive role in the resolution of the play, even employing perfume as she torments Cinesias.[88] A lengthy deferral of satisfaction ensues as Myrrhine runs off to fetch bedding, a pillow, a blanket, and, finally, some perfume (μύρον, 938).[89] She returns clutching an *alabastos* (947, also called an *alabastron*), a container that was commonly used to hold perfumes.[90] The phallic aspect of the vessel is fully exploited as Myrrhine commands, "Take this *alabastos*," and the distraught Cinesias replies, "I have one!"(947). Myrrhine, clutching an *alabastos* (and as we shall see, metaphorically cultivating a garden of Adonis), bears a striking resemblance to a terracotta figurine (fig. 23) that has been identified as a young woman tending a garden of Adonis.[91]

The transformation of the Acropolis into a space rather like a rooftop, the appearance of the "boar" and myrrh, women playing the role of Aphrodite—these activities seem to be distinctively Adonia-like behavior. Thus far, I have focused on the women of the play. At this point we must see what happens to the men in relation to women playing the role of goddesses.

Astutoi *(Impotent Men)*

By the end of the play, the young men are in such a state of arousal that they appear to be nothing but their erections. This is made clear near the end, when a Spartan herald comes onstage and has a long exchange with Cinesias. His erection is the subject of banter during the entire sequence. First, Cinesias refers to the herald as a Conisalus, a Priapic-type divinity. Then Cinesias asks if he holds a spear, or if instead his groin is inflamed from the long ride. By the end of the exchange, the herald's member is described as a *skutalê,* a wooden stick device by means of which messages are sent (991–92). It turns out that this is a particularly apt metaphor. Plutarch offers a description of the instrument in his *Life of Lysander* 19.5.[92] Plutarch's description reveals that meaning is produced through the *combination* of parchment and two *skutalai*. If you have only the parchment and no stick, you have no message. More pertinent for the Spartan herald of *Lysistrata*, if you have only the stick and no parchment, signification does not take place. Cinesias's remarks emphasize the utter ineffectiveness of the men's devices. At this point in the play, the men are powerless inasmuch as they are unable to wield their members in the way that they want. The men of *Lysistrata* all have Spartan sticks. In fact the two equivalent *skutalai* ("then this too is a Laconian *skutalê*!" 992) suggest the equivalence of Spartan and Athenian men, but the instruments have become decidedly ineffective as they are powerless to use them properly, that is, in sexual relations with their wives. One would think that in their Priapic state, the men of the play would be powerful, potent figures. Instead, despite the proliferation of the verb *stuein* in the play and the attention to the men's erections, the young men of *Lysistrata* are figuratively impotent.

In chapter 2, I introduced the myth of the goddess and her mortal lover, a story pattern that informs the Adonia. Such narratives tend to resolve with the demise of the man, who, in a union with a goddess, becomes literally or figuratively impotent, a resolution that offers a way of negotiating the competing hierarchies, immortal/mortal and male/female. Adonis too is linked with death and impotence (discussed in chapter 1), inasmuch as he is killed by a boar and associated with lettuce, a vegetable that, in the Greek mind, inhibited male virility. In a fragment of Eubulus (*PCG* v fr. 13), a speaker from a play titled, significantly, *Astutoi* (Impotent Men) describes lettuce as food for corpses and associates Adonis with the vegetable. The passage turns on a joke in which old men who are sexually decrepit are frequently referred to as "dead," a "corpse," a "tomb."[93]

In *Lysistrata*, the chorus of old men are called *tumbos*, "tomb" (372), and the Official, also an older man, is told to buy a σορός, "coffin" (600). *Tumbos* and *soros* are generic epithets used of old men, but in *Lysistrata* the terms also speak to the men's diminished sexual capacity, a fact that becomes apparent in the scene between Lysistrata and the Official when he remarks, "Well, anyone who can still get an erection (στῦσαι)" 598.[94] Lysistrata's response is to cut him off midsentence and retort, "Why on earth don't you die already! Here is a plot. Go buy a coffin (σορός)!" (599–600). At this moment, Lysistrata silences the Official, metaphorically killing him. Like the figure of Aphrodite in stories told about Adonis, Lysistrata (forcibly) lays this "Adonis" in a bed of lettuce.[95]

In *Lysistrata*, as the women play the role of Aphrodite, all the men—young and old—exhibit characteristics of powerlessness vis-à-vis the women. As we have seen, the young men are metaphorically impotent as a result of their erections, which, despite all appearances, render them weak and ineffective. The old men are repeatedly referred to as "corpses," an appellation that connotes an inability to exhibit arousal. The men, then, young and old, take on characteristics of mortal men in goddess-mortal pairings, as the women play the role of Aphrodite.

Gardens of Adonis

One of the more puzzling aspects of this play is the fact that Lysistrata's plan to deny sex to the men *works*. There are, certainly, many other options open to the men for relieving their plight—sex with boys, slaves, prostitutes, or masturbation. The very fact that Lysistrata's scheme is successful underscores the notion that this play focuses on the denial of a specific kind of sex—sex between men and women within the confines of marriage.[96] It is for this reason that the play contains the drawn-out scene between the married couple Myrrhine and Cinesias rather than a scene between, say, two lovers.

The women of *Lysistrata*, however, are certainly not ensconced in the *oikos* producing more children or taking care of the ones that they already have. They are, rather, up on top of the Acropolis, decked out in finery and looking very seductive and, as I have argued, they are playing the role of Aphrodite. In her consideration of *Lysistrata*, Nicole Loraux argues that the women become *parthenoi*: "The women of Athens make themselves into young girls once again—on the Acropolis, and to serve the needs of Aphrodite's cause."[97] Each woman undergoes this metamorphosis "to recover all the seductive allure of a young girl and thus entice her husband."[98] Sarah Stroup, by contrast, argues that the women of *Lysistrata* are "comically 'hetairized'—recreated as pseudo-*hetairai*."[99] How is it that two readings of *Lysistrata* reach such opposite conclusions? To be sure, Aristophanes's *Lysistrata* presents a puzzling situation. The women refuse sex with men. But rather than wander the hills like Artemis, the quintessential *parthenos*, the women of the play are decidedly urban. They align themselves with a different *parthenos*, the patron deity of Athens—Athena. On the other hand, while Lysistrata and her allies embody an excessive seductiveness and commitment to *aphrodisia*, they are engaged in a rejection of men—not the approach of the average fifth-century *hetaira*. The fact that Loraux associates the women of the play with *parthenoi* while Stroup is able to see them as "hetairized" underscores the fact that it is their status as *nonreproductive* women that is important. The scene with Myrrhine and Cinesias makes this clear. A vast gulf exists between the sphere that Cinesias inhabits and the space atop the Acropolis. It is the presence of her child, in the end, that convinces Myrrhine to descend. When Myrrhine responds, "What a significant thing is motherhood; I must go down" (οἷον τὸ τεκεῖν. καταβατέον 884), she emphasizes the fact that the space where the women are located is nonreproductive space.

This theme of women as nonreproductive figures in *Lysistrata* finds parallels in the ritual planting of gardens of Adonis. After all, the seeds planted in *ostraka* bear no fruit, becoming proverbial for that which came to no issue. "More fruitless than the gardens of Adonis," runs the proverb.[100] And in Plato's *Phaedrus,* Socrates emphasizes this aspect of the gardens, when he characterizes the planting involved in the Adonis festival as the antithesis of proper farming (276b).[101] Translated into sexual terms, the cult of the Adonia involves a suspension of marital, reproductive sex, precisely the situation in *Lysistrata.*

Plant imagery is employed in Aristophanes's play to characterize the women's actions. As we have seen, the Official describes the actions of the women as Ἀδωνιασμός, "Adonis festival activity," and τρυφή, "feminine excess/depravity," a characteristic of foreign cult that he considers destructive to the *polis.* But the Official also uses a specific metaphor to describe the actions of the women when he remarks, "When we ourselves sink to their level and teach the women to be depraved (τρυφᾶν), such schemes bloom (βλαστάνει) from them," 404–6. The Official employs the verb βλαστάνειν, "to bloom," an action associated with plants. As far as the Official is concerned, the women connected with Lysistrata are growing terrible plots. To him, the women atop the Acropolis are cultivating gardens of Adonis, putting the *polis* in a state of disarray.

But this is only one view of the women's actions. The Official's use of the verb βλαστάνειν echoes the use of the same word by the old women in the battle between the two choruses, an elemental battle in which the women are armed with water, and the men are armed with fire. The old men, horrified that they have been doused and that their weapon—fire—has become unusable, ask the women what they mean by their action. The women respond that they are watering the old men so that they will grow, βλαστάνειν (383–85). The women are watering the men to quench their fiery desire for war so that civic order can be established and so that proper "farming" (that is, proper sexual relations) can begin again.[102] The women want to grow a healthy *polis.*

While Aristophanes rarely underscores the passage of time in his plays, he seems to emphasize it in *Lysistrata.*[103] In *Phaedrus,* Plato's Socrates asserts that a garden of Adonis takes eight days to grow (276b). When Cinesias remarks, "Do you not pity your child, unwashed and unfed for the sixth day now?" (880–81), it is tempting to conclude that the women of *Lysistrata* are atop the Acropolis for approximately the amount of time that is needed to cultivate a garden of Adonis.[104] In the end, what appears merely to be frivolous gardening for fun is, instead, productive and serious. The very women who point out that they are qualified to give advice to the *polis* because they provide Athens with children who are sent off to war (589–90, 651) suspend normative (but irregular, unsatisfactory, wartime) sexual relations with their husbands during the run of the play in order to return to them on a permanent and more uninterrupted basis after a cease-fire has been established—a very fruitful plan.

Lamentation Then and Now

Recent work on lamentation and burial practices (introduced in chapter 1) makes clear that it is incorrect to think of rituals surrounding death during the Classical period as *simply* private events. Laws allegedly passed by Solon to restrict funeral rituals confirm the fact that funeral rituals were public activities and that groups of keening women had the potential to become disruptive. Indeed, lamentation was one of the few avenues open to women by which they could voice opinions on matters to those in authority. Given that typical lamentation at Athens did not take place on a rooftop, it is likely that the dirges performed by women at an Adonia would have been still more visible and audible than conventional funeral *thrênos*. Certainly Aristophanes constructs the situation in *Lysistrata* to make Demostratus's wife particularly audible (387–98), as does Menander in *Samia* (38–49).

The Adonia described by the Official in *Lysistrata* functions as an expression of dissident opinion by means of lamentation. What the Official remembers so vividly when he recalls the Adonia before the Sicilian expedition are the lamentations of Demostratus's wife on the rooftop, audible to him during the discussions under way in the assembly. It tends to go unnoticed that, as the Official describes it, the lamentation sung on the rooftop at the Adonia invades the male space of debate. Since Demostratus's wife is foretelling the deaths that will occur as a result of the failed military undertaking, the play asserts the validity of the voice of the individual participating in what the Official dismisses as a nonmainstream ritual. On the eve of the expedition the public arena does, in fact, seem to be distracted and troubled by the lamenting woman, since the lone voice of Demostratus's wife can be heard in the assembly.

By 411, when *Lysistrata* was produced, the Athenians had had a year or two to attempt to come to terms with the devastating and traumatic events in Sicily. As it turns out, the Official of *Lysistrata* is not the only one who associates a foreign cult with the momentous events in Sicily. In his *Life of Alcibiades* (18.2) and *Life of Nicias* (13.7), Plutarch relates that the fleet sets sail amid ominous portents.[105] In both *Lives* Plutarch describes the wailing women and the funeral rites for Adonis. The lamenting women make everyone wonder if heading to Sicily is such a good idea after all.[106] No explicit reference to the gardens of Adonis appears in the passages. Instead, the mention of the plants that, like Adonis, die without issue is displaced onto the Athenian fleet, which, despite its splendor and excellence, many fear will wither away (μαρανθῇ, *Life of Nicias* 13.7).[107] In retrospect, the lamenting women that the Official and Plutarch describe appear to have been predicting the death and destruction that would come about, rehearsing for the lamentation that would occur if the Athenians sailed to Sicily. The youth Adonis is implicitly likened to the sons who would be sent off to war, and who would—like him—die young. Indeed, it has been suggested that the Adonia functioned as an improvised war protest.[108] Although I do not claim that a historical Adonis festival took place before the fleet set sail, the Adonia recalled by the Official serves as a critique of the Sicilian expedition at least within the context of *Lysistrata.* Its use in this way by Aristophanes indicates Athenian understanding of its potential function as a means of dissent.

In *Lysistrata,* the Official has come onstage to get money for oars to equip the fleet, of course, years *after* the Sicilian expedition has already sailed. He finds himself surrounded by women, and he likens them to Demostratus, whom he describes as the instigator of the destructive military venture. But the women atop the Acropolis are not, in fact, a force of destruction; they are, instead, like Demostratus's wife at the Adonia that the Official remembers from a few years past, foretelling destruction if war is *not* stopped. However, unlike the women described by Plutarch, and unlike Demostratus's lamenting wife, the women of *Lysistrata* manage to achieve a cease-fire.

The antiphonal element of the Adonia is the focus of the Official's description, and, indeed, what he recalls from a few years past parallels the recent interaction between the chorus of old men and women. Although the Official's description of the Adonis festival is structured like the amoebaean exchange of a leader and choral respondents, it lacks the component that is so prominent in other representations of the Adonia, namely, the chorus of responding women. Instead of the group of *korai* respondents seen, for example, in a Sappho fragment (fr. 140 Voigt), or the chorus of Moirai and mountain nymphs who lament Adonis in Bion's *Epitaph on Adonis,* it is only one *gunê,* Demostratus's wife, dancing alone (ὀρχουμένη, 392) atop the roof. Demostratus can thus be seen as a kind of lament leader, battling it out with his wife. He urges: "Sail to Sicily!" and his nameless wife calls back: "Alas for Adonis!" He shouts: "Marshal Zakynthian troops!" and she responds: "Beat your breasts for Adonis!" Unfortunately for the fleet and the city of Athens, as the Official points out, Demostratus's words had *bia,* "force" (ὁ δ' ἐβιάζετο, 396), perhaps in part because of the solo (rather than choral) performance of Demostratus's wife.[109]

While the Official and Plutarch describe women lamenting at an Adonis festival as decisions are made regarding Sicily, it is the *men* of *Lysistrata,* and not the women, who are doing the mourning. Lysistrata and her allies have *bia* within the context of the play. While the aptly named Demostratus turns the unfortunate *dêmos* into a *stratos,* Lysistrata, working in solidarity with a group of women, manages to dissolve (*luein*) the *stratos.* As mentioned above, the choral nature of the Official's description of the Adonia parallels the most recent action of the play—the battle between the chorus of old men armed with fire and the chorus of old women armed with water. In this case, it is the group of men who are defeated and are thus the ones doing the lamenting: they are the ones who cry out, *oimoi talas*! (382).[110] The Official as a representative of a newly created civic office (*proboulos*) embodies broad powers. He could, as Demostratus did years ago, levy troops and allot funds. But the women of the play are the ones who dominate.

The wailing on the roof by the unnamed wife of Demostratus represents the *failure* of an Adonia to put a stop to the impending Sicilian expedition; the same is so for the passages from Plutarch's *Lives*. By contrast, if we see the Adonis festival as a kind of cultural script that underlies *Lysistrata*, as I have argued, the metaphorical Adonia performed by Lysistrata and her friends represents a choral success. As the play ends, the two choruses join together. The women clearly dominate, and the men join up reluctantly, all the while muttering and complaining.[111] The defeated men are subsumed into *Adôniazousai* (Women at the Adonis Festival)—even Lysistrata disappears eventually—leaving a unified collective that sings of abundance and plenty, dangling delights before the audience, while each time denying their presence or in some way hindering access to the treats.[112]

In *Lysistrata*, then, the metaphorical performance of an Adonia operates as a means of resistance, as the women offer an effective dissident voice to stop a war. It is significant that Lysistrata and her friends put a stop to the war by appropriating a practice that showcases *thrênos*. As seen in chapter 1, Helene Foley has documented the ways that, in tragedy, female figures manipulate funerary ritual to counter those in authority. Given Solon's laws aimed at restricting women's roles in mourning, as well as tragedy's tendency to showcase elements that appear to have been outlawed, it seems likely that lament continued to inhabit an ambiguous position in the *polis*.

While lamentation may praise the dead, the focus is on loss and, in particular, individual loss, as mourning women call to mind the cost of war, and the women tend to lament their own fate.[113] Lamentation may offer a critique of the rhetoric of the *polis*, in particular, that of funeral oration, which praises the dead and focuses on the value of their sacrifice to the state. As Foley remarks, "The themes developed in lamentation are often subtly at odds with the rhetoric of the public funeral oration and thus with the public ideology at Athens. . . . By concentrating on the negative effects that death and war itself have on survivors, lamentation can offer a muted reproach of the dead and of the ambitions of the dead for immortal fame celebrated in funeral oration."[114]

As many ancients and moderns alike have noted, the *epitaphios logos* was no place for the sorts of questions that *thrênoi* and unfettered keening might raise.[115] The extant *epitaphioi logoi*, the speeches that participate in the genre of funeral oration, comprise our best evidence for the ritual of the state funeral.[116] Enough complete speeches survive to provide insight into the genre of funeral oration: Thucydides 2.35–46 (which includes the speech of Pericles), Lysias (2), Plato's *Menexenus* (which includes Aspasia's speech related by Socrates, 236d–249c), Demosthenes (60), Hyperides (6), and fragments of Gorgias (frs. 5a, 5b, 6 D–K).[117] These texts indicate that unrestrained lament was an inappropriate activity. For example, near the end of his funeral oration, Lysias remarks, "But really I do not know why we should lament (ὀλοφύρεσθαι) such things" (77). He explains that, after all, we are mortal; death comes to all; and the fallen are blessed. Plato has Socrates assert that the living must not join in lamentation (συνοδύρεσθαι, 247c) with mournful fathers and mothers; he even has the dead assert that it is "not by singing dirges or by lamenting (οὐ θρηνοῦντες οὐδὲ ὀλοφυρόμενοι, 248b) that they will most gratify us." Finally, Hyperides insists on the necessity of restricting grief as much as possible (41), explaining that the dead did not suffer a fate worthy of dirges (θρήνων, 42).[118]

It is a typical rhetorical flourish, then, to claim that *thrênos* misses the true point. In fact, even Pericles's famous remarks (as rendered by Thucydides) to the widows of the deceased warriors should likely be viewed within the context of mourning and funerary practices. It has been suggested that "the words to the widows . . . contain a barely encoded warning not to go to excess with the laceration and self-mutilation which had been restricted by the Solonian laws. This funeral should be marked by self-control and moderation. Individual mourners were not to make a spectacle of themselves."[119] Indeed, at the end of his lengthy speech, Pericles offers a concise directive with regard to mourning: "And now, having lamented whom it is appropriate for you to lament, be on your way" (νῦν δὲ ἀπολοφυράμενοι ὃν προσήκει ἑκάστῳ ἄπιτε, 2.46.2).[120] Lament has a place, but not in the *epitaphios logos* itself because of the ways in which mourning dwells on loss. In funeral oration, instead, the dead are praised; in death they have become a noble, virtuous collectivity.

As we have seen, the Adonia features lamentation. I suggest that, just as *thrênos* may serve as a critique of the rhetoric of *epitaphios logos*, the women of *Lysistrata*, who harness the lament-featuring Adonia as a vehicle for dissent, incorporate and critique aspects of the tradition of *epitaphios logos*.[121] In extant funeral oration, Athens's reputation as the salvation of Greece is emphasized.[122] Lysias explains, "The power of the [Athenian] *polis* was the savior (σωτηρία) of Greece" (2.58).[123] Demosthenes concurs: "They [the Athenians] established themselves as the cause of the salvation (σωτηρία) of all Greece" (10).[124] As discussed above, the Athenian Lysistrata and her allies assert that they will save Greece: "The preservation (σωτηρία) of all Hellas is in the hands of women" (29–30), and the repetition of the verb σώσειν (41, 46) further underscores the fact that the security and well-being of Greece are at stake. In *Lysistrata*, then, the salvation of Greece is at issue, but it is in the hands of *women.*[125]

In Pericles's speech as preserved by Thucydides, a speech that draws on conventional elements of the genre of *epitaphios logos*, Pericles makes striking metaphorical use of the term *eranos*, "contribution," to describe the value of the fallen Athenians.[126] The Athenians die "offering a most splendid contribution (ἔρανος) to the city" (2.43.1). This metaphorical use is paralleled in *Lysistrata*, where the women claim a right to speak on behalf of the *polis* because of their "contribution" (ἔρανος): they supply the city with men (651).[127] In Pericles's speech, the contribution—death in war—of the fallen men is praised. In *Lysistrata*, the metaphor instead describes the contribution of women rather than men, women who are currently trying to stop further deaths from occurring, so that men will avoid continuing to make the contribution described by Pericles. Thucydides's Pericles presents a vision of progress over time, as each generation receives its patrimony and increases it for the next generation. In *Lysistrata*, by contrast, the female chorus-leader claims that the chorus of old men, representatives of contemporary Athenians, neither increases nor maintains the assets acquired from the preceding generation ("there is no share to you wretched old men, since you have squandered the *eranos* from the Persians and you don't pay taxes to replenish it," 652–54). Here, the *eranos* metaphor is manipulated again to denounce the conduct of the men and to suggest that the women should advise (παραινέσαι, 648) the *polis*.

Furthermore, Pericles suggests that the citizens of Athens become *erastai* of the *polis* (2.43.1).[128] *Lysistrata* offers a different spin on Pericles's injunction to become lovers of the city, as the men who have been denied sex become highly aroused and agree to a peace treaty. Meanwhile, Lysistrata and her allies certainly present a marked contrast to the silent women of Pericles's funeral oration.[129] In the scene with the Official, Lysistrata describes women keeping silent in the past as their husbands made decisions about the war (507–22). No more, she says. Now Lysistrata and her friends let loose their tongues and hold a symbolic funeral for the Official, first dressing him as a woman and then as a corpse (599–613).

Elements from the tradition of *epitaphios logos*, then, appear in *Lysistrata*, but critiqued: the women of *Lysistrata* stand in place of Athenian men who tend to appear as "saviors" of Greece in the speeches. While men offer their lives as contribution (*eranos* as death) in Thucydides, in *Lysistrata* women insist on their own contribution in the form of sons (*eranos* as life), who, they insist, should no longer make additional contributions of their lives in war. Finally, the vocal women of *Lysistrata* stand in stark contrast to the silent war widows described by Thucydides.

Just as the Adonis festival has the potential to draw on the wedding, but to critique and invert it (as seen in chapter 2), so too, I suggest, the Adonis festival may draw on, critique, and invert features seen in *epitaphios logos.* I do not suggest that the Adonis festival always served this function in Classical Athens. But the points of contact outlined above between Aristophanes's *Lysistrata* (*Adôniazousai*) and funeral oration suggest that the cult had the potential to operate in this way. The *epitaphios logos* is marked, generically, by the fact that it is a speech that takes place at the gravesite (ἐπιτάφιος), and the τάφος tends to be mentioned at the beginning of the speeches.[130] It is significant that the Adonia is an imitation of a funeral and that, notionally at least, women at the Adonia are mourning at the grave of Adonis, a youth who is represented by the gardens of tender plants.

As we have seen, funeral oration honors men who have died young in war by limiting mourning and, at least according to Thucydides, highlighting one man chosen by the city who delivers an address (*logos*). By contrast, the Adonia mimics a funeral for a youth who dies young, featuring audible lamentation by a group of women. The Adonia's focus on lamentation contrasts with the trope of praise of dead and the topos that lamentation does not have a place in *epitaphios logos*. In contrast to the war-ethic-affirming funeral oration, which formed an important part of the state funeral during winter or early spring, the Adonia took place during the summer, when the weather was warm and the seas traversable, in other words, in the midst of the fighting season.[131] In funeral oration, Athenians are insistently characterized as autochthonous, descended from individuals sprung from the earth, and it has been suggested that, "the funeral oration . . . in its repeated references to the collective autochthony of Athenian citizens, dispossesses the women of Athens of their reproductive function."[132] By contrast, the Adonia focuses on women's important role in human reproduction, inasmuch as participants cultivate gardens of Adonis, plants that represent Adonis that the women ritually rear, stand-ins for the sons and lovers and husbands they will lose or have lost already in war.[133]

As I have argued, *Lysistrata* mobilizes elements from the Adonis festival that would have registered with an audience familiar with the cult, and the action of the play is bound up with the ritual. The end of the play enacts an end to the Peloponnesian War and a conclusion to *Lysistrata* or *Women-at-the-Adonis-Festival.* This is signaled when an Athenian remarks: "Now I want to get naked and farm (γεωργεῖν)!" (1173). The Athenian's words suggest a return to proper sexual intercourse between married men and women. The Adonis festival is over. There will be no more fruitless gardens of Adonis, but rather proper farming will be reestablished, as husband stands by wife (ἀνὴρ δὲ παρὰ γυναῖκα καὶ γυνὴ/ στήτω παρ' ἄνδρα, 1275–76).

Yet it is, after all, a metaphorical Adonis festival that led to the cease-fire, an Adonis festival that led to the reestablishment of intercourse between married men and women. The peace is, in the end, explicitly described as "that which the Cyprian goddess (Aphrodite) made" (1289–90). This reading of *Lysistrata* with attention to the Adonia—the oath-taking ceremony in which women seize the "boar," the way in which Lysistrata and her allies play the role of Aphrodite, the use of myrrh/perfumes to stop the war, the manner in which the men of the play are turned into Adonis figures, and lamentation as means of dissent—calls into question frequent assertions that the Adonia was frivolous and peripheral, and that gardens of Adonis were *simply* fruitless and inconsequential, given that the ritual proves to be a serious and productive undertaking within the confines of the play. While the earlier solo performance by Demostratus's wife as she took part in a private foreign cult, though unsettling to the assembly, failed to halt the Sicilian expedition, the symbolic Adonia that Lysistrata and her allies convenes puts an end to the Peloponnesian War.

As for the place of the Adonia at Athens during the Classical period, this play suggests that a ritual frequently dismissed as private or foreign can be imagined to have significant effects on the *polis*. In *Lysistrata*, the Adonis festival takes center stage in unexpected ways on the Acropolis, in the heart of the Athenian *polis*, and indeed as a focus for the whole of Hellas. Even the Official, a figure who embodies such a prominent political position, takes part (against his will) in the ritual of the Adonia. As the women of *Lysistrata* manipulate elements associated with the Adonia, as they alter the political landscape, not only are they being seen; they are also being heard.

4 Philosophy

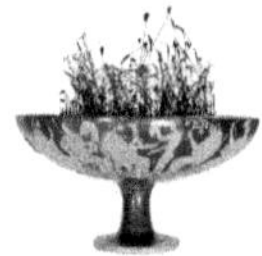

Gardening for Fun in Plato's Phaedrus

A dialogue of Plato might seem a strange place to go hunting for information about the Athenian Adonia. Why would a foreign women's cult that featured mourning hold appeal for a philosopher whose dialogues frequently express a strong distaste for lamenting women and *thrênos*? In *Republic*, for example, Socrates argues that it is unseemly for men to lament. He grants that women may indulge in such activity, but even then, the serious of these will refrain from outward expressions of mourning (387e–388a). Socrates goes on to suggest that certain passages of the *Iliad* be forbidden: the portrayal of Achilles in mourning; Priam's lamentation; and gods and goddesses in the throes of *thrênos*. Socrates remarks (in fine paradoxical fashion) that we should rather *laugh* at such passages. In *Laws,* too (in Magnesia, the "second-best" city), excessive emotion on the part of female mourners will be carefully controlled: loud lamentation will not be permitted outside the house (960a).[1]

The curbing of lamentation is also a theme in *Phaedo*. At the beginning of the dialogue, as he prepares to die, Socrates curtly dismisses the wailing women (who include his wife). And at the end of the dialogue, when his friends begin to mourn audibly, he silences them. Before he drinks the hemlock, he prepares his own body for burial by washing himself. Thus, by the end of *Phaedo* Socrates has usurped the activities that women typically perform in rituals surrounding death, as he carries out the rites himself and repeatedly emphasizes the immortality of the soul.[2] Socrates, then, co-opts funerary ritual in *Phaedo* for his own ends, in the service of his philosophic project. As I will suggest, a similar co-optation of funerary ritual occurs in *Phaedrus*, as Socrates exploits the Adonis festival, which, as we have seen, features an imitation of a funeral.

In chapters 2 and 3, I argued that the Athenian Adonia offers a commentary on both the wedding and the funeral, as women at the Adonia incorporate elements of these two prominent rituals. In this chapter, I argue that Plato recognizes the dissident messages that the Adonis festival has the potential to carry and uses the cult to craft his portrayal of Socrates, who inhabits a paradoxical position in the Athenian *polis*.

The Adonia is mentioned near the end of *Phaedrus* when Socrates uses the festival to make a point about writing. Cultivation of gardens of Adonis, like writing, is described as something done "for the sake of play and festivity" (παιδιᾶς τε καὶ ἑορτῆς χάριν, 276b). Planting *Adônidos kêpoi* is opposed to the serious work of proper farming, just as writing is opposed to engagement with a living interlocutor.[3] In scholarship on *Phaedrus*—even in work attentive to the religious aspects of the dialogue—one finds little or no discussion of the Adonis festival.[4] This is somewhat surprising given how much ink has been spilled over Plato's (or Socrates's) views on writing. As I will show, Plato is a keen cultural critic and observer of Athenian ritual, and his mention of the Adonia demands careful analysis as evidence for the significance of the festival at Athens during the Classical period. In this chapter, I suggest that the opposition between seriousness and play that Socrates uses to contrast proper farming with the cultivation of gardens of Adonis appears in connection with such an important theme in Plato's work as the practice of philosophy, inasmuch as Socrates is characterized as a practitioner of serious play.

When Socrates mentions the gardens of Adonis, he remarks that a serious farmer (one who has νοῦς, "sense") would be unlikely to plant in this way:

> Σω. τόδε δή μοι εἰπέ· ὁ νοῦν ἔχων γεωργός, ὧν σπερμάτων κήδοιτο καὶ ἔγκαρπα βούλοιτο γενέσθαι, πότερα σπουδῇ ἂν θέρους εἰς Ἀδώνιδος κήπους ἀρῶν χαίροι θεωρῶν καλοὺς ἐν ἡμέραισιν ὀκτὼ γιγνομένους, ἢ ταῦτα μὲν δὴ παιδιᾶς τε καὶ ἑορτῆς χάριν δρῴη ἄν, ὅτε καὶ ποιοῖ· ἐφ' οἷς δὲ ἐσπούδακεν, τῇ γεωργικῇ χρώμενος ἂν τέχνῃ, σπείρας εἰς τὸ προσῆκον, ἀγαπῴη ἂν ἐν ὀγδόῳ μηνὶ ὅσα ἔσπειρεν τέλος λαβόντα;

> Socrates: Tell me this, would a farmer who had sense (νοῦν), if he had seeds that he cared about and wanted them to bear fruit, would he in all seriousness (σπουδῇ), during the summertime, sow them in gardens of Adonis (εἰς Ἀδώνιδος κήπους) and rejoice seeing them becoming beautiful (καλούς) in eight days? Or would he rather do these things for the sake of amusement (παιδιᾶς) and festivity (ἑορτῆς), if he did them at all? The seeds he was seriously concerned about (ἐσπούδακεν), employing his farming skill, having sown them in a fitting place (εἰς τὸ προσῆκον), would he not be well pleased with as many things as he planted coming to fruition in the eighth month? (276b)

Socrates explains that a serious farmer would only plant gardens of Adonis—if he ever did such a thing at all—on two conditions: for the sake of amusement (παιδιά) and for the sake of festivity (ἑορτή). The seeds the farmer was truly concerned about (σπουδάζειν) he would care for in the proper way; he would see to it that they reached their telos in the appropriate time. Socrates thus sets up an opposition between proper and improper farming, and the distinction between the two concerns where one plants (on the one hand, εἰς Ἀδώνιδος κήπους, on the other hand, εἰς τὸ προσῆκον) and the time that elapses before maturation (eight days versus eight months). Thus, Socrates appears to disparage *Adônidos kêpoi* as unfitting places to sow one's seeds; the practice appears to be characterized as a trivial and mindless undertaking.

Indeed, given the context of the discussion between Socrates and Phaedrus, the contrast between the serious farmer and the playful gardener is analogous to the contrast between the philosopher and the nonphilosopher. The philosopher grows *logoi* in his own soul. These *logoi* are not fruitless but produce seeds that are planted in other souls (276e–277a). If the seeds are planted in appropriate places, the process continues, and the *logoi* have the potential to become immortal.[5] Socrates, then, would be aligned with the serious farmer (who has *nous*), the kind of farmer who would rarely, if ever, deign to do such a silly thing as plant gardens of Adonis.[6] He would rather plant in a fitting place and watch his seeds achieve their *telos* in the appropriate time.

While to some extent Socrates surely represents the serious farmer in *Phaedrus*, the situation is not so straightforward in a dialogue whose primary movement consists of performing a *logos* and then subsequently pronouncing it untrue. After Socrates's first "Lysianic" speech, the speech in praise of the nonlover, he recants, quoting Stesichorus's palinode, "this story is not true" (οὐκ ἔστ' ἔτυμος λόγος οὗτος, 243a). He then promptly delivers a second speech, one that is sometimes referred to as the "Great Speech," in which he discusses the soul's immortality. It is a challenge, as a reader, to get one's footing in this dialogue set on the banks of the Ilissus River. Concerned as it is with *erôs* and *mania*, *Phaedrus* is one of Plato's more slippery works.

As I demonstrate in this chapter, despite appearances to the contrary, Socrates is, ultimately, playing the role of the individual gardening for fun in a festal context in *Phaedrus*. More importantly, Socrates's practice of philosophy in Plato's works is described in the same terms as the cultivation of gardens of Adonis. Like writing, the cultivation of gardens of Adonis is described as something done for fun, and in his description of both practices, Socrates echoes an opposition that appears frequently in Plato's dialogues—that between the *geloion*, the "silly," the "trivial," or "funny," and the *spoudaion*, the "serious," or "important"—aligning gardens of

Adonis (and writing) with the *geloion*. Socrates's practice of philosophy is similarly associated with play, hovering between the poles of the *geloion* and *spoudaion*. Although Plato characterizes Socrates as playful, his message is deeply serious.

In this chapter, I examine the two conditions on which Socrates suggests that a serious farmer might plant gardens of Adonis—for amusement (παιδιά) and in a festal context (ἑορτή)—to show that, in *Phaedrus,* Socrates takes on the characteristics of one who cultivates gardens of Adonis. First, I show that play (παιδιά) is an important theme in many of Plato's works and that Socrates regularly engages in serious play. Play is of particular concern in *Phaedrus*, too, and the dialogue incorporates elements of comedy, the playful genre par excellence. Next, I argue that Socrates's exploitation of the metaphor of the Adonis festival is part of a larger tendency toward manipulation of religious language in Plato's works. A look at Plato's use of festival (ἑορτή) to situate his other dialogues, as well as an investigation into religious language specifically in *Phaedrus*—in particular, the language associated with ecstatic rites—reveals that *Phaedrus* takes place in a festal context, the second reason for indulging in ritual planting. This chapter, then, argues that cultivation of gardens of Adonis is described in the same terms as the practice of philosophy. Gardens of Adonis should be taken seriously in *Phaedrus*, and this argument serves as justification for the close reading of *Phaedrus* and the attention to Adonis festival elements that follows in the final section of this chapter.

In *Phaedrus,* Socrates and Phaedrus walk along the Ilissus River. But, significantly, they walk through an area known as *Kêpoi,* "the Gardens," and Phaedrus takes on the characteristics of a plant that Socrates cultivates. The dialogue equivocates about the outcome of Socrates's gardening for fun. Just as writing has the potential to awaken truth, so too the day spent with Phaedrus may prove to be philosophically productive. Ultimately, the metaphor of the philosopher as cultivator of gardens of Adonis is fitting, inasmuch as diverging opinions exist concerning the "work" that the philosopher performs in the *polis.* Just as outsiders to the Adonia might view the cult's ritual planting as fruitless, so too those who are not philosophically inclined see Socrates's practice of philosophy as fundamentally nonproductive.

The Ritual Play of Philosophy: Socrates and *paidia*

Throughout Plato's works, Socrates's approach is decidedly ludic. In *Symposium*, for example, Alcibiades says that Socrates "spends his whole life playing around (παίζων) with people," 216e. Socrates often seems to say one thing and mean another, giving rise to (the infamous) "Socratic irony." He is regularly described as *geloios*, so regularly, in fact, that *geloios* has been described as one of "*the* Socratic epithets."[7] But Socrates's play conveys a serious message, and it has been suggested that "the more Plato discloses of truth for understanding readers, the more he denotes the conversation as a παιδιά."[8] The serious work of philosophy in Plato is bound up with trivial and playful elements, the *spoudaion* with the *geloion*.[9]

In Plato's works, the game of *pessoi* is a metaphor for dialectic, and Socrates is a master *pessoi* player who corners his interlocutors in a game played not with tokens but with words (e.g., *Gorgias* 461d; *Republic* 487b–c). Why is the philosopher so bound up with games? In part, because play carries with it great potential for education. In *Laws*, the Athenian stranger explains that in order to be good at something, one should play at it beginning in childhood: "and through games (*paidia*) to try to turn the pleasures and desires of the children in the direction of their goal (*telos*)," 643b–c. Children should play at pursuits, he suggests, amusing themselves as little farmers, playing at tilling land, so that they grow into adult farmers (643c).[10] Ultimately, education, which includes play, is defined as training to create proper citizens, who know how to rule and how to obey (643e).[11]

Socrates is associated with play perhaps nowhere so much as in *Phaedrus*.[12] His second speech, the "Great Speech," is frequently taken to be the *serious* speech—the true words of the philosopher—when compared with his lighthearted revision of Lysias's speech in praise of the nonlover. Or—another way of looking at it—Socrates is planting gardens of Adonis as he delivers his first speech but transforms into the philosophic farmer when he delivers the second. Yet near the end of the dialogue, in reference to his second speech, Socrates says, "We played out (προσεπαίσαμεν) a mythic hymn moderately and auspiciously in honor of Eros, your lord and mine," 265c1–3. This is not the only time the verb παίζειν is used to describe Socrates's and Phaedrus's activities. As *Phaedrus* draws to a close, the *entire* discussion held by Socrates and Phaedrus on the banks of the Ilissus is characterized as nothing more than a diverting game: "So now we have played around enough with words" (οὐκοῦν ἤδη πεπαίσθω μετρίως ἡμῖν τὰ περὶ λόγων, 278b).[13]

Socrates's practice of philosophy, then, is characterized by serious play, especially in *Phaedrus*, and when Socrates asserts that a farmer might cultivate gardens of Adonis "for fun," he is drawing on an opposition that pervades Plato's works. Not only are writing, the cultivation of Adonis gardens, and the practice of philosophy described as seriously playful activities, but also, in Plato's works, the dramatic arts are so described. Tragedy and comedy are both described as amusements. In *Laws*, comedy is characterized above all as a genre concerned with play and with that which is *geloion*: "those funny amusements (γέλωτα . . . παίγνια) which we all call comedy," 816e. In contrast to comedy, tragedy is concerned with serious things, *spoudaia*. Yet Plato undercuts such a simple distinction in *Laws* by having the Athenian stranger refer to the tragic poets as "our so-called serious poets" (τῶν δὲ σπουδαίων, ὥς φασι, τῶν περὶ τραγῳδίαν ἡμῖν ποιητῶν, 817a), while, in *Republic*, Socrates explains that tragedy is a playful mimesis that should not be taken seriously (ἀλλ' εἶναι παιδιάν τινα καὶ οὐ σπουδὴν τὴν μίμησιν, 602b; cf. 608a).

Socrates famously asserts that tragic and comic *paidia* must be carefully controlled. What appears to be merely amusing has the capacity to become threatening. The potential for the dramatic arts to promote disorder is particularly clear in a passage from *Republic* where *mousikê*, "music and the arts," is described as *paidia* that has the potential to overthrow the entire order of things (424d–e). *Mousikê* carries significant dangers if left unregulated, a notion that comes as no surprise, given the concerns that Socrates frequently expresses about poetry. Yet *philosophy* is described as *mousikê* in *Phaedo* (ὡς φιλοσοφίας μὲν οὔσης μεγίστης μουσικῆς, "since philosophy is the greatest *mousikê*," 61a), and, indeed, far from excluding poetry from his works, Plato constantly *uses* poetry in his dialogues in an attempt to carve out a place for philosophy, a genre that, it has been convincingly argued, Plato himself creates.[14]

Yet although Plato incorporates a variety of genres including the dramatic arts in his work, it has been suggested that Plato is "more indebted to comedy than to any other literary genre."[15] Plato's dialogues share formal characteristics with comedies, with many of Plato's characters taking on the appearance of comic actors.[16] What is more, "both genres claim authority on the basis of the 'fact' that they 'dare' to utter the truth. Or, to be more precise, both genres feature a 'voice,' which claims to speak the truth."[17] Plato is said to have had the writings of Aristophanes with him at his death.[18] This apocryphal detail serves to illustrate something apparent to any careful reader of Plato's dialogues: Plato takes comedy seriously. Comedy, of course, is not *just* funny. As the chorus explains in Aristophanes's *Frogs*, it will say many silly things and many serious things (καὶ πολλὰ μὲν γελοῖά μ' εἰ-/πεῖν, πολλὰ δὲ σπουδαῖα, 389–90).[19] Plato is clearly aware that, for such a playful genre, comedy has powerful effects. Indeed, in *Apology* he has Socrates express the idea that Aristophanes's comic portrayal of him cost him his life.[20] Like the *spoudogeloios* philosopher, who blends jest with sincerity, comedy treads a fine line between the playful and the serious.

Plato incorporates the playful genre par excellence—comedy—into *Phaedrus*, thus thematizing *paidia* within the context of the dialogue. *Phaedrus* partakes of many of the conventions of a comic play, complete with *phallos* jokes (Socrates wants to know what Phaedrus is holding in his left hand beneath his cloak at 228d–e).[21] The dialogue contains role reversal (Socrates and Phaedrus each in turn play the part of *erastês* and *erômenos*, discussed below), a chorus of cicadas (230c), and a cast of nymphs and Pan as κωφὰ πρόσωπα (mute persons). At the end of his comedies, Aristophanes tends to have his characters leave the dramatic space and head home for a feast or celebration, and many of his plays end in prayer, hymn, or *paiôn* (e.g., *Frogs*, *Peace*, *Birds*, *Lysistrata*). *Phaedrus* offers a "comic" ending, inasmuch as Socrates and Phaedrus take their leave of the dramatic setting to head back to the city, closing with a prayer to Pan.

There is no explicit mention of sex between Socrates and Phaedrus at any point in the dialogue, but it is hard to read *Phaedrus* without noting its affinity to a prolonged and heavily coded seduction scene.[22] Socrates's reference to Lysias's manuscript that Phaedrus is holding beneath his cloak (or thinly veiled reference to Phaedrus's sexual excitement, 228e) is followed up with a description of the grass as "perfect for laying one's head upon" (230c). As they perform the first and second speeches, Socrates and Phaedrus in turn occupy the positions of *erastês* and *erômenos*.[23] As the dialogue begins, Socrates plays the part of the *erastês* of *logoi* (228c), while Phaedrus plays the part of the *erômenos* who has just the speech Socrates wants to hear. Phaedrus, like a good *erômenos*, is coy and demure when Socrates demands to hear the *logos*.[24] Finally, though, despite Phaedrus's reluctance (which Socrates says is feigned coyness, laying bare the mechanics of their dance), Phaedrus gives in and produces the first speech, compelled by threat of force (*bia*, 228c).

After Phaedrus delivers Lysias's speech, the roles are reversed, and it is Socrates's turn to play the coy *erômenos*. When Phaedrus demands that Socrates deliver a speech in praise of the nonlover, he too threatens Socrates with force (236c–d). Socrates complies. As they perform the first and second speeches, then, Socrates and Phaedrus in turn occupy the positions of *erastês* and *erômenos*.

At the start of the third speech, Socrates wonders aloud—where is that boy (*pais*) I was talking to? And Phaedrus responds—right here beside you (243e).[25] The positions have shifted once again. In the end, it is Phaedrus who is portrayed as a (healthy, fit, attractive) *young* man and is addressed as such (ὦ νεανία, 257c; ὦ παῖ, 267c).[26]

Phaedrus is most visibly comic when Phaedrus is appalled to find that he and Socrates are taking on the role of actors in a comedy. Phaedrus remarks: "For you must, above all, speak as you are able, so that we are not compelled to produce the base material of the comics (τὸ τῶν κωμῳδῶν φορτικὸν πρᾶγμα), exchanging jabs with one another" (236c). Phaedrus casts the conversation generically as a descent into the world of comedy because the two are so obviously playing roles that have just been reversed. Earlier, Socrates had said, "O Phaedrus, if I don't know Phaedrus I have forgotten myself" (ὦ Φαῖδρε, εἰ ἐγὼ Φαῖδρον ἀγνοῶ, καὶ ἐμαυτοῦ ἐπιλέλησμαι,

228a), as he played the role of *erastês*. Phaedrus quotes that very line, changing only the name Phaedrus to Socrates ("Watch it and don't make me say, 'O Socrates if I don't know Socrates I have forgotten myself,'" 236c). Phaedrus plays Socrates's prior role as *erastês*, quoting still another of Socrates's earlier lines (from 228c): "He wanted to speak but feigned coyness" (236c).

As we have seen, Plato's works take *paidia* seriously, characterizing complex and significant issues such as writing, the activity of the philosopher, and the performance of drama (especially comedy) as play. Socrates is particularly playful in *Phaedrus,* and the dialogue emphasizes the theme of *paidia* inasmuch as it draws on comedy. An Adonia characterized as *paidia* within *Phaedrus* thus warrants serious scrutiny, since the opposition between the playful individual who gardens for fun (*paidia*) and the serious farmer is part of a more general (and complicated) discussion in Plato's dialogues. I have suggested that Socrates is gardening for fun in *Phaedrus*, but how exactly is he gardening within the context of religious festival (*heortê*), the second occasion on which a farmer might cultivate gardens of Adonis?

Ritual Planting: Socrates and *heortê*

Just as *paidia* plays an important role in Plato's works (especially in *Phaedrus*), so too *heortê* is a significant theme in them and is particularly pronounced in *Phaedrus*. Furthermore, as I will argue, the opposition between the laughable and the serious that I have discussed maps onto religious practices, with foreign rites associated with women (for example, Corybantic and Bacchic practices) aligned with the *geloion*.[27] But just as play may convey messages of substance, so too religious practices that appear trivial at first glance are not what they seem in *Phaedrus*.

Many fifth- and fourth-century Athenian authors describe festival, *heortê*, as the opposite of work, a leisure activity, something done for fun.[28] So it stands to reason that Socrates would mention *heortê* in connection with *paidia*. Just as *paidia* is a concern in Plato's dialogues, so too festival appears regularly and is similarly connected with education. For example, in *Laws*, *heortê* is crucial for the creation of law-abiding citizens. The properly educated individual is one who hates what should be hated and loves what should be loved (653b–c). However, as people age they grow forgetful of what should be hated and loved. Festivals provide a remedy for this (653c–d). *Heortê* provides relief from work, but it is also a means by which one makes a citizen straight (ἐπανορθῶνται, 653d). Festival serves as a quiet reminder to recall whatever has been forgotten. *Paidia* and *heortê*, then, make for the proper education of individuals, which results in the proper running of the state.[29]

Heortê, then, is bound up with education, and just as he does with *paidia,* Plato often employs festival as a setting for his philosophical dialogues. In *Phaedo,* the annual *theôria* to Delos delays Socrates's execution (61a), and he owes to *heortê* the time that remains of his life (as well as the opportunity to discuss the soul's immortality with his friends). In the very first lines of *Republic,* Socrates explains that he went down to Piraeus the day before to offer prayers to the goddess and to see the festival (*heortê,* 327a).[30] It is then that he runs into a group of friends who take him to Polemarchus's house, where the philosophical discussion takes place. *Timaeus* also takes place during the festival of the "goddess" (26e); *Ion* begins as Ion comes from the festival of Asclepius at Epidaurus (530a); the occasion for the dialogue in *Parmenides* is the Great Panathenaea (127b); *Lysis* opens with a mention of a festival of Hermes (206d); *Symposium* takes place just after the Great Dionysia (173a). As Socrates moves about the city, going to and from festivals, he runs into individuals who become his interlocutors, for on these occasions, there is leisure to talk.[31]

I have suggested above that *Phaedrus* is particularly concerned with *paidia*; the dialogue is also especially keen to emphasize *heortê.* As we have seen, state-sanctioned civic festivals often frame Plato's dialogues, and the cast of characters subsequently moves to a more private setting to be "feasted" on *logoi.*[32] A different kind of *heortê* is operative in *Phaedrus,* since the dialogue underscores foreign rituals that tend to be associated with women. In *Phaedrus,* the setting is outside the *astu,* and this special topos on the outskirts of Athens is repeatedly described as "sacred" (e.g., 230b), so much so that Socrates himself is overcome by religious experience: he represents himself as a nympholept (238d, 241e; cf. 263d, 278b), as well as engaged in Corybantic (228b–c) and Bacchic *mania* (234d).[33] Early on, Phaedrus comments on Socrates's oddness, explaining that Socrates never leaves the city and that outside the city, Socrates is "most out of place" (ἀτοπώτατος, 230c).[34] He is like "some foreigner being led around and not like a native" (ξεναγουμένῳ τινὶ καὶ οὐκ ἐπιχωρίῳ ἔοικας, 230c–d). Socrates explains that he loves learning and that the land (χωρία) and the trees are not likely to teach him anything at all; it is people in the city who do (230c–d).

The setting has a profound effect on Socrates. *Phaedrus* is the only dialogue that takes place outside the walls of Athens, and it has been suggested that "Socrates, who is the embodiment of reason in Athens, seems to lose his composure, if not his mind, the moment he leaves the city."[35] While in other dialogues Plato presents a Socrates who cuts an odd figure (for example, standing barefoot in the snow for hours and generally lacking in social graces), the Socrates of *Phaedrus* is still more eccentric. In *Phaedrus,* Socrates calls upon the Muses and mentions Sappho and Anacreon (235c); he quotes Ibycus (242c–d) and Stesichorus (243a–b);

he exclaims that he is nearly spouting dithyrambic poetry (238d); he marvels that he is speaking in hexameter (241e); and he describes the "palinode" as "poetic" (τοῖς ὀνόμασιν . . . ποιητικοῖς, 257a).[36] The composition of *Phaedrus*, too, calls attention to itself as peculiar when compared with other Platonic texts, as it contains three lengthy speeches, two delivered by Socrates, who is more accustomed to engage in dialogue.[37]

Socrates's strangeness, his "foreignness" (230c–d), is presented specifically in religious terms. Socrates remarks: "But tell me this too—for I cannot really remember on account of my state of divine possession (διὰ τὸ ἐνθουσιαστικόν)—did I define *erôs* at the start of my speech?" (263d). In crossing the boundary that separates the city from the rustic countryside (χωρία, 230d), Socrates enters a space where limit setting becomes challenging, not only with regard to defining terms within speeches (ὡρισάμην ἔρωτα, "Did I define [literally, "set a boundary" concerning] *erôs*?") but also with regard to ritual experience. Socrates becomes "enthused," as speeches not his own exit through his bewitched (καταφαρμακευθέντος, 242e) mouth. He begins to invoke foreign, female religious practices, describing himself as a participant in ecstatic cults—the same sorts of cults that I have discussed in chapter 3, and which provide a context for Athenian ways of thinking about the Adonis festival.

For religious authority, Plato often defers to the religious "center," Delphi. In *Republic,* when he designs his perfect state, Plato entrusts religious matters to Delphic Apollo, explaining his reasoning thus: "For this god [Apollo] is the ancestral interpreter for all people, concerning such things; sitting at the center of the earth (ἐν μέσῳ τῆς γῆς) at the navel (ἐπὶ τοῦ ὀμφαλοῦ), he pronounces his interpretations" (*Republic* 427c).[38] Links between Apollo and Socrates abound, for example, the discussion of Apollo and his oracle in *Apology*, as well as Socrates's commitment to the Delphic maxim: know thyself.[39] Indeed, attention to this Delphic maxim is the opposite of the *geloion*, the "ridiculous," in *Philebus* (48c).[40] To know thyself is deeply serious.

In *Phaedrus*, too, Plato gives Apollo and Delphi a programmatic role near the beginning of the dialogue when Phaedrus inquires about Boreas and Oreithyia. Are he and Socrates not, Phaedrus wonders, walking right near the very place where Oreithyia was raped by Boreas? Socrates quickly brushes this nonsense aside and remarks curtly: "I am not yet able, as the Delphic inscription says, to know myself. And it seems to me laughable (γελοῖον), since I still don't know this, to investigate the things of others," 229e. Socrates would like to begin his investigation with himself. This is the serious matter at hand, in contrast to a discussion of the wind god and his escapades. Yet despite Socrates's avowal at the beginning of *Phaedrus* that he will attend to serious and central concerns, the dialogue is preoccupied with the playful, as well as with madness and a loss of *nous*, "rational sense."

Socrates represents himself as a Corybant, dancing with Phaedrus outside the city. Soon after Socrates and Phaedrus meet, Socrates gives a description of what he imagines Phaedrus's reaction would have been upon hearing Lysias's speech. Phaedrus would have urged Lysias to repeat it, borrowed the manuscript, and sat reading for a while. Then he would have gone for a walk, memorized the speech, and headed outside the walls of Athens to practice it. Socrates then remarks: "Meeting one who is sick over hearing speeches, he rejoiced on seeing him because he would have a co-Corybant (συγκορυβαντιῶντα) and he kept telling him to lead on" (228b–c).

Most of our evidence for Corybantes comes from Plato, and the picture of Corybantic ritual, incomplete as it is, looks much like Bacchic madness and maenadic worship of Dionysus, with frenzied group dancing to the music of pipes and *tympana*.[41] "Have you gone truly mad or are you in a Corybantic frenzy?" asks Xanthias in the opening lines of Aristophanes *Wasps* (ἀλλ' ἦ παραφρονεῖς ἐτεὸν ἢ κορυβαντιᾷς; 8). Just as Dionysus and Bacchic practices were associated with madness, the *teletai* associated with Corybantes seem to have provoked (and homeopathically cured) a kind of madness.[42] Corybantic and Bacchic practices are frequently linked in Plato's works, as they are in *Phaedrus,* where, in addition to describing himself as a Corybant, Socrates also describes himself as a Bacchant (234d).[43]

Elsewhere in Plato's works, Corybantic and Bacchic rituals are described in ambiguous if not downright unappealing terms; yet in *Phaedrus,* Socrates embraces such practices. In *Euthydemus*, Socrates takes the hapless Cleinias aside and tries to give him encouragement: the sophists who are barraging him with questions are acting like Corybantic dancers, initiating him into their cult. Here, Corybantic initiation is described as *paidia* (277d) and is associated with the verbal gymnastics of the sophists. And in *Ion*, Socrates mockingly likens poets to Corybantes and Bacchantes, who are unable to explain what they do because they are possessed and not in their right mind. The divinity is the one speaking through the poet, who does not have his wits about him and lacks cognitive understanding.[44] It has been suggested that "there is no reason to suppose that the philosopher viewed the [Dionysiac] rites in any other way than he did those of the Korybants, with which he everywhere brackets them. They are amusing for many and therapeutic for some, and are tolerated in the ideal state, though not endorsed."[45]

In *Phaedrus*, Socrates indulges in these practices that are bound up with play. When Phaedrus asks for Socrates's reaction to his recitation of Lysias's speech, Socrates responds, "It is divine my friend! I am completely bowled over (ὥστε με ἐκπλαγῆναι).[46] And I suffered this because of you, O Phaedrus, looking at you, because you seemed to sparkle delighted by the speech while you were reading it. So, thinking that you understand more than me about such things, I followed you, and following you I joined in with you in Bacchic revel (συνεβάκχευσα μετὰ σοῦ, 234d)."[47] Socrates explains that, while watching Phaedrus performing Lysias's speech with such verve, he was entirely overcome and became a Bacchic reveler following in Phaedrus's train. But surely Socrates jests. Indeed, it is specifically Socrates's characterization of himself as a Bacchant that prompts Phaedrus to question his earnestness: "Well! So you are resolved to mock it (παίζειν)?" Socrates responds cryptically, "Do I seem to you to be joking and not to be serious (δοκῶ γάρ σοι παίζειν καὶ οὐχὶ ἐσπουδακέναι)?" (234d).[48]

Play, then, is bound up with religious language in *Phaedrus*, specifically with Corybantic and Bacchic practices—foreign cults associated with women and a loss of *nous*. Just as Socrates revels in Bacchic worship, so too does he delight in Phaedrus's difficulty in distinguishing between the playful and the serious, an opposition that the notion of the reasonable philosopher as Bacchant calls into question and that recalls the contrast between the serious farmer and the playful gardener. Although at the beginning of *Phaedrus,* Socrates says that he will concern himself with serious things like the Delphic maxim, he begins to play the Corybant and engage in Bacchic activities. Plato's deployment of ritual practices is connected with his complicated manipulation of the opposition between the *spoudaion* and the *geloion*—serious attention to the Delphic maxim, on the one hand, playful Bacchic and Corybantic excess, on the other.

The idea that the sober philosopher would play the Bacchant is laughable, as silly as the notion that Socrates would cultivate gardens of Adonis. Surely Socrates would prefer to have his wits about him. Surely he would condemn practices that involve such emotional paroxysms. Just as Cadmus's and Tiresias's cross-dressing in *Bacchae* is described by Pentheus as "ridiculous" (πολὺν γέλων, 250), so too Phaedrus considers Socrates playing a Bacchant to be *geloion*. In *Bacchae*, Pentheus explains why he believes the actions of Cadmus and Tiresias are funny. "Your old age lacks *nous*," says Pentheus when he sees his grandfather decked out in maenadic attire during a moment in Euripides's tragedy that contains strong elements of comedy.[49] Socrates, too, could be seen as too old for this sort of adolescent exuberance and decidedly lacking in *nous*.[50] Yet *Bacchae* reveals the importance of incorporating Dionysiac mania into the *polis*, and similarly *Phaedrus* insists on the importance of erotic *mania* within the context of the philosophic project.

Just as Plato *uses* literature—reshaping generic conventions—as he creates the new genre of philosophy, so too he uses ritual language and supernatural metaphors in innovative fashions.[51] Socrates has a *daimonion* that no one else seems to have, and while the Eleusinian mysteries were well known to the Athenians, the mystery language that peppers dialogues such as *Symposium*, *Phaedrus*, and *Phaedo* must originally have sounded revolutionary to Athenians because of the very particular ways that Socrates connects the familiar language of initiation with the philosophic ascent.[52] In *Phaedrus*, Socrates actually seems to be "initiating" Phaedrus as he discusses the role of erotic *mania* in philosophy.[53] Of course, in the end, Socrates was famously tried and executed on a charge of impiety (*graphê asebeias*).[54]

Socrates's practice of philosophy was deeply troubling and disruptive, at least to a segment of the Athenian population. Just as the *paidia* associated with dramatic performances has the potential to become disruptive if not carefully regulated (for example, spectators watching a tragic performance may become habituated to excessive mourning and may go on to engage in such practices), so too playful practices like Bacchic and Corybantic rituals are troubling, precisely because they are infectious; the activities may result in the production of *more* Dionysiac revelers. In *Symposium*, Alcibiades associates Socrates's effects on others, his philosophic madness, with Bacchic rites and Corybantic practices. Alcibiades explains that he himself reacts like a Corybant when he listens to Socrates: "For whenever I hear him, I am more moved than the Corybantes. My heart leaps and tears pour out because of his words. And I see many others suffering the same things" (215e). According to Alcibiades, he and many others are profoundly affected by Socrates's words, just as the Corybantes are moved during their rites. Alcibiades continues, explaining that those present at the drinking party "have all partaken of [Socrates's] philosophic mania and Bacchic frenzy" (218b).

Such ecstatic practices tend to break down the distinction between the spectator and the participant. In chapter 3, I suggested that certain kinds of foreign cult—nonmainstream Dionysiac practices and maenadic ritual—are described in precisely the same terms as the Adonis festival and that representations of such practices emphasize the ways in which the boundary between the spectator and the participant is blurred. So it is that, in *Bacchae*, the prudish young king Pentheus is pulled into the Bacchic sphere, as he dresses as a maenad and heads out to Mount Cithaeron.[55] Like Bacchic and Corybantic activities, the Adonis festival was a similarly infectious foreign rite. In Menander's *Samia,* Moschion begins as a spectator of the Adonis festival, but he soon becomes involved in the ritual, so involved that he gets a girl pregnant and an illegitimate child is produced (38–49). In *Phaedrus*, Socrates and Phaedrus are outside the *astu*, where their *paidia* will have no such ill effects on others. Nevertheless, Socrates marks his Bacchic and Corybantic religious experience as a group activity, inasmuch as he employs verbs that carry the συν- prefix, συγκορυβαντιῶντα (228b) and συνεβάκχευσα (234d).

I have suggested that Socrates's mention of gardens of Adonis must be viewed within the context of his larger tendency to rework familiar ritual language for the purposes of his philosophical project. As seen above, in *Phaedo*, Socrates co-opts funerary practices, washing himself before he drinks the hemlock, and doing away with noisy lamentation by dismissing his wife and the women who accompany her and criticizing his friends when they begin to mourn. So too, in *Phaedrus* Socrates manipulates the metaphor of the Adonia, a ritual that features lamentation, in unexpected ways. While mourning is an important element of representations of the Adonia, in *Phaedrus* Socrates makes no mention of lamenting women in connection with the festival. Instead, he replaces the lamenting women atop roofs with a male "farmer." While in other texts, the Adonis festival is described as *paidia*—as we saw in chapter 3 *paidia* can be a common critique of foreign cult, associated with "frivolity" in the minds of many Athenians—the festival is not simply a game in *Phaedrus*.[56]

As we have seen, in *Phaedrus* Socrates portrays himself as a Corybantic and a Bacchic reveler, religious practices that involve madness (Socrates is *not* characterizing himself and Phaedrus as, for example, visitors to Delphi).[57] These rites are appropriate activities for Socrates and Phaedrus. After all, they have left the confines of the city and are relaxing outside the walls, on the margins of the *astu*, where Socrates is a "foreigner," and where they discuss *erôs* as the best kind of *mania*. Socrates, whom one would think would be a serious farmer, a farmer with *nous*, planting properly in a fitting place, instead aligns himself with foreign, ecstatic rituals, as he gardens for the sake of *paidia* and *heortê*—the very conditions that characterize the cultivation of gardens of Adonis. The circumstances are right, then, for ritual planting, and we can now investigate the more specific ways in which Socrates is a cultivator of *Adônidos kêpoi* in *Phaedrus*.

Gardening for Fun in Plato's *Phaedrus*

Thus far, I have argued that in his works Plato describes Socrates's practice of philosophy in precisely the same terms he uses to characterize cultivation of gardens of Adonis in *Phaedrus*, echoing an opposition between and inversion of play and seriousness that pervades his dialogues. The mention of gardens of Adonis in *Phaedrus* should be taken seriously. In what follows, I examine specific elements associated with the Adonia that appear in the dialogue to argue that Socrates's allusion to the cultivation of gardens of Adonis is an element integral to *Phaedrus* as a whole. As Phaedrus and Socrates take their rest and converse on the banks of the Ilissus River just outside the city walls of Athens, the setting begins to resemble a garden of Adonis. As the sun beats down on the pair, Phaedrus takes on characteristics of the plants around him, while Socrates is figured as a cultivator of young Phaedrus. Depending on how Phaedrus responds to Socrates's attempts to convert him to the philosophical life (and the dialogue equivocates here), the *kêpos* that Socrates tends has the potential to go in two opposite directions: to become "more fruitless than a garden of Adonis" or, alternatively, to become a philosophically productive *kêpos*.[58] Ultimately, I suggest that the cultivation of gardens of Adonis is a fitting metaphor for Socrates to employ to describe the practice of philosophy. Just as gardens of Adonis may be seen as a productive activity by participants of an Adonia but as a fruitless undertaking by outsiders to the cult, so too the "work" of the philosopher may be characterized as a worthwhile contribution or an idle pastime.

"The Gardens" and Adônidos kêpoi

To a greater extent than in most of Plato's dialogues, the setting in *Phaedrus* is described with relish.[59] Indeed, it has been suggested that the background does not stay put: "Topography becomes the topic of conversation in a highly obtrusive manner. . . . The background will not stay where it belongs."[60] As Socrates and Phaedrus arrive, Socrates describes the delightful place at length (230b–c), and the description of this bucolic setting is one of the earliest examples of what becomes known as "pastoral." The landscape of *Phaedrus* is extremely lush and well watered, with blooming plants and trees, soft grass, and a cool stream. But this is not some vague and unidentifiable *locus amoenus*. Athenians would have been quite familiar with the location that the dialogue describes—a place known as "the Gardens," where a temple of Aphrodite stood and where Aphrodite "in the gardens" was worshipped.[61] In the opening lines of *Phaedrus*, Socrates and Phaedrus meet up in the city near the Olympieum (227b) just inside the walls, and Phaedrus explains that he is going for a walk "outside the wall" (ἔξω τείχους, 227a). The pair then amble along the Ilissus River, southeast of the Acropolis, through an area where, as Thucydides tells us, many ancient cults were situated (2.15.4).[62]

Pausanias describes this place, just after discussing the Olympieum and the Pythion: "Concerning the place, which is called 'the Gardens' (ὃ Κήπους ὀνομάζουσι) and the temple of Aphrodite, no story is told by them, nor about the Aphrodite, which stands near the temple" (1.19.2). Lucian, too, refers to the area known as "the Gardens," when he mentions a heifer sacrificed to Aphrodite Ourania, the one "in the Gardens" (*Dial. Court.* 7.1).[63] *Phaedrus*, then, calls to mind the luxuriant area just outside town near the Ilissus River, a place known as *Kêpoi*, one of "the two most important religious zones in Athens."[64]

But what is growing in this *kêpos*?[65] Readers from ancient times to the present recall the plane tree when they think of *Phaedrus*.[66] The plane tree is a decisive presence, so much so that it intrudes on their conversation ("but, my friend, to interrupt our discussion, isn't this the tree that you were leading me to?" 230a), and Phaedrus even swears by it (236e).[67] At the beginning of the dialogue, Phaedrus indicates the tree off in the distance: "Do you see that very tall plane tree (ὑψηλοτάτην πλάτανον)?" Socrates responds, "Of course, why?" And Phaedrus explains, "There is shade there and a measured breeze and grass to sit on, or if we want, to recline on" (229a–b).

Plane trees were common in Greece.[68] They are mentioned in ancient texts for the shade that they provide, since their broad leaves offered relief from the blazing sun during the summer.[69] And, in fact, the plane tree keeps the pair cool as they converse. It is hot on this summer day: Phaedrus and Socrates remark on the intensity of the heat repeatedly, and Socrates's second speech is delivered at the hottest moment of the day (242a).[70] The plane tree provides welcome relief.

But while plane trees offer shade, that is pretty much all they offer; they were considered to be unproductive trees, and Aesop's fable about the travelers and the plane tree (Fable 175 Perry) plays on this aspect of fruitlessness.[71] In the fable, some travelers are worn out by the scorching heat, and when they see a plane tree, they recline and take their rest. Looking up at the tree, they remark, "How useless (ἀνωφελές) and fruitless (ἄκαρπον) for humans is this tree!" The tree responds, "Oh you ingrates! Do you still call me useless and fruitless while enjoying the benefit of my kindness?"

The situation described by Aesop is remarkably similar to that of *Phaedrus* as two travelers take their rest, reclining beneath a plane tree in an attempt to avoid the midday heat.[72] In *Phaedrus*, given the intense heat and the prominence of such a tree—a sort of emblem of sterility—it would seem that Socrates, who tends to do his "planting" in the city, instead tends to a kind of garden of Adonis as he loses his mind (*nous*), performing an idiosyncratic sort of planting in an atypical sort of space. Phaedrus is presented as an impressionable young man, the sort of person who tends to be taken in by the latest fad and who is unlikely to be converted by Socrates's words to the serious work of the philosophical life. When Socrates prays to Eros to turn Phaedrus to philosophy, as Phaedrus "wavers" (ἐπαμφοτερίζῃ, 257b) between Socrates and Lysias, Socrates is not really taking Phaedrus seriously.[73] The youth thus possesses an unfitting soul in which to plant one's philosophical seeds. It seems that the conversation between Phaedrus and Socrates will bear no fruit. Phaedrus will not be converted to the philosophical life, and the discussion held between the pair will come to naught, as Socrates playfully practices a decidedly unproductive kind of planting.[74]

Yet just as in the Aesop passage, where the travelers are misguided to call the tree useless and fruitless, given the shade that the tree offers, so too it would be misguided to call Socrates's "planting" in *Phaedrus* fruitless. In Aesop's fable, the travelers are (surprisingly) rebuked by the tree. We might imagine that, in interpreting the dialogue thus, we too are rebuked by the tree, πλάτανος, whose name sounds an awful lot like the genitive of its creator, "of Plato," Πλατῶνος. A play on Πλατῶνος/πλάτανος is credible, given how much Plato loves etymologies (e.g., *Cratylus*). *Phaedrus* too is chock full of wordplay.[75] Although the dialogue equivocates about the productive potential of the *kêpos*, the verdant area known as "the Gardens" also evokes the isolated spaces where vulnerable young girls become prey to abductors. It is a familiar *topos* in Greek literature: the garden or meadow externalizes the reproductive potential of the maiden.[76]

Goddesses and Mortals, or Aphrodite (Socrates) **en kêpois**

In literary texts, young girls frequently play in open spaces where they become sexually vulnerable, and a garden (κῆπος) or meadow (λειμών) signifies impending abduction or marriage.[77] In the *Homeric Hymn to Demeter*, Persephone, the quintessential *korê* and quintessential abducted maiden, is playing (παίζουσαν, 5) with other young *korai* in a soft meadow (λειμῶν' ἄμ μαλακόν, 7), when she is seized by Hades. In the *Odyssey*, Nausicaa and her friends play ball in an isolated spot (6.99–101) just before the sexually charged scene with Odysseus. Euripides's Hippolytus is figured as a *korê* who refuses to make the transition to adulthood because of his aversion to Aphrodite and his disdain for marriage. He speaks of culling flowers for a garland for Artemis from an "untouched meadow" (73–74), a kind of foreshadowing of the disaster to come. The meadow mirrors Hippolytus's "pure" state, and the similarities between the grassy spaces (gardens and meadows) are emphasized, since it is a meadow (λειμών) that is being described, yet "Aidôs tends it like a garden (κῆπος) with wet streams" (Αἰδὼς δὲ ποταμίαισι κηπεύει δρόσοις, 78).

Phaedrus has stumbled into just such a space. At the beginning of the dialogue, Phaedrus wonders if he and Socrates are walking in the area where Oreithyia was abducted, remarking that the place is certainly "fit for girls (*korai*) to play (*paizein*) near" (229b). Socrates explains that, indeed, that is precisely what Oreithyia was doing when Boreas snatched her away; she was playing (παίζουσαν, 229c) with Pharmakeia.

Phaedrus is a young man, of course, and we saw above the ways in which he occupies the role of *erômenos*. Yet in the case of the *erômenos*, as well as the *korê* and *nymphê*, what is important is that the transition to *gunê*, "woman," or *anêr*, "man," has not yet occurred, and the individual occupies the position of desirable object. Socrates's quotation (or invention) of the hexameter "wolves love lambs just as *erastai* love a boy" (241d), underscores the potential for violence in the spot near where Oreithyia was abducted, as does the etymological connection that Socrates offers between *erôs* and "force" (ῥώμη, 238c). Phaedrus, playing around in the lush landscape outside the city, resembles a susceptible *korê* or *nymphê* ready for the transition to womanhood as he teeters on the brink of philosophic conversion and maturation.[78]

Phaedrus, like Adonis, shares characteristics with maidens abducted from gardens as they play. In chapter 2, we saw how the narrative of Aphrodite and Adonis represents one of a series of stories told about goddesses and their mortal paramours. Such stories complicate conventional gender roles. Specifically, in the case of Aphrodite and Adonis, we saw that Adonis is figured as a bride. The narrative of Adonis's abduction in Panyassis's account (Apollodorus *Bibl.* 3.14.4) is similar to Persephone's abduction in the *Homeric Hymn to Demeter*—but with gender roles inverted. Just as Hades abducts Persephone when she plays in a meadow, Persephone takes possession of Adonis. Her unwillingness to return Adonis to Aphrodite after Aphrodite places him in a *larnax* (chest) and entrusts him to Persephone results in an intervention by Zeus by which Adonis is to remain for one part of the year by himself, one part with Persephone, and one part with Aphrodite (ultimately, Adonis gives over his own share to Aphrodite). Such a time-share resembles the division of the year seen in the narrative of Hades and Persephone. Although Adonis is certainly not explicitly described as abducted from a garden by Persephone, when asked in the underworld what is the most beautiful thing he has left behind, Praxilla's Adonis (fr. 1 Page = *PMG* 747) says he misses ripe cucumbers, apples, and pears—all that blooms in a well-bounded, well-tended *kêpos*.

As we have seen, *Phaedrus* is filled with oblique references to sex. In Plato's works in general, Socrates tends to call into question traditional hierarchical sexual positions and gender roles by insisting on an erotic and philosophic reciprocity.[79] In his relationship with Alcibiades (described by Alcibiades in *Symposium*), he turns the typical *erastês-erômenos* relationship on its head; Alcibiades believes at first that Socrates is the pursuer only to discover later that Socrates is the pursued.[80] In *Phaedrus,* Socrates offers a twist on the institution of pederasty by his radical insistence that it is better not to consummate an erotic relationship.[81] Furthermore, Socrates delights in appropriating female reproductive imagery for his own philosophic project.[82] In *Symposium*, for example, he exploits the figure of male pregnancy with his description of giving birth to the beautiful, all the while taking on a female persona and ventriloquizing through the mouth of the priestess Diotima.[83] Socrates is figured as a midwife in *Theaetetus*, delivering his interlocutors of ideas that are deemed either fruitful or sterile.[84]

As we have seen, the theme of erotic reciprocity is especially pronounced in *Phaedrus*, as Socrates and Phaedrus exchange roles, switching between the position of *erastês* and *erômenos*. And given Socrates's tendency to interrogate traditional sexual roles, the gender inversion and hierarchical complications in the narrative of Aphrodite and Adonis lend themselves to Socrates's project. Phaedrus, like the young Adonis, can be seen to be shared between two "divinities"—Lysias and Socrates—inasmuch as both are competitors for his attentions. Phaedrus has the potential to give over his own portion to either Socrates or Lysias, depending on what he decides after this afternoon spent outside town.

In myth, as we have seen, Adonis spends a portion of each year with Persephone in the underworld. In the ritual of the Adonia, too, the focus is on death, since inasmuch as Adonis returns each year, he returns to be mourned by the Athenian women. The myth and ritual of Adonis, perhaps, appeal to a philosopher so concerned with developing new (to the Athenians) notions concerning the afterlife (e.g., *Republic*, *Phaedrus*, *Phaedo*), an individual who insists on the idea that true philosophers practice dying (οἱ ὀρθῶς φιλοσοφοῦντες ἀποθνῄσκειν μετελῶσι, *Phaedo* 67e).

In *Phaedrus*, Socrates associates philosophic lovers with various gods and goddesses. Some follow Zeus; some follow Hera; still others are dedicated to Apollo (252e–253b).[85] Aphrodite, however, is not mentioned as Socrates enumerates the divinities on whom the philosophical souls attend. Instead, Socrates, with his focus in his second speech on the philosophic lover, himself plays the role of Aphrodite, though he does not mention her name. As Socrates and Phaedrus wander through "the Gardens," an area sacred to Aphrodite, the goddess is referred to as the inspiration of the best kind of divine madness (265b). Socrates is veiled during his first speech, and for his second speech he performs a palinode in the manner of Stesichorus, recanting all that he had earlier said. Like Aphrodite, who unveils herself in the *Homeric Hymn to Aphrodite* to reveal not a chaste and defenseless maiden but a powerful goddess standing before the terrified Anchises, Socrates removes his veil and delivers his second speech before the mystified Phaedrus.[86]

In the myth of Aphrodite and Adonis—as in other stories told about goddesses and mortal men—a powerful goddess desires a beautiful youth whom she removes from civilization and the human sphere. In *Phaedrus*, a skillful philosopher—closest to divinity and so like a god(dess)—removes Phaedrus from civilization for a time and converses with him in a wild region where Pan and the nymphs roam, and where young Phaedrus becomes as vulnerable as a maiden in an empty field.[87]

The Cultivation of kalos *Phaedrus, or Beautiful Boys and Beautiful Plants*

Socrates was famously accused of "corrupting" (*diaphtheirein*) the young.[88] In *Euthyphro*, vegetal metaphors enhance this charge, since the future of the Athenian *polis* is figured specifically as a young plant in need of care from a good farmer. At the beginning of the dialogue, Socrates explains to Euthyphro that Meletus has brought a charge against him:

> And he alone of all the political men seems to me to begin correctly. For it is right to take care of the young first, so that they may be the best possible, just as it is reasonable for a good farmer (γεωργὸν ἀγαθόν) to take care of his young plants (τῶν νέων φυτῶν) first, and after this the rest. And so Meletus, perhaps, is first clearing us away, who corrupt the young shoots, as he says (καὶ δὴ καὶ Μέλητος ἴσως πρῶτον μὲν ἡμᾶς ἐκκαθαίρει τοὺς τῶν νέων τὰς βλάστας διαφθείροντας, ὥς φησιν). (2d–3a)

As seen in chapter 1, young men are frequently described in vegetal imagery in Greek texts.[89] Thus, Thetis mourns Achilles in the *Iliad* (18.54–60) and compares her son to a young tree and a plant (*ernos*, *phuton*).[90] It also is common to find agricultural imagery describing female bodies. Marriage takes place specifically for the "sowing" of children, and a bride is frequently likened to a field to be plowed. Nouns like "seed" (*sperma*), and "fruit" (*karpos*), as well as verbs like "to sow" (*speirein*), and "to bloom" (*blastanein*) have the potential to operate on several levels, and while agricultural language may function simply to describe the growth of crops and plants, it may also metaphorically describe human reproduction.[91]

The Greek medical writers—especially the writers who dealt with embryology—certainly describe the human body as a plant. Though the writers of the Hippocratic corpus often cast about for a likeness—occasionally comparing the growth of humans in the womb to sacrificial animals or to chickens—more often than not, they settle on plants as the most apt comparison for a human body. The author of *The Nature of the Child*, describing the growth of the child in the womb, makes his case as clear as possible through a lengthy digression on plants: "Nutrition and growth depend on what arrives from the mother into her womb; and the health or disease of the child corresponds to that of the mother. In just the same way, plants growing in the earth receive their nutriment from the earth and the condition of the plant depends on the condition of the earth in which it grows" (*The Nature of the Child* 22, trans. I. M. Lonie).[92] After the writer makes this connection between the development of the child and of plants, the discussion of human embryos is entirely abandoned. Instead, for several pages, he provides a lengthy discussion of the growth of a seed, the manner in which roots are produced, the differences between plants grown from seedlings and plants grown from cuttings, as well as a discourse on grafting. At the end, he reports, "If you review what I have said, you will find that from beginning to end the process of growth in plants and in humans is *exactly the same*" (*The Nature of the Child*, 27, trans. I. M. Lonie, emphasis mine).[93]

Like the Greek medical writers, Plato tends to describe humans in plant-like terms. Parts of *Timaeus*, in particular, read like an embryological treatise. Bodies are complicated systems with irrigation channels, and a human being is explicitly described as a "heavenly plant" (φυτὸν . . . οὐράνιον, 90a), with a head/root (τὴν κεφαλὴν καὶ ῥίζαν, 90a) suspended from the upper regions.[94]

While agricultural seeds produce fruit if planted and cared for properly, philosophical seeds produce philosophical knowledge and philosophers (if the circumstances are right), and in *Phaedrus*, the lover's potential (or lack thereof) for philosophical production is paralleled by the use of vegetal imagery, most obviously with regard to the vividly depicted landscape where Phaedrus and Socrates find themselves but also in connection with the realm of truth and the soul. Not only is the realm of truth described as a meadow in Socrates's second speech (248b–c), but Socrates also explains that when humans are embodied, a soul is planted in a man like a seed.[95] The soul is figured as a plant, and the human body is a kind of soil with varying degrees of fertility. The soul is, of course, more generally described as a charioteer with two horses that becomes winged by loving. This winged chariot is also, however, decidedly vegetal: the wings need to be "watered," like a plant, by the vision of the beloved.[96]

When the beloved is glimpsed, a stream of beauty (τοῦ κάλλους τὴν ἀπορροὴν, 251b) is received through the lover's eyes. The wing is watered, and it grows: "As the nourishment flows upon him, the stem of the wing swells and expands from the root under all the form of the soul" (ἐπιρρυείσης δὲ τῆς τροφῆς ᾤδησέ τε καὶ ὥρμησε φύεσθαι ἀπὸ τῆς ῥίζης ὁ τοῦ πτεροῦ καυλὸς ὑπὸ πᾶν τὸ τῆς ψυχῆς εἶδος, 251b). The wing grows, like a plant with a stem (καυλός, 251b) and root (ῥίζης, 251b)—from exposure to the beloved. The "roots" of the wings sprout and, eventually, bloom (βλαστάνειν, 251b).

When Phaedrus remarks that it is a noble thing to discourse on justice and the other subjects that Socrates tends to discuss, Socrates replies:

> So it is, my dear Phaedrus. But I think seriousness (σπουδή) concerning them is far better, whenever someone employs the dialectic method, having seized upon a fitting soul (ψυχὴν προσήκουσαν), and plants and sows (φυτεύῃ τε καὶ σπείρῃ) *logoi* with knowledge, which are able to help themselves and the one who planted (φυτεύσαντι) them and are not fruitless but contain seed (καὶ οὐχὶ ἄκαρποι ἀλλὰ ἔχοντες σπέρμα) from which other *logoi* sprouting (φυόμενοι) in other minds are able to make this process immortal for all time and make the possessor happy to the extent that it is possible for a human. (276e–277a)

As we saw above, when Socrates describes gardens of Adonis, he opposes the proper farming performed by the farmer with *nous*, who plants "in a fitting place" (*eis to prosêkon*, 276b). Here, the contrast between the farmer and the playful gardener is echoed, as the same word (προσήκουσαν) is being used to describe a fitting *soul*. Phaedrus is akin to a plant that Socrates cultivates by means of his dialectic method.[97]

Written Gardens

Near the end of *Phaedrus*, Socrates tells the tale of the invention of writing by the Egyptian god Theuth and its condemnation by Thamus. The Adonia is subsequently mentioned as analogous to writing. Together, the story of the invention of writing and the mention of the improper planting that takes place at an Adonia make an important point: while writing may act as an aid to memory, overdependence on writing can lead people to believe they possess knowledge, when in reality they do not. Thus, Socrates argues, it is preferable to engage in dialogue—a living, animated dialogue (λόγον . . . ζῶντα καὶ ἔμψυχον, 276a)—with a speaker who is present, who plants seeds of philosophical truths properly within the soul of his interlocutor, than to depend on a defective medium that has the potential to be misread. True knowledge, Socrates argues, should be "written in the soul" (ἐν τῇ . . . ψυχῇ, 276a; cf. 278a), not in texts.[98]

Socrates describes writing in the same terms in which he describes the planting of gardens of Adonis:

> SOCRATES: Not in earnest (σπουδῇ) will he write them in water, sowing (σπείρων) them in black ink with a pen, with words that are unable to help themselves with spoken word and unable to teach true things sufficiently.
>
> PHAEDRUS: No, certainly not.
>
> SOCRATES: But gardens of letters, as it seems, he will sow and write for the sake of play, whenever he writes . . . and he will rejoice looking upon them growing into tender shoots (ἀλλὰ τοὺς μὲν ἐν γράμμασι κήπους, ὡς ἔοικε, παιδιᾶς χάριν σπερεῖ τε καὶ γράψει, ὅταν [δὲ] γράφῃ . . . ἡσθήσεταί τε αὐτοὺς θεωρῶν φυομένους ἁπαλούς. (276c–d)

Someone with knowledge of the just, the beautiful, and the good will not sow gardens of letters "in earnest" (σπουδῇ) but will write only for the sake of play (*paidia*). Socrates draws out the metaphor, describing writing specifically in agricultural terms, with the same opposition between the trivial and the serious—*geloion* and *spoudaion*—associated with the playful gardener and the serious farmer.[99] Writing is thus opposed to serious speech (*logos*), just as the cultivator of gardens of Adonis is opposed to the farmer with agricultural sense. Writing, then, is positioned on the same side of a structurally homologous opposition as gardens of Adonis; like *Adônidos kêpoi*, writing is linked with the playful, the trivial, the *geloion*.

Socrates's statements concerning writing have sparked a great deal of debate about his (and Plato's) views on writing, with some scholars taking the extreme position that Socrates/Plato did not believe that truth should or could ever be written down. Yet despite appearances, writing is not *simply* fruitless and trivial.[100] After all, *Phaedrus* is a written text. *Phaedrus* also begins with a written text: Lysias's manuscript (*biblion*, 228b) prompts the entire discussion.[101] Socrates says that he is being led like an animal who hungrily trails after a piece of fruit, as Phaedrus tempts him with *logoi* in *biblia* (230d–e). With this formulation, Socrates equates writing (*logoi* in *biblia*) with fruit (*karpos*), precisely the goal of the farmer with *nous*. The line between the living, present *logos* and the written speech is blurred from the beginning: when Socrates sees the manuscript, he claims that Lysias himself is present (*parontos* . . . *Lusiou*, 228e). With this remark, he conflates the manuscript—a piece of writing that he describes as the *logos autos*—with the living man. What is more, a *written* artifact is Socrates's professed motto: the Delphic maxim that Socrates takes so seriously is referred to as a *gramma* (229e). The faulty and deficient system of writing is thus bound up with the production of truth, and writing is connected to the *serious* activity of philosophy for Plato: "We are not to forget that each dialogue is a literary construction, a game that Plato plays, albeit a serious one. . . . It may be that a written discourse is less serious than the living discourse in the soul, but this does not entail that it may not awake serious reflection through its play."[102]

But why do gardens of Adonis (of all things) come to mind when Plato wishes to characterize writing? Why is it specifically an Adonis festival onto which the tensions surrounding writing are displaced (since certainly concerns about writing are being expressed in *Phaedrus*, even if writing is not entirely or simply a negative practice)?

Writing is characterized as an *eidôlon*, a lifeless "image" or "representation" of living, breathing *logos* (276a). Socrates's description of the *eidôla* produced by writing—not living *logoi*, but a remove or two from truth—has a parallel in the Adonis festival. Not only was the festival essentially an imitation of a funeral, a pale shadow of *real* lamentation (because the women involved in an Adonia were mourning not real family members but rather Adonis); also, according to some accounts, each year participants in the Adonia brought out effigies, *eidôla*, of

Adonis. These representations of Adonis are mentioned in Plutarch's account of the ritual in his *Life of Alcibiades* (18.3, cf. *Life of Nicias* 13.7). In an imitation of a funeral (ταφὰς ἐμιμοῦντο), women at the Adonia employed *eidôla*, not true but imitation corpses (νεκροῖς ἐκκομιζομένοις ὅμοια), not the real Adonis but effigies of Adonis.

In *Phaedrus*, Socrates explains that written words are like paintings, inasmuch as they say the same thing over and over again (ἕν τι σημαίνει μόνον ταὐτὸν ἀεί, 275d). Similarly, women at the Adonis festival seem to say the same thing over and over again each year, as they lament on the rooftops. Furthermore, Socrates argues that writing is like a bastard son, lacking a father, as opposed to a legitimate son (γνήσιος, 276a). Written words thus resemble Adonis, born from Myrrha's incestuous relationship with her father, lacking legitimacy. Finally, Socrates explains that written words are unable to defend or help themselves (οὔτ' ἀμύνασθαι οὔτε βοηθῆσαι δυνατὸς αὑτῷ, 275e), a characterization that fits Adonis. After all, he died in a hunting accident, unable to defend himself from a wild boar.

Written texts are not stationary. They may travel far from home, and they are promiscuous in terms of whom they address: "Whenever it is written, every word roams about everywhere to those who understand as well as to those who have no concern with it. And it does not know to whom it should speak and to whom not to speak" (ὅταν δὲ ἅπαξ γραφῇ, κυλινδεῖται μὲν πανταχοῦ πᾶς λόγος ὁμοίως παρὰ τοῖς ἐπαΐουσιν, ὡς δ' αὔτως παρ' οἷς οὐδὲν προσήκει, καὶ οὐκ ἐπίσταται λέγειν οἷς δεῖ γε καὶ μή, 275d–e). The Adonia, one of a number of foreign festivals imported to Athens from the East, shares in the mobility of the written text. In fact, a variety of foreign cults practiced at Athens were associated with written texts—especially "Orphic" and Bacchic practices—at least in the minds of the contemptuous individuals who characterize them negatively.[103] For example, in Euripides's *Hippolytus*, Theseus insults Hippolytus the best way he knows how, by connecting the youth with "fringe" Orphic/Bacchic religious practices: "Feel proud! And traffic in your vegetarian diet! Revere Orpheus as lord and go mad with Bacchic worship, honoring the smoke of many books!" (πολλῶν γραμμάτων τιμῶν καπνούς, 952–54).[104] In *On the Crown,* Demosthenes mocks Aeschines by connecting him with deviant (in his view) cults associated with writing ("After you became a man, you read the sacred books for your mother while she performed the initiations and you organized the rest of the hocus pocus," ἀνὴρ δὲ γενόμενος τῇ μητρὶ τελούσῃ τὰς βίβλους ἀνεγίγνωσκες καὶ τἄλλα συνεσκευωροῦ, 259). Finally, in "the most celebrated text that relates to unlicensed religion in Athens,"[105] Plato complains of "the din of books associated with Musaeus and Orpheus" (βίβλων δὲ ὅμαδον παρέχονται Μουσαίου καὶ Ορφέως, *Republic* 364e).[106]

The Greeks told many stories about the invention of writing, attributing the technology to Palamedes, Cadmus, and Prometheus, among others.[107] But the Phoenician syllabary truly was an import from the East.[108] A book (*biblion; byblion*), of course, was made of papyrus (*byblos*). These two words were derived from the name of the important Phoenician city Byblos, which was said to have been one of the oldest cities in the world.[109] Like Egypt, where, as the Greeks were aware, writing had existed for millennia, Byblos (which was in fact under Egyptian domination) was bound up in the Greek mind with the invention of writing and the production of technologies for writing.[110] In addition to supplying the Greeks with their words for papyrus and book, Byblos also happened to be a major center of Adonis cult activity: [Lucian]'s *On the Syrian Goddess* describes the Adonis festival that took place there each year, and Byblos was said to contain the grave of Adonis, as well as a river bearing his name.[111]

Windflowers

For many Athenian outsiders to philosophy, the practice of philosophy as a way of life was as new, foreign, and unproductive as the improper farming involved at an Adonia. Certainly a great many Athenians thought Socrates was bizarre, and Socrates set himself apart, constantly underscoring his own idiosyncratic nature and the special nature of philosophers. In *Republic,* Socrates describes the philosopher as a "foreign plant in alien soil" (ὥσπερ ξενικὸν σπέρμα ἐν γῇ ἄλλῃ, 497b).[112] A fragile creature, the philosopher tends to become overpowered and absorbed by the native growth and die out. In *Gorgias*, Callicles describes the practice of philosophy (in a truly negative and contemptuous tirade) as a kind of child's play,[113] suggesting that it is an appropriate enterprise when one is young but that older philosophers are simply ridiculous (καταγέλαστοι, 484e). Too entrenched in the "life of the mind," the philosopher does not understand how to conduct business transactions and is hardly a productive member of society (484d).[114] Such a portrayal of philosophy as ridiculous and unprofitable emphasizes the marginal status of the philosopher at Athens. At least some Athenians must have wondered what Socrates and his followers were *producing* anyway. The cultivation of gardens of Adonis—inasmuch as it is associated with that which is *geloion* and "child's play," as we have seen, thus becomes a fitting metaphor for the "work" that the philosopher does in the *polis*.

As Socrates exploits the metaphor of gardens of Adonis, he forces us to reconsider how productive such playful farming can be. After all, Socrates's own activities had a profound effect on the *polis*, inasmuch as he cultivated young men who became deeply involved in politics. One has only to think of Alcibiades and Critias and Charmides, and, more to the point here, Phaedrus, who was implicated in the profanation of the mysteries and denounced for mutilating the herms.[115] In the end, the marginal, laughable, and playful practices of the philosopher are enough to have Socrates put to death.

According to Socrates, the practitioner of normative farming watches his seeds reach their *telos* in the eighth month. By contrast, he explains, seeds planted in gardens of Adonis are characterized by the much more rapid trajectory of only eight days. These seeds will wither and die long before they produce fruit. Yet while seeds planted in a garden of Adonis do not reach the *telos* associated with normative planting, it is noteworthy that, at least in Socrates's formulation, the farmer rejoices seeing them becoming beautiful (καλούς) in eight days.

Phaedrus and Socrates repeatedly mention a beautiful (*kalos*) boy in their conversation.[116] At the start of the dialogue, Phaedrus remarks that Lysias had described "one of the beautiful" (τινα τῶν καλῶν, 227c) being propositioned. When Socrates delivers his first speech, he begins, "Once upon a time, there was a boy or rather a youth, extremely beautiful" (ἦν οὕτω δὴ παῖς, μᾶλλον δὲ μειρακίσκος, μάλα καλός, 237b). After the interruption of Socrates's first speech, Socrates returns to the "boy" (238d), just as he does when he prepares to deliver his second speech. Phaedrus, as we have seen, so identifies himself (243e). In Socrates's second speech, Socrates explicitly addresses Phaedrus when he says, "This experience, my beautiful boy, to whom my speech is addressed" (252b), and he refers to the "boy" again at 256e. Over the course of the dialogue, then, Phaedrus is identified with the *kalos* boy.[117] When Socrates refers to the seeds in the gardens of Adonis that become *kalos* after eight days, the gardens of Adonis merge with *kalos* Phaedrus, whom Socrates has been tending throughout the dialogue.

At the end of the dialogue, the heat subsides, and Socrates and Phaedrus can return to Athens. But before they return, Socrates suggests that they pray to Pan and the divinities of the place: "Dear Pan and other gods, as many as are in this place, grant that I become *kalos* on the inside. And as many things as I have on the outside, let them be *philia* with my insides," Ὦ φίλε Πάν τε καὶ ἄλλοι ὅσοι τῇδε θεοί, δοίητέ μοι καλῷ γενέσθαι τἄνδοθεν· ἔξωθεν δὲ ὅσα ἔχω, τοῖς ἐντὸς εἶναί μοι φίλια, 279b–c).[118] Socrates prays that he become beautiful, *genesthai kalos*, on the inside, a phrase that echoes the activity of the playful farmer, who looks upon his seeds becoming beautiful in eight days (*genesthai kalous*).

But what does this summer's day spent in a *locus amoenus* amount to? As I mentioned above, in Plato's *Theaetetus,* Socrates likens himself to a midwife who delivers ideas. His philosophical midwifery, he explains, can have two very different results: the production of a proper birth or the production of a mere wind egg, that is, an egg that is sterile or otherwise imperfect. Socrates remarks, "But come now, let's examine this together, whether it is a proper offspring or a wind egg" (ἀλλὰ φέρε δὴ αὐτὸ κοινῇ σκεψώμεθα, γόνιμον ἢ ἀνεμιαῖον τυγχάνει ὄν, 151e). The opposition continues throughout the dialogue (157d; 161a), and the *Theaetetus* closes with Socrates's question: "Then does our art of midwifery say that all these things that have been born are wind eggs and not worth rearing" (οὐκοῦν ταῦτα μὲν πάντα ἡ μαιευτικὴ ἡμῖν τέχνη ἀνεμιαῖά φησι γεγενῆσθαι καὶ οὐκ ἄξια τροφῆς).[119] Theaetetus agrees: "Yes, Socrates it does" (Παντάπασι μὲν οὖν, 210b). And so ends *Theaetetus*. Nothing but wind. But this aporetic dialogue has the potential to be fruitful for Theaetetus, since it is possible that Theaetetus learned a great deal after all through a discussion of the nature of knowledge with Socrates, and perhaps the dialogue will prove fruitful for the reader as well.[120]

After Adonis meets his death, the youth is associated with the anemone, the windflower. Bion's *Epitaph for Adonis* has Aphrodite shedding tears, as Adonis's blood drenches the earth; the tears and blood produce the rose and the anemone, respectively: "The Paphian pours out as many tears as Adonis pours out blood, and everything on the ground becomes flowers; his blood produces the rose, and her tears produce the anemone" (δάκρυον ἁ Παφία τόσον ἐκχέει ὅσσον Ἄδωνις / αἷμα χέει, τὰ δὲ πάντα ποτὶ χθονὶ γίνεται ἄνθη· / αἷμα ῥόδον τίκτει, τὰ δὲ δάκρυα τὰν ἀνεμώναν, 64–66).[121] Nicander, by contrast, has Adonis's *blood* produce the anemone (fr. 65 Schneider = Σ Theocritus 5.92), a detail echoed by Ovid in book 10 of his *Metamorphoses*.[122] Venus speaks after Adonis has died:

> Monuments of my grief will remain forever (*luctus monimenta manebunt/ semper*), Adonis, and an imitation of your death repeated yearly will produce a likeness of our lamentation; but your blood will be changed to a flower. (725–28)

After these words, Venus sprinkles the blood with nectar, and soon afterward

> a flower sprouted, the color of blood, the sort that pomegranates which hide their seed under clinging bark are accustomed to bear. But its enjoyment is fleeting, for the same winds which provide its name shake the flower clinging so frail and light and prone to fall. (731–39)

The windflower is short-lived (*brevis*, 737). It is a fragile flower, blown about by the winds, from which it gets its name. Like Plato's aporetic dialogues that end in wind eggs, *anemiaia*, the windflower, anemone, is all that remains of Adonis after his death, a delicate plant that lives only briefly and then passes away.[123] But at the same time, the brilliant blood-red flower is not nothing at all but rather, as Venus explains, a monument for all time, an eternal, recurring reminder of Adonis (*luctus monimenta manebunt/ semper*, 725–26).

Like *Theaetetus*, *Phaedrus*—a dialogue that begins with a discussion of the wind god Boreas and his abduction of Oreithyia—may seem to result in nothing but wind, as Socrates and Phaedrus head back to town at the end of a diverting day. But the possibility exists that the seeds Socrates plants as he gardens for fun may lead to philosophical fruit, as might Plato's written "monument." After all, like the windflower that lives on when Adonis dies, the *logos*, the story of Socrates, of what he did and what he said, lives on, long after the death of the philosopher.

Conclusion

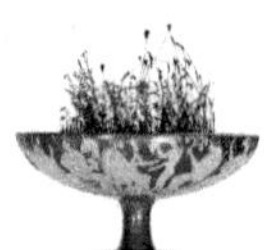

Although the Adonia tends to be neglected in modern scholarship and is frequently dismissed as merely a "private" ritual (a term best avoided when discussing Greek religion), this study argues that, in iconographic and literary texts, the festival is bound up with three culturally significant activities: weddings, funerals, and philosophy. Iconographic and literary representations of Adonis and his cult incorporate nuptial elements, as we saw in chapter 2, with Adonis in the role of bride and Aphrodite in the dominant role. Such an inversion of typical wedding scenes suggests that Athenian women had the potential to offer a critique of the wedding in their performance of the Adonis festival, as they take on the persona, not of Persephone, the "bride of death" par excellence, whose myth lies behind the conventional wedding, but of the powerful goddess Aphrodite, whose mortal consort, Adonis, assumes the characteristics of the bride, inverting traditional gender roles before he dies. Inasmuch as women perform the role of Aphrodite rather than Persephone at the Adonia, the festival offers them a different perspective on the typical wedding.

In chapter 3 we saw that in Aristophanes's *Lysistrata*, Lysistrata and her allies manipulate Adonis festival elements that would have been recognizable to an Athenian audience, familiar as it was with the cult. In so doing, the women manage to end the Peloponnesian War, suggesting that this foreign cult was not imagined to be private and apolitical, as the Official characterizes it. Instead, at least within the context of the play, the Adonia is shown to carry potential for political dissent. What is socially peripheral becomes symbolically central.[1]

Recent scholarship on lamentation has shown that it offered a vehicle for public expression and, what is more, that it offered a critique of the rhetoric of the Classical Athenian *polis,* more specifically, the ideology conveyed by funeral oration. While funeral oration praises the war dead and provides impetus for the continuation of war, lamentation emphasizes individual loss and the cost of war. I have argued that the Adonia, with its incorporation of lamentation, is imagined to be a vehicle of dissent that critiques the rhetoric of funeral oration within the context of *Lysistrata*. The Adonia works as a metaphor of dissent within the play because the Adonis festival, with its emphasis on lamentation, offers a space where Athenian women can speak publicly.

Chapters 2 and 3, then, although they deal with representations of the Adonia in two very different media—the visual arts and a comedy, respectively—form a unit. The representations of the Adonia in each case suggest ways in which Athenian women may have employed the Adonia to offer a counter-ideological message about marriage and death. Athenian women had the potential to harness the story of Adonis and Aphrodite for their own ends, to make use of the Adonia to offer a coded message of resistance to two rituals that on some level impacted the lives of all Athenians, and women particularly: the wedding and the funeral.

Plato, always the innovator, does something new with the Adonis festival, connecting it more generally with his philosophical enterprise and employing the metaphor of cultivation of gardens of Adonis to characterize the philosopher. Plato's exploitation of the festival for his own ends in *Phaedrus* (discussed in chapter 4) speaks to the very real effects of the ritual on the Athenian *polis*. Plato incorporates the Adonia to make a point about writing in an exchange between two men; the festival is intimately bound up with his project of philosophy. Certainly, it is possible to take Plato's co-optation of the festival in a negative light: just as Plato appropriates female imagery such as midwifery elsewhere and uses it to his own ends in the service of his project, so too he uses the Adonis festival, a women's festival, to make his points. But another interpretation is equally valid: Plato saw the dissident messages the cult offered. He incorporates the myth and cult of Adonis, a youth associated in the minds of Athenians with the anti-aphrodisiac lettuce, whose cult includes gardens known proverbially for sterility. In so doing, he reveals, paradoxically, the fruitful significance of the myth and cult vis-à-vis his project of philosophy.

This study has examined the work the Adonia does within its larger cultural and textual context, allowing us to make some suggestions about the work that it performs within the fifth- and fourth-century Athenian *polis*. This book turns basic assumptions about the Adonia on their head; no longer can the ritual be characterized simply as private, apolitical, or fruitless. Although I begin chapter 1 as a study of a given cult tends to begin, with a survey of the evidence for Adonis and his cult, I have been able to offer a profoundly different interpretation by means of a new approach taken in chapters 2, 3, and 4. This book, then, illustrates what insights can be gained when the evidence for Greek religion is studied with appropriate attention to textual and cultural context.

I have offered new suggestions concerning the meanings of the Adonia by resisting the tendency to take information about the Adonis festival at face value—all too common when a few lines are removed from their textual context. Instead I have teased out the complex role that the cult plays within the texts themselves. Although, at first glance, red-figure vase paintings appear to depict ladders—a touch of realism—that lead either to the rooftops or to a second story, these ladders are shown instead to be loaded signifiers that carry complex nuptial meanings. In *Lysistrata*, the Official's remarks, which on the surface seems to be a factual characterization of the festival as merely a foreign women's cult with no impact on the politics of Athens, instead is shown to be a stereotype concerning foreign rituals that were troubling to some. In *Phaedrus*, while Socrates seems to make a simple point about fruitless cultivation of gardens of Adonis and to connect it with the faulty system of writing, instead he is saying something far more profound about the productive nature of play and festivity, as well as the written *logos*.

Religion tends to be characterized as a conservative feature of society, and especially within the field of classics, ritual tends to be seen in light of its community-building aspects. This, in part, is why until now it has been so hard to see the Adonia as a ritual that interrogates and questions mainstream Athenian society. It is challenging to see a ritual functioning as an expression of dissent where dissent is taken to undermine community. In this case, however, the dissenting voice is one that advocates for the inclusion of a new portion of the population in communal discourse. This study has provided a complex picture of the functions the Adonia served in the *polis*, suggesting that we must avoid divorcing information about individual cults from context. If we want to see what work a given ritual does in the *polis*, we must first see what work it does in the larger text in which it is embedded.

I have focused on Classical Athens in this study. But Adonis and his cult have an afterlife.[2] Indeed, Plato's use of the metaphor of gardens of Adonis appears in the works of later philosophers who also draw on it for its potential. Aristotle (*Physics* 5.230a–b) gives examples of violent growing against nature, and Simplicius saw in that a reference to gardens of Adonis (*in Phys.* 911.13).[3] Epictetus, too, mentions gardens of Adonis (*Discourses* 4.8.36), in connection with people who rush into philosophy. After Plato, a general association exists between gardens and philosophers.[4] The Academy itself was such a *kêpos*, purchased by Plato and dedicated to philosophical "fruit."[5] Epicureans were called *kêpologoi* because they taught in a garden.[6]

During the Hellenistic period outside Athens, Adonis and his cult enjoyed increased popularity. Adonis was the subject of poems by Dioscorides, Glycon, Lycophron, and Euphorion.[7] Ptolemy IV Philopator wrote a tragedy titled *Adonis*, as did Dionysius I of Syracuse.[8] Callimachus, too, was interested in the youth.[9] Sotades wrote a poem titled *Adonis*, and Bion's *Epitaph for Adonis* is an extended meditation on the death of the youth.[10] A papyrus survives from the Fayum containing a list of purchases dating from the time of Ptolemy Philadelphus (*P. Petrie* 3.142), and among the expenses are "garlands for Adonis."[11]

When the Adonia appears in Classical Athenian literary texts, the festival is shunted to the periphery, even if, as we have seen, the festival does take on symbolically central importance. Theocritus, by contrast, depicts an Adonia situated front and center, at the royal palace in the city of Alexandria.[12] Instead of a fleeting mention of the Adonis festival, Theocritus's entire poem concerns itself with the ritual, as *Idyll* 15 describes the journey of two women, Praxinoa and Gorgo, from Praxinoa's home to the palace of Arsinoë II, the queen of Egypt, where they witness the Adonia. The Adonis festival that Praxinoa and Gorgo attend is a carefully orchestrated, centrally located, and public event. The lavish performance bankrolled by the ruling family is no impromptu rooftop gathering. Theocritus's representation of the Adonia is an inversion of what we have seen thus far.[13]

In sharp contrast to the city of Athens, with its strong tradition of continuous habitation and autochthony, the urban center of Alexandria was an artificial creation by the Macedonians. Everything was imported to the new city, the materials, as well as the inhabitants.[14] As a result, Alexandria was a city of displaced peoples from many different locales: "under Macedonian rule, as a whole, Alexandria attracted expatriates from over fifty separate Greek states, as well as twenty-odd African, Italic, Balkan, and Asiatic ethnic groups."[15] At Alexandria the question, "Where are you from?" was applicable to everyone, not just metics and slaves as at Athens: "from its historical inception, Alexandria was a city where to be an outlander was paradoxically the norm."[16] Indeed, the term *metoikos* was not used at Alexandria, since the city was entirely composed of metics.

Alexandria's cultural and ethnic diversity provided an appropriate setting for the Adonia to take root. After all, modern scholars, as well as ancient writers, have frequently asked the question, "Where is he from?" of Adonis. To classical Athenians, as well as more recent critics, Adonis would seem to be ever alien, a foreigner from the East, always translated. Adonis and his cult, then, lend themselves to this city of displaced people, taking center stage, no longer on the sidelines.[17]

While it is Adonis's foreignness that, I suggest, allows him to play a more pronounced role in the Hellenistic imagination, his strangeness, too, appealed to Classical Athenians who made use of his myth and cult. This book has suggested that, with its inversion of taken-for-granted roles, the narrative told by Classical Athenians about Aphrodite and Adonis is representative of the "strange" and "foreign" with regard to constructed Athenian norms. Although scenes of Aphrodite pursuing Adonis across the visual field do not survive in Classical Athenian red-figure vase painting, the pursuit by the goddess Eos of the mortal Tithonus is documented on hundreds of Athenian vases. In iconographic scenes of pursuit, the image of Zeus pursuing Ganymede offers a model for the *erastês'* (active male lover's) pursuit of the *erômenos* (passive male beloved).[18] In the case of Eos and Tithonus, however, the female figure is put in the dominant position of pursuer, analogous to Zeus, while the male is the pursued. What sort of model, then, do scenes of Eos's pursuit of Tithonus offer to Athenian women?

One scholar has remarked, "To imagine such a female pursuit is to imagine something without correlates in 'real life.' Worse than that, it is to imagine something that, if instantiated in real life, would overturn established social structures and destroy the household as Athenians knew it. Eos's wings are all that keep her subversive power at bay, signaling that hers is an unavailable transgression."[19] This transgression is purported to be unavailable; it is, then, merely a myth that corresponds in no way to lived experience. Yet this study suggests otherwise. Women did have such a lived experience available to them. The Adonia provided Athenian women with the opportunity to perform a purportedly unavailable role. Within the context of the festival, women take on the persona of Aphrodite, the powerful goddess who pursues a mortal youth. And although their performance of the role of Aphrodite at the Adonis festival is, to be sure, different from the "real-life" bearded male's pursuit of the youthful beloved, it is, nevertheless, closer to the realities of Athenian life than simply an entirely imaginary mythical paradigm. Through the performance of the ritual, the myth of Aphrodite and Adonis is enacted and lived, as women's voices offer a critique of mainstream practices in the public arena.

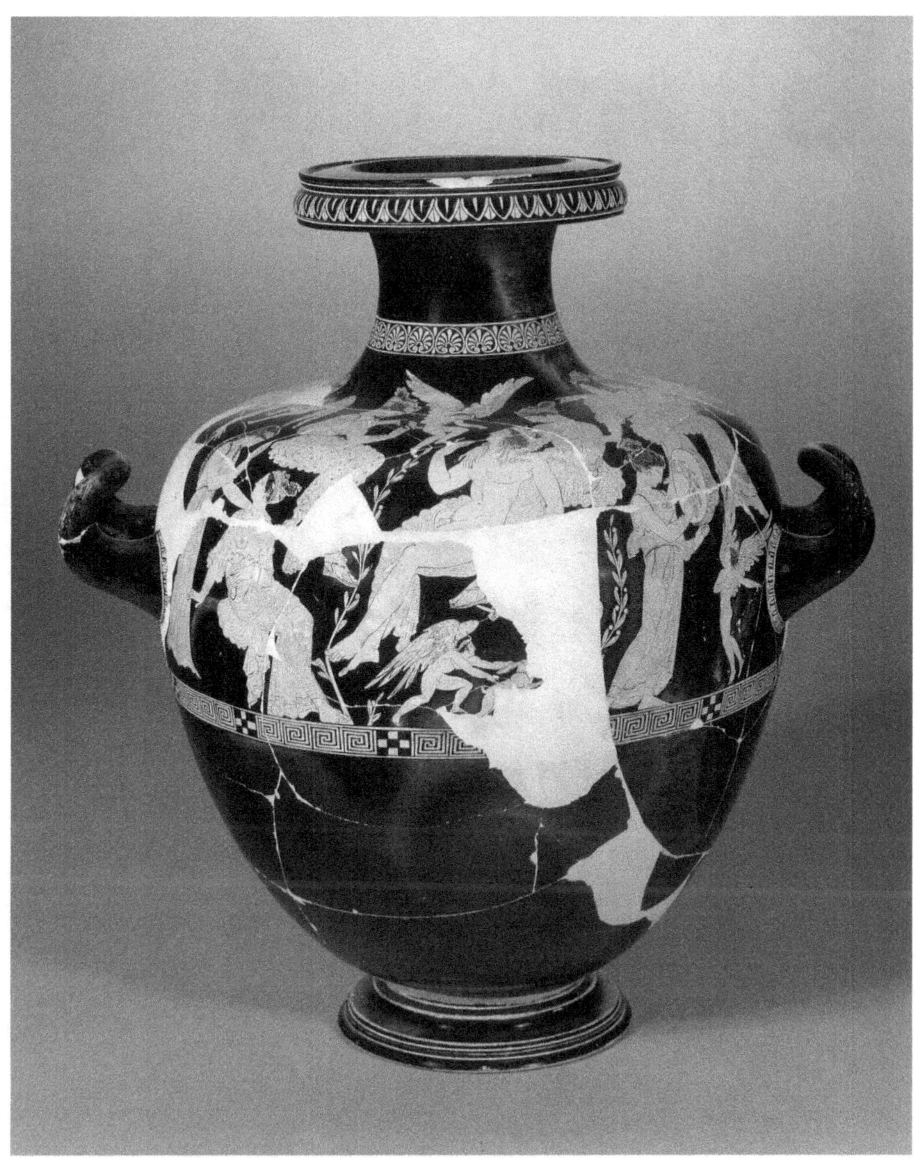

Figure 1. Red-figure hydria attributed to the Meidias Painter, Florence, Museo Archeologico 81948. Used with the permission of the Soprintendenza Archeologia della Toscana–Firenze.

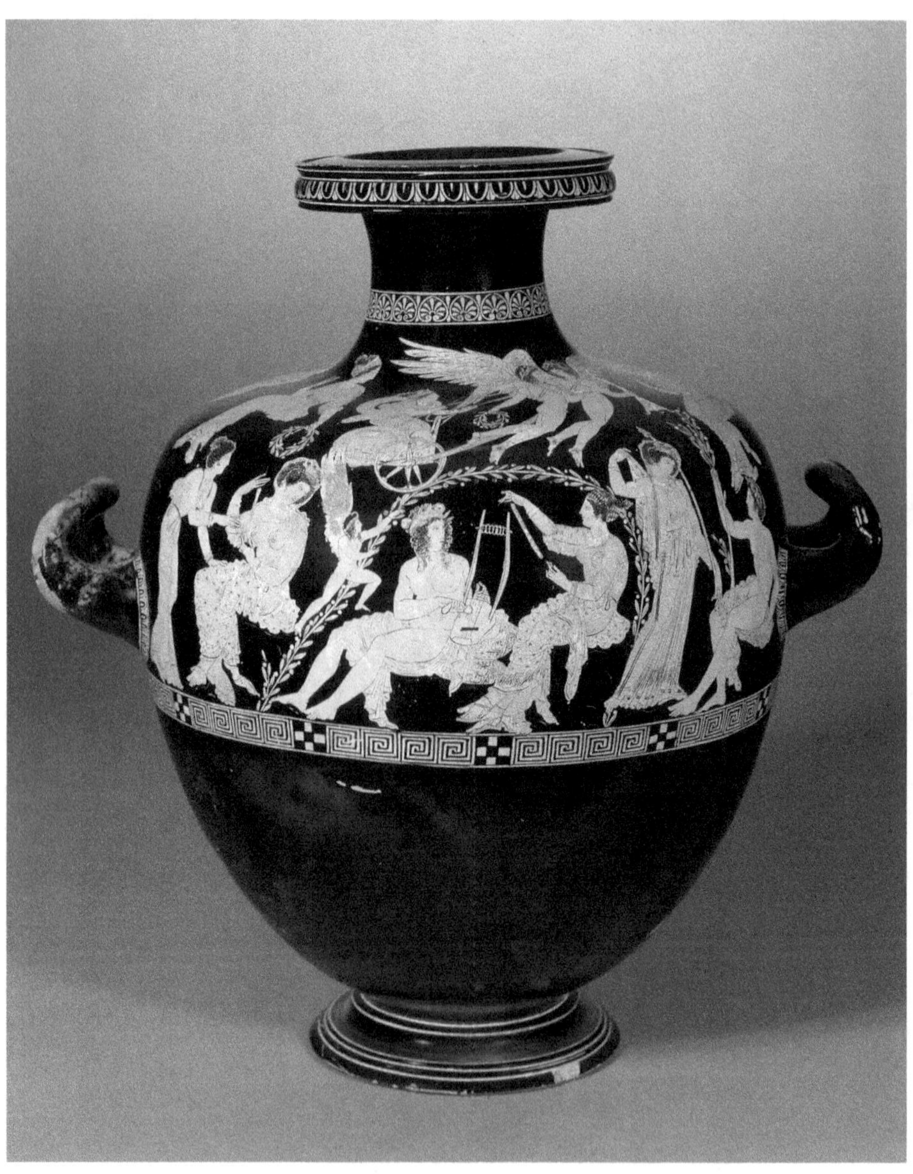

Figure 2. Red-figure hydria, Florence, Museo Archeologico 81947. Used with the permission of the Soprintendenza Archeologia della Toscana–Firenze.

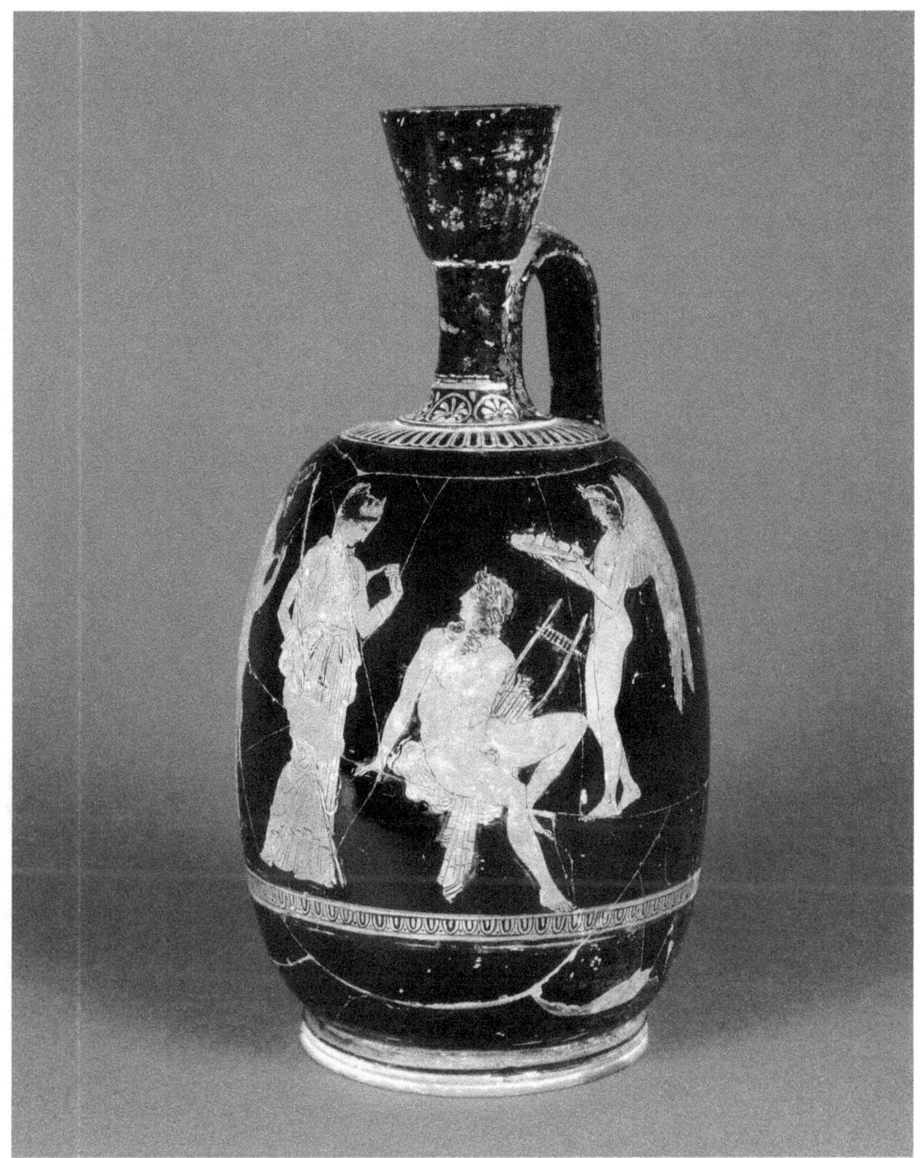

Figure 3. Red-figure aryballos lekythos attributed to Aison, Paris, Musée du Louvre MNB 2109. © Musée du Louvre, Dist. RMN-Grand Palais/ Hervé Lewandowski/ Art Resource, NY.

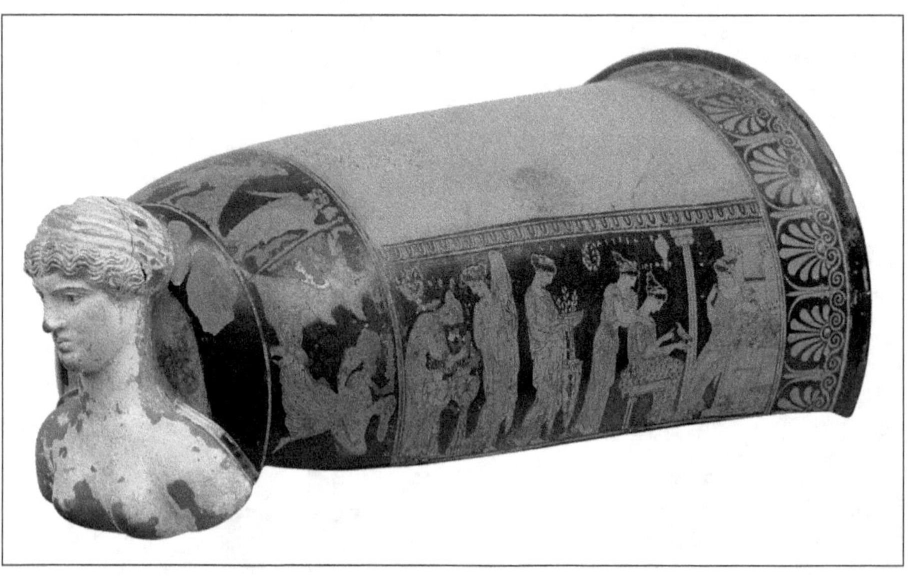

Figure 4. Red-figure epinêtron by the Eretria Painter, Athens, National Museum 1629. National Archaeological Museum Athens (Patrikianos). © Hellenic Ministry of Culture, Education, and Religious Affairs/Archaeological Receipts Fund.

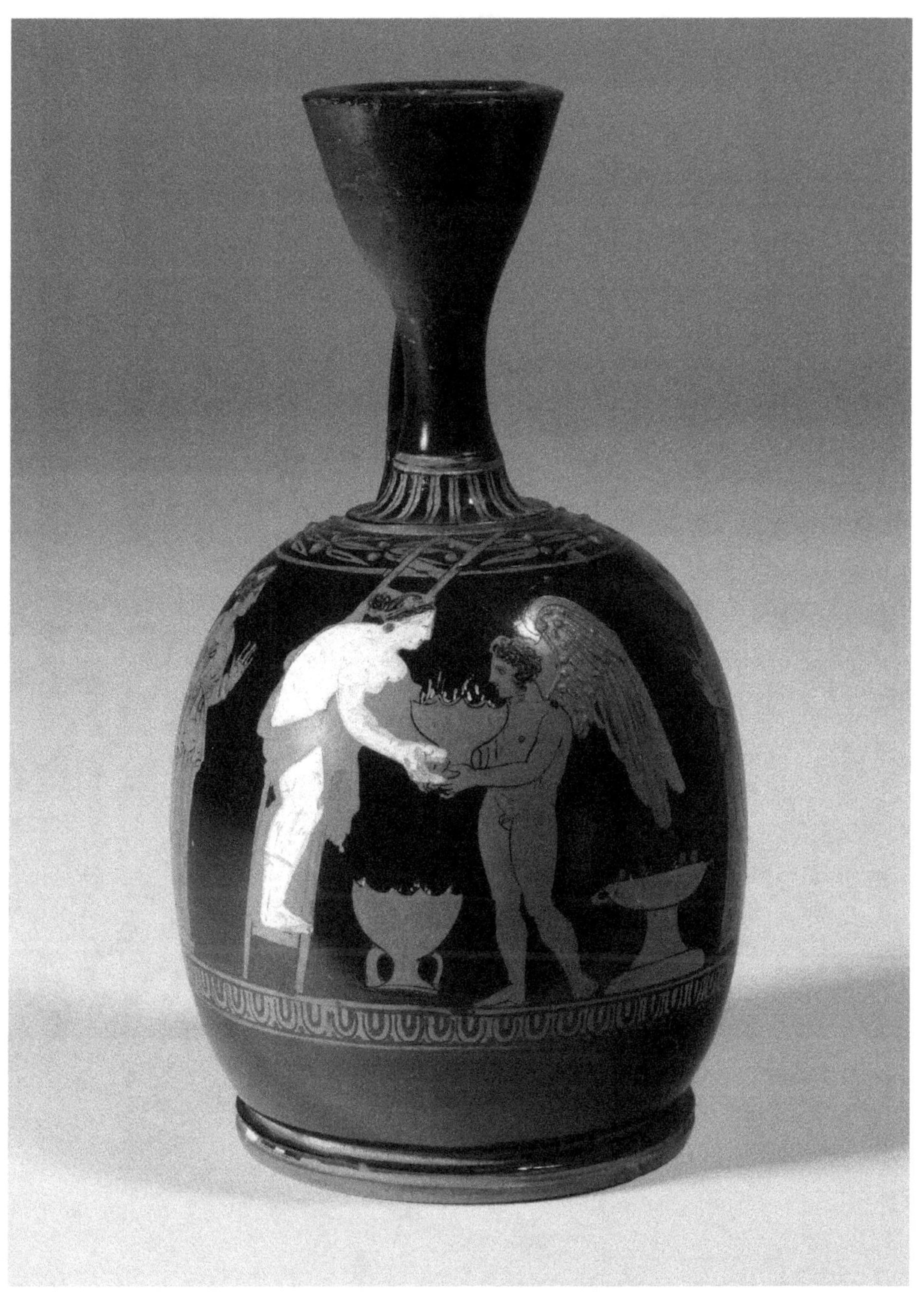

Figure 5. Red-figure squat lekythos (circle of the Meidias Painter), Karlsruhe, Badisches Landesmuseum, B39. Photo by Thomas Goldschmidt.

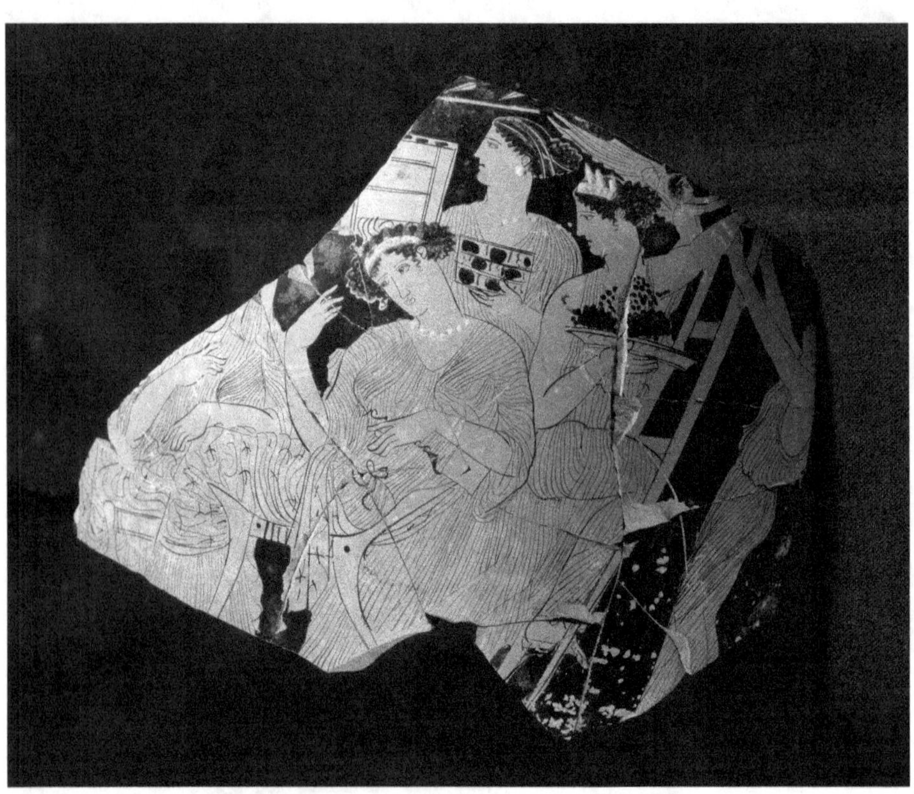

Figure 6. Fragment of a red-figure lebes gamikos, attributed to the Painter of Athens 1454, Paris, Musée du Louvre CA 1679. © Musée du Louvre, Dist. RMN-Grand Palais/ Hervé Lewandowski/ Art Resource, NY.

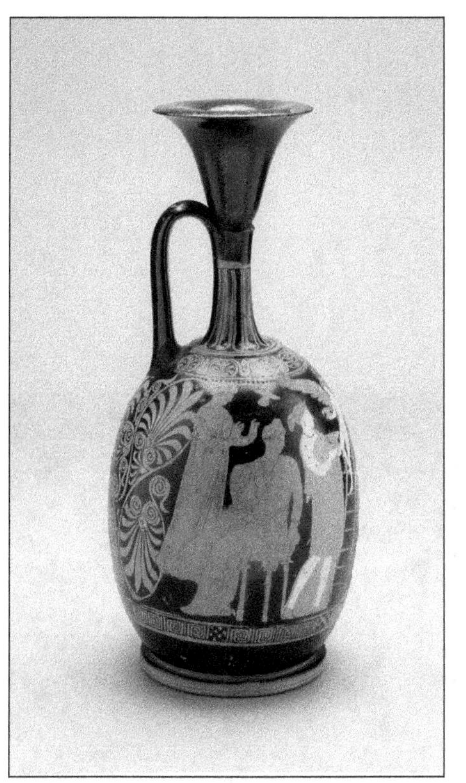

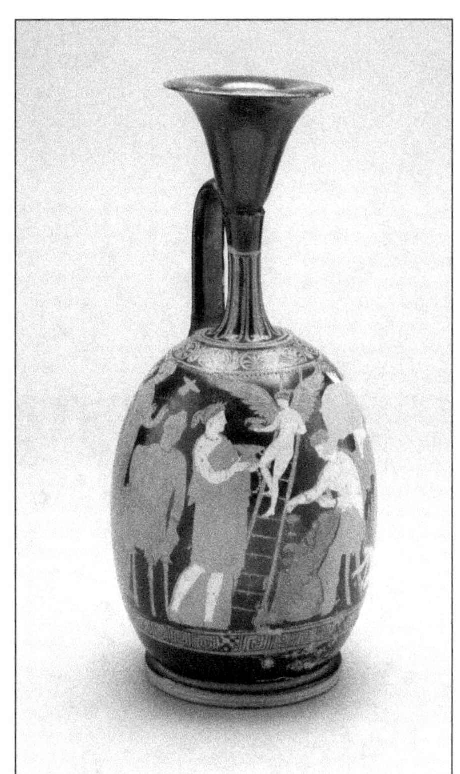

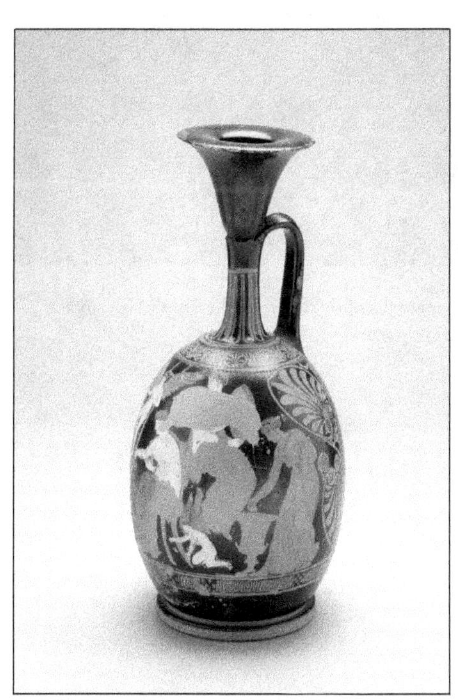

Figure 7. Red-figure aryballos lekythos, St. Petersburg, State Hermitage Museum 928. © The State Hermitage Museum. Photos by Pavel Demidov.

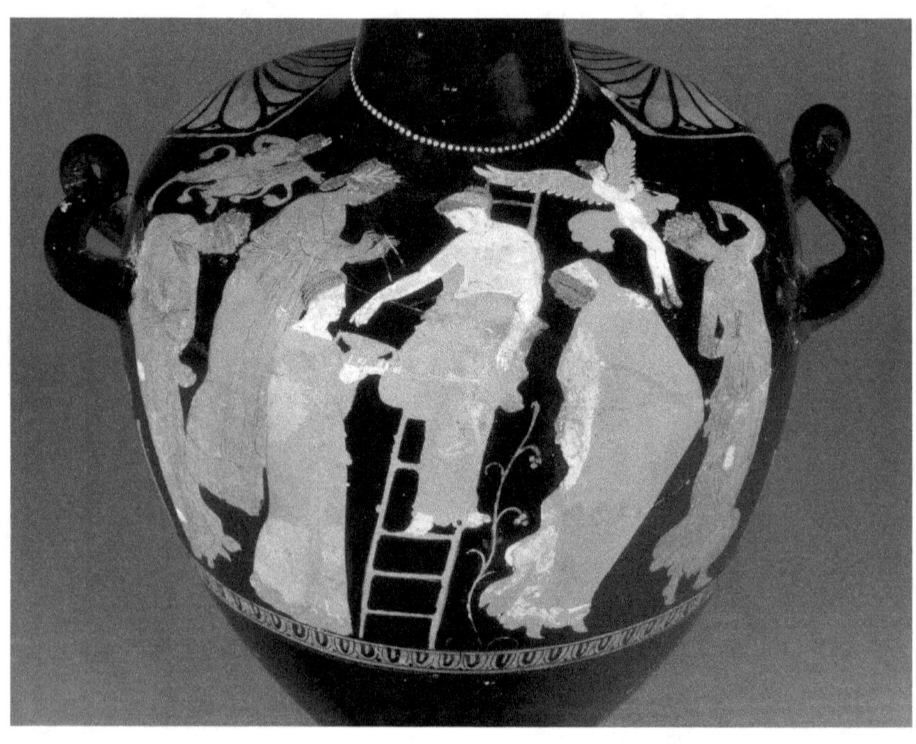

Figure 8. Red-figure hydria, Cyrenaica, London, British Museum E 241. © Trustees of the British Museum.

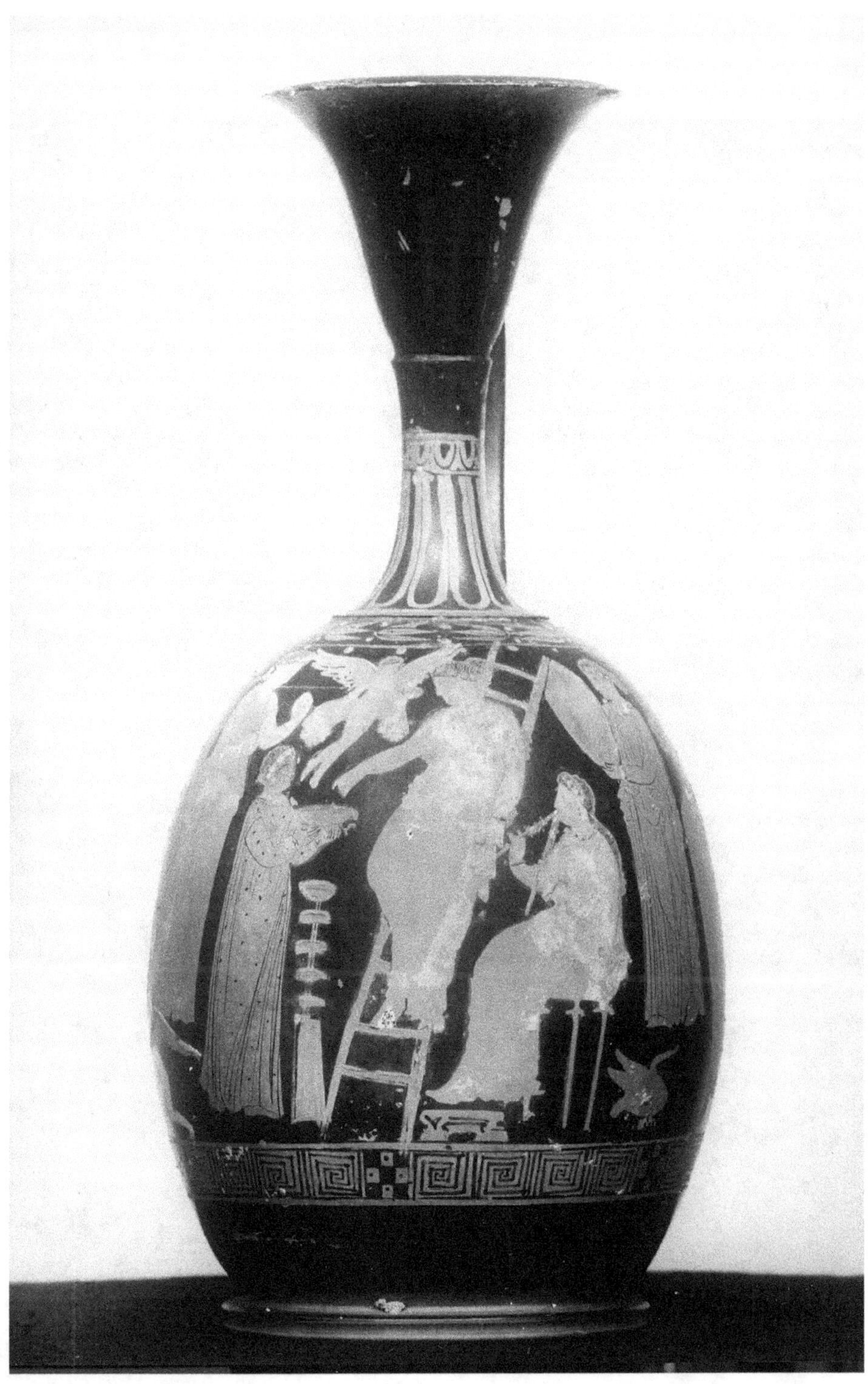

Figure 9. Red-figure aryballos lekythos, Berlin, Antikensammlung 3248. Antikensammlung, Staatliche Museen zu Berlin, Preussischer Kulturbesitz.

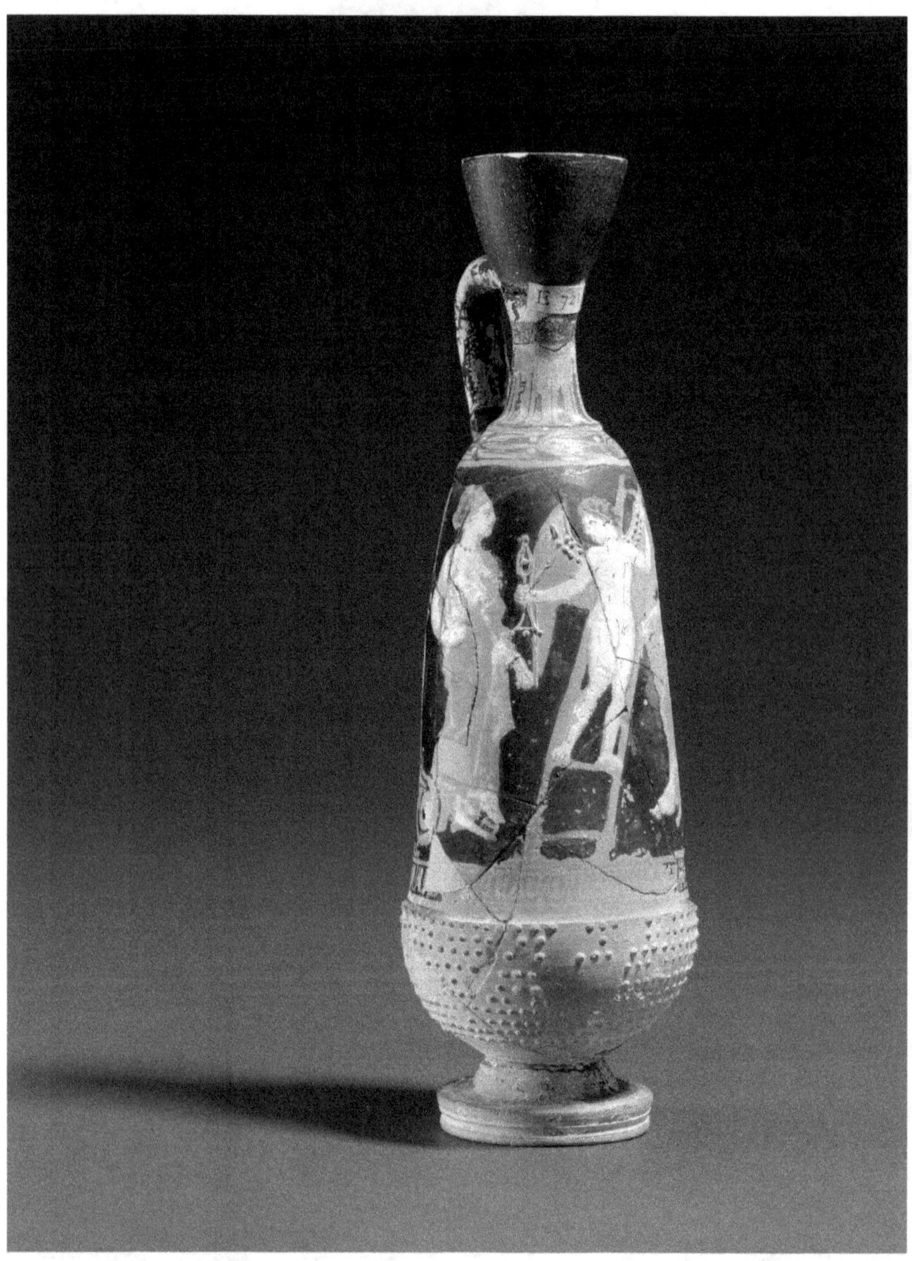

Figure 10. Red-figure lekythos, London, British Museum E 721. © Trustees of the British Museum.

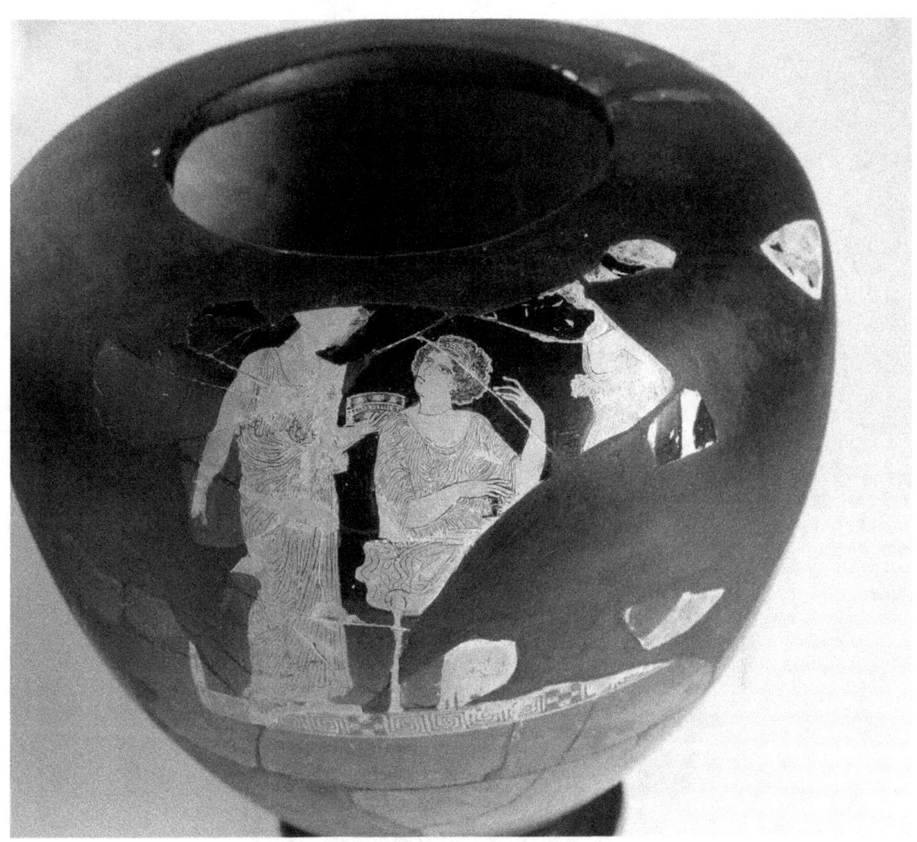

Figure 11. Red-figure hydria, attributed to the Meidias Painter, Athens, National Museum 1179. National Archaeological Museum, Athens (Xenikakis). © Hellenic Ministry of Culture, Education, and Religious Affairs/Archaeological Receipts Fund.

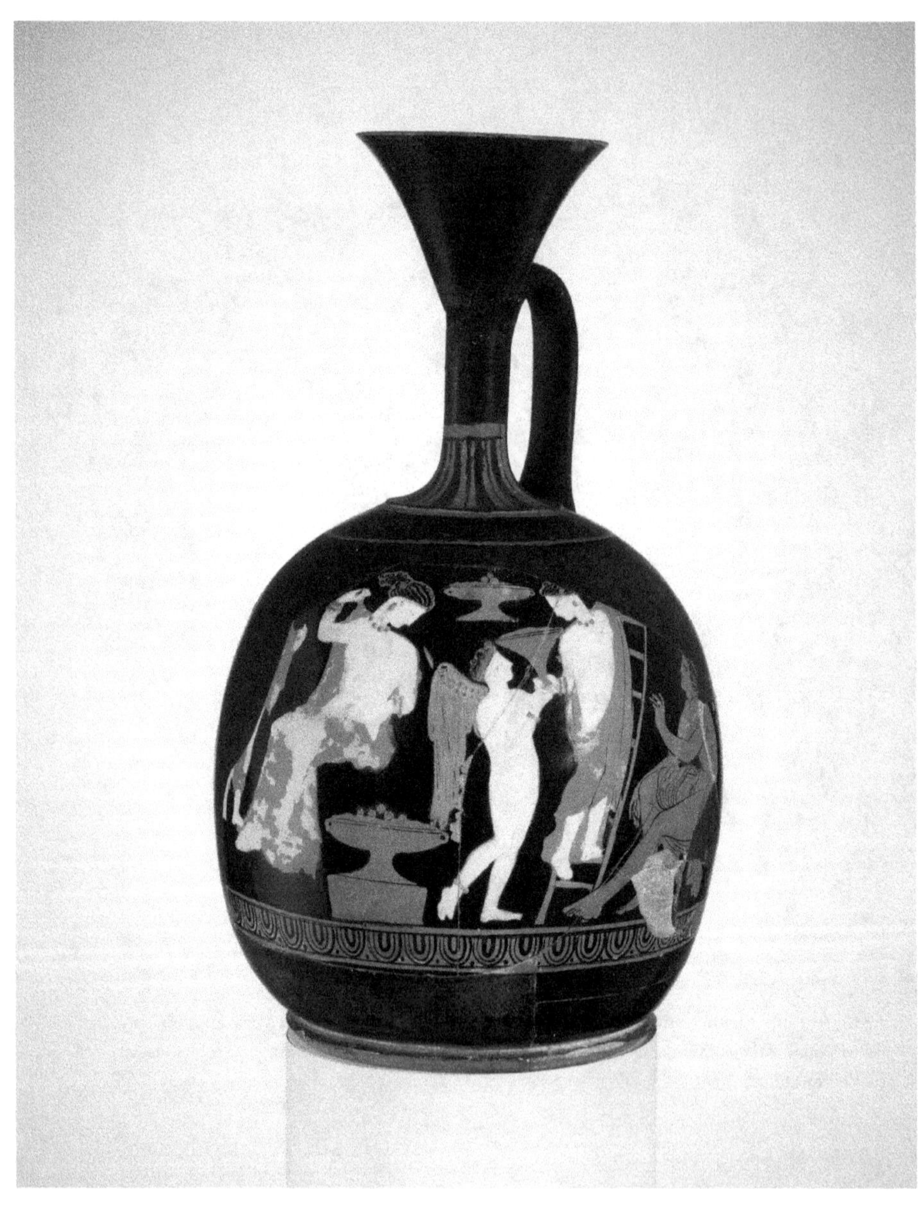

Figure 12. Red-figure aryballos lekythos, New York, Metropolitan Museum (1922) 22.139.26.

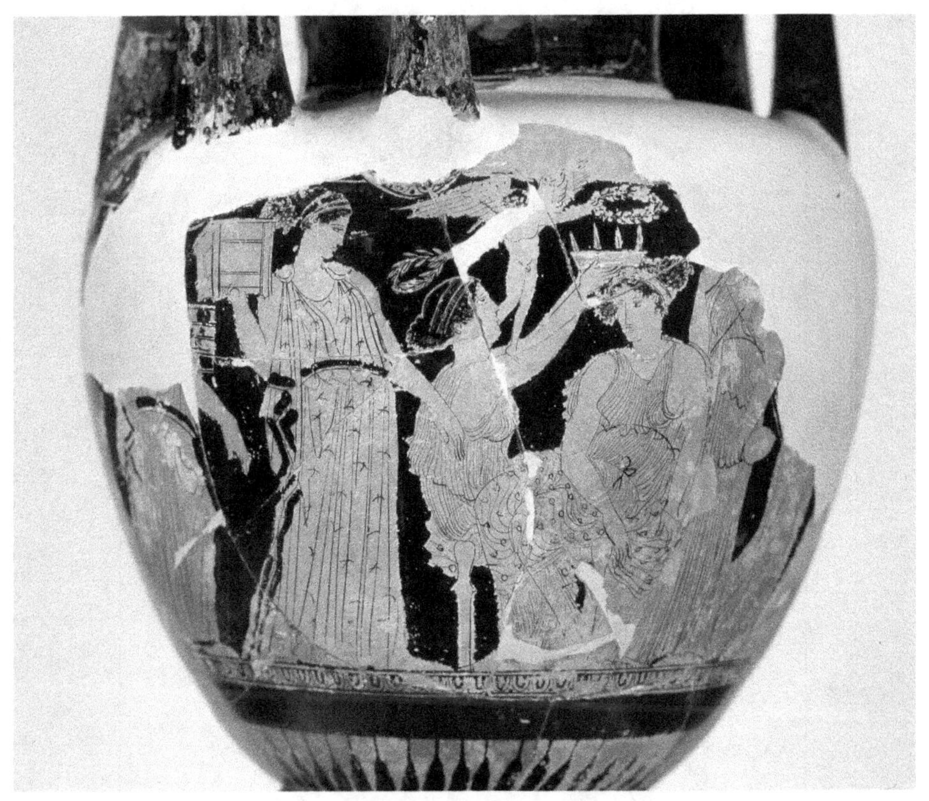

Figure 13. Red-figure lebes gamikos, Athens, National Museum 1454. National Archaeological Museum, Athens (Stournaras). © Hellenic Ministry of Culture, Education, and Religious Affairs/Archaeological Receipts Fund.

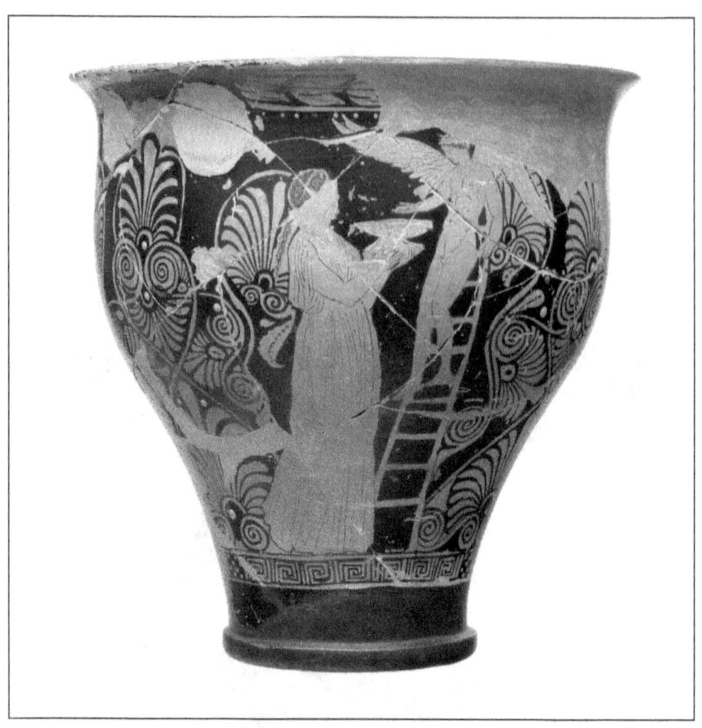

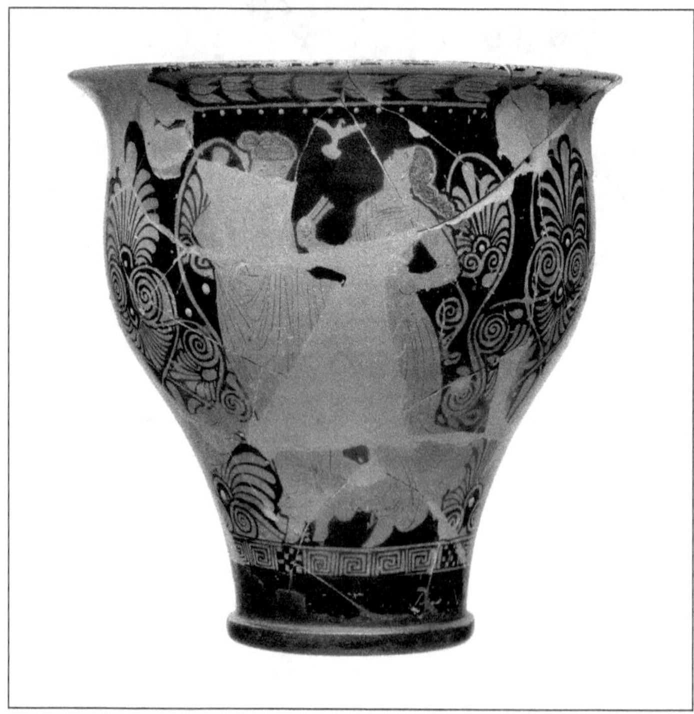

Figure 14. Red-figure skyphos, Athens, Acropolis Museum 1960-NAK 222. © Acropolis Museum. Photo by Socratis Mavrommatis.

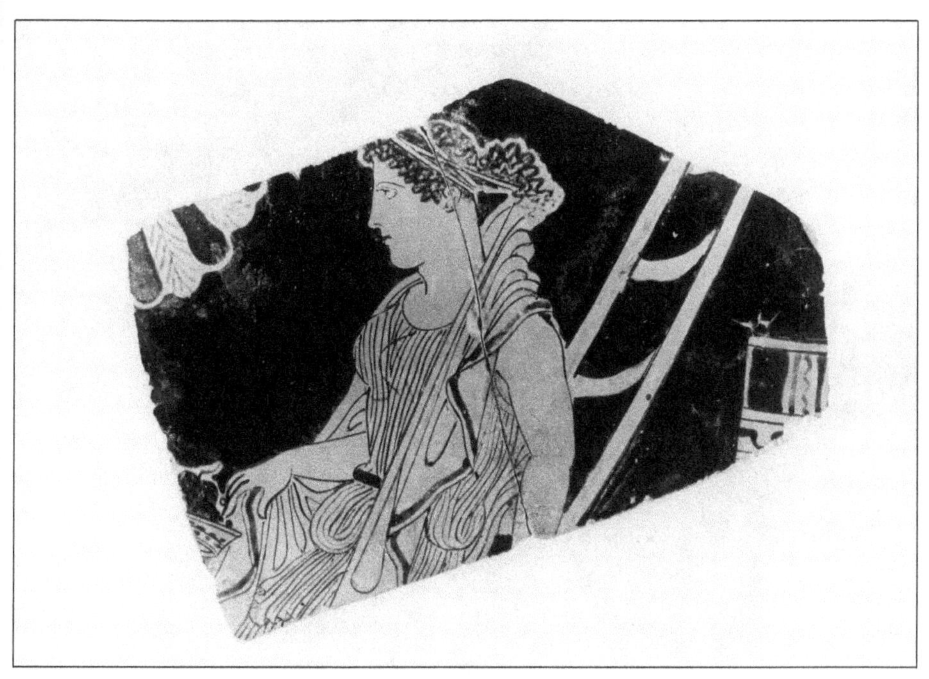

Figure 15. Fragment of a red-figure hydria or stamnos, Athens, National Museum 19522. National Archaeological Museum, Athens (Konstantopoulos).

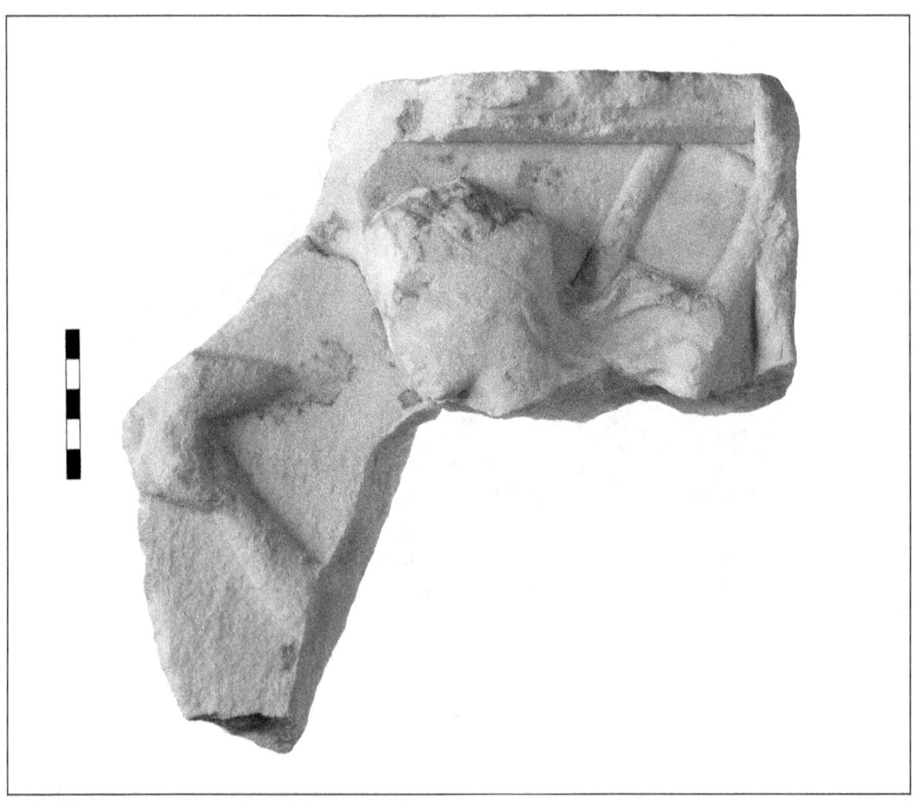

Figure 16. Fragments of a votive relief, Agora S 3344. American School of Classical Studies at Athens: Agora Excavations.

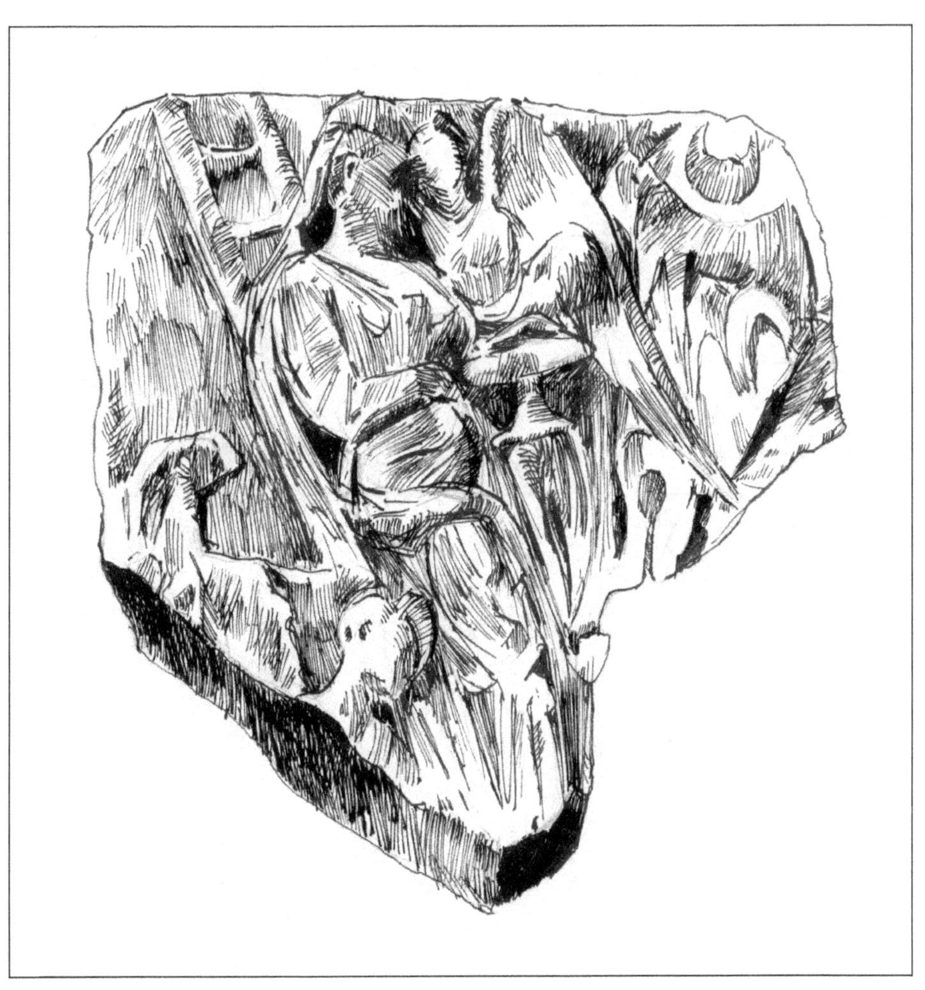

Figure 17. Votive relief (now lost), formerly Museo Kircheriano. Drawing by Alexander Hollmann (after Watzinger 1928, fig. 1).

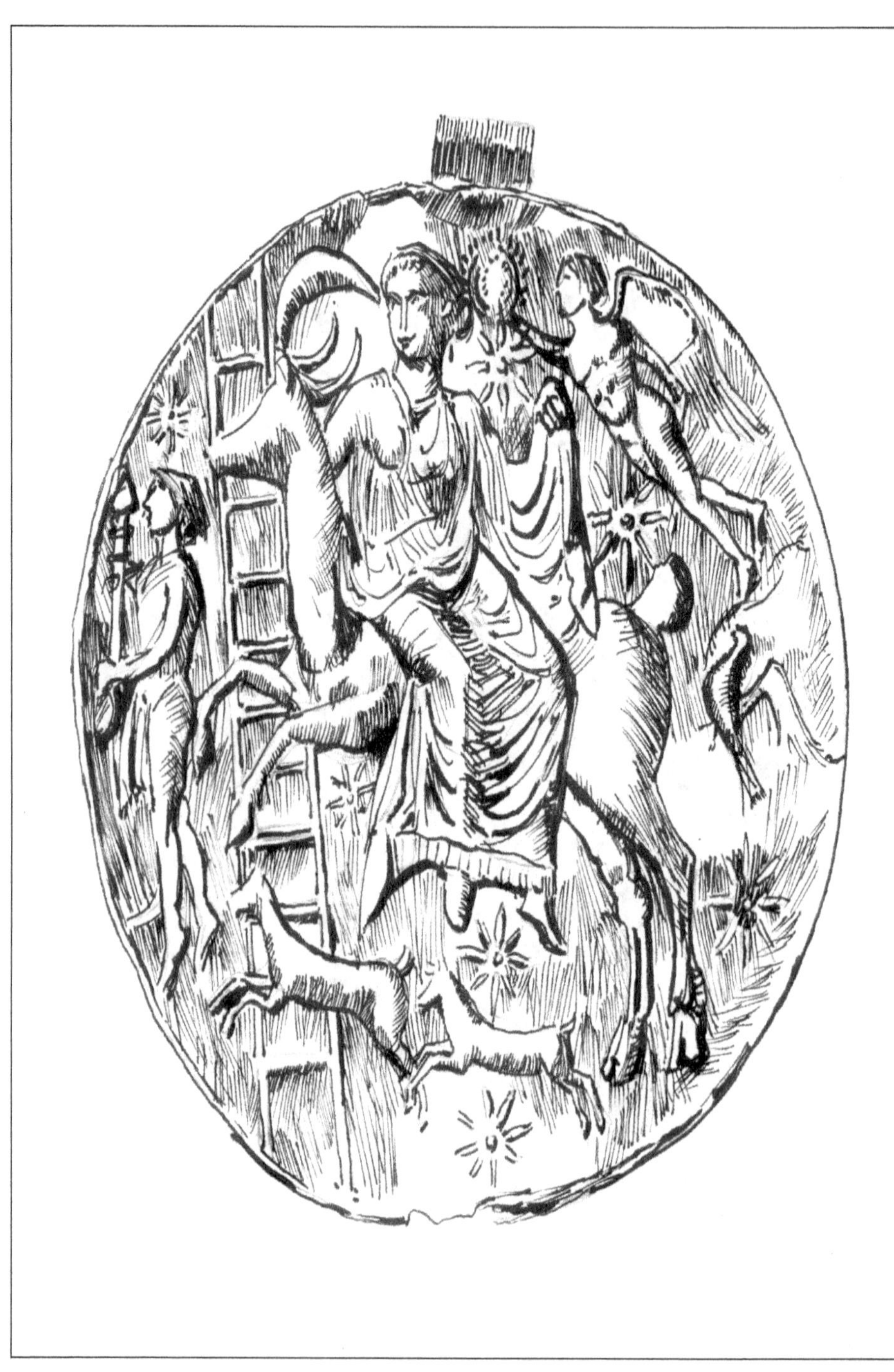

Figure 18. Silver medallion from Building Z, Athens, Kerameikos M 374. Drawing by Alexander Hollmann.

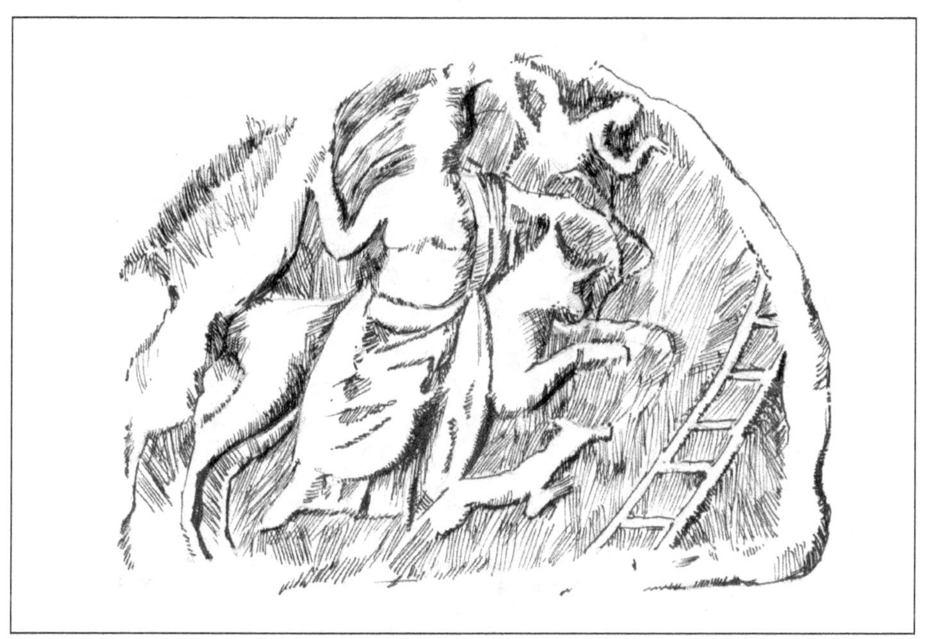

Figure 19. Relief, Sparta Museum 17. Drawing by Alexander Hollmann.

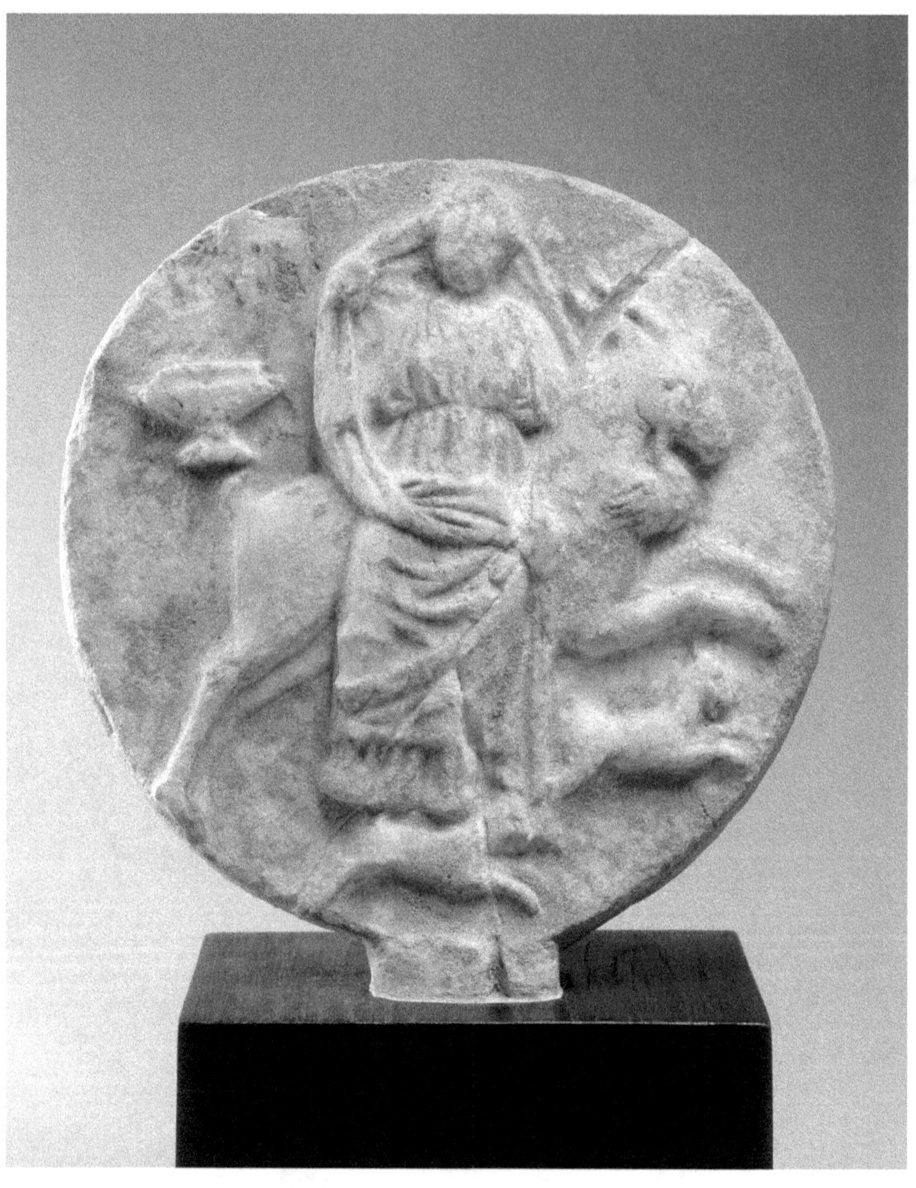

Figure 20. Marble relief medallion, Paris, Musée du Louvre MA 2701 = MNC 978. © Musée du Louvre, Dist. RMN-Grand Palais/ Hervé Lewandowski/ Art Resource, NY.

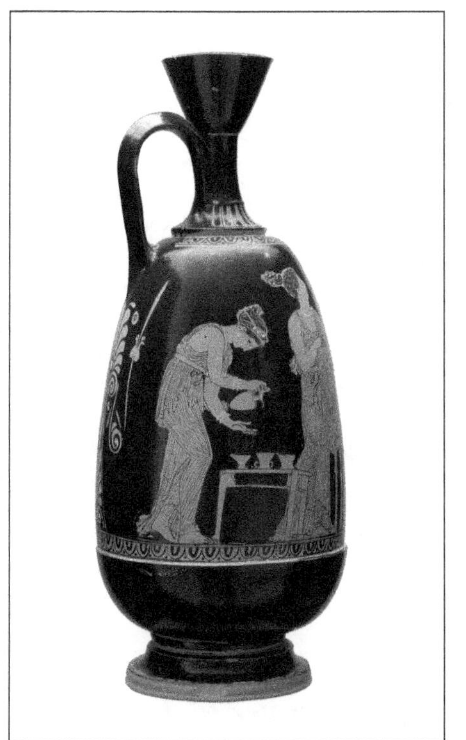

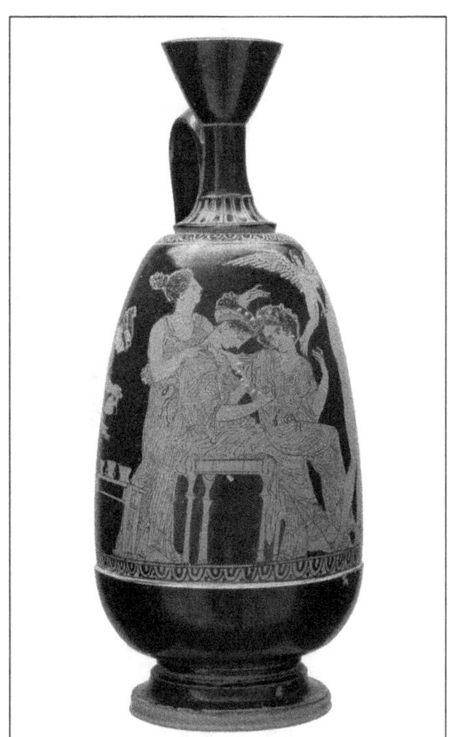

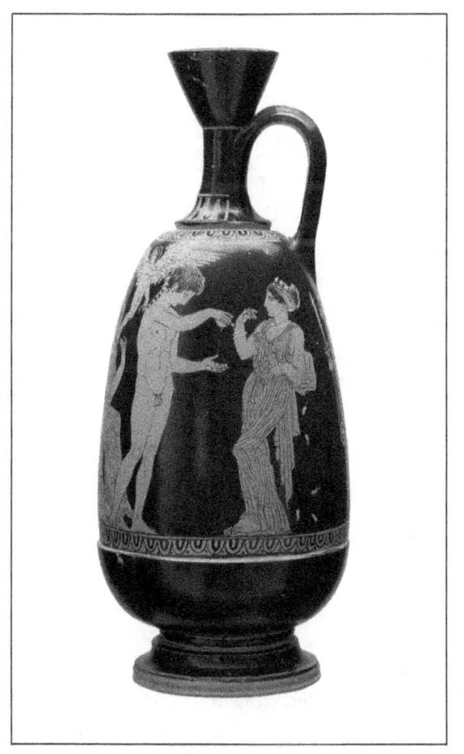

Figure 21. Red-figure acorn lekythos attributed to Aison, Athens, Acropolis Museum 6471. © Acropolis Museum. Photo by Socratis Mavrommatis.

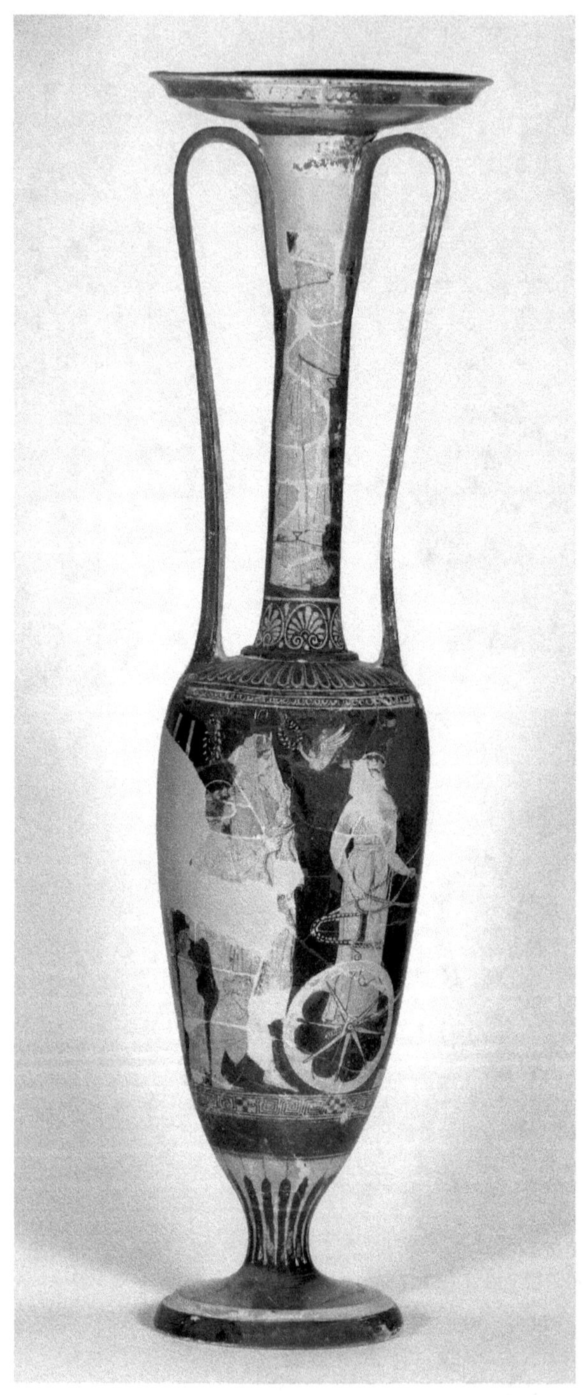

Figure 22. Red-figure loutrophoros, Berlin, Staatliche Museen F 2372. Antikensammlung, Staatliche Museen zu Berlin, Preussischer Kulturbesitz.

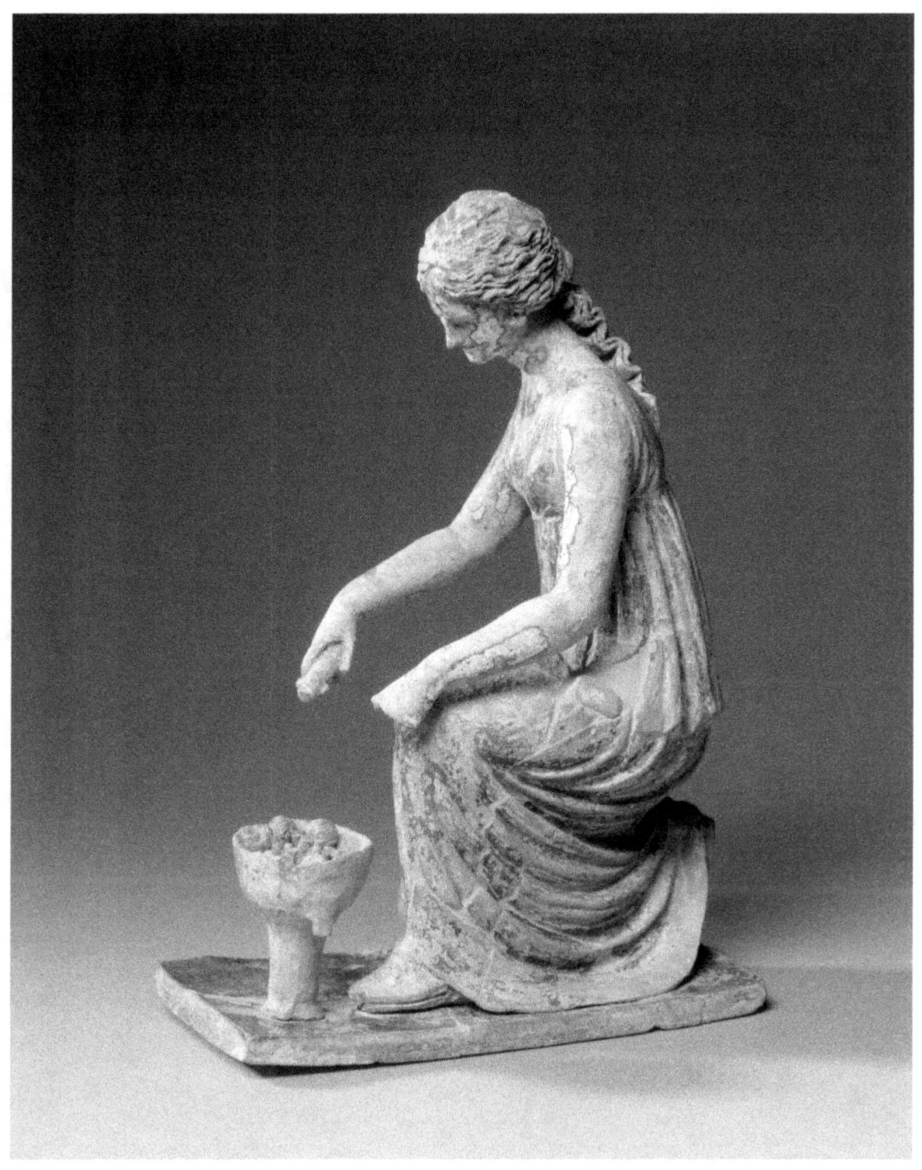

Figure 23 Hellenistic terracotta figurine from Myrina, Paris, Musée du Louvre Inv. Myr. 233. © Musée du Louvre, Dist. RMN-Grand Palais/ Hervé Lewandowski/ Art Resource, NY.

Notes

INTRODUCTION

1. For the citizenship of women as different from that of men, see, e.g., Patterson 1986, and more recently Kamen 2013, 87–96.

2. For the Adonia as a private festival, see, e.g., Detienne (1972) 1994, 100; Reed 1995, 319.

3. It is unclear how much of Apollodorus's account derives from Panyassis. Because Philodemus (first century BCE) *On Piety*, N 243 IV (HV^2 40 upper fragment) 3–12 (p. 12 G.) explains that Panyassis told of the shameless love of Aphrodite for Adonis, it is likely that Panyassis's narrative contained more than just genealogy. See Matthews 1974, 120–25, for arguments for attributing the entire passage to Panyassis.

4. For another treatment of the myth of Adonis, see Ovid's *Metamorphoses* 10.519–59, 708–39. Apollodorus also gives alternative accounts of Adonis's parents, discussed later in the introduction.

5. In other accounts, Adonis's mother is named Myrrha. Myrrha and Smyrna are both Greek words for myrrh, "perfume," or "incense." Σμύρνα is the Aeolian form of Μύρρα (cf. Athenaeus 14.688c).

6. On Adonis's birth and genealogy, see Atallah 1966, 23–47.

7. Cf. Σ Lycophron, *Alexandra* 829; Antoninus Liberalis *Met.* 34.

8. In this case the incest story does not seem to be part of the narrative. For other accounts that name Kinyras as father, see, e.g., Plato Comicus *PCG* vii fr. 3; Σ Theocritus 1.109a (Wendel); Σ Lycophron, *Alexandra* 831; Hyginus *fab.* 248, 251, 271; Ovid *Met.* 10.298–739. Kinyras is usually said to be king of Cyprus and to have established a temple of Aphrodite there (Pindar *Pyth.* 2.15–17). But [Lucian] reports that he founded the temple of Aphrodite in Byblos (*de dea syria* 9). Cf. Strabo 16.2.18.

9. Cf. [Probus] on Verg. *Ecl.* 10.18: *Adonis, <ut> Hesiodus ait, Phoenicis Agenoris et Alphesiboeae* (= fr. 139 Merkelbach-West). Adonis is the son of Zeus, conceived without female intercourse (*ex Iove sine ullius feminae accubitu procreatus*), [Probus] on Vergil *Eclogues* 10.18, cf. Philostephanus *FHG* 3 31 fr. 14 Müller.

10. This detail also appears in book 10 of Ovid's *Metamorphoses*, 725–39. By contrast, in Bion's *Epitaph on Adonis*, Aphrodite's tears produce the anemone, while Adonis's blood produces the rose, 64–66. Adonis and anemones seem to be associated in the fragmentary

second century BCE P. Hamb. II 121 = *Supplementum Hellenisticum* 902.16–18. Cf. Reed 1997, 233; 2006, 80.

11. The Arabic word for anemone contains the title "pleasant," attested for Western Semitic gods, and a passage in Isaiah (17:9–11) that refers to plants for Na'aman has been translated as "gardens of Adonis," as well as "gardens of anemones." Cf. Albright 1964, 172–73; de Vaux 1971, 213; Delcor 1978. See Reed 1997, 233, on the increased popularity during the Hellenistic period of tales of humans becoming plants.

12. For an insightful discussion of the Alexandrian Adonia, see Reed 2000.

13. For rooftop ritual at Athens, see, e.g., Aristophanes's *Lysistrata* 389; Menander's *Samia* 45 (and see further discussion in this volume).

14. Cf. Plutarch, *de sera numinis vindicta* 560b–c.

15. The vases and iconography associated with the Adonis festival will be discussed in chapter 2. Cf. a Hellenistic terracotta figurine from Myrina (fig. 23) depicting a woman cultivating a garden of Adonis in a broken pottery vessel.

16. It must be noted, however, that Socrates is opposing eight days needed for the ritual with eight months needed for proper farming. The number eight, then, may be meant as a useful contrast to the eight months that he indicates are needed for agriculture rather than a reflection of reality (cf. Yunis 2011, 232). Nevertheless, some number of days are needed for the germination and growth of the seeds, even if it is unclear exactly how many and whether the festival continues throughout the period.

17. Cf. Hunter 1996a, 123, 131. The poem is frequently taken to reflect reality. See, e.g., Dillon: "Theocritus is obviously describing an actual occurrence of the Adonia as celebrated at Alexandria" (2002, 163).

18. Theocritus fashioned *Idyll* 15 after a mime by Sophron, titled "Women Watching the Isthmia" (Σ Theocritus Wendel 305). See Hordern 2004, 49–50. Little survives of Sophron's mimes, but Gorgo and Praxinoa certainly call to mind female characters from the extant mimes of Herodas. Cf. Dover 1971, 197; Griffiths 1981, 256; Lambert 2001. For mime as an influence on Theocritus, see Griffiths 1979; Hunter 1996a, 116–23; Kutzko 2007–8. For other mimes or "playlets," cf. *Idylls* 1, 2, 3, 4, 5, 10, and 14.

19. Cf. Hunter 1996a, 119; Gutzwiller 2007, 33–34.

20. For Theocritus and Sicily, see Gow 1952, 1:xv–xviii; Dover 1971, xix; Griffiths 1979, 84, 109. Cf. J. B. Burton 1995; Hunter 1996a. The difficulty (or ease) that the women have in gaining entrance to Arsinoë's palace can thus be interpreted as a comment on Theocritus's access to his patrons. For Sicily in Theocritus's poems, cf. 11.7 and 28.16; *AP* 9.434 = GP 27. Because of Theocritus's influence, bucolic poetry was seen to be "Sicilian" or "Syracusan" (Hunter 1999, 1).

21. Griffiths 1979, 84. Oddly, the stranger who mocks the Doric accent of Gorgo and Praxinoa seems to speak a dialect similar to that of the two women, and Hunter remarks: "To call attention to linguistic differences within a linguistically uniform poem highlights the mimetic artifice of a poetic form which claims on the surface to offer an unmediated representation of 'reality'" (1996b, 157). On the stranger's Doric, see Gow 1952, 290; J. B. Burton 1995, 201–2n57; Kutzko 2007–8.

22. For a discussion aiming at comprehensiveness with regard to Adonis in iconography and literature, see Atallah 1966; for Adonis in iconography, see also Servais-Soyez 1981. For a more traditional project of reconstruction of the Adonis festival, see Reed 1995.

23. Frazer 1906.

24. Discussion of the Adonia in conjunction with the Thesmophoria has persisted since Detienne's (1972) 1994 analysis, for example, R. Parker's examination of the Adonia appears in a chapter titled "Women's Festivals: Thesmophoria and Adonia" (2005, 270–89). Cf. Winkler's chapter in *Constraints of Desire* (1990) titled "The Laughter of the Oppressed: Demeter and the Gardens of Adonis," and Neils 2008, 242–49.

25. R. Parker 1996, 2005; Burkert 1985; Goff 2004; Cole 2004; Alexiou (1974) 2002; Foley 2001; Dillon 2002; Connelly 2007. I have also been influenced by Foley's 1985 work on ritual and tragedy. Outside of the field of classics, I have found Bell's (1992 and 1997) work on ritual extremely helpful. New historicist approaches such as those of Stallybrass and White 1986 and Gallagher and Greenblatt 2000 have also contributed to my reading of the Adonis festival.

26. In his *Greek Religion*, Burkert devotes only a few pages to Adonis, in a section fittingly titled "The Remainder of the Pantheon," under a subheading "Foreign Gods" (1985, 176–79). The Adonia occupies few pages in other comprehensive works on Greek or Athenian religion. In Simon's *Festivals of Attica*, Adonis receives a one-sentence mention in a list of divinities that were mourned at festivals (1983, 91). Cf. Farnell 1907; Deubner (1932) 1969; Simon 1983, 91; Bremmer 1994, 80; R. Parker 1996, 160n29, 162n33, 194, 197–98, and 2005, 270–89; Larson 2007, 124. The festival does not receive a mention in Parke's *Festivals of the Athenians* (1977).

27. Winkler 1990.

28. R. Parker 1996, 2.

29. R. Parker 1996, 2.

30. For the importance of historical context when dealing with evidence for the Adonia, see Reed 2000.

31. Aristophanes's *Peace* does mention the Adonia, and the play survives intact, but for my purposes it is more useful to consider *Lysistrata* as a test case because of a scholion on line 389 (Σ 389 Hangard) that indicates that the play was alternatively titled *Adôniazousai*, "Women at the Adonis Festival."

32. G. Ferrari 2002; Hedreen 2009; Lissarrague 2012; Topper 2012a and 2012b. Similar approaches to images were articulated as early as 1989 in Bérard and Bron, *City of Images*.

33. Peirce 1998, 61.

34. Fragment of a red-figure lebes gamikos, attributed to the Painter of Athens 1454, Paris, Louvre CA 1679; *ARV*[2] 1179.3; *Paralipomena* 460; *Addenda*[2] 340; BAD 215618; *LIMC* I Adonis 46; Weill 1966, 668–74; Reeder 1995, 234, no. 59; Rosenzweig 2004, fig. 50; Kaltsas and Shapiro 2008, 242, 261, no. 120.

35. Hauser 1909, esp. 99. Hauser was one of the few to suggest a fall date; as we will see in chapter 1, most scholars argue for summer, while a few believe the festival was performed in the spring. Cf. Deubner (1932) 1969, 221.

36. Nock (1934) 1986, 290–92.
37. Weill 1966, 675–98.
38. Edwards 1984; Dillon 2003, 10–11.

Chapter 1. Adonis and the Adonia

1. Antimachus of Colophon: fr. 92a Matthews (from [Probus] on Vergil's *Eclogues* 10.18), *'Adonis' . . . ut Antimachus ait, <Cinyrae qui> regnavit in Cypro*. Philodemus *On Piety*, N 243 IV (HV^2 40 upper fragment) 3–12 (p. 12 G.) reads]χος. Vogliano suggested Antimachus (contra Philippson's "Callimachus"), discussed by Henrichs 1972, 93–94. For Adonis in *Lyde*, see Matthews 1996, 256.

2. This information comes by way of Philodemus, *On Piety*, N 243 IV (HV^2 40 upper fragment) 3–12 (p. 12 G.) with Henrichs's (1972, 92–93) correction of Epimenides for the erroneous reading of Hesiod.

3. Dioscorides (*AP* 7.407.7–8 = GP 1565–74) portrays Sappho herself lamenting Adonis. Pausanias reports that Sappho sang of Adonis: Σαπφὼ δὲ ἡ Λεσβία τοῦ Οἰτολίνου τὸ ὄνομα ἐκ τῶν ἐπῶν τῶν Πάμφω μαθοῦσα Ἄδωνιν ὁμοῦ καὶ Οἰτόλινον ᾖσεν, "Sappho of Lesbos learned the name of Oitolinos from the hymns of Pamphos and sang of Adonis and Oitolinos together," 9.29.8. Later writers attest to Sappho's interest in Adonis: According to Comes Natalis, Sappho told the story of Adonis and his associations with lettuce: *scriptum reliquit Sappho Adonim mortuum fuisse a Venere inter lectucas depositum*, *Myth.* 5.16 (531 ed. Francof. 1581) = fr. 211c Voigt.

4. Cf. Alexiou (1974) 2002, 55; Atallah 1966, 309; West 1992, 339–40, and 1997, 530; Lardinois 1994, 65–66; Reed 1995, 333–34; H. Parker 1996, 180; F. Ferrari 2010, 150.

5. Cf. West's suggestion for fr. 96.23 (West 1970, 328). For the exclamatory accusative within the ritual context of lament, see Bulloch 1985, 200; Reed 1995, 334; Acosta-Hughes 2002, 246. Cf. *Lysistrata* 393, αἰαῖ Ἄδωνιν; Bion *Epitaph* 32, αἲ τὸν Ἄδωνιν; Callimachus *Iambus* 3, 37–38. See also West 1997, 263 for the similarities between Jeremiah 22:18 (where a dead king is lamented with the phrase *hôy 'ādôn*, "Alas, lord!") and the ritual cry at the Adonia seen in Sappho fr. 168 Voigt, and see later in the chapter for the relationship between Adonis's name and the Semitic word for "lord."

6. Aristophanes, Cratinus, Pherecrates, and Plato Comicus used the accusative Ἀδώνιον for Ἄδωνιν (Photios s.vv. *Adônios*, *Adônia*: Pherecrates *PCG* vii fr. 181, 213; Plato Comicus *PCG* vii fr. 4; Cratinus *PCG* iv fr. 404; Aristophanes *PCG* iii 2 fr. 759).

7. Antiphanes *PCG* ii fr. 14–16; Ararus *PCG* ii fr. 1–3; Nicophon *PCG* vii p. 63; Philiscus *PCG* vii p. 356; Plato Comicus *PCG* vii fr. 1–8.

8. The Adonia is mentioned by Cratinus *PCG* iv fr. 17; Pherecrates *PCG* vii fr. 181. The festival appears in Aristophanes *Peace* 416–20; Philippides *Women-at-the-Adonis-Festival*: *PCG* vii fr. 1–3; Aristophanes *Lysistrata* as *Adôniazousai*: Σ 389 Hangard.

9. Cf. Reed 1995, 339.

10. The fragment describes the disparaged individual only as the "son of Cleomachus." Athenaeus, who preserves the fragment, believes that the individual was Gnesippus, though

this has been disputed. For discussions of the fragment, see Davidson 2000; Hordern 2003; Prauscello 2006.

11. Gnesippus has been variously characterized by scholars as a tragic, comic, and lyric poet. Davidson 2000 claims that Gnesippus wrote lyrical mimes called παίγνια.

12. Zenobius 4.21 (*CPG* i.89); Apostolius 8.53 (*CPG* ii.445).

13. For the Heracles anecdote, see, e.g., Σ Theocritus 5.21 (Wendel); Hesychius and Suda s.v. οὐδὲν ἱερόν. Atallah 1966, 106n2, suggests that the proverb was known during the Classical period. Cf. the scholion on *Iliad* 24.23 (that probably goes back to Aristarchus on *Iliad* 24.23–30, the allusion to the Judgment of Paris). Regarding the contest between Athena and Aphrodite, the note reads, "as if Heracles should contend with Adonis" (ὡς εἰ καὶ Ἡρακλῆς ἀγωνίζοιτο πρὸς Ἄδωνιν). The results are predetermined in a contest between one known for martial prowess and one known for beauty.

14. Zenobius 1.49 (*CPG* i.19). See Reed 1995, 324n30 and 338.

15. Cf., e.g., Theophrastus *CP* 1.12.2; Detienne (1972) 1994, 101–6, 135–36, and see further discussion of gardens of Adonis later in the chapter.

16. Detienne (1972) 1994, 99–100, italics mine.

17. Winkler 1990, 188–209.

18. Winkler 1990, 205. For attention to the participants, see Simms 1997–98, 122, 130. Just as Winkler's (1990) approach offers a more positive view of the festival than Detienne's, at least from the perspective of the participants, so too, in a different (though far less convincing) manner, Baudy (1986) suggests an interpretation for the gardens that does not carry the negative associations of Detienne's. Baudy argues that the cultivation of gardens of Adonis was a productive, economically based practice because gardens of Adonis were used to test seeds (cf. Versnel 1990, 104n28), an economic interpretation of the function of the gardens that radically shifts the discussion away from sterility and death. Baudy's ritual seed testing theory relies on evidence from a much later period than fifth- and fourth-century Athens and is ultimately not persuasive; nevertheless, he is able to take the actions of the women at the Adonia seriously, at least on some level, and it is this aspect of his argument that is compelling.

19. Goff 2004, 59. Cf. Burkert, who remarks, "The 'garden' ritual is to be understood as play-acting the failure of planting in order to ensure by contrast the success in reality" (1979, 107). Even more dismissively, Dillon (2002) questions the ability of the participants to understand what they were doing. After summarizing a number of interpretations of the Adonia, including Frazer's argument that the festival represented a fertility ritual (discussed later), and the views of Detienne and Winkler just mentioned, Dillon remarks: "All of these explanations are too ingenious and dress up the evidence in interpretations too complex for the women at the Adonia to have understood" (2002, 166). He concludes, "They celebrated the Adonia because the cult of Aphrodite and Adonis entered Greece, just like those of Cybele and Sabazios" (166). Yet just as myths do not simply appear out of nowhere but gain popularity because a group of people make use of them for some reason, so too cults do not simply materialize ready to be celebrated. The Adonia held an appeal at Athens during the Classical period for the women who took part in the ritual.

20. Adonis is not quite mortal; neither is he wholly immortal, an ambiguous status that is underscored, for example, with a mention of his "ambrosial" blood in a fragmentary elegiac poem (*P. Oxy.* 4711). Cf. Reed, who comments, "Shifting between the Underworld and Heaven, he has both and neither. And on earth he achieves immortality after a fashion, in earthly things that reappear every year" (2006, 82). Adonis has the epithet ἄμβροτος in [Orph.] *Hymn* proem. 41 and 55.26. He is called demigod (ἡμίθεος) in Theocritus *Idyll* 15 (137). As for Adonis's *death* as preoccupation, ancient authors enjoyed imagining Adonis in the underworld: Praxilla (fr. 1 Page = *PMG* 747) has Adonis speaking from the land of the dead, as he is interviewed about what he misses most. And Euphorion (third century BCE) has Adonis receive ministrations from the "river of wailing," when he relates, "Kokytos alone washed off Adonis's wounds" (Κώκυτός ‹τοι› μοῦνος ἀφ' ἕλκεα νίψεν Ἄδωνιν, fr. 43 Powell). Ptolemy Chennus preserves the line from Euphorion's *Hyacinth* (Photius *Bibl.* 146b). Reed (2000, 341) sees Egyptian influence.

21. See Ribichini 1981, 133n82, for Adonis's "doppia esperienza di morte."

22. Clearchus (fr. 101 Wehrli = Ath. 8. 332b; cf. Aelian *NA* 9.36) mentions an amphibious fish that is called "Adonis" because both the fish and the youth travel between two spheres that tend to be kept distinct. Theocritus refers to this aspect of the Adonis story (*Idyll* 15. 136–37), as do Lucian (*Dialogues of the Gods* 19) and Alciphron (*Letters of Courtesans* 4.14.3). A scholion on Theocritus *Idyll* 3.48 (3.48d Wendel) reports an alternative tradition that Adonis spends equal time with each goddess—six months with Aphrodite and six months with Persephone. The story of Adonis shared by Aphrodite and Persephone later informs the allegorical interpretation of the myth, since Adonis's disappearance and reappearance are linked to the seasonal cycle. The time he spends with Persephone is understood to be winter, and the time with Aphrodite spring/summer. The myth also is represented in the visual arts, although it is rare. See, e.g., M. Turner 2005, 81, for an Apulian lebes in Sydney (Nicholson Museum, 83.04; *CVA* Sydney I pl. 92–94 [72–74]), where Adonis rises from the ground into the arms of Aphrodite (though the figures are not inscribed). An Apulian pelike (Naples, Museo Archeologico Nazionale SA 702; *LIMC* I 233, Adonis 5; Charbonneaux 1972 fig. 366) depicts Adonis (labeled) reclining on a couch with Artemis, Aphrodite, and Persephone. See also Cambitoglou 2009 for three (uninscribed) Apulian vases that he argues depict Adonis and Persephone. De Grummond (2004, 362) discusses a Praenestine mirror from Orbetello (ca. 400 BCE) depicting Venus, Jupiter, and Proserpina, along with a chest. Unfortunately, nothing definitive can be said about the votive pinakes from Italian Locri that show a seated woman opening a chest with a child inside. It has been suggested that the child is Adonis; Persephone is certainly the subject of other pinakes and may be the seated woman. For discussions of the pinakes, see, e.g., Dillon 2002, 234; MacLachlan 1995; Redfield 2003, 346–85.

23. ὀλεῖτον (translated here as "will destroy") is Jacobs's reading for transmitted εχειτον or ἔχετον.

24. Reed characterizes the fragment as a "bisexualized burlesque on the Panyassian rivalry between Aphrodite and Persephone" (1995, 335). For ἐλαύνω used in a sexual sense, see Aristophanes's *Assemblywomen* 39.

25. Cf. Stehle 1996, 206.

26. Cf. Hunter 1983, 104. A passage from Amphis's *Ialemos* (*PCG* ii fr. 20) also describes lettuce as an anti-aphrodisiac:

> ἐν ταῖς θριδακίναις ταῖς κάκιστ' ἀπολουμέναις,
> ἃς εἰ φάγοι τις ἐντὸς ἑξήκοντ' ἐτῶν,
> ὁπότε γυναικὸς λαμβάνοι κοινωνίαν,
> στρέφοιθ' ὅλην τὴν νύκτ' ἂν οὐδὲ ἓν πλέον
> ὧν βούλεται δρῶν, ἀντὶ τῆς ὑπουργίας
> τῇ χειρὶ τρίβων τὴν ἀναγκαίαν τύχην
>
> A curse upon destructive lettuces! When attempting intercourse with a woman, if someone not yet sixty years old should eat them, he would toss and turn the whole night long without accomplishing even a single one of his desires, rubbing off with his hand his doom imposed by fate instead of rendering his services.

Cf. Hipp. *Vict.* 2.54.20 (explanation for anti-aphrodisiac qualities: coolness of the lettuce).

27. On Adonis and lettuce, see Detienne (1972) 1994, 67–71, 108–9.

28. Nicander reports in the second book of his *Glosses* that βρένθις is used by the Cypriots for *thridax* (lettuce). See Reed 1996 for an alternative interpretation of βρένθις.

29. The Egyptians apparently had a very different take on the effects of lettuce and believed that the vegetable promoted *fertility*. See Reed 2000, 343, for an interpretation of the Callimachus passage in an Egyptian context.

30. For discussion of the death of Adonis and the boar, see Atallah 1966, 53–91; Reed 1995, 335; 1996, 382. The boar is possibly alluded to in Ararus *PCG* fr. 1, and Dionysius I of Syracuse *TrGF* fr. 1, and certainly mentioned in Lycophron (*Alexandra* 831–33); Glycon (*PMG* Adesp. 1029 = Hephaestion, *Ench.* 10.2); Bion *Epitaph on Adonis*; Plutarch *Symp.* 4.5.3; Philostephanus ([Probus] on Verg. *Ecl.* 10.18, *FHG* 3 31 fr. 14 Müller); Hyginus *Fables* 248.

31. Other sources name different deities who send the boar or who are the boar: the Muses (Lycophron *Alex.* 831 with schol.); Apollo (Ptolemy Chennus in Photius *Bibl.* 146b); Jupiter (Servius on Vergil *Eclogues* 10.18); Hephaestus (Nonnus *Dion.* 42.320–21). Cf. Atallah 1966, 53–56; Reed 1995, 336.

32. Frazer 1906.

33. For criticisms of Detienne (1972) 1994, see Piccaluga 1974; Winkler 1990, 199–203; Pirenne-Delforge 1994, 24–25; Reed 1995, especially 321–22; Stehle 1996, 200–202.

34. Cf. Menander *Samia* 38–49.

35. The category rising/dying god has since been thoroughly dismantled. See, e.g., J. Z. Smith 1990; M. S. Smith 1998. Mettinger 2001, however, offers a reappraisal of the evidence and continues to find the category useful to some extent. For a discussion of the category in scholarship on Greek religion (and its replacement by theories of initiation), see Versnel 1990.

36. For Frazer and Christian views, see M. S. Smith 1998, 268.

37. For interpretations of the passage, see Atallah 1966, 261–63, and see also Lightfoot 2003, 309–11, for the tradition in which Aphrodite goes searching for Adonis and finds him to be "alive." For Adonis's afterlife, see Reed 2002.

38. Kowalzig remarks, "Aetiological myth is the primary form through which myth plays a function in ritual, and thence in society" (2007b, 8). Cf. *Homeric Hymn to Demeter* (270–74), which explicitly connects the mysteries at Eleusis with the mythical story in which Demeter comes to Eleusis in search of her daughter. In the same hymn (202), Iambe makes the sorrowful Demeter laugh, and Apollodorus (1.5.3) explains that this is why women joke at the Thesmophoria (γραῖά τις Ἰάμβη σκώψασα τὴν θεὸν ἐποίησε μειδιᾶσαι. διὰ τοῦτο ἐν τοῖς θεσμοφορίοις τὰς γυναῖκας σκώπτειν λέγουσιν, "A certain Iambe, joking around with the goddess made her laugh. On account of this they say the women at the Thesmophoria joke"). So too Diodorus Siculus accounts for *aischrologia* (*Bibl.* 5.4.7) in contemporary ritual practice by appealing directly to Demeter's laughter in the mythical past at such bawdy humor.

39. See Schibli 1990, 50–77. For etiology and the Greek wedding, see, e.g., Faraone 1999, 70–72.

40. For discussions of the ritual, see, e.g., Oakley and Sinos 1993, 136; G. Ferrari 2002, 186–90.

41. Whether the rituals that Euripides mentions were accurate representations of cultic reality is not important for my purposes. See, e.g., Scullion 1999–2000; Seaford 2009.

42. For the cult, see W. S. Barrett 1964, 3–6.

43. Of course, the relationship between myth and ritual is not unidirectional. The performance of the Adonis festival, without a doubt, influenced poetic treatments of the story of Adonis. For example, it may well have been Eubulus's knowledge of the cultivation of the gardens of Adonis during the ritual of the Adonia that led him to compose the lines concerning lettuce and the unfortunate youth. Yet even if this story serves to explain the ritual, once the story has been created participants in the ritual believe they are enacting the ritual because of past events.

44. Cf. Reed 1995, 327–28; Simms 1997–98.

45. Hesychius (s.v. Ἀδώνιδος κῆποι) makes the connection between the myth and the ritual explicit when he explains that participants prepare gardens for Adonis "because they say that he was laid out by Aphrodite in lettuce."

46. The scholion on the *Lysistrata* passage remarks: "For the women used to celebrate a festival for Adonis and they used to carry garden-thingies up to their rooftops," ἑορτὴν γὰρ ἐπετέλουν τῷ Ἀδώνιδι αἱ γυναῖκες καὶ κήπους τινὰς εἰς τὰ δώματα ἀνέφερον (Σ 389 Hangard). The Suda defines "fruits of Adonis" as "gardens high-in-the-air," μετέωροι κῆποι. Suda, s.v. Ἀδώνειοι καρποί. Cf. Reed 2005. Archaeological evidence indicates that roofs could be pitched or flat. See, e.g., Jameson 1990, 181, fig. 18, for a flat roof on a fourth-century BCE Athenian house. For more-recent work on houses, see, e.g., Nevett 1999, 2010; Ault 2005; Ault and Nevett 2005; J. Morgan 2010.

47. It is likely that whatever was convenient, available, and quick to sprout did the job of providing lush shoots for the ritual. The scholion on Theocritus 15.112–13 (Wendel) explains that the gardens contained wheat and barley, while Hesychius and the Suda s.v. Ἀδώνιδος κῆποι mention lettuce and fennel. For discussions of gardens of Adonis, see Sulze 1930; Atallah 1966, 211–28; Winkler 1990; Reed 1995; Simms 1997–98; Dillon 2002, 162–69; R. Parker 2005, 284–89.

48. The hymnist in Theocritus *Idyll* 15 sings that "Adonis" will be taken to the sea on the following day (132–33, with scholia), and this seems to refer to some sort of lightweight effigy of Adonis (cf. Gow 1952, 299–300). In Alciphron's (second century CE) *Letters* 4.14.8 (which draw on fourth-century BCE cultural norms), a participant at the Adonia is told to come bringing a little garden (κηπίον) and a κοράλλιον, which likely refers to a figurine of Adonis. Cf. Zenobius 1.49 (*CPG* i.19), Hesychius s.v. Ἀδώνιδος κῆποι, Photius *Lex.* s.v. Ἀδώνια. Suda s.v. Ἀδώνια explains that the effigy was called the Ἀδώνιον; Suda, s.v. Ἀδώνιδος κῆποι; *Etym. Magn.* s.v. Ἀδωνιασμός, Ἄδωνις. The gardens (and the figurines if used) were disposed of somehow. Eustathius, like the hymnist in Theocritus, reports that the gardens were thrown into the sea: *Od.* 1701.45–50 (on *Odyssey* 11. 590). Cf. Dioscorides *AP* 5.53 and 193. But according to Zenobius (second century CE), the gardens were carried out with the dying god and thrown into a *spring* 1.49 (*CPG* 1.19).

49. Simms 1997–98, 129.

50. For gardens of Adonis in iconography, see figures 5, 21, and 23, and for discussion, see chapter 2. Broken pottery vessels that may or may not function as a mythical *aition* for gardens of Adonis (nothing conclusive can be said) also appear on an aryballos lekythos in Kassel (Staatliche Museen Kassel, Antikensammlung, T389, early fourth century; *LIMC* III 928, Eros 955; Atallah 1966, 197, fig. 53). For discussions of the vase, see Boehlau 1901; Metzger 1951; Picard 1953; Atallah 1966, 195–201; Simon 1972. A winged youth fleeing a boar drops a hydria from his right hand. Another hydria, apparently broken in half (the top part is depicted, and it is upside down), hovers in the air above the boar's back. A female figure with her arms stretched out to meet the youth runs in from the left, and a second female figure prepares to strike the boar with the top portion of another hydria. The youth has been identified as Eros (Boehlau 1901) as well as Adonis (Metzger 1951). For a winged Adonis, an Etruscan mirror has been adduced as parallel; it depicts a winged youth with the inscription Atunis, the Etruscan name for Adonis (Metzger 1951, 90). On the connections between Eros and Adonis, two youths who are closely associated with Aphrodite and who appear to have been confused from time to time, see Meritt 1935, 574; Walton 1938, 71–72; Atallah 1966, 199–201.

51. For a youth as ἔρνος, see, e.g., *Iliad* 18.56; for θαλλός, see, e.g., *Homeric Hymn to Demeter* 66. For generations of humans as leaves, see *Iliad* 6.146–49. When Odysseus encounters Nausicaa in book 6 of the *Odyssey*, he thinks immediately of a palm tree he once saw at Delos (163). The words that are believed to have been said at marriage ceremonies are preserved in several passages of Menander: ἀλλ' ἐγγυῶ παίδων ἐπ' ἀρότῳ γνησίων / τὴν θυγατέρ' ἤδη, μειράκιόν, σοι, "I pledge my daughter to you, young man, for the plowing of legitimate children" (*Dys.* 842–6). Cf. *Mis.* 444–46 Sandbach; *Pk.* 1013–14 Sandbach; *Sam.*

726–28 Sandbach; cf. *P. Oxy.* 429. See Cole 2004, 153. For agricultural imagery and the wedding ceremony, see Redfield 1982; duBois 1988.

52. In later allegorical accounts, Adonis is clearly identified with grain. Cf. Σ Theocritus 3.48d (Wendel), which connects Adonis explicitly to σῖτος, "grain," that spends six months in the earth just as Adonis spends six months with Persephone. Cf. Cornutus *de natura deorum* 54–55; Porphyry in Euseb., *P.E.* 3.11.9 = Porph. *Agalm.* 7 Bidez; Sallustius *de deis* 4.3; Amm. Marc. 19.1.2, 22.9.15; Macrob. *Sat.* 1.21.1–4; [Clem. Rom.] *Hom.* 6.9; Jo. Lyd. *Mens.* 4.64.

53. Cf. [Orph.], *Hymn* 56.8.

54. R. Parker comments, "On the old fertility/agricultural interpretation Adonis the god was a metaphor for the natural world; his death and supposed rebirth represented the annual cycle of the plants. But in Greek sources the metaphor often goes the other way, with young humans being spoken of as if they were young shoots. Whatever the origin of the gardens, such was surely their significance in Athens. They were a second embodiment of Adonis" (2005, 287). Cf. Reed 1995, 327–28.

55. Cf. Atallah 1966, 325–27; Detienne (1972) 1994, 2–3, 63–64. The frankincense tree and the myrrh tree produced substances that could be used as perfumes, burned as incense, or employed for medicinal purposes. Frankincense (*libanos*) and myrrh were imported from South Arabia via Phoenicia (Burkert 1985, 62). The two substances tend to be mentioned together (e.g., Herodotus 2.40.3; Theophrastus *Odors* 3.12) and often seem to have been used interchangeably. For myrrh used as perfume, see, e.g., Theophrastus *Odors* 4.17, 6.29; for myrrh used as incense, see, e.g., Theophrastus *Odors* 3.12; Euripides *Trojan Women*, 1064–65.

56. Cf. *Greek Anthology*, 5.113.3, where a woman addresses her lover as "my perfume, my tender Adonis" (μύρον καὶ τερπνὸν Ἄδωνιν).

57. Oakley and Reitzammer 2005; Jeammet and Bonora Andujar 2010, 194–95.

58. Additional vases that depict scenes involving incense will be discussed in chapter 2. On incense and the Adonia, see also Hauser 1909, 97; Burkert 1985, 62.

59. A puzzling passage from [Lucian]'s *de dea syria* (6) mentioned earlier may provide evidence for the use of myrrh in ritual during the Imperial period. [Lucian] explains that after offerings are made to Adonis as to a corpse, on the next day they say that he lives and "they send [Adonis] into the air," ἐς τὸν ἠέρα πέμπουσι. Lightfoot 2003, 321–22, notes that the passage must refer to the myth in which Adonis is shared between Aphrodite and Persephone. Burkert (1979, 194n15) suggests that it may refer to a fire ritual (cf. ἐξαεροῦν, "to turn into the air," of burning, Luc. *Peregr.* 30), and the suggestion is intriguing. Like Adonis, who travels between spheres, spending part of the year with Persephone in the underworld and part with Aphrodite, the smoke of incense wafts up from earth to the gods. Myrrh, for example, is described as "ethereal," or "heavenly" in Euripides's *Trojan Women* (σμύρνης αἰθερίας τε κα- / πνόν, 1064–65).

60. Most scholars follow Detienne (1972) 1994, 106. See, e.g., Nagy 1985, 62; Stehle 1996, 198; Goff 2004, 59.

61. See Atallah 1966, 229–58, for a thorough discussion of the season of the Adonia. The issue is controversial and spring, summer, and fall have all been proposed. Scholars

who argue for a summer date include Baudissin 1911, 126–33; Cumont 1927, 1935; Atallah 1966, 255–58 (argues for a springtime festival followed by a summer festival); Weill 1966; Detienne (1972) 1994, esp. 100–101, 106; Burkert 1979, 106; Robertson 1982, 342–46; Servais 1984, 83–93; Winkler 1990, 189; Reed 1995, 319–20; Simms 1997, 52–53; Goff 2004, 36; Burnett 2012, 185. Proponents for a springtime date will be discussed later.

62. For *theros* used loosely, see Nock (1934) 1986; Weill 1966, 687–90. For example, Thucydides reports that the original meeting when it was decided to sail to Sicily occurred during "the next summer, early in the spring" (τοῦ δ'ἐπιγιγνομένου θέρους ἅμα ἦρι, 6.8.1). Here *theros* is qualified by a word for spring (cf. Thucydides 2.31.1, where *theros* is qualified by a word for autumn).

63. Dillon (2003, 8), who argues for a springtime Adonia (rather than a summer festival), produces a strained reading of the Theophrastus passage (*Hist. plant.* 6.7.3) in an attempt to argue against Theophrastus's use of "in summer" to describe the time of the cultivation of gardens of Adonis. The passage is as follows: "Southernwood/wormwood grows better from the seed than from the root or from a cutting, though it grows with difficulty from the seed. It is grown in *ostraka*, like gardens of Adonis, in the summer," ἀβρότονον δὲ μᾶλλον ἀπὸ σπέρματος βλαστάνει ἢ ἀπὸ ῥίζης καὶ παρασπάδος· χαλεπῶς δὲ καὶ ἀπὸ σπέρματος· προμοσχευόμενον [δὲ] ἐν ὀστράκοις, ὥσπερ οἱ Ἀδώνιδος κῆποι, τοῦ θέρους. In Dillon's reading, the phrase "in summer" refers only to the planting of wormwood.

64. See Weill 1966, 695–98. For summer and the Adonia in Spain, see Cumont 1927; for summer and the Adonia in Syria, see Cumont 1932 and 1935.

65. For scholars who argue for a springtime Adonia, see Nock (1934) 1986 (he suggests that perhaps an additional summer celebration took place); Meritt (1935, 574–75) argues for the date of Mounychion 4 for the Adonia; Walton 1938, 69; Atallah 1966, 255–58 (also suggests the possibility of a spring and summer festival); Henderson 1987, 119 (the Adonia took place "prior to the campaign season"); Dillon 2002, 163, and 2003.

66. *Lysistrata* names Demostratus as the speaker who is in favor of the military undertaking. Thucydides says that "a certain Athenian" spoke (6.25.1) at the second meeting of the Assembly. Plutarch *Nicias* 12.6 names Demostratus apparently as one who spoke in response to the lengthy speech of Nicias described in Thucydides, suggesting to some that Demostratus himself spoke at the second meeting of the assembly and that the Aristophanes passage refers to that meeting. Yet as Hornblower (1991–2008, 3:311–12) points out, it is impossible to know at which assembly meeting Demostratus spoke. He may even have spoken at the meeting discussing reinforcements held two years later.

67. Although Dillon discusses the literary aspects of the Plutarch passage at great length, he takes the Aristophanes passage at face value in his arguments for a spring Adonia, remarking, "The testimony of Aristophanes is clear and irrefutable" (2003, 8). For a different take on the apparent chronological discrepancy of Aristophanes, see Furley 1988, who argues that a historical Adonis festival must have been held in 415 BCE, not during the normal time of the Adonia (summer), but as an improvised war protest during the spring while the Sicilian expedition was being debated. Cf. Keuls, who also connects the Adonia with the mutilation of the Herms (1985, 391, 395).

68. Cf. Dillon 2002, 165, and see 339n165. For the point that no evidence links the death of the plants to the sun, see also Reed 1995, 325; Simms 1997–98, 129; Dillon 2003; R. Parker 2005, 285.

69. Ἀδώνιδος κῆποι· ἐπὶ τῶν ἀώρων καὶ μὴ ἐρριζωμένων. ἐπειδὴ γὰρ Ἄδωνις ἐρώμενος ὤν, ὡς ὁ μῦθος, τῆς Ἀφροδίτης, προήβης τελευτᾷ, οἱ ταύτῃ ὀργιάζοντες, κήπους εἰς ἀγγεῖά τινα φυτεύοντες ἢ φυτεύουσαι, ταχέως ἐκείνων διὰ τὸ μὴ ἐρριζῶσθαι μαραινομένων, Ἀδώνιδος αὐτοὺς ἐκάλουν. This passage contains both the masculine and the feminine participle to describe cultivators of gardens of Adonis. See my later discussion of the possibility of male participation at the Adonia.

70. Simplicius (*in Ph.* 9.911.13, cf. 10.1212.18–19) suggests that Aristotle (*Physics* 5.230b2) refers to gardens of Adonis when he likens youths who come to manhood early "by luxury" to "grains of wheat not firmly compressed in the ground." See Detienne (1972) 1994, 104–5, on the passage. Cf. Epictetus *Disc.* 4.8.36.

71. See Amendola 2010 on the passage.

72. Cf. Σ *Phaedrus* 276b, where the gardens are proverbial for things "out of season" (ἀώρων), "of short duration" (ὀλιγοχρονίων), and "not firmly established" (μὴ ἐρριζωμένων).

73. Cf. Dioscorides (GP 1565–74 = *AP* 7.407).

74. For a recent summary of scholarship on ritual both inside and outside the field of classics, see, e.g., Kowalzig 2007b. See also Bell 1992 and 1997.

75. For this point, see Kowalzig, who remarks, "Especially in Classics, ritual is still relatively rarely studied as a productive force, a dynamic agent, which derives its power not from a fixed relation, but from a dialogue, with its own past" (2007b, 34).

76. Hugh-Jones remarks, "It is through ritual that the categories of thought can be manipulated to produce effects" (1979, 260).

77. Goff 2004, 14.

78. For the visibility accorded those on rooftops, see an inscription from Thasos (*SEG* 42.785) discussed by Henry 2002.

79. Cf. Reed 1995, 318. Aristophanes's *Lysistrata* has the wife of Demostratus lamenting the youth (393). The fourth-century comic poet Diphilus suggests that courtesans were involved (*PCG* v fr. 42.38–41; *PCG* v fr. 49). Menander's *Samia* (38–46) portrays a citizen wife and a Samian courtesan celebrating together. Later texts, too, consistently represent married women as well as prostitutes. Theocritus *Idyll* 15 concerns two married women; Alciphron includes courtesans (14.3, 14.8, cf. 10.1); Dioscorides (5.53 and 5.193) portrays highly sexualized participants at the Adonia. Burnett has recently attempted to account for the involvement of both prostitutes and married women at the Adonia by arguing that Athenian mothers mourned the loss of sons leaving their homes and entering the world of heterosexual activity. She suggests that prostitutes and mothers joined each year "in a symbolic action meant to ensure that the youthful familial seed, planted in the wrong season, outside the house, and in imperfect receptacles, should leave no trace" (2012, 189). Yet one wonders why, for example, prostitutes would *want* to be involved in such celebrations.

80. Although the Adonia was a women's festival, there does seem to have been a concern that men might be pulled into the female Adonis festival sphere, and this will be

discussed in chapter 3. For example, in Menander's *Samia* (38–49), Moschion himself becomes involved in the festivities. Cf. Burton 1998; Scullion 2013, who mentions the possibility of men at the Adonia within a larger discussion of male maenadic activity during the Classical period. For the male speakers in Theocritus *Idyll* 15 (72, 74, 87–88) as spectators attracted to the women's ritual, see Gow 1952, 303. Cf. Dover 1971, 209. As seen above, [Diogenianos] 1.14 (*CPG* 1.183) contains masculine and feminine participles to describe cultivators of gardens of Adonis.

81. R. Parker has stressed the problems associated with the public/private distinction with regard to Greek religion, remarking, "Antitheses of this type sometimes appear in Greek texts, and may have clear meanings in specific contexts; but a general distinction between 'public' and 'private' in religion cannot be maintained" (1996, 5). A number of conferences have been devoted to the relationship between religion and the categories public and private with subsequent publications, for example, de Polignac and Schmitt Pantel, 1998; Dasen and Piérart, 2005; Macé, 2012. Cf. Kindt's 2009 and 2012 critiques of "*polis* religion."

82. For the month Ἀδωνιών attested for the Argive colony Iasus, see Hicks 1888, 342.

83. We have no record that the Adonia took place in a public building at Athens, though when Pausanias discusses Argos and the sanctuary of Zeus Sôtêr, he reports a structure (οἴκημα) nearby where the women lamented Adonis (2.20.6). Pausanias also mentions a joint temple (ἱερόν) of Adonis and Aphrodite at Amathus on Cyprus (9.41.2); see also Aupert 2008. Cf. [Lucian]'s *de dea syria* 6 (Byblos); Steph. Byz. s.v. Ἀλεξάνδρειαι p. 71.14–15 Mein., for an Ἀδώνιον in Alexandria in Latmos (in Caria). For recent discussion (with bibliography) of the second-century CE temple that Adonis shared with Atargatis in Dura Europos (the only securely identified temple to Adonis), see Lightfoot 2003, 53–56.

84. A scholion reports (*Lysistrata* 389 Hangard) on Ἀδωνιασμός that women celebrated sacrifices (θυσίαι) that were "not at public expense and irregular" (οὐ δημοτελεῖς οὐδὲ τεταγμένας). As R. Parker remarks, "The most important Greek word that suggests the idea of 'public' cult is δημοτελής, 'paid for by the people,' which can be applied to sacrifices, festivals, sacred precincts, and even gods" (1996, 5). The rites at the Adonia, then, were "*not* paid for by the people" (οὐ δημοτελεῖς). Yet this does not mean that the Adonia lacked public characteristics.

85. Cf. R. Parker 2005, 284.

86. For lamentation, Alexiou's ([1974] 2002) seminal account remains influential. See also Monsacré 1984; Holst-Warhaft 1992; Murnaghan 1999; Derderian 2001; Foley 2001; Pantelia 2002; Dué 2002, 2006; Tsagalis 2004; Suter 2008. Simms (1997–98) is one of the few to underscore the role of lamentation at the Adonia. She argues that women who mourned Adonis were lamenting their own losses, such as family members who died during the Peloponnesian War. I build on her work to suggest that women at the Adonia are not simply mourning but are offering dissident messages on cultural practices, publicly and audibly, through the ritual.

87. Foley points out that "a non-Western or rural Mediterranean audience, for example, might well respond differently and . . . more appropriately to the complex variety of scenes

revolving around death rites and lamentation in tragedy, instinctively seeing in them a far greater range of purpose and nuance. South Africans or Palestinians, for example, would know that funerals are often political events, opportunities to foment revolution, resistance, or revenge under the cover of one of the few mass events that those in authority do not feel comfortable in suppressing altogether, even if they do their best to control them" (2001, 21). For Plato and lament, see, e.g., *Laws* 959e–960a, where the Athenian stranger forbids loud mourning outside the house, as well as lamentation during the *ekphora*. The funeral party is required to be outside city limits before the sun rises. See Morrow 1960, 368–69, on *thrênos* in *Laws*. In *Republic*, we have a "mournful part" (τοῦ θρηνώδους) in our soul that must be carefully watched over (606a–b). The guardians should not be allowed to imitate women, especially a woman "in misfortune and possessed by grief and mourning" (ἐν ξυμφοραῖς τε καὶ πένθεσι καὶ θρήνοις ἐχομένην, *Republic* 395e).

88. On the legislation, see Alexiou (1974) 2002, 14–23; Humphreys 1983; Garland 1989, 1–15; Holst-Warhaft 1992, 114–19; Rehm 1994, chapters 1–2; Foley 2001.

89. Of course the laws may have been attributed to Solon after the fact. Regarding legislation attributed to Solon, it is always difficult, if not impossible, to judge what the historical Solon did, because of the tendency for later Athenians to attribute all manner of laws and reforms to him. See, e.g., I. Morris 1989, 50; Frost 2002, 41; Noussia Fantuzzi 2010, 19–21. The legislation allegedly passed by Solon is mentioned by three different ancient authors: [Demosthenes] *Against Macartatus*, 43.62; Cicero *Laws* 2.59; and Plutarch *Solon* 21.

90. I. Morris comments, "The traditions, even if the details are quite wrong, suggest that the *poleis* felt threatened by lavish funerary expenditure, which in turn suggests not only that the scale of rites was being used by the wealthy as a symbol of power and status, but, most importantly, that it was understood by the community as a whole as an overt statement on the social order and the relative significance of its members" (1989, 51). Cf. Garland 1985, 121. For women as primary targets of the legislation, see Foley 2001, 22; Garland states, "The stress on the part played by women at funerals is highly significant. As all three testimonies indicate, it was a characteristic of Solon's legislation, as of all funerary legislation, that many of the provisions were aimed primarily at women. There can be no doubt that in Greece, as commonly throughout the Mediterranean to this day, the task of mourning the dead fell chiefly to women, whose displays of grief, unless checked, might amount to a social nuisance," (1989, 4–5). Cf. Humphreys, who remarks, "Convention required that men should maintain self-control in mourning, whereas women were encouraged to display wild grief: therefore to restrict female participation in *prothesis* and funeral procession *ekphora* to kin and women over sixty markedly reduced both the aural and the visual impact of the procession" (1980, 100).

91. Cf. the burial of Hector's body after nine days in book 24 of the *Iliad*.

92. Solon's laws insist that only the person who is being buried be mourned (Plutarch's *Solon* 21). It is evident as early as Homer's *Iliad* that a funeral was an opportunity for women to bemoan their own fate or the death of another loved one (ὣς ἔφατο κλαίουσ', ἐπὶ δὲ στενάχοντο γυναῖκες / Πάτροκλον πρόφασιν, σφῶν δ' αὐτῶν κήδε' ἑκάστη, "So she spoke, weeping, and the women groaned in response. They mourned for Patroclus, but also each

bemoaned her own sorrows," 19.302–3). Cf. Garland 1989, 4. Plutarch provides a historical context for the legislation, explaining that it came about because of the feuding that resulted after Cylon was assassinated by Megacles. Garland remarks, "The clear implication is that funerals were being used to foment jealous rivalries between kin groups" (1989, 4). Similarly, Alexiou comments, "In the inflammatory atmosphere of the blood feud between the families of Megakles and Kylon that was raging in Solon's time, what more effective way could there be to stir up feelings of revenge than the incessant lamentation at the tomb by large numbers of women for 'those long dead'?" ([1974] 2002, 21).

93. Foley 2001, 25. From the Archaic to the Classical period, we see restrictions on private death rituals as new forms develop, like the state funeral for the war dead at Athens. On the state funeral, see, e.g., Loraux 1986 and chapter 3. In other *poleis*, sixth-century hero cults involving public lamentation replace aristocratic clan cults. See Seaford 1994, chapter 4, who argues that Athenian tragedy allows for collective mourning as the hero cults did in other *poleis*. Funerals continue to present volatile possibilities in Xenophon's *Hellenica* (1.7.8), where Theramenes dresses up relatives in funeral garb to stir up the assembly after Arginusae.

94. For lament in Homer, see also Dué 2002, 2006; Tsagalis 2004. For *thrênos* in tragedy, see Holst-Warhaft 1992; Suter 2008; Swift 2010.

95. For Helen's general association with lamentation, see Richard Martin 2008.

96. Foley 2001, 33. See also her discussions of Sophocles's *Electra* and *Antigone*.

97. Foley 2001, 27. Karanika suggests that Attic tragedy uses lament "as women used it in real life, namely, to utter a voice on public matters" (2008, 181).

98. Adonis has no identity apart from Aphrodite, and the Adonia is by its very nature linked to Adonis as well as Aphrodite (cf. Σ *Peace* 420c Holwerda). The late paroemiographer [Diogen.] 1.14 indicates that the festival is celebrated solely in honor of Aphrodite. Contra Reed (1995, 318, 320), who argues that the festival was celebrated in honor of Adonis alone at Athens during the Classical period. Few public buildings are attested for Adonis at all, but those that are mentioned tend to be joint temples of Aphrodite and Adonis (as seen earlier).

99. For a detailed and authoritative account of Aphrodite, see Pirenne-Delforge 1994. For critiques of the view of Aphrodite as goddess of love and beauty, see, e.g., Pirenne-Delforge 2010a; Pironti 2010.

100. Pironti (2007, 2010) connects Aphrodite to warfare, and especially to Ares. For Aphrodite and the Athenian fleet, see Papadopoulou 2010. For Aphrodite's political role in connection with the island of Thasos, see Croissant and Salviat 1966. Cf. Sokolowski 1964. For thorough discussion of the Athenian Aphrodite, see Pirenne-Delforge 1994, 15–82.

101. On participant identification with Aphrodite at the Adonia, see Stehle 1996, 217, and Lardinois 2001, 77. Reed remarks, "Once a year in the privacy of her own home, she could be Aphrodite" (1995, 346). As a discussion of the important role of lamentation at the Adonia has demonstrated, however, the Adonis festival is not limited to the privacy of the home. On the identification of ritual participants with original actors, see Kowalzig, who has suggested that a suspension of time occurs with regard to festival *aitia*, as participants in some festivals oscillate between being themselves in real time, on the one hand, and

performing a mythical role, on the other: "The key to understanding the social efficacy of myth and ritual lies in the collapse of the distinction between mythical past and ritual present in choral performances, allowing for a continuous reformulation of the worshipping group that any given song delineates. Myth-ritual performances thus lend themselves to radical redefinitions of social and power relations within the worshipping group that myth and ritual claim to embrace" (2007b, 8). Cf. R. Parker 2011, 199–200.

102. For work on women as ritual agents, see Gilhuly 2009. Winkler 1990, like Connelly 2007, is interested in ritual practice as a space of empowerment for women. He emphasizes women's dissident role, as does Goff 2004.

103. Connelly 2007.

104. Stehle 1996, 225.

105. Reed comments that the poem "simulates a funereal lament with a leader (Bion's narrator) and a responding chorus" (1997, 196).

106. Prauscello 2006, 61n55.

107. See Hordern 2003, 612, for the spectacle of the festival. Demostratus's wife is dancing atop the roof (ὀρχουμένη, 392) in *Lysistrata*, as is a group of women celebrating the Adonis festival in Menander's *Samia*. ὠρχο]ῦντ' (46) is West's suggestion, followed by Sandbach. In Classical Athenian vase painting, too, the Adonia is associated with music and dancing. The Meidias Painter's hydria (fig. 1, discussed in chapter 2), which features Adonis and Aphrodite relaxing in a garden surrounded by female figures, includes Pannychis (All-Night-Festival), her *tympanon*, and a dancing Himeros, and on other vases associated with the Adonia, dancers appear, along with various musical instruments: *krotala*, *tympana*, and *auloi*. For *Auloi*: figs. 8, 9. *Krotala*: figs. 8 and 14. *Tympana*: figs. 7 and 9. Dancers: fig. 8. For music and the Adonia, see Servais-Soyez 1984. The youth was so bound up with an instrument called the *gingras*, a shrill pipe used by the Phoenicians in mourning songs, that he himself was called Gingras (Athenaeus *Deipn.* 174f–175a). See Atallah 1966, 187–88, for the suggestion that the pipes depicted on the British Museum hydria (fig. 8) and the aryballos lekythos from Berlin (fig. 9) are examples of the *gingras*. Not only is Adonis associated with a musical instrument, but the name of Adonis's father, Kinyras, also seems to be related to an Ugaritic word for lyre. See Baurain 1980; West 1997, 57.

108. For the importance of *choreia*, one has only to think of Plato's *Laws*, where choral performance is the hallmark of an educated individual (654a–b). For a recent discussion of chorality and Plato's *Laws*, see Kowalzig 2013. For the possibility that women were involved in choral performances at the Anthesteria, see Bravo 1997; P. Wilson 2000, 32.

109. Kowalzig 2004, 48.

110. Budelmann and Power 2015.

111. Scholarship on *choreia* is immense; see, e.g., Calame (1977) 2001; Stehle 1997; P. Wilson 2000.

112. On the alignment of choral harmony with civic harmony (and vice versa), see, e.g., Calame (1977) 2001; Nagy 1990, 338–80; Stehle 1997. Within the so-called Debate of the Constitutions, for example, Herodotus uses a choral metaphor to characterize civic discord (3.82.3), as competitive individuals within the ruling elite (oligarchs) each wish to

become κορυφαῖος, "leading figure." The term κορυφαῖος is a general one and is related to κορυφή, "top" or "summit," but it also functions to describe choral performance during the fifth century and means "chorus leader." In the Herodotus passage, the political struggle between competitive individuals—which is cast specifically as a choral competition—results in feuding, civil strife, murder, and eventually leads to monarchy. The passage emphasizes a "complete interpenetration of political and choral domains" (Kurke 2007, 78). See also Nagy 1990, 368–69. The notion of a discordant chorus also appears in Plato's *Laws* (662b), when the Athenian stranger wishes to emphasize that the interlocutors disagree. Agreement would be possible, he says, εἰ θεὸς ἡμῖν, ὡς ἔοικεν, ὦ φίλοι, δοίη τις συμφωνίαν, ὡς νῦν γε σχεδὸν ἀπᾴδομεν ἀπ' ἀλλήλων, "if a god should grant to us, as it seems, musical concord, since now we sing at discord with one another."

113. For characters on the rooftops, see the opening lines of Aeschylus's *Agamemnon* and Aristophanes's *Wasps*. For rooftop space in Athenian drama and the tendency for divinities to inhabit the space, see Mastronarde 1990.

114. For Adonis's Eastern connections, in particular, the Greek view of Adonis as effeminate (opposed to Greek concepts of masculinity), see Ribichini 1979, 1981.

115. Cf. Robertson 1982, 322; Reed 1995, 328; West 1997, 57. Robertson (1982, 340–42) argues that attestation of the Corinthian month Phoinikaios is evidence for an Adonia in Corinth.

116. Panyassis's "Assyria" is likely used loosely, since in ancient sources it may refer to any region at one time under the control of the Assyrian Empire. Cf. Reed 1995, 329.

117. Panyassis used the name Ἠοίης for Adonis (Hesychius s.v. Ἠοίην). Ἠοίης is an epic form of the Cypriot name for Adonis Ἀῷος, and from this Matthews (1974, 123) argues for Cypriot connections in Panyassis's account. It is thought that Adonis reached mainland Greece by way of Cyprus. See, e.g., Nock (1934) 1986, 291.

118. Cf. Atallah (1966, 315), who points out that to account for the origin of the cult and myth of Adonis is challenging in the extreme—all we can say with certainty is that Adonis is attested in mainland Greece in the middle of the fifth century BCE and during the sixth century among Greeks in Ionia.

119. For Adonis as Eastern in the minds of Athenians, see Detienne (1972) 1994, 128.

120. For Adonis and *adôn*, see Burkert 1979, 105–6, 192n3, 193n15; 1985, 177; Lipiński 1995, 90; West 1997, 57. See Atallah 1966, 303–8, for arguments against other etymologies of Adonis's name, especially that of Kretschmer 1915, and cf. Baudissin 1911, 65–71. The Greeks were calling the youth Adonis by the Archaic period as seen in Sappho's fragment. Still, in different regions, he continued to be known by other names. Cf. Atallah 1966, 306; Rudhardt 1975, 119–20; Burkert 1979, 106–107; Pirenne-Delforge 1994, 365. He was known as Abobas in Perge, Pamphylia (Hesychius, s.v. Ἀβώβας). According to Athenaeus (4.174), the Phoenicians called him Γίγγρας. On Cyprus he was known as Ἀῷος (*FGrH* 758 fr. 7 = *Etym. Magn.* Gaisdorf 117.33, and see Matthews 1974, 123) and Γαυάς (*FGrH* 758 fr. 8; Σ Lycophron, *Alexandra* 831), among other names.

121. Tammuz and Ishtar replace Sumerian Dumuzi and Inanna under the Akkadians. See Burkert 1979, 105–11; Penglase 1994, 177–78; Brown 1995, 244–46; Reed 1995, 317–21;

West 1997, 57; Anagnostou-Laoutides and Konstan 2008. Jerome identifies Tammuz with Adonis (*Epist.* 58.3).

122. Burkert 1979, 106; Reed 1995, 317–18; R. Parker 2005, 284.

123. Burkert 1979, 105–11; Baudy 1986, 37–38; Reed 1995, 317–18.

124. Burkert 1979, 110; Penglase 1994, 179; Reed 1995, 330.

125. For problems with the text and attribution to Lucian, see Lightfoot 2003, 184–208; Oden 1977, 7–14, 41–43, 46.

126. The earliest evidence that connects the Adonia and Adonis to Byblos is Lycophron's *Alexandra* (third century BCE), where the "city of Myrrha" is Byblos (828–33 and Σ 829, 831). Cf. Strabo 16.2.18. See Soyez 1977, 9–12. As Lightfoot (2003, 307) explains, Adonis appears in Byblos precisely at the time when Greek authors begin to be interested in Byblos, after Alexander's conquest of the city.

127. On Adonis's grave, see Σ Lyc. 831 (who reports that it was in Byblos) and Σ Dionysius Periegeta 509. For the river Adonis, see Strabo 16.2.19; Ptol. *Geog.* 5.15.4; Jo. Lyd. *Mens.* 4.64, p. 119 Wünsch; Nonnus *Dion.* 3.107–9; 4.81–82; 20.144; 31.127. On the discoloration of the river, see Soyez (1977, esp. 44–75), who suggests a connection with the Nile flood, and see Lightfoot's arguments against this theory (2003, 316–17).

128. The building has not been securely identified. As we have seen, evidence for public buildings for the Adonia is scanty and certainly does not appear in Athens, where rooftop celebration was the norm.

129. Lightfoot remarks, "Near Eastern sources do reveal that this Adonis—even if a synthetic Greek creation—was carried back and implanted in Syria under his Greek name. What is next to impossible to determine in each case is the extent to which he is an import, and that to which he overlies some indigenous deity" (2003, 307).

130. The decrees are dated to 302/301, 301/300, and 300/299 BCE. For discussions, see Foucart 1879; Deubner (1932) 1969, 222; Meritt 1935; Reed 1995, 318; Simms 1985, 264–73; 1997–98, 125n24; Baslez 1986, 303. R. Parker 1996, 160–61n29; Dillon 2002, 168–69; Kloppenborg and Ascough 2011, 59–65; Demetriou 2013, 221–22.

131. Baslez (1986, 303) connects the sacrifice and procession described in the inscription to the ritual at Byblos.

132. Foucart 1879, 514; Dillon 2002, 168–69.

133. For discussions of the inscription, see Tod 1948, 250–51; Baslez 1986, 293; Rhodes and Osborne 2007, no. 91; Kloppenborg and Ascough 2011, 26–32. ἔγκτησις meant that foreigners could own land and establish a temple on private land. The cult would then not be recognized as official, but it was publicly acknowledged. Cf., e.g., Demetriou 2013, 202.

134. R. Parker 1996, 160–61n29. For the Aphrodite and Astarte cult on Cyprus, see Nicolaou 1976, 105–8. A fifth-century BCE metic had the name Adonis. He was a goldsmith from Melite and earned 166 drachmas for 166 gilding leaves on the rosettes on the ceiling of the north porch of the Erechtheion (*IG* I^3 476.291–95, 301–2). Dillon suggests that this may be connected with the Kitians and their temple of Aphrodite (2002, 340–41n184). It is possible that *IG* II^2 337 refers to a cult of Aphrodite Ourania (Garland 2001, 112–13; Kloppenborg and Ascough 2011, 31). Two fourth-century dedications to Aphrodite

Ourania from Piraeus date from approximately the time when the sanctuary was founded (*IG* II^2 4636; 4637).

135. See, e.g., R. Parker 1996, 160–61n29; Demetriou 2013, 226.

136. Cf. Reed 1995, 318; Dillon 2002, 168–69; Kloppenborg and Ascough 2011, 62; Demetriou 2013, 222. For the importance of inscriptions to the study of Greek religion, see R. Parker 2012. Unfortunately, in the case of the Adonia, the epigraphic evidence does not help us out that much.

Chapter 2. Weddings

1. Karlsruhe, Badisches Landesmuseum B39; BAD 361; *CVA* Karlsruhe 1 Germany 7 32–33, pl. 27.1–4; *LIMC* I pl. 169, Adonis 47; Nicole 1908, pl. 8.3; Deubner 1932, pl. 25.1; Bérard and Bron 1989, 97, fig. 131; Rosenzweig 2004, fig. 46; Oakley and Reitzammer 2005, pl. 7; Parker 2005, 285, fig. 15. Edwards (1984) remarks that denial of the Karlsruhe lekythos's association with the Adonia would be "perverse," 62 and 71. Oakley and Sinos characterize it as "the only clear example of Adonis cult" (1993, 139n8). R. Parker explains, "not every vase showing a woman on a ladder need relate to the *Adonia*, but one on which an Eros passes a 'garden' planted on half a pot to a woman is perhaps the clearest illustration of a specific festival that survives to us" (2005, 284). For other recent discussions of the vase, see also Bérard and Bron 1989, 96–97; Reeder 1995, 236–38; Dillon 2002, 162–63.

2. The gardens of Adonis depicted on the Karlsruhe lekythos are remarkably similar to the garden that appears on a Hellenistic terracotta figurine (fig. 23), as well as the middle vessel depicted on an acorn lekythos from Athens (fig. 21), both discussed later.

3. Identified as Aphrodite, see, e.g., Edwards 1984, 71; Oakley and Sinos 1993, 40; Dillon 2002, 162. *Possibly* Aphrodite, according to Reed 1995, 320; Reeder 1995, 238.

4. The challenge of separating mythical elements from contemporary religious practice in scenes that depict ritual is similar to the problems associated with separating true genre scenes (scenes from daily life) from mythical scenes in vase painting more generally, see, e.g., G. Ferrari 2002, 2003. Cf. Lissarrague 2012.

5. The ladder cannot be seen in figs. 11 and 13. In fig. 11, the ladder appears to the right of the photographed scene and is only partially preserved. In fig. 13, the ladder is to the right of the central seated figure who is being crowned. The vases were made in Athens and found scattered in disparate locations, e.g., Italy, Bulgaria, and Libya. Metzger (1951, 99) suggests that individuals may have traveled to Athens, participated in the Adonia, and then returned home with a vase, as a kind of souvenir. For a discussion of the grapes depicted in figure 6 and the relationship to the Adonia, see introduction. Figure 7: red-figure aryballos lekythos, St. Petersburg, State Hermitage Museum 928; *ARV*^{2} 1482.6, 1695; *Addenda*^{2} 382; BAD 230498; *LIMC* I Adonis 48a. Figure 8: red-figure hydria, London, British Museum E241; *ARV*^{2} 1482.1, 1695; *Addenda*^{2} 382; BAD 230493; *CVA* London, British Museum 6 III, pls. 96.4, 97.4 (371, 372); *LIMC* I Adonis 48b; Rosenzweig 2004, fig. 47; Kaltsas and Shapiro 2008, 246, fig. 3. Figure 9: red-figure aryballos lekythos, Berlin, Antikensammlung 3248; *ARV*^{2} 1482.5, 1695; *Addenda*^{2} 382; BAD 230497; *LIMC* I Adonis 48; Rosenzweig 2004, fig. 48.

Figure 10: red-figure lekythos, London, British Museum E 721; BAD 44575. Figure 11: red-figure hydria, attributed to the Meidias Painter, Athens, National Museum 1179; *ARV*[2] 1312.3; *Paralipomena* 477; *Addenda*[2] 361; BAD 220495; Nicole 1908, pl. 4. Figure 12: red-figure aryballos lekythos, New York, Metropolitan Museum 22.139.26; BAD 6986; *LIMC* I Adonis 49; Deubner 1932, pl. 25.1; Richter and Hall 1936, pl. 168. Figure 13: red-figure lebes gamikos, Athens, National Museum 1454; *ARV*[2] 1178.1, 1685; *Paralipomena* 460; BAD 215616; Oakley and Sinos 1993, figs. 28–29. Figure 14: red-figure skyphos, Athens, National Museum 1960-NAK 222; *LIMC* I Adonis 48c. Figure 15: fragment of a red-figure hydria or stamnos, Athens, National Museum 19522; *Paralipomena* 400; *Addenda*[2] 272; BAD 275774; *LIMC* I Adonis 45; Rosenzweig 2004, fig. 51; Kaltsas and Shapiro 2008, 260, no. 119.

6. Although lekythoi and hydriai are vases that may be used by women, and the lebes gamikos was a vase used in a nuptial context, it is difficult to establish a connection between vase imagery and shape. On such challenges, see, e.g., G. Ferrari 2002, 9; and Topper 2012a.

7. The controversy seems to have originated with discussions between Jahn (1845) and de Witte (1846). It continued with Nicole 1908; Hauser 1909; Metzger 1951; Neppi Modona 1951–54; Atallah 1966. For more-recent discussions, see Servais-Soyez 1981; Edwards 1984; Simms 1985; Oakley and Sinos 1993, 39–40; Pirenne-Delforge 1994, 21–25; Rosenzweig 2004; Kaltsas and Shapiro 2008.

8. Weill remarks, "En définitive, un détail à lui seul autorise à conclure qu'un tableau de ce genre évoque bien les Adonies: c'est l'échelle, que les Ἀδωνιάζουσαι empruntent pour monter jusqu'aux toits" (1966, 671).

9. See Neppi Modona 1951–54; Edwards 1984. Dillon (2002, 168) identifies figure 6 as a wedding scene (he does not discuss the other vases). For a general discussion of the *epaulia*, see Oakley and Sinos 1993, especially 38–42.

10. For women's quarters and challenges faced in locating them given our scant evidence, see Jameson 1990, 104; Oakley and Sinos 1993, 39, 139n7. For more-recent scholarship on ancient Greek houses, see, e.g., Nevett 1999, 2010; Ault 2005; Ault and Nevett 2005; Morgan 2010. For houses at Olynthus (a site that has provided scholars with a tremendous amount of information about ancient Greek houses), see Cahill 2002.

11. Pirenne-Delforge explains, "L'échelle signifie l'action d'Aphrodite *Ourania*, à la fois dans les représentations religieuses dont le symbolisme astral est patent, et dans les illustrations de la vie quotidienne: *Ourania*, qui unit la terre au ciel, réunit l'homme et la femme" (1994, 23). Cf. Oakley and Sinos 1993, 39–40; Rosenzweig 2004, 66–67.

12. Naples H 3256 (81.667) Dareios Painter. *LIMC* II Aphrodite 1406. For the ladder as an attribute of Aphrodite, see Pirenne-Delforge 1994, 23; cf. Edwards 1984, 68.

13. For the xylophone, see Cumont 1917, 101–2; Keuls 1979; Nelson 1986; West 1992, 126–28.

14. Salapata 2002, 420. Cf. Salapata 2001, where she discusses the relief iconography on two terracotta altars, identifying two of the figures depicted as Aphrodite and Adonis. In addition to Aphrodite and Adonis, three female figures appear in procession, one holding a *tympanon*, another holding the xylophone/ladder object. An Apulian lebes gamikos in Sydney (Nicholson Museum 83.4) depicts a youth who has been convincingly identified as

Adonis in an *anodos* scene. A female figure to his left holds the xylophone object. See also Cambitoglou's (2009) discussion of a pelike in Naples attributed to the Painter of the Copenhagen Dancer (National Museum, 3224 inv. 82302, *RVAp* II, 509, 18/127). Cambitoglou identifies Adonis (though no inscription appears) and a female figure above him holds the xylophone in her right hand.

15. Ultimately, Pirenne-Delforge (1994, 24) also interprets the scenes that Edwards (1984) had tied to the *epaulia* (figs. 6, 11, 13, and 15) as wedding scenes, when she remarks that the images that depict boxes and fruit must represent a wedding and not an Adonia, because it is hard to believe boxes and fruit would be taken up to the roof.

16. For the phrase preserved by Menander, and for agricultural metaphors in weddings, see chapter 1, n51. For the anti-agricultural function of the Adonia, see, e.g., Detienne (1972) 1994, esp. 102–5; Goff 2004, 59.

17. Cf. Gow 1952, 301. The adjective is used of Eos in Sappho's poetry (58.19 Voigt). Cf. West 2005; Greene and Skinner 2010.

18. For the age of the bride and the groom, see Hesiod *Works and Days* 696–98; Solon 27.9–10 (West); Plato *Republic* 460e, *Laws* 721b–d, 772d–e, 785b; Aristotle *Politics* 7.1335a27–30.

19. For example, Reed comments, "In myth Adonis is for [Aphrodite] only a romantic diversion, not a consort" (1995, 320).

20. Adonis is never called "bride"; yet it is challenging to categorize Adonis, and written texts trace this challenge. As we will see, he is *habros* in Sappho (fr. 140 Voigt), a word that may be used to describe a bride. In Bion's *Epitaph on Adonis*, Adonis is called "boy" (παῖδα, 18) as well as "husband" (πόσιν, 24, 54; ἄνδρα, 29). Throughout the poem (with great obsession), he is characterized as *kalos*, and he is described as "white" (8, 10, 27), an adjective that is commonly used of women (cf. Reed 1997, 199). In Lucian's *Dialogues of the Gods*, Adonis is called *erômenos* of Aphrodite (19); so too in Alciphron's *Letters of Courtesans* (4.14). The *erastês/erômenos* metaphor coexists with the groom/bride metaphor, since maidens (*parthenoi*) and young men are regularly described as similar. See, e.g., G. Ferrari 2002, 91 (Bacchylides 17 provides a good example, since for part of the poem there is a conflation between maidens and young boys, all of whom Minos desires).

21. Rather than describing the union of Aphrodite and Adonis as a "perverted" marriage, I prefer to speak of the gender roles as inverted, as R. Parker (2005, 287) does. To say that the union of Aphrodite and Adonis is "perverted" assumes that one form of union is the norm, while the other is deviant. This is to assume the normative point of view, rather than addressing it.

22. On Aphrodite and *aphrodisia*, see, e.g., Pirenne-Delforge 2010a. For "the works of Aphrodite" (ἔργα Ἀφροδίτης) as "sex," see, e.g., Hesiod *Works and Days*, 521; see also J. S. Clay 1989, 156.

23. For *pothos* and *himeros*, see, e.g., *Iliad* 23.14; 24.507; *Odyssey* 4.113 and 183, 10.398; see also Vermeule 1979. For *terpsis*, see *Iliad* 23.10, 98; *Odyssey* 11.212; cf. 19.213; 21.57. Cf. Euripides *Andromache*, 91–95. For the erotic dimension of lament, see Dué 2006, 75.

24. See Richard Martin, who argues that throughout the *Iliad* and the *Odyssey* Helen's language evokes lament. He remarks, "Her other speeches, even though they are

not called laments, more often than not contain the strategies and phrases of that genre" (2008, 122).

25. Dué (2002, 74) emphasizes the evocation of the role of wife in the Briseis passage (19.282), as well as in two passages from the *Odyssey* where Penelope is compared to Aphrodite (17.36–37; 19.53–54). Although I suggest that the goddess-mortal relationship lies beneath the moments when mourning women are compared to Aphrodite, as will become clear, the goddess-mortal relationship incorporates nuptial elements. For slightly different but important connections between lament and Adonis, see Dué 2006, 68–69, 70–73, 75.

26. For lament in Homer, see Murnaghan 1999; Pantelia 2002; Dué 2002, 2006. Derderian argues that lament functions as a complement to heroic activity in epic poetry and "becomes the linguistic and generic inverse of heroic *kleos*" (2001, 32). For a recent discussion of *thrênos*, see Swift 2010, 298–366, and see further chapter 1.

27. Diggle 1970, 151. G. Ferrari (2008) disagrees and suggests that the one who is hidden in the ether refers not to Hymenaeus but to Phaethon.

28. Cf. Zeitlin 1996, 249n65.

29. Pindar fr. 128 Maehler. Cf. a fragment from Euripides *Phaethon* (227–35 Diggle).

30. On the cult, see W. S. Barrett 1964, 3–6.

31. Stehle 1996. On goddesses and mortals, see also Giacomelli [Carson] 1980 and Williamson 1995.

32. Stehle 1996, 202. Stehle comments, "The story's potential for subverting the male/female hierarchy must have been felt" (1996, 209). Just as the goddess who desires a mortal male is beset by problems not experienced by male divinities who rape mortal women, similarly, attempts by goddesses to produce children apart from male gods typically result in problems associated with these offspring, e.g., Hera's production of Typhaon (*Homeric Hymn to Apollo*) and Hephaestus (Hesiod *Theogony*).

33. Youths paired with goddesses tend to be beautiful in similar ways. For Tithonus's beauty, see Ibycus *PMG* 289, Tyrtaeus 12.5 (West), and Sappho 58.11 Voigt (cf. West 2005; Greene and Skinner 2010). Cf. Selene's description of Endymion in Lucian *Dialogues of the Gods* 232. *Kalos Adonis* appears repeatedly as a refrain at line endings in Bion's *Epitaph on Adonis*.

34. Stehle 1996, 195. Stehle describes Adonis (and structurally similar males) as a "non-man" (1996, 207). She explains, "If a man who is subordinate to a goddess is also subordinate to another man, then his position with respect to the goddess does not establish a model of female control that would threaten the male/female hierarchy" (1996, 206). Winkler remarks, "He whom a goddess loves ceases to be a phallic man, enters instead a state of permanent detumescence" (1990, 204).

35. The structural equivalence can be seen, for instance, in the fact that in each case the goddess "abducts" her paramour. Cf. Nagy 1973, 157. Eos abducts Tithonus (*Homeric Hymn to Aphrodite* 218; Sappho's Tithonus poem, fr. 58); Eos Cleitus (*Odyssey* 15.250); Eos Orion (*Odyssey* 5.121–24); Aphrodite Phaethon (Hesiod *Theogony*, 988–90); Eos Cephalus (Euripides *Hippolytus* 455).

36. Inasmuch as brides are frequently likened to wild animals (unyoked horses, fillies, etc.), this passage may speak to the dysfunctional marital paradigm within which Circe is

working, because she wishes to turn Odysseus into an animal so that she may then tame him.

37. Cf. Stehle: "[Odysseus's] escape can therefore be read as his triumph. Narrative in this case requires male predominance over the immobilizing goddess" (1996, 204).

38. See, e.g., the word used to describe Zeus in his relationship with Hera in Homer's *Iliad* 15.91. Cf. Sophocles *Trachiniae* 525.

39. The word seems to be composed of alpha-privative and the word μένος. On the valence of ἀμενηνός, see Giacomelli [Carson], who remarks, "Beginning from the image of the movement of the male seed, the Greeks characterize as μένος that which moves as shooting fluid in nature, in the human body, or in the spirit" (1980, 4). Μένος, then, is a word of broad valence, used to refer to life force or vital energy, including sperm. Cf. J. S. Clay 1989, 182–83.

40. See Giacomelli [Carson] 1980; J. S. Clay 1989, 199–200. Cf. Gow 1952, 23–24; Sophocles *TrGF* 4 (Radt) fr. 373.2–3; Vergil *Aeneid*, 2.649, Servius *ad loc* and 1.617.

41. On the boar, lettuce, and Adonis, see chapter 1.

42. Although Stehle (1996) does not discuss marital elements in her examination of the goddess-mortal relationship, Winkler briefly alludes to (though does not explore) the "marriage" of a goddess and mortal when he remarks that the pattern "is a reversal of the patrilocal or virilocal pattern prevalent (though not universal) in Greek towns" (1990, 203); he also suggests that "the implied permanence of the union [goddess-mortal] makes it a quasi-marriage" (203).

43. See, e.g., Euripides *Trojan Women* 445 (Cassandra); *Hecuba* 368 (Polyxena). The "marriage to death" is the focus of Rehm's 1994 investigation. See also, e.g., Seaford 1987. Cf. Phrasikleia *IG* I^3 1261.

44. Cf. Rehm 1994, 36.

45. Rehm 1994, 59–71.

46. A fourth-century epigram by Erinna (GP 1789–1796 = *AP* 7.712) is particularly representative of this tendency. The shift from wedding to funeral is a common theme in Hellenistic epigrams. See GP on line 1793; cf. Lattimore 1962, 192–94.

47. Alexiou and Dronke 1971; Alexiou (1974) 2002, 120–22; Vermeule 1979, 145–78; Redfield 1982, 188–91; Burkert 1983, 58–67; Jenkins 1983; Loraux 1987, 23–42; Seaford 1987; Dowden 1989; Barringer 1991; Rehm 1994. G. Ferrari (2002, 190–94; 2004, 255, 258, which includes discussion of the *Antigone* passage mentioned earlier) offers a welcome adjustment to what has become a commonplace in scholarship, as she argues that, despite their fundamental correspondences, marriage and death were construed not as equivalent but as opposites. She makes the important point that marriage is reversible while death is not and that when the bride dies something has gone fundamentally wrong, a point that is frequently ignored. I suggest that a distinction is to be made between marriage from the point of view of the male participant—where marriage may in fact be seen as the opposite of death—and from the perspective of the bride—where marriage is figured as a symbolic death.

48. Rehm explains that "on occasion weddings and funerals intermingle to such an extent that the two rites become inseparable" (1994, 4).

49. Wedding and funeral loutrophoroi are remarkably similar (though with different iconography) and are used only for these two rituals.

50. "Hades" is always short for "the house of Hades" in Homer and tragedy. Hesiod's *Theogony* presents Tartarus as a place where the divinities are imagined to live in houses (e.g., οἰκία, 744, 758; δόμος, 751). On the actions performed at weddings and funerals, see Rehm 1994, 11–29; for iconography, 30–42. For iconography associated with weddings, see also Oakley and Sinos 1993; for iconography associated with funerals on white-ground lekythoi, see Oakley 2004.

51. Seaford 1987, 106–7.

52. Cf. Bion's *Epitaph on Adonis*, 79; Nonnus *Dion.* 6.365; Proclus *H.* 1.26; ἁβροκόμης in [Orph] *H.* 56.2.

53. On the association of the adjective with the *parthenos*, see Chantraine 1968–80, 1:4–5; Lombardo 1983; Kurke 1992, 99. See Hesiod fr. 339 Merkelbach-West; Alcaeus fr. 42.8 L-P; Aeschylus *TrGF* fr. 313. Kurke argues that *habros* and related words like *habrosynê* have a particular valence during the archaic period and are bound up with a complicated negotiation for status and power. When Sappho proclaims, "I love *habrosynê*" (ἔγω δὲ φίλημμ' ἀβροσύναν, fr. 58.25 Voigt), she essentially means, "I align myself with an aristocratic elite that has strong ties with the East" (1992, 96). On *habros*, see also Nagy 1985, 60–63; 1990, 263–90.

54. Cf. *Idyll* 18, "Epithalamion of Helen," where Menelaus locks Helen in (κατεκλᾀξατο, 5), as a troop of twelve maidens sings outside the door, and where the same word for bride (νυός, 15) refers to Helen.

55. For discussion, see chapter 1.

56. For other appearances of the myth (in literature and iconography) in which Adonis is shared by Persephone and Aphrodite, see introduction and chapter 1.

57. For ἀνακαλέω (94) as a technical term for summoning the dead, see Reed 1997, 248.

58. For the textual problem in line 63, see Faulkner (2008, 146–48), who adopts the conjecture ἑδανῷ; see also West 2001, 2003; West translates the adjective as "bridal" (2001, 122–23 [with discussion], and 2003, 165). It is an epithet of oil.

59. ἄδμητος means literally "unsubdued," "untamed" and is an adjective commonly used in epic to describe animals that have not been broken; it is also used to describe a *parthenos* who has not yet been "mastered." See Olson 2012, 183. Cf. the similar adjective "unyoked," e.g., *Bacchae* 694 (παρθένοι . . . ἄζυγες).

60. See Murnaghan 2005 and further later in this discussion.

61. Cf. J. S. Clay: "Aphrodite has established her credentials as a nubile maiden of royal stock, who has been properly brought up and sheltered in accordance with the standards of aristocratic society; in addition to her evident beauty and desirability, she is a valuable commodity" (1989, 176).

62. For the evocation of the Circe episode, see Faulkner 2008, 222. Cf. J. S. Clay 1989, 179.

63. Faulkner 2008, 227.

64. See Foley 1994, 81; Murnaghan 2005. At Locri, a Greek colony in southern Italy, girls who were about to marry offered dedications to Persephone and Hades. For a discussion of this cult, see Sourvinou-Inwood 1991, 147–88; MacLachan 1995; Redfield 2003. Foley comments, "This cult was unique to this location but the use of the myth as a literary paradigm for marriage in Attic tragedy . . . indicates that the analogy was not confined to Greek Italy" (1994, 81n7, 80–81). Cf. Jenkins 1983.

65. See, e.g., Seaford 1987; Oakley and Sinos 1993, 13.

66. On a bride's physical movement to another household see, e.g., Osborne 1985, 127–53.

67. On the gesture, see Jenkins 1983; Oakley and Sinos 1993, 32, 45, 137n4, 141; Rehm 1994, 14. The description of the rape of Creusa evokes this gesture in Euripides *Ion* (ἐμφὺς καρποῖσιν / χειρῶν, 891–92).

68. Oakley and Sinos comment, "To try to distinguish between weddings and abductions may be a modern rather than an ancient concern" (1993, 13). They point out elsewhere that "the figure of a woman holding a wreath, a conventional way of depicting a bride, sometimes appears in scenes in which the woman is being pursued. The nuptial motif not only clarifies the sexual nature of the pursuit but also likens it to the legitimate form of sexual union, the wedding, much as in literature abductions are sometimes called 'weddings'" (1993, 8).

69. Foley 1994, 82.

70. G. Ferrari 2002, 181–86; 2004.

71. G. Ferrari argues against the prevailing etymological derivation of the word from *guion*, the "hollow" or "palm of the hand." Instead, she agrees with Chantraine that we should look to a derivation of the word from *gue*, *guia*, and *gualon*, "a group of terms that go back to the notion of 'hollow,' 'vault'" (2002, 184).

72. G. Ferrari 2002, 186. The process can go horribly wrong, and Seaford (1990) has examined examples of imprisoned and immured women in tragedy.

73. Ebbott 2003, 13–14.

74. Ebbott 2003, 16. See Lissarrague 1995 for boxes and chests depicted in vase painting, which he argues are associated with women's spaces and emphasize notions of interiority and confinement, e.g., the storage of the embryo in the womb.

75. Of course, *larnax* can also mean "coffin," and here the word certainly resonates within a funereal context as well. For the notion that placing a child in a container may indicate ritual adoption by the deity, see Sourvinou-Inwood 1978, 114–18 (she is discussing the cult of Persephone at Locri).

76. For Calypso and καλύπτειν, see Dimock 1962, 111. Although Aphrodite does not literally "cover" or "conceal" Anchises, such an action is perhaps hinted at in *Homeric Hymn to Aphrodite*. As soon as Anchises realizes that he has slept with a goddess (just before he begs her not to make him ἀμενηνός), he covers (καλύπτειν) his face in the blanket from his bed (183). A bit later, Aphrodite explains that old age will cover Anchises (νῦν δέ σε μὲν τάχα γῆρας ὁμοίιον ἀμφικαλύψει, 244). The goddess-mortal narrative marks an inversion of the concealment in the myth of Demeter and Korê, where Persephone moves beneath the

earth after Hades possesses her and is hidden from her mother. In response, Demeter "hides" the seed while Persephone is beneath the earth (*Homeric Hymn to Demeter* 307, 353).

77. For the popularity of goddesses and mortals during the Classical period, see Williamson 1995; Stehle 1996.

78. Plato *PCG* vii frs. 188–98; Antiphanes *PCG* ii fr. 213.

79. Cratinus *PCG* iv fr. 370.

80. Alcaeus *PCG* ii frs. 10–13. For Euripides *Phaethon*, see Diggle 1970.

81. For Athenian comedy and Adonis, see chapters 1 and 3.

82. Although fifth- and fourth-century vase painters could choose from a number of goddess-mortal stories, when they depicted scenes of female divinities and youths, they limited the subject to Eos and Tithonus (or Cephalus). On the confusion between Tithonus and Cephalus, see Weiss, *LIMC* III.1, 776–77. Attic vases include many examples of pursuit scenes in which immortals swoop down on hapless mortals. Most scenes, however, portray *male* gods paired with either mortal men or mortal women (e.g., Zeus and Ganymedes, Boreas and Oreithyia). The bibliography on pursuit scenes and, more specifically, scenes of goddesses abducting mortal men is extensive. See Kaempf-Dimitriadou 1979; Keuls 1985; Zeitlin 1986; Sourvinou-Inwood 1991; Shapiro 1992; Stewart 1995; Osborne 1996; Stehle 1996; Lefkowitz 2002; Topper 2007.

83. A few representations of Eos and her mortal lover appear to indicate a more reciprocal relationship; see Stehle 1996 for a discussion.

84. An exception is the late fourth-century BCE bronze mirror support from Locri (London, British Museum 303, *LIMC* I Adonis 14). Cf. Boardman and La Rocca 1978, 142. Plautus mentions a mural that portrays the same scene (*Menaechmi* 143–4). Most surviving visual representations portray Adonis and Aphrodite together harmoniously, a favorite subject for Etruscan mirrors (see, e.g., de Grummond 2004).

85. On wedding iconography, see, e.g., Reilly 1989; Oakley and Sinos 1993; Sabetái 1993 and 1997; Oakley 1995; Vérilhac 1998; G. Ferrari 2002 (who discusses the *anakalyptêria*), 186–90, and 2004; Oakley 2012.

86. Personifications are usually female. The Greeks had no word for "personification," as Shapiro (1993, 12) is quick to point out at the beginning of his thorough book on the subject. And G. Ferrari urges caution: "To define certain figures as 'personifications' is to draw a line between mythological characters and embodiments of abstractions—a line that may have been drawn differently or not at all in Archaic and Classical Greece. In this view, Eros, for instance, falls on one side, although he is the embodiment of love and the word for 'love,' his mythological associations being stronger than for other personifications, while his brother Himeros falls on the other" (2002, 46). See also, e.g., Burn 1987, 32–40; Stafford 2000; Stafford and Herrin 2005; A. Smith 2011 and 2012. The interpretation of such scenes can become somewhat literal-minded. So Borg comments, "If, for example, on a fragment from Ullastret, Dike (Justice) or Nike (Victory) . . . steps up to Eukleia sitting on a rock to present her a necklace, or if, on a lid in Mainz, Eukleia offers the seated Eunomia a box, then these gestures of giving and serving can well be transferred metaphorically to

the personified concepts themselves: Justice—as well as victory—certainly contributes to good repute and a good reputation is a substantial contribution to good order" (2005, 195). While in some cases readings like this offer useful interpretations, one wonders why Justice (or Victory) has a necklace and why Good Repute would like to have one. As I argue later, at times it makes more sense to see these images as drawing on the "bands of maidens" from myth, as G. Ferrari (2002) suggests.

87. Pyxis, in the manner of the Meidias Painter. Metropolitan Museum of Art, Rogers Fund, 1908 (09.221.40); *ARV*[2] 1328.99; *Addenda*[2] 364; *Paralipomena* 479; BAD 220655; Rosenzweig 2004, fig. 13.

88. In a thorough analysis of the iconography of red-figure interior scenes depicting spinners (scenes that include the New York pyxis mentioned earlier), G. Ferrari has convincingly argued that in such settings the female figure "belongs to the group of her peers. No less than their elegant clothes and conspicuous jewelry and the fact that they are at home in a palace, the articulation of the figures into main characters and attendants is the visual equivalent of the way in which the image of a girl outstanding for beauty and rank is cast in poetry and myth. In Greek myth, girls come in packs: the Nereids, the Minyads, the Proetids, and the Danaids, to name only a few" (2002, 44–45).

89. Young women tend to be abducted from such spaces in poetry. For erotic meadows, see *Iliad* 14.346–51; Archil. fr. 196a W; Sappho frs. 2, 94, 96, 122 Voigt; Ibycus fr. 286 *PMG*. On eroticized meadows and maidens, see Swift, who comments, "Being linked to a meadow signifies readiness to marry" (2006, 127). Cf. Bremer 1975; Foley 1994, 33–34; P. Rosenmeyer 2004.

90. In a discussion of female choruses in myth and tragedy and their connections with marriage, Murnaghan remarks, "In mythology . . . the female chorus participates in a dynamic scenario in which one member of the group is separated out and embarks on an often-complicated course toward the settled state of marriage" (2005, 186). Cf. J. S. Clay: "Frequently mentioned in Greek legends, the dance in honor of Artemis by girls approaching the age of marriage performed the function of a debut or showcase for the display of marriageable maidens, who were generally kept in seclusion" (1989, 176). On choruses to Artemis, see also, e.g., Boedecker 1974, 47–49; Calame (1977) 2001, 91–101.

91. On abduction scenes and gestures of fear, see, e.g., Kaempf-Dimitriadou 1979; Zeitlin 1986; Sourvinou-Inwood 1987; Stewart 1995; Frontisi-Ducroux 1996; Osborne 1996; McNiven 2000; Topper 2007.

92. Cf. the adornment of Pandora by the Horai, the Graces, Peitho, and Athena in Hesiod's *Works and Days*, 72–76 (cf. *Theogony* 573–80). Pandora is similarly arrayed in finery, and an alluring bride is created. Cf. Oakley and Sinos 1993, 19. As G. Ferrari suggests, "Aphrodite, Persephone, Pandora are all variations upon the paradigm of the *numphê*, the bride: Persephone is the bride of Hades; Pandora the first mortal bride" (2004, 252).

93. Adonis is not easily identified in visual depictions because he has no attribute. Unlike Hermes with his wand or Athena with her warrior paraphernalia, nothing sets Adonis apart from the many attractive young men seen in Athenian vase painting. Cf. Salapata 2001, 36. For thorough discussions of Adonis in the visual arts, see Atallah 1966; Servais-Soyez

1981. I have chosen to discuss the vases typically taken to be *mythical* depictions of Aphrodite and Adonis first, and to examine vases associated with the *ritual* in the next section. Although I have organized the chapter somewhat artificially in this way, I do not make a rigid distinction between representations of myth and ritual; instead, the decision to deal with mythical before ritual iconography is motivated primarily by ease of exposition. As I have suggested in chapter 1 and at the beginning of this chapter, an understanding of the merging of myth and ritual is crucial to our conception of the Adonia. As we shall see, the portrayal of the cult is imbued with mythical elements, just as the "mythical" images include ritual elements.

94. Attic red-figure hydria, Florence, Museo Archeologico, 81948. Beazley, *ARV*[2] 1312.1; *Paralipomena* 477; *Addenda*[2] 361; BAD 220493; *CVA* Florence 2 III I pls. 60–63 (644–47); *LIMC* I Adonis 10; Nicole 1908, pl. 3.2; Burn 1987, pls. 22–25a; A. Smith 2011, figs. 5.1–5.2, 5.11, 8.3. For an account of Meidian painting, see Burn 1987. For discussions of this vase, see, e.g., Atallah 1966, 201–3; Burn 1987, 40–44; Shapiro 1993, 63, 86, 70, 129, figs. 16, 39, 70, 81.

95. The Meidias Painter was fond of gardens, and nearly all his scenes are set amid rocky outcroppings, flowers, and trees. These gardens are populated, for the most part, with female figures and the goddess Aphrodite. No other god or goddess was as central to the Meidias Painter's workshop. Indeed, Burn (1987, 29) believes that his painting evokes Aphrodite specifically in her guise as Aphrodite *en kêpois*.

96. Attic red-figure hydria, Florence, Museo Archeologico, 81947. *ARV*[2] 1312.2; *Paralipomena* 477; *Addenda*[2] 361; BAD 220494; *CVA* Florence 2 III I, pls. 60.2, 61.2, 64.1–3, 65.1–3 (644–45, 648–49); *LIMC* VII Phaon 2; Burn 1987, pls. 27–29; Stewart 1997, 150, fig. 90. For discussions, see Burn 1987, 40–44; Shapiro 1993, 67–68. The two vases were, according to Burn, "surely designed as a pair" (1987, 44).

97. Cf. Simon, Hirmer, and Hirmer 1981, 148; Burn 1987, 43; Shapiro 1993, 67–68; Stewart 1997, 150–51. Elsewhere Dêmonassa is the wife of Phaon and the mother of Philoctetes, or she is the daughter of the Argive seer Amphiaraus.

98. Other representations of Phaon and Adonis (it is often difficult to tell the two apart) are discussed by Burn 1987, 40–44. Cf. Beazley 1950, 320–21. For depictions of goddesses with mortal men, who are figured as *paidika*/*erômenoi*, see, e.g., Dover 1978, 172; Porter 2003. After 480, bridegrooms tend to be depicted beardless on red-figure vases (Sutton 1992, 26–27). Couelle (1989) discusses the late fifth-century tendency for heroes to appear in relaxed poses surrounded by women, in contrast to earlier depictions, where heroes actively engage in exploits such as the defeat of beasts.

99. Burn 1987, 41.

100. Cf. Nonnus *Dion.* 11.500, where one of the Horai "was weaving the *kômos* for Adonis and Kythereia" (ἔπλεκε κῶμον Ἀδώνιδι καὶ Κυθερείῃ). Just as the Horai accompany Adonis from the underworld to earth, so, too, in some accounts, they lead Persephone up to earth ([Orph.] *Hymn* 43; cf. *Hymn* 29.9). Cf. Griffiths 1979, 66; Foley 1994, 58–59.

101. For the posture, see Shapiro 1986, 17; 1993, 76n148. Antikenmuseum, F2705. *ARV*[2] 1317, 2 (Painter of the Frankfort Acorn); *JdI* 102 (1987) 185–89, figs. 1–3.5–6; *LIMC*

IV.1 49 Eukleia 1; *LIMC* IV.1 63 Eunomia 3; *CVA* 8 pl. 46, 484; Shapiro 1993 pl. 25 p. 75. For discussion of the vase, see Wehgartner (1987), who found the Adonis inscription (Beazley had identified the youth as Phaon), and who suggests that the lyre belongs to Adonis and the fruit evokes the Adonia. Certainly Aphrodite herself is also closely bound up with wedding imagery in vase painting in general and in particular on vases attributed to the Meidias Painter. For visual representations of Aphrodite in general, see, e.g., Rosenzweig 2004. Concerning scenes attributed to the Meidias Painter, Burn remarks, "The Meidian scenes suggest a special connection between Aphrodite and weddings" (1987, 30). The depiction of Aphrodite and Adonis on the Meidias Painter's hydria evokes images of Ariadne and Dionysus that have been connected to wedding iconography. See Hedreen 1992, 31–51; Topper 2012b, 114–21.

102. Cf. Burn 1987, 43. See Herodotus 5.20.14. Pandaisia is not a common personification. She appears on a squat lekythos in London (British Museum E698; *ARV*^{2} 1316; BAD 220518), holding a tray of fruit and accompanied by Eudaimonia, Eros, and an unknown youth labeled Polykles. Shapiro 1993, 63–64; A. Smith 2011, 84–85.

103. Stehle 1996, 198.

104. See Menander *Samia* 46. "Rape at a pannychis" becomes a literary motif (R. Parker 2005, 166, 172, 182–83; Furley 2009; Bathrellou 2012). Cf. Reed 2000, 323n19. For *tympana* playing at the Adonia, see Aristophanes *Lysistrata* 388.

105. For *paidia* and festival, see chapter 4. For *paidia* and the Adonia, see Menander *Samia* 41–42; Plato *Phaedrus* 276b.

106. Attic red-figure aryballos lekythos, Paris, Louvre MNB 2109, *ARV*^{2} 1175, 7; *Addenda*^{2} 339; BAD 215563; *LIMC* I Adonis 8; Shapiro 1993, 181, figs. 137–38; A. Smith 2011, fig. 5.13. Shapiro (1993, 180) notes that Paidia is a popular personification for a short period of time from about 425–400.

107. The object is depicted on at least three vases (late fifth to early fourth century), and is held by Eros or women, 117. Cf. Wehgartner 1987; Böhr 1997. Shapiro (1985) argues that objects from the agora identified as "bobbins" are in fact *iunges*.

108. On the *iunx*, see Faraone 1993; 1999, 60–69, 140–49; Johnston 1995; see Detienne (1972) 1994, 83–85, on the *iunx* and Adonis.

109. E.g., Simaitha in Theocritus's *Idyll* 2. For the dedication of an *iunx* to Aphrodite, see GP Anon. 35 (3798–803) = *AP* 5.205. For the tendency of men to use the *iunx*, with courtesans coopting the practice, see Faraone 1999, 64–69 and 149–60. For Lysistrata's use of the *iunx* in Aristophanes's *Lysistrata* (1110), see Faraone 2006, 217.

110. See Burn 1987, 43; Böhr 1997, 116; Turner 2005, 81. Cf. Detienne (1972) 1994, 84–86.

111. Böhr 1997; Turner 2005.

112. Attic red-figure epinêtron, Athens, National Museum 1629; *ARV*^{2} 1250.34, 1688; *Paralipomena* 469; Beazley *Addenda*^{2} 354; BAD 216971; Oakley and Sinos 1993, figs.128–30; Shapiro 1993, 105, fig. 58; Rosenzweig 2004, fig. 11; A. Smith 2011, fig. 5.6. For recent discussions, see, e.g., Oakley and Sinos 1993, 40–41; Kousser 2004; Topper 2012a. The epinêtron, or onos, was used for wool working and covered the leg and knee of the wool worker. Three

mythological weddings are represented on this epinêtron: the marriage of Harmonia, the rape of Thetis by Peleus, and Alcestis's *epaulia*. This particular epinêtron also includes a sculpted bust of a nude female.

113. Cf. Hauser 1909.

114. Cf. Swift (2010, 244–45), who comments, "The only authentic and certain examples of Greek *hymenaios* come from Sappho" (244). On *hymenaios* and *epithalamia*, the distinction between the two terms, and bibliography, see Swift (2010, 242–97), who prefers *hymenaios* as a "catch-all term to refer to any kind of wedding song" (243). See also Maas 1914; Page 1955, 72–74, 119–26; Diggle 1970, 149; Calame (1977) 2001, 83–85.

115. Williamson 1995; Most 1996; Foley 1998, 40n3. At least six plays were named after Sappho: Antiphanes (*PCG* ii frs. 194–95); Diphilus (*PCG* v frs. 70–71); Timocles (*PCG* vii fr. 32); Ephippus (*PCG* v fr. 20); Amipsias (*PCG* ii fr. 15); Amphis (*PCG* ii fr. 32). Other comedies likely dealt with Sappho: Plato Comicus *Phaon* (*PCG* vii frs. 188–98); Antiphanes *Phaon* (*PCG* ii fr. 213); *The Leucadian* by Menander (*PCG* vi 1 Leucad. fr. 1); Diphilus (*PCG* v fr. 52); Alexis (*PCG* ii frs. 135–137); Antiphanes (*PCG* ii frs. 139–140); and Amphis (*PCG* ii fr. 26). The comic poet Epicrates speaks of Sappho's love songs (*PCG* v fr. 4), and a handful of vase paintings survive inscribed with the poet's name. Cf. Yatromanolakis 2001.

116. See also Page 1955, 126–28.

117. Cf. West's suggestion for fr. 96.23 (1970, 328).

118. Sappho's wedding fragments: 103b, 107, 108, 109, 110a, 111, 112, 113, 114, 115, 116, 117 Voigt and probably also 104ab, 105ac Voigt. For Eastern elements (in general) in Sappho's wedding songs, see West 1997, 529–31. Williamson (1995, 14) points out that Dioscorides is closer in time to Sappho and more precise in his characterization of her poetry than later poems of this type.

119. Σ Theocritus 18 Wendel: ᾄδουσι δὲ τὸν ἐπιθαλάμιον αἱ παρθένοι πρὸ τοῦ θαλάμου, ἵνα τῆς παρθένου βιαζομένης ὑπὸ τοῦ ἀνδρὸς ἡ φωνὴ μὴ ἐξακούηται, λανθάνῃ δὲ κρυπτομένη διὰ τῆς τῶν παρθένων φωνῆς.

120. Hesychius 8. 957 θυρωρός· ὁ παράνυμφος, ὁ τὴν θύραν τοῦ θαλάμου κλείων; Pollux 3.42 θυρωρός, ὃς ταῖς θύραις ἐφεστηκὼς εἴργει τὰς γυναῖκας τῇ νύμφῃ βοώσῃ βοηθεῖν.

121. Other evidence emphasizes the distressed bride and the ways in which a wedding was not necessarily a positive experience, e.g., Aeschylus *Suppliants*; see Seaford 1987. The yearning that the companions of the bride feel for their lost age-mate is expressed in Theocritus *Idyll* 18 (Helen's *epithalamion*), where her friends remember Helen just as lambs remember their mother's teat (μεμναμέναι ὡς γαλαθηναί / ἄρνες γειναμένας ὄιος μαστὸν ποθέοισαι, 41–42).

122. For praise of the bride and groom, see Hague 1983; Swift 2010, 245–46. Ares and Aphrodite serve as a mythical paradigm for the human wedding of Habrocomes and Anthia in Xenophon of Ephesus *Ephesian Tale* 1.8.

123. For the sexual innuendo in the phrase "bigger by far than a big man," see Kirk 1963; cf. Lloyd-Jones 1967. Zellner (2006), by contrast, believes the "supra-superlative" is typical of Sappho.

124. Roof for *oikos*, see, e.g., Homer *Iliad* 2.414.

125. Loraux 1987, 24.

126. Cf. Roland Martin 1987.

127. Attic red-figure loutrophoros. Berlin, Staatliche Museen F 2372.

128. A Sapphic fragment addresses the *gambros* and makes clear that the *gambros* possesses the *parthenos*, the object of his desires. Aphrodite is present as a source of honor in this exchange, fr. 112–17 Voigt.

129. Loraux 1987, 24.

130. οἷον τὸ γλυκύμαλον ἐρεύθεται ἄκρῳ ἐπ' ὔσδῳ, / ἄκρον ἐπ' ἀκροτάτῳ, λελάθοντο δὲ μαλοδρόπηες· / οὐ μὰν ἐκλελάθοντ', ἀλλ' οὐκ ἐδύναντ' ἐπίκεσθαι.

131. R. D. Griffith 1989. Cf. Himerius *Orationes* 9.16.

132. Plutarch *Advice to the Bride and Groom* 138d; *Roman Questions* 279f; cf. *Solon* 20.3, which preserves information about laws handed down from Solon that required *epiklêroi* (heiresses) to eat a quince (*kudonian mêlon*) as bride while confined to the bridal chamber. While it is never clear whether laws attributed to Solon are to be trusted as such, most scholars accept this law; see, e.g., Lacey 1968, 29–30. An etiological myth preserved by Pherecydes tells that the goddess Earth caused apple trees to grow at the wedding of Zeus and Hera (*FGrH* 3 fr. 17); cf. Apollodorus 2.5.11. On fruit at weddings and iconography, see Oakley and Sinos 1993, 35; Rehm 1994, 17.

133. Attributed to Polygnotus, ca. 430–20 BCE. Toronto, Royal Ontario Museum 929.22.3; *ARV*[2] 1031.51; *Addenda*[2] 317; BAD 213434. Cf. the chain of pomegranates that appears over a bride's head on a red-figure hydria attributed to the Orpheus Painter in New York. Metropolitan Museum of Art, 17.230.15, Rogers Fund, 1917 (*ARV*[2] 1104.16; *Addenda*[2] 329; Sutton 1997–98, fig. 15).

134. After death, Praxilla's Adonis (fr. 747 *PMG*) himself says he misses ὡραίους σικύους καὶ μῆλα καὶ ὄγχνας, "ripe cucumbers, apples, and pears." Reed suggests that the Suda entry on "fruits of Adonis" brings to mind Sappho fr. 105a V, since "'fruits high up' represent the choicest and hardest-to-reach fruits on the tree" (2005, 363). The Suda records Ἀδώνειοι καρποί· λέγονται οἱ μετέωροι κῆποι (Suda α 514 Adler). Reed suggests textual corruption and would restore Ἀδώνειοι καρποί· λέγονται οἱ μετέωροι καρποί, "fruits of Adonis: fruits high up are so called." Both the Adonia and the Athenian wedding feature plant metaphors: at the Adonia, women cultivate gardens of Adonis, while ancient Greek weddings involve a bride handed over for the "plowing of legitimate children." And, indeed, in another of Sappho's *epithalamia* fragments, agricultural imagery is employed to describe the bridegroom, as the speaker wonders what she might use as an appropriate comparison (fr. 115 Voigt) and settles on likening him to a "slender sapling" (ὄρπακι βραδίνῳ). The same adjective is employed in another Sapphic fragment to modify *Aphrodite* (fr. 102 Voigt): γλύκηα μᾶτερ, οὔ τοι δύναμαι κρέκην τὸν ἴστον / πόθῳ δάμεισα παῖδος βραδίναν δι' Ἀφροδίταν. For the similarity between the phrasing of the rhetorical question in Sappho's fragment and the Lamentations of Jeremiah, see West 1997, 530.

135. For this convention, see Alexiou (1974) 2002, 183; Lardinois 2001; and see, e.g., *Iliad* 24.725–26; Euripides *Hippolytus*, 848. Cf. Sappho fr. 107 Voigt.

136. Swift (2010, 259) follows other scholars in suggesting that Sappho fr. 104a Voigt, where Hesperus takes a child from her mother (φέρης ἄπυ μάτερι παῖδα, 2), and 105b Voigt, where a hyacinth is trampled by shepherds (οἴαν τὰν ὐάκινθον ἐν ὤρεσι ποίμενες ἄνδρες / πόσσι καταστείβοισι, χάμαι δέ τε πόρφυρον ἄνθος), may have formed part of a single poem along with fr. 105a 1–2 Voigt. For the *parthenos* as flower, cf. Sophocles *Women of Trachis* (144–50), where Deianeira describes the unmarried *parthenos* as a flower that neither heat nor rain nor wind disturbs. Such a "young life" (νεάζον, 144) enjoys a pleasurable existence and a life of no toil, "until she is called a woman instead of a girl" (ἕως τις ἀντὶ παρθένου γυνὴ / κληθῇ, 148–49), at which point she takes on a multitude of cares and anxieties. For Adonis and the anemone, see chapter 1 and chapter 4.

137. Occasionally, Eros appears on the ladder (figs. 7, 10, 14) and the female figure (or figures) is beside the ladder.

138. For visual representations of ladders and ships, see Edwards 1984, 63–64. For ladders and siege warfare, see, e.g., Thucydides 3.20; 4.135; 5.56. For ladders to roofs, see, e.g., Homer's *Odyssey* 10.557–59 (cf. 11.61–64); Aristophanes *Clouds* 1486–88. When women do appear with ladders, the scenes are marked as distinctive. In Euripides *Iphigenia among the Taurians*, a ladder is given to Iphigenia (1351–53), but she is too frightened to climb it, so Orestes puts her on his shoulder and carries her to the ship (1380–83). In Euripides *Helen* 1570–71, as Helen climbs aboard a ship with Menelaus, we are invited to dwell on her foot. Allan comments, "The detail of Helen's shapely foot has the effect of a cinematic closeup" (2008, 333). Ladders also appear in scenes of adultery, e.g., Xenarchus *PCG* vii fr. 4 = Ath. 569b–c.

139. For speech-making, see Quintilian 9.3.54 on Demosthenes's use of the *klimax*.

140. On ladders as stairways to the gods, see, e.g., Cook 1925, 125–30. The best-known heavenly ladder is, perhaps, Jacob's ladder in the book of Genesis (28:10–19). For Egyptian texts and heavenly ladders, see Edwards 1984, 66n50.

141. For example, a ladder to the heavens that fails to serve its function is described in Aristophanes *Peace*. Trygaeus, who wishes to speak with Zeus in order to stop the Peloponnesian War, first tries to reach the upper regions by means of a ladder (69), but he is forced to settle on a dung beetle for transport.

142. Cf. Apollodorus 1.7.4.

143. Euripides *Phoenician Women* 1172–86 describes Capaneus's attempt to take Thebes by means of a ladder; his attack is figured as an unsuccessful assault on the heavens. The moment in which he goes beyond the upper reaches of the wall carries cosmic repercussions, as the earth resounds loudly, and Zeus blasts Capaneus with a thunderbolt, hurling him back to earth, where he belongs. For other examples of heights and negative connotations, cf. the overweening *dêmos* in Euripides *Suppliants* that reaches beyond its station and functions as a contrast to the brave general described by the messenger, 726–30; Pentheus's climb to the top of the fir tree in *Bacchae* (1064–74); in Aristophanes *Clouds*, once he learns Socrates's teachings, Strepsiades is promised he will have "*kleos* that stretches to the heavens," κλέος οὐρανόμηκες, 461; Sophocles *OT* 872–80.

144. In addition to a cult at Athens in the northwest corner of the agora, she had major shrines at Cyprus, Cythera, and Corinth. The epithet is also used of gods in general (e.g., *Homeric Hymn to Demeter* 55) and for other divinities (e.g., Zeus, Herodotus 6.56).

145. Travlos 1971, 361–64; Servais-Soyez 1983, 196n45, 201–2; Pirenne-Delforge 1994, 23–24; Rosenzweig 2004, 67; R. Parker 2005, 442–43.

146. Pirenne-Delforge 1994, 23–24.

147. For discussions of these representations of "Aphrodite" on a ladder, see Atallah 1966, 177–95; Edwards 1984; Pirenne-Delforge 1994, 21–25; Rosenzweig 2004, 63–81.

148. The relief was published by Edwards (1984). He identifies the figure specifically as Aphrodite Ourania, dates the relief to the late fifth century (60), and connects the votive relief with the sanctuary of Aphrodite Ourania in the agora.

149. See Edwards 1984 (61 and 61–62n17). It has been suggested that, like the votive ladder at the shrine of Nymphê, the fragment of the votive relief was a dedication to Aphrodite Ourania within a marital context. See Edwards 1984, 61; Pirenne-Delforge 1994, 24.

150. Atallah describes it as "un vase ventru avec deux anses sur les bords, une sorte de coupe géante" (1966, 196). See also Watzinger 1928, who published a photograph of the relief, provided a description, and dated the relief to the early fourth century BCE; Edwards 1984, 66–67, who suggests that the relief is late Hellenistic in style; Rosenzweig 2004, 79.

151. It is unclear what object is depicted in the lower left, near the head and wing of another Eros. Watzinger (1928) saw a *klinê*; Edwards saw the prow of a ship (1984, 67n53).

152. Kerameikos M 374. For discussion and dating of the disk, see Knigge 1982, 153–70, pl. 31, and Knigge 1991, 93, fig. 86. See also Edwards 1984, 66; Pirenne-Delforge 1994, 36–38; Treister 1999, 572–73.

153. Aphrodite appears on a goat most famously in the statue of Aphrodite Pandêmos by Scopas for the city of Elis described by Pausanias (6.25.1). Aphrodite is called Epitragia (Goat-Rider) in two late sources: an inscription for a seat in the theater of Dionysus reserved for the representative of the goddess's cult (second century CE); and Plutarch's *Life of Theseus* 28. See Pirenne-Delforge 1994, 35–40.

154. In a discussion of this medallion, Knigge (1982, 164–65) argues that in iconography Aphrodite Ourania rides a swan and is goddess of the morning star, while Aphrodite Pandêmos rides a goat and is goddess of the evening star. Such classification is overly rigid. Although some scholars identify the "Aphrodite" on a ladder as Aphrodite Ourania (e.g., Edwards 1984), the iconography of the ladder is also at times connected with the "goat-rider" Aphrodite who is frequently identified as Pandêmos. Oikonomides (1964, 7–8) believes the "Nymph" cult continued in the temple of Aphrodite Pandêmos. Cf. Pirenne-Delforge (1994, 24), who also points out the affinities between Aphrodite and marriage, as well as between Aphrodite Ourania and Pandêmos. Cf. Larson 2007, 117–18. See also Rosenzweig for a discussion of "lack of cult specificity" (2004, 4–5) with regard to depictions of Aphrodite.

155. Sparta Museum 17; Mitropoulou 1975, 7–8; Knigge 1982, 158, pl. 33.1; Rosenzweig 2004, 79; *LIMC* II Aphrodite 955.

156. Paris, Louvre MA 2701. Mitropoulou 1975, 13–14; Treister 1999, 573; *LIMC* II Aphrodite 957. Collignon identifies the hovering vessel as a kylix (1894, 147).

157. The goat-rider Aphrodite also appears on a Berlin hydria, seminude, with Eros and incense burner to left (Berlin, Antikensammlung, Staatliche Museen, F2635; *ARV*[2] 1483.2; BAD 242922; *LIMC* II Aphrodite 952). For depictions of partially naked Aphrodite on a goat, see Miller 1979, 38–40, pl. 22a, b. Miller discusses a circular pendant relief medallion from Pelinna (*LIMC* II Aphrodite 970) that portrays a bare-breasted, goat-riding Aphrodite, along with a kid, a bird, and a ladder. Concerning the ladder, Miller remarks, "The explanation for this seemingly curious (and generally misunderstood) attribute is undoubtedly to be found in the festival . . . of the Adonia" (40). Cf. two second century BCE gold medallions from Delos (*LIMC* II Aphrodite 967 and 968) on which a horizontal ladder appears, above which the goat-rider Aphrodite flies (see Mitropoulou 1975, 21–23; Miller 1979, pls. 23c, d).

158. Cf. G. Ferrari's (2003) discussion of the depiction of fountain scenes (which vary in individual details) as evocations of mythical-historical springs rather than references to particular springs.

159. Cf. Edwards 1984, 61. While these two vases are not categorized as *epaulia* scenes, they are occasionally interpreted as depictions not of an Adonia but of unknown rituals associated with Aphrodite (see, e.g., Edwards 1984) because no telltale garden of Adonis appears. Yet the distinctive iconographical element of the female figure and the ladder as well as the movement of vessels unites these two vases with the Karlsruhe lekythos.

160. Cf. Detienne (1972) 1994, 114–15.

161. Edwards 1984, 67. Cf. a Hellenistic *thymiatêrion* in the Corinth museum, C 2007-11 (James 2010, cat. no. 203, pl. 17). Haider (2011–12) has published fragments of an Attic vase from Sidon that depict Eros with a *thymiatêrion*. She suggests that the vase depicts an Adonia. On *thymiatêria*, see, e.g., Zaccagnino 1998.

162. Thucydides mentions incense (θυμιατήρια, 6.46.3) in connection with Aphrodite; Empedocles mentions myrrh and frankincense (D-K 128). Cf. Pindar fr. 122 (Maehler), where *libanos* is offered to Aphrodite Ourania; and see Alciphron 4.13.5. Aphrodite and Eros are depicted with incense burners. For Eros, see, e.g., the relief plaque from the north slope of the Acropolis (Kaltsas and Shapiro 2008, 120–21, cat. no. 52). On incense and cults of Aphrodite, see Metzger 1942, 233, 241–42.

163. See, e.g., the Attic red-figure lekanis lid attributed to the Eleusinian Painter (St. Petersburg, State Hermitage Museum, ST 1791; *ARV*[2] 1476.3; *Addenda*[2] 381; *Paralipomena* 496; BAD 230433; Sutton 1997–98, fig. 17) and the Attic red-figure squat lekythos (St. Petersburg, State Hermitage Museum, yu.o.27 St. 1929; BAD 6554), where a statue of Aphrodite holds a *thymiatêrion* in her right hand (and a *phialê* in her left hand); another incense burner sits on the ground in front of the horses.

164. Cf. Aristophanes *Wealth* 529–30 for myrrh as perfume for the groom.

165. Hauser compares this vessel to those used in Eleusinian cult and suggests that it is an incense burner (1909, 92); Metzger states, "à droite d'Eros, sorte de vasque à pied ou de dinos" (1951, 92); Edwards describes the object as "a vase on a stand" (1984, 62). Gloria

Ferrari (personal communication) comments on the strangeness of the vessel, remarking that it looks like a Middle Geometric pedestaled krater.

166. Richter and Hall 1936, 219n4. Cf. Rubensohn 1898. For depictions of kernoi from Eleusis and from the Athenian agora that seem to have been used in the Mysteries and that certainly resemble the container depicted on the Karlsruhe lekythos, see Pollitt 1979. See also Mitsopoulou 2010 and 2011. Although the Adonia never had the state backing of a mystery cult like the Eleusinian Mysteries, Burkert (1987, 75–76), likens the Adonia to a mystery cult, and it is interesting that objects like Eleusinian kernoi (if they are to be identified as such) are represented in connection with the Adonia.

167. Richter and Hall 1936, 219.

168. Richter comments, "On top of the 'kerchnos' is an area of discolored glaze with traces of green (besides the round objects)" (Richter and Hall 1936, 219n5).

169. For other depictions that seem to combine gardens of Adonis and myrrh, see the acorn lekythos from Athens (fig. 21) and the Hellenistic terracotta figurine (fig. 23). The terracotta figurine, like the "kernos" on the Karlsruhe lekythos, holds round objects.

170. See, e.g., G. Ferrari 2003; Hedreen 2009; Topper 2012b.

171. See, e.g., G. Ferrari's 2002 discussion of the Brauron krateriskoi, esp. 175. For depictions of primitive ritual, see Hedreen 2014.

172. Several other vases also include mythical elements. On the hydria from the British Museum (fig. 8), Pan flies in on the left. Elsewhere, indications of an outdoor setting alongside interior-space elements seems to indicate an imagined, mythical setting. On the aryballos lekythos from Berlin (fig. 9), a fruit tree appears to the left of the ladder, while a female *aulos* player is seated on a chair to the right (along with a swan behind her). On an aryballos lekythos from New York (fig. 12), a nude male is seated on a chair.

173. The nudity of the figure on the ladder on the Karlsruhe lekythos has puzzled scholars. Creuzer (1839, 66) interpreted the figure as Aphrodite and argued that her dress was in disarray because she was upset by the news of Adonis's encounter with the boar. For other interpretations, see Edwards 1984, 62. For discussions of nudity in general, see, e.g., Sutton 1997–98, 41–42; and, more recently, Kousser 2004, 2011.

174. See, e.g., G. Ferrari 2002, 163.

175. Oakley and Sinos 1993, 42, fig. 41.

176. Kousser 2004.

177. On the textual problems here, see Reed (1997, 209–11), who accepts Ahrens's emendations.

178. See Reed 1997, 207, 210.

179. Gow comments, "Presumably they unfasten the περόναι on their shoulders so that the upper part of their χιτῶνες falls from the girdle before and behind, leaving the upper part of the body bare, though if, as is usual at this period, the girdle is worn below the breast rather than round the waist, the falling drapery will hardly reach their ankles" (1952, 302).

180. Cf. GP 1475–78 = *AP* 5.53, another epigram of Dioscorides on the same subject, with similar language.

181. Lamenting women commonly rend their garments, as in Sappho's Adonis fragment (fr. 140 Voigt), and occasionally lamenting women expose their breasts, as in book 22 of the *Iliad*, when Hecuba weeps and appeals to Hector: "She groaned, pouring forth tears, and she loosened the folds of her robe and with her other hand she exposed her breast," ὀδύρετο δάκρυ χέουσα / κόλπον ἀνιεμένη, ἑτέρηφι δὲ μαζὸν ἀνέσχε, 79–80. Of course, Hecuba's breast exposure makes a particular point, as she is Hector's mother. Cf. Polybius 2.56.7.

182. Cf. the Washing Painter's lebes gamikos in the Benaki Museum, which depicts a loutrophoros with protruding branches (Oakley and Sinos 1993, fig. 22). Oakley and Sinos suggest that the branches might have been used for sprinkling water, (1993, 17 and 134n49).

183. Hauser 1909; Atallah 1966, 191–92; Edwards 1984, 63n28.

184. London, British Museum E774; *ARV*[2] 1250.32; *Paralipomena* 469; Oakley and Sinos 1993, figs. 32–35. On Nereids and wedding iconography, see Barringer 1991 and 1995.

185. It is possible that the object identified as a "fan" on the fragmentary figure 15 is a large wing, since occasionally wings do appear as alternating light and dark bands. It is reminiscent of the wings of both Sleep and Death, who move Sarpedon on the Attic red-figure calyx krater from the late sixth century. Rome, Mus. Naz. Etrusco di Villa Giulia L.2006.10; BAD 187; *LIMC* VII 697 Sarpedon 4. Sleep: Vermeule 1979, 38 fig. 27; Death: 149 fig. 2. Metzger suggests that (on the vases, which he believes depict the Adonia) Eros "remplit ici les fonctions d'un esclave domestique" (1951, 96).

186. An Eros tends to suggest to scholars that a scene is "erotic"—not a terribly satisfying conclusion for our purposes—while Erotes fluttering by the head of an unnamed female figure may indicate that she is Aphrodite. See, e.g., Edwards 1984. For discussions of Eros and Erotes, see, e.g., *LIMC* III.1 850–942 Eros; Shapiro 1992; Sutton 1997–98. On the tendency of Eros to proliferate and become Erotes, see Shapiro 1993, 28. For Eros as (beardless) *erastês*, see Shapiro 1992.

187. Vermeule 1979, 157.

188. *Kalos* inscriptions, of course, appear in other contexts. For discussions, see, e.g., Robinson and Fluck 1937; Immerwahr 1990.

189. Attic red-figure loutrophoros, Boston, Museum of Fine Arts, 03.802; BAD 15815; Oakley and Sinos 1993, figs. 1, 105–7. To the right of the wedding procession, a female figure observes an Eros while raising her palms in the same gesture seen on the Karlsruhe lekythos (fig. 5).

190. Athens, National Archaeological Museum, Acropolis Collection 569 (*ARV*[2] 890.172; *Addenda*[2] 302; BAD 211735; Sutton 1997–98, fig. 6). On a red-figure hydria attributed to the Orpheus Painter, *kalos* is written over the head of the bride, as well as over the head of the groom (New York, Metropolitan Museum of Art, 17.230.15, Rogers Fund, 1917; Sutton 1997–98, fig. 15). Sutton argues that, because vase painters tend to write a single letter for a double consonant, *kallos* should be read over the head of the bride, rather than the masculine adjective *kalos* (1997–98, 47n66). Similarly, on an alabastron in Paris that draws on wedding iconography, a young woman seated before a wool basket holds a wreath while a small figure standing behind her offers an alabastron (Paris, Cabinet des Médailles 508, unattributed: *ARV*[2] 1610; BAD 21648; Reilly 1989, pl. 80; Sutton 1997–98, 31). To her

right a young man holds a sash or fillet. On this alabastron, the *kalos* name of Timodemos appears, as well as ἡ νύμφη καλή (the bride is beautiful).

191. 1, 2, 5, 7, 29 (implicitly at 55), 37, 38, 61, 63, 67, 71, 92. Reed calls it "a standing epithet of Adonis" (1997, 194). Cf. Estevez 1981.

192. Athens, Acropolis Museum 6471; *ARV*[2] 1175, 11; Beazley *Addenda*[2] 339. For discussions, see Stafford 1997; Sutton 1997–98. Zarkadas (1989) believes that the scene to the far left represents the preparation of gardens of Adonis, the middle scene depicts the participation of women in the festival, and the scene to the right represents a divine group (Aphrodite, Adonis, and Eros).

193. Beazley identified the containers as "Adonis plants," and described the scene as an "unexplained subject." Stafford remarks, "The three plant pots are of unusual shape, the middle one having very oddly placed handles, and they make most sense as the up-ended necks of broken amphorae, just such as those depicted containing gardens of Adonis on a lekythos in Karlsruhe" (1997, 202). For a different interpretation of the scene, see Sutton, who argues that the vase might represent a "civilian version of Paris and Helen" (1997–98, 42). He refers to the three gardens of Adonis as "mugs . . . and kalathoi" and argues that these containers are "a distinctively Laconian shape appropriate for a Spartan setting" (42). Interestingly, although Sutton does not believe that the vessels on the acorn lekythos from Athens depict gardens of Adonis, he suggests that the planters recall the branches arranged in lebetes gamikoi and loutrophoroi in wedding scenes.

194. Brouskari 1974, 111; Delivorrias 1984. Cf. Reed 1995, 320n15. By contrast, Stafford believes that the appearance of the nude youth makes an identification of this as a wedding scene doubtful. She concludes that the scene represents the "visit of a lover to his mistress' courtyard . . . commenting on the newly popular cult of the Adonia" (1997, 202). But even if an illicit event is depicted here, the painter is clearly drawing on "chaste" wedding iconography and adornment scenes. It is noteworthy that no scholar describes the depiction of Aphrodite and Adonis in a garden on the Meidias Painter's hydria as a "visit of a lover to his mistress" because the figures are inscribed and therefore understood to be mythical.

195. Stafford 1997, 200. For example, on a lebes gamikos in Athens (fig. 13), a bride drapes herself atop another woman who prepares to crown her. Likewise, the Berlin amphoriskos by the Heimarmene Painter depicts a veiled Helen with downcast eyes sitting on the lap of Aphrodite (Berlin, Antikensammlung, Staatliche Museen 30036; *ARV*[2] 1173.1; *Paralipomena* 459; *Addenda*[2] 339; BAD 215552; Stafford 1997, pl. 4). Lap-sitting is common in Helen and Aphrodite scenes, Stafford 1997, 200. Cf. the Meidias Painter's Adonis hydria (fig. 1, discussed earlier), where Paidia is seated on Hygieia.

196. Cf. Lysias 1.6: ἐπειδὴ ἔδοξέ μοι γῆμαι καὶ γυναῖκα ἠγαγόμην εἰς τὴν οἰκίαν, "after I decided to marry and I led my wife to my house." *Agein*, of course, does not exactly mean "to marry" but refers to the closely linked transfer of the bride and is often used as a proxy for "to marry." Cf. *Iliad* 18. 490–96. The Horai are, as Theocritus quickly explains, "always carrying something" (αἰεί τι φέροισαι, 105), and Theocritus's characterization of the Horai as conveyers of objects between spheres (Adonis included) is consistent with their representation in ancient texts where they frequently carry flowers or ambrosia to mortals. Cf.

Quintus of Smyrna, *Fall of Troy* 4.133–36; Pindar *Pythian* 9.59–65. The famous procession of Ptolemy Philadelphus included the Horai, each carrying fruits. See Athenaeus 5.198b; cf. Rice 1983.

197. The two female figures on the Karlsruhe lekythos that flank the central scene of "Aphrodite" on a ladder gesture with elbows bent, palms raised. The gesture of raised palms may be yet another detail that has both nuptial and Adonis festival associations. The St. Petersburg lekythos and the hydria from the British Museum (figs. 7 and 8) also include a female figure with her palms raised on the left side of the tableau, just as on the Karlsruhe lekythos. Figure 12 depicts a nude youth seated on a chair, and he makes the same gesture. The gesture also appears in a nuptial context, for example, on an Attic red-figure loutrophoros, Boston, Museum of Fine Arts, 03.802 (Oakley and Sinos 1993, figs. 1, 105–7). To the right of a wedding procession, a female figure observes an Eros while raising her palms. Cf. the figure with palms raised on an Attic red-figure squat lekythos in Malibu (attributed to the Painter of the Frankfurt Acorn, Malibu, J. Paul Getty Museum, 91.AE.9; *ARV*[2] 1317.3; BAD 220525). See Oakley and Sinos 1993, 36; and Sutton 1997–98, 37, for discussions of this vase. The gesture on the Karlsruhe lekythos has been interpreted as "surprise and ecstasy at the deity's epiphany" (Edwards 1984, 71); "adoration" (Dillon 2002, 162); and prayer (Simon 1972, 23–24).

198. Campbell translates, "(There is no) road to great Olympus for mortals."

199. Cf. Sappho fr. 52 Voigt ψαύην δ' οὐ δοκίμωμ' ὀράνω, "I do not expect to touch the heavens." At the Adonia, however, perhaps the heavens may be touched. And cf. fr. 96 Voigt, where the speaker (possibly) exclaims, "It is not easy to be like the goddesses in form" and then after a lacuna (possibly) mentions Adonis.

Chapter 3. Funerals

1. Portions of this chapter were previously published (Reitzammer 2008).

2. See, e.g., Detienne (1972) 1994, 65, 99–100; Reed 1995, 319.

3. Henderson contrasts the chorus of old men, with whom he suggests many Athenians might have identified, with the Official, whom he describes as "unsympathetic" and "unredeemable" (1987, 99).

4. Σ 389 Hangard. In addition, another title is given for *Lysistrata*: *Diallagê* (Σ 1114 Hangard). Concerning ancient titles, M. Griffith remarks, "It seems that most ancient works of literature did not bear formal titles such as we are accustomed to; they were generally known either by their subject matter . . . or by their opening words . . . or often by both together. Authors sometimes cited their own or other people's works by different names at different times, and alternative titles seem often to have been equally well established" (1977, 242). Cf. 231, 236–37. On ancient titles, see also Nachmanson 1941 (1969); Taplin 1975; 1977, 164n1.

5. On the dating of the play see, e.g., Sommerstein 1977; Westlake 1980; Henderson 1987, xv–xvi; Slater 2002, 294–95n5; Tsakmakis 2012.

6. Ten older men (we know, for example, that the tragedian Sophocles served as *proboulos*) held the post, as a sort of advisory board. For their age, see Thucydides 8.1.3. For the number of *probouloi*, see *Ath. Pol.* 29.2 (cf. Σ. *Lys* 421 and Suda s.v. πρόβουλοι), Androtion *FGrH* 324 F 43 and Philochorus *FGrH* 328 F 136. Cf. Henderson 1987, 117–18. Aristotle, writing years later and speaking of *probouloi* generally, and not just the Athenian manifestation, associates the office with oligarchy: *Politics* 6.5.13 (1323a); 4.12.8 (1299b); cf. *Ath. Pol.* 29.1–5.

7. Like a raging fever, or a spark from a flint stone, which will grow into a roaring fire, the τρυφή of the women has flared up once more. ἐκλάμπειν can be used of a (potentially) powerful force. See, e.g., Aristotle *HA* 516b11 (fire out of flint stones); Hippocrates *VM* 16 (fever). Cf. Henderson 1987, 118.

8. Furley (1988) examines much of the same evidence analyzed in this chapter, arguing that the Official refers to a historical Adonis festival that was held in 415 BCE on the eve of the Sicilian expedition.

9. At first the Official appears to refer to many celebrants, when he refers to τῶν γυναικῶν ἡ τρυφή (387), τυμπανισμός (388), and πυκνοὶ Σαβάζιοι (388); but once he fastens on the Adonia, he describes a single woman (γυνή, 392) lamenting Adonis atop a roof. The significance of the performance of an Adonia by a lone woman (and not a group of women) will be discussed later.

10. For the women as "hated by the gods" (like Demostratus), see 283, 371, 622.

11. According to Kurke (1992), τρυφή and its compounds appear in the last third of the fifth century in place of *habros* and its compounds, which were popular during the Archaic period. While words like *habrosunê* did not necessarily have a negative valence during the Archaic period (cf. Sappho fr. 58. 25–26 Voigt, ἔγω δὲ φίλημμ' ἀβροσύναν, "I love *habrosunê*") and were not bound up with effeminacy, but instead evoked a certain lifestyle and were tied to a specific set of politics, by the end of the fifth century the signification had shifted. For more on τρυφή, see Kurke 1992, 105. See also Detienne (1972) 1994, 66, 119, 123.

12. Although Henrichs (1978) points out that there is no unambiguous evidence for real maenadic practices in classical Athens (cf. Henrichs 1982, especially 144), Athenians clearly loved to think about maenads, and they appear regularly with *tympana* in Athenian texts and on Athenian vase paintings during the fifth century. Versnel suggests that "the existence of an official 'maenadic' festival is established by the very name 'Lenaia'" (1990, 149). For images of maenads, see Frickenhaus 1912, 16; Lawler 1927, 107–8; Dodds 1940; Jameson 1993, 51, fig. 5; *LIMC* III.2 296–406 Dionysus. See also Hedreen (1994), who argues that many "maenads" on vases are in fact nymphs who have assumed the characteristics of maenads in the context of satyr play; see also Carpenter 1997 and Peirce 1998 for discussions of maenads/nymphs. For Dionysus and *tympana*, see also, e.g., Euripides *TrGF* fr. 586. For Archaic images of Dionysus, see Isler-Kerényi 2007.

13. Dionysus also mentions that the *tympana* are native to Phrygia and are his invention (as well as Rhea's). Cf. *Bacchae* 124, where this time the chorus gives the etiology for the instruments, though now they sing about their invention by the Corybantes.

14. For other parallels between Pentheus and the Official, see Henderson 1987, 66, 136, 146–47; Levine 1987; and discussion later in this chapter.

15. For a thorough discussion of the material culture associated with Sabazius, see Vermaseren 1983; Lane 1985, 1989. On Sabazius generally, see Dodds 1940 and Versnel 1990, 114–18. For fifth-century new gods, see R. Parker 1996, 152–98, and Garland 1992. For a discussion of the comic fragments associated with Sabazius, see Delneri 2006.

16. R. Parker 2005, 325; Versnel 1990, 149n212. Cf. Amphitheos *FGrH* 431 fr. 1; Plutarch *Quaest. conv.* 671e–672b. For Sabazius and kettledrums, see Dodds 1940; Versnel 1990, 114; Demosthenes 18.284, 259–60, and discussion later in this chapter. For *tympana* and the Great Mother, see Pindar fr. 70b9 Maehler; for *tympana* and Cybele, see Euripides *Helen* 1340–50; Herodotus 4.76.3–4. For Kotyto and *tympana*, see Aeschylus *TrGF* iii fr. 57. There were at least two plays titled *Tambourine Players*: Autocrates's play *Tympanistai* (*PCG* iv test. 1–2; frs. 1–3) and one by Sophocles by the same name (*TrGF* iv frs. 636–45).

17. For other mentions of Aeschines's mother, see Demosthenes 19.199, 249, 281.

18. For Sabazius's associations with women and slaves, see Aristophanes *Wasps* 9–10; *Birds* 873; *PCG* iii 2 fr. 578. See also Johnson 1981–84. See Lane 1989, 49–60, for the problems associated with the textual evidence for Sabazius. Lane chooses to focus on the archaeological and epigraphical evidence because, as he sees it, the literary evidence is so troublesome. As long as we acknowledge that Demosthenes is hardly writing from a pro-Sabazius position and that he does not offer any information about rites for Sabazius as actually practiced, the passage may be used to shed important light on *conceptions of* Sabazius worship at Athens during the classical period. I am interested here in the ways that Athenians thought about Sabazius worship and foreign cult, rather than actual practices in honor of Sabazius or original (pre-imported) rituals for Sabazius.

19. Cf. Versnel 1990, 114–18.

20. We might compare Theseus's insults to his son, Hippolytus, in Euripides *Hippolytus*, when Theseus accuses Hippolytus of being an Orphic and engaging in Bacchic rites (952–54). See W. S. Barrett 1964, 342–45, on the passage. Lane suggests that the cult of Sabazius "would seem to have had the same kind of reputation in antiquity that, say, the Scientologists, the Moonies, or the Hare Krishnas enjoy in the United States in the present day" (1989, 50).

21. Cf. R. Parker 1996, 159.

22. R. Parker 1996, 159. On foreign cults, cf., e.g., Roller 1988; Versnel 1990, 1:96–123; Garland 1992; Allan 2004; Demetriou 2013, 217–27.

23. Cf. R. Parker (1996, 158), who cites (surprisingly) Dodds (1940, 171–76), as an example of a scholar who describes foreign cult as an infection.

24. R. Parker explains that foreign cults are "Greco-Roman products stamped 'made in Egypt' or 'Persia'" (1996, 159). Cf. Versnel 1990, 156. Strabo 10.3.18 indicates that the Athenians were particularly hospitable to foreign gods (Ἀθηναῖοι δ' ὥσπερ περὶ τὰ ἄλλα φιλοξενοῦντες διατελοῦσιν, οὕτω καὶ περὶ τοὺς θεούς. πολλὰ γὰρ τῶν ξενικῶν ἱερῶν παρεδέξαντο ὥστε καὶ ἐκωμῳδήθησαν, "Just as the Athenians continue to be hospitable to things from

elsewhere, so also with regard to the gods. For they received so many of the foreign cults that they were even ridiculed in comedy").

25. R. Parker 1996, 158–59, 163; 2011, 273–77.

26. R. Parker explains, "One can scarcely insist enough on the paradox that ecstatic dancing, the mark *par excellence* of an 'eastern' cult, was, in all seeming, indigenous in Greece" (1996, 160).

27. R. Parker 2005, 284.

28. On ancient criticisms of nonestablished cults, see R. Parker 1996, 162n33. In a discussion of Euripides *Bacchae*, Versnel surveys the foreign gods to argue that Euripides's play is modeled on historical religious phenomena. As he explains, with regard to the rituals associated with these divinities, we find characterized a mode, a way of being, and a lifestyle that is worrisome to many: "The very nature of the notion 'foreign' evoked various unpleasant associations: the smell of magic and profit-making, connotations of licence or ecstasy, revelry and sexual promiscuity and a special appeal to women and people of low social status. Foreign cults also tended to be associated with private or secret ritual, which in its turn fostered all kinds of suspicions, especially when it involved participation by Athenian citizens" (1990, 121–22). He continues, "This fear and disapproval from the side of the *polis* . . . dominates our sources and entirely outvoices the experiences or expectations of the initiated" (156). What interests Versnel (and what interests me) is not so much what *really* happened when foreign gods were worshipped, nor the original practices in the deity's homeland, rather, the *associations* that such rituals carry in the minds of outsiders to the cult.

29. R. Parker 1996, 162. For παιδιά and the Adonia, see Menander *Samia*, 41; Plato *Phaedrus*, 276b (and see chapter 4). For παιδιά used to describe Orpheus initiators, see Plato *Republic*, 364e–365a. Cf. Theophrastus *Characters* 16.11a; Plato *Euthydemus*, 277d (παιδιά) of Corybantic initiations; see also Foucart 1873, 153–77.

30. The *polis* in question is Thebes, not Athens, but Euripides's drama draws on Athenian conceptions of foreign ritual, specifically, maenadic ritual. See Zeitlin 1990 on the representation of Thebes in Greek tragedy.

31. Versnel 1990, 110. Cf. Vernant 1985, 50, on Dionysus's alterity at the heart of the *polis*, discussed by Versnel (1990, 150n213).

32. An ancient Greek could refer to sex by alluding to *ta aphrodisia*, "the things of Aphrodite," or ἔργα Ἀφροδίτης, "the works of Aphrodite." See, e.g., Homer *Iliad* 5.429 (ἔργα γάμοιο, directly connected with Aphrodite); Hesiod's *Works and Days* 521; *Homeric Hymn to Aphrodite*, 1, 6 (ἔργα Κυθερείης), 9, 21; Solon fr. 26 West.

33. Cf. Pentheus's remark that Dionysus has the "wine-dark graces of Aphrodite in his eyes," 236. See also 354, 402–8, and 459. Henrichs remarks, "Doubt about the morality of the maenads was presumably not so much a real issue in fifth-century Athens as an invention of Euripides or Aeschylus as playwrights who exploited it as a dramatic foil for Pentheus' own prurient curiosity" (1978, 135). The association between maenads and sex was, I suggest, a "real issue in fifth-century Athens," inasmuch as the association between maenads and sex was a stereotype. Descriptions of maenads and other similarly described foreign cults (discussed later) indicate that nonmainstream cult activities produced a certain amount of

anxiety (worries that such activities might indeed become infectious) in the minds of Classical Athenians.

34. See, e.g., Schlesier 1993, 90; Segal (1982) 1997, 374. Kowalzig (2007a) builds on Henrichs's (1994–95) notion of choral self-referentiality, moments when the chorus insists on a merging of myth and ritual, play and *polis*. Kowalzig argues that, in these moments, *choroi* tend to become specifically choruses of Dionysus. Ultimately, she suggests that the spectators themselves are on some level pulled into the orchestra during the plays: "Passages of choral self-referentiality do not project the choros into a distant realm of Dionysiac revel but rather project the audience into the orchestra and make it part of the 'ritual' occurring on stage" (2007a, 236). In a Dionysiac context, then, what separates the actor from the audience may dissolve. Cf. Segal (1982) 1997, 218, 225; J. Barrett 2002.

35. Henrichs (1978, 133) argues that maenadic activity is exclusively associated with women in Greece until the Hellenistic period. Yet maenadic ritual, at least in the Athenian imagination—I am not as concerned about maenadism as actually practiced (or not)—was troubling to Classical Athenians, and texts that underscore the breakdown between spectator and participant and showcase unsuspecting men drawn into the Dionysiac sphere emphasize these concerns. Cf. Bremmer 1984; Versnel 1990, 119–20n94; Scullion 2013.

36. Ιων· ἐθιάσευσ', ἢ πῶς τάδ' αὐδᾷς; Ξο. Μαινάσιν γε Βακχίου.
Ιων· ἔμφρον' ἢ κάτοινον ὄντα; Ξο. Βακχίου πρὸς ἡδοναῖς.

I: He brought you into their *thiasos*, or what do you mean?
X: . . . the maenads of Bacchus.
I: Did you have your wits about you or were you drunk?
X: I was in the throes of Bacchic pleasures (552–53).

37. For a recent discussion of rape at a festival in Menander, see Bathrellou 2012.

38. Cf. 403–23. The women of *Lysistrata* are very much associated with sex and "the works of Aphrodite" through their *denial* of sex, since, as they deny *ta aphrodisia* to their husbands, they become all the more desirable.

39. Seaford 1993.

40. For the troubling position of lamentation in the *polis*, see chapter 1. For mourning women as bacchants, see, e.g., Aeschylus *Seven against Thebes*, 835; Euripides *Hecuba* 684–87; *Phoenician Women* 1489–90. Cf. Andromache in Homer's *Iliad* 6.389; 22.460. See Segal, who remarks, "Euripides could . . . draw upon a certain interchangeability between the release of intense emotion among women in Bacchic ritual and the sharing of intense emotion in funeral lament. In this way he characteristically explores aspects of social behavior that his culture found threatening. Both bacchantic rites and funerary lament set women apart from men in a collective and exclusively female activity. In both cases this collective, segregated, and female activity is perceived as dangerous to the women themselves and as potentially subversive of civic order" ([1982] 1997, 363–64). On Dionysiac mourning women, see also Schlesier 1993; Seaford 1993, 119–20.

41. See Bowie 1993, 178–204; Loraux (1993, 147–83) has greatly influenced my reading of this play, in particular, her attention to the notional space of the Acropolis discussed later in the chapter; Gilhuly 2009, 140–79; Bierl 2012.

42. At the promontory of Kolias, not far from Athens (the location of Kolias seems to be near Phaleron, cf. Herodotus 8.96), Aphrodite had a major sanctuary. Pausanias reports that he saw there an *agalma* of Aphrodite Kolias and the "goddesses called Genetyllides," 1.1.5. Stephanus of Byzantium (s.v. Κωλιάς) also reports that there was a temple of Aphrodite at Kolias. For Kolias and Genetyllis and τρυφή, see Aristophanes *Clouds* (49–52), where Strepsiades provides a definition of τρυφή that includes Kolias and Genetyllis. Cf. Aristophanes *Thesmophoriazousai* 130. For the intentionally archaizing writers Alciphron (*Letters of Farmers* 2.8.2) and [Lucian] (*Amores* 42), Genetyllis and Kolias are linked with τρυφή and "new" (or nonestablished) divinities. Although Kolias and Genetyllis clearly evoke Aphrodite and "feminine excess" in the minds of Athenians, their precise relationship, as well as the relationship of the two to Aphrodite, is unclear. Some evidence instead connects the Genetyllides with Artemis (Pirenne-Delforge 1994, 76–78).

43. On Pan, see, e.g., Borgeaud 1988; R. Parker 1996, 163–68. In *Lysistrata*, during the memorable scene in which Myrrhine torments her sexually afflicted husband, Cinesias, Cinesias suggests that the pair satisfy their desires in the grotto of Pan (911). The rape of Creusa by Apollo (Euripides *Ion* 10–13) took place in the grotto of Pan, where Cinesias and Myrrhine meet. In *Lysistrata*, once the women begin to feel the effects of Lysistrata's plan, they start sneaking off to reunite with their husbands. One of the defectors overcome by desire tries to dig her way out through the cave of Pan, 721. Cf. 997–98, where Cinesias asks the Herald if Pan caused his erection.

44. A scholion on the lines reads: "for the women used to celebrate many festivals outside of the state rituals (i.e., 'not paid for by the people'), gathering together privately" (καὶ γὰρ πολλὰς ἑορτὰς αἱ γυναῖκες ἔξω τῶν δημοτελῶν ἦγον ἰδίᾳ συνερχόμεναι, Σ 1 Hangard). Versnel suggests that the passage contains a reference to "female *thiasoi* of a private nature," likening the rituals to the private *teletai* of Sabazius (1990, 149 and 149n212). R. Parker comments, "The reference seems to be to informal festivals of women, like the mourning for Adonis, but held in this case not in a house but at public shrines" (1996, 161). Cf. R. Parker 2005, 325; see also Seaford 1994, 262–75.

45. Cf. MacDowell 1995, 242–43.

46. For the Lysistrata-Lysimachê connections, see D. M. Lewis 1955; Foley 1982; Henderson 1987, xxxviii–xl; Loraux 1993, 179–81; Connelly 2007, 62–64; Gilhuly 2009, 148–49. For a different view, see Dover's assertion that Aristophanes chose the name Lysistrata in order to *avoid* an identification between the two women, even though he wanted a name meaning "ending war" (1972, 152n3). On Myrrhine's connections with the priestess of Athena Nike who was also named Myrrhine, see Papadimitriou 1948–1949; Connelly 2007, 62–64.

47. There are two exceptions—the naming of Lysistrata and the naming of the character Dionysus in *Frogs*. On (not) naming respectable women, see Schaps 1977; Sommerstein 1980; Olson 1992.

48. In the opening scenes, Lysistrata is named not only at 6, but also at 21, 69, 135, 186, 189, 216. Later her name appears at 746, 1086, 1103, 1147.

49. Cf. Herodotus 5.72, where the priestess of Athena Polias speaks on behalf of the city at a moment of crisis. On priestesses in general, see, e.g., Dillon 2002, 73–106; Goff 2004, 61–69; Connelly 2007.

50. Cf. Aristophanes *Peace*, where Trygaeus prays to Peace: "Release the battles and the tumult, so that we may call you *Lysimachê*" (991–92).

51. When the Official arrives onstage, he sees rampant female sexuality and Ἀδωνιασμός. But the women who confront him at first are not marriageable young women; they are older matrons, well past their prime. Why is the Official worried about female sexuality getting out of control? The Official sees what he wants to see (so too Pentheus, whose prurient imagination conjures up visions of women and sex on Mount Kithairon even as the Messenger proves him wrong).

52. Philippides's *Women-at-the-Adonis-Festival*: *PCG* vii fr. 1–4.

53. Elderkin 1940; Stroup 2004. Loraux 1993, 147–83.

54. Aristophanes's extant plays, with the exception of *Peace* and *Wealth*, are named after groups and choruses rather than individual characters. The name *Lysistrata* is somewhat anomalous. Foley remarks, "*Lysistrata* is the only extant Greek comedy named after a single individual, and the play may well have been the first old comedy with a female hero" (1982, 8). The chorus in *Lysistrata* is distinctive; it is split between old men and old women during the run of the play. How can *Adôniazousai* refer to this idiosyncratic chorus? As I will argue, the two choruses merge in the end, becoming a collective with the women dominating, as the men join together with the *Adôniazousai*. For another quirky Aristophanic chorus, compare *Frogs*, where the chorus of *Batrachoi* give their name to the play, yet the chorus of initiates play the main role. I do not argue that the only figures who can be seen to be women-at-the-Adonis-festival are the chorus. As will become clear, I believe that Lysistrata and the other individually named characters also take on this role.

55. Many articles on *Lysistrata* begin with an attempt to deal with what is seen as an inherent contradiction throughout the play. See Richard Martin 1987, 83n19, for a survey of this tendency, and see Hulton 1972 for the formulation of the two plans as "A" and "B."

56. Loraux 1993, 151. Cf. Elderkin 1940.

57. Loraux remarks: "What, then, is the secret portion of the play that has too often been ignored? In a word—the Acropolis . . . the *Lysistrata* is not a play about the Acropolis, but the Acropolis functions as something like an essential comic *operator* within the work" (1993, 148).

58. Revermann's 2006 work on Aristophanes and staging does not consider this particular aspect, though he does examine other performative concerns in *Lysistrata.*

59. Mastronarde 1990.

60. Mastronarde 1990, 259. He provides a thorough discussion of the probable staging of tragic and comic plays. For his discussion of *Lysistrata*, see 261–62 and 282.

61. Cf. 864, 873, 874, 883, 912. For the women's shift in position, cf. Lysistrata's pronouncement of the "oracle" (770–73). See also Henderson 1980, 159; and 1987, xli, for more on staging.

62. See Loraux 1993, 147–83, for a discussion of the relationship between the real space of the Acropolis to the space of the play.

63. Pausanias 1.27.3; Broneer 1932, 39–55; Langlotz 1954, 28–29; Glowacki 1991. And near the Nike temple on the southwest slope was the shrine to Peitho and Aphrodite Pandêmos. On Aphrodite Pandêmos, see further discussion later in the chapter.

64. Cole has referred to Athena as "goddess of the secured height," remarking, "some of the earliest epigraphical evidence for political unity is associated with an *akropolis*. The earliest fortified communities identified the security of these heights with Athena, called Polias not because she was goddess of the city but because she was goddess of the secured height. Her title had a strictly spatial reference that defined her as guardian of the πόλις in its original meaning as *akropolis*" (2004, 17).

65. In the world of the play, the Acropolis is simply Athena's space (241, 302–3), even though the space was in reality associated with other divinities.

66. For a description of the rites of the Adonis festival as *orgia*, see [Lucian] *de dea syria* 6.

67. Cf. Cinesias's remark to Myrrhine: "It's been so long since you celebrated the rites of Aphrodite" (τὰ τῆς Ἀφροδίτης <δ'>ἱέρ' ἀνοργίαστά σοι / χρόνον τοσοῦτόν ἐστιν, 898–99).

68. Lysistrata notes Cinesias's location at 835, when she remarks that Cinesias is by Chloe's shrine. Pausanias mentions this shrine in his approach to the Propylaia, coming from the southwest (1.22.3). During the seduction scene, Myrrhine remarks that she will no longer be "pure" (*hagnos*) when she returns to the Acropolis (*Lysistrata* 912). *Aphrodisia*, then, appears to be permitted in the lower area near Pan's grotto—where, in fact, a precinct to Eros and Aphrodite was located—but not atop the Acropolis.

69. See Scullion 1998 for discussion of Corybantic rites and how they relate to rituals in honor of Dionysus.

70. Foley 1982, 7.

71. For the rooftop as an advantageous location given the perspective it affords one who looks down from it, see Callimachus *Hymn to Demeter* 3–4, where the uninitiated are not permitted to look down from above on the procession. They would then be able to see the sacred objects carried in the basket. Cf. Aristophanes *Acharnians*, where Dicaeopolis celebrates the rural Dionysia and tells his wife to watch him from the roof (262). For the ability to be seen from a rooftop, see the inscription from Thasos (*SEG* 42.785) discussed by Henry 2002.

72. Cf. Menander *Samia* 38–49.

73. And just as Medea flies off to Athens. The *skênê* roof seems particularly associated with temporary occupation.

74. For oaths and Aristophanes, see Dillon 1995; for the scene in *Lysistrata*, see Fletcher 2012, 220–40.

75. Burkert (1985, 71) explains that *sphagia*, the shedding of blood not necessarily within the context of a meal, often occurs before a battle (as in *Seven against Thebes*, to which Lysistrata alludes). This is particularly germane as the women of *Lysistrata* will wage a battle (though a battle for *peace*). For the notion that *Lysistrata* is not *simply* a peace play, see Gilhuly 2009. She argues that while the play is superficially concerned with peace, violence and aggression toward the Spartans lurk beneath the surface. On the scene as a disruption of a normative sacrifice, see Fletcher 1999; as a disruption of a normative symposium, see Pütz 2003. The jug (*stamnion*) is simultaneously diminutive and supersized, as Revermann (2006) points out.

76. Elderkin (1940) is one of the few to comment on the fact that the *stamnion* is called a "boar." On Adonis and the boar, see chapter 1.

77. Boars were used in oath-sacrifice ceremonies (*Iliad* 19.251; see also Lupu 2005, 188, for a handful of other references). Individuals who took the oath of the Areopagus stood over the severed pieces of a boar, ram, and bull and invoked destruction on themselves and their households if they perjured themselves (Demosthenes 23.67–69; on the oath see Antiphon 1.8, 1.28, 5.12, 6.16; Lysias 10.11; Isocrates 18.56; Aeschines 2.87; [Demosthenes] 59.10; see also Sommerstein 1989, 15–16). In general, a κάπρος appears as a sacrificial animal far less frequently than a domesticated pig (ὗς, χοῖρος). Cf. Jameson 1988, 99. For an analysis of visual representations of animal sacrifice in Archaic and Classical Greece, see Van Straten 1995 and Gebauer 2002. Boars appear infrequently in Van Straten's discussion (though see 54, 76, 201, 216, 218, 288). A useful table (176) "Prices of Victims in Attic Sacrificial Calendars" shows entries for ὗς, ὗς κυοῦσα, χοῖρος but not κάπρος. As Van Straten points out, it is at times difficult to identify an animal from a vase painting. See, e.g., fig. 110 (V147; Paris Louvre G 112), which Van Straten identifies as a pig, but which appears to have the bristles of a boar. Apparently, because of the existence of the Greek hairy pig, it is difficult to distinguish between a boar and a pig. Cf. Durand 1989, 94. In visual representations, we lack labels identifying the animals as κάπρος, ὗς, or χοῖρος. But even if we did have such labels, κάπρος may occasionally refer to a domesticated pig (see Lupu 2005, 188).

78. On the boar hunt in Greek myth, see Felson 1983; Felson and Sale 1984; Davies 2001.

79. As soon as the two choruses (divided through nearly the entire play) join together, they sing of a piglet (δελφάκιον, 1061) that they have sacrificed. And shortly after this, the Spartans are described as "having a pigpen around their thighs" (ὥσπερ χοιροκομεῖον περὶ τοῖς μηροῖσιν ἔχοντες, 1073), a joke that, regardless of its specific meaning (their erections cause their clothing to stick out and thereby resemble a pigpen?) is another mention of domesticated swine. Cf. Henderson 1987, 192.

80. Cf. Pandora's adornment scene (Hesiod *Works and Days* 69–82; *Theogony* 571–84); see also West 1978; Zeitlin 1996, 53–86. See also Hera's "arming"/preparation in *Iliad* 14 (159–92), in which she calls on Aphrodite for help. And see Brillet-Dubois for a reading of Aphrodite's adornment scene in the *Homeric Hymn to Aphrodite* as a "love *aristeia*" (2011, 109).

81. While *kosmos*/*kosmein* and the like do not appear in the play, similar language is employed, as in the language connected with "saving" Greece, discussed earlier. Also the women hope to ward off war and madness from Greece (ἀλλὰ πολέμου καὶ μανιῶν ῥυσαμένας Ἑλλάδα καὶ πολίτας, 342–43); they hope to "straighten" the men out (ἐπανορθώσαιμεν ἂν ὑμᾶς, 528); they are described as patriotic (φιλόπολις, 546); they plan to join together diverse elements (ξυνάγειν καὶ ξυναθροίζεν, 585); their goal is peace (Ἡσυχίας, 1289). On their interest in the politics of harmony, *eunoia*, see Reckford 1987. For a discussion of *kosmos* from a variety of perspectives, see Cartledge, Millett, and Reden, 1998.

82. For this interpretation of Aphrodite Pandêmos, see, e.g., Halperin 1990, 104–6. Pausanias 1.22.3 reports that Theseus established the cult when he brought the Athenians together. Cf. Apollodorus *FGrH* 244 fr. 113. For a similar argument connecting Aphrodite Pandêmos with civic harmony, see Petre 1992–94; Rosenzweig 2004, 13. Cf. Simon 1983, 48–51; Pirenne-Delforge 1988, 1994; Frost 2002. On the advances in recent scholarship relating Aphrodite to civic cult, see chapter 1.

83. Sappho, for instance, has Peitho as the daughter of Aphrodite (Sappho 90a col. II 7–8 Voigt; 96.26–29 and test. 200). Even when the familial relationship between Aphrodite and Peitho is not emphasized, the two tend to be mentioned in the same breath (Ibycus 288.3 *PMG*, where Euryalus is nursed by Kypris and Peitho). On Peitho in Greek tragedy, see Buxton 1982.

84. Pausanias mentions the sanctuary (1.22.3), and it has been securely identified (*IG* I^2, 700 (= I^3, 832); II^2, 659 (*SIG*^{3} 375), 4596, 4862). See Dontas 1960, 4–9; Beschi 1967–68, 517–25; Simon 1983, 48–51; A. Smith 2011, 55–57.

85. *Homeric Hymn to Aphrodite* 7. On Aphrodite and persuasion, see, e.g., Sappho 1.18 Voigt. Pindar refers to *hetairai* as *amphipoloi Peithous* and speaks of them flitting up to the heavens to Aphrodite (fr. 122 Maehler; cf. fr. 123).

86. See Sokolowski 1969, 39, for a procession to wash what is possibly the image of Peitho in the Klepsydra. A quick rinse in the Klepsydra is exactly what Cinesias suggests that Myrrhine do if she wishes to be pure upon her return to the Acropolis. This is apt, since surely at this moment Myrrhine embodies "persuasion."

87. Cf. Elderkin 1941, 122.

88. Cf. Henderson 1987, 174, on the common use of "myrtle" to mean female genitalia; Detienne (1972) 1994, 62–64 on the Myrrhine scene.

89. "Would you like some perfume?" says Myrrhine (βούλει μυρίσω σε; 938), using the verb μυρίζειν, which means to anoint one with μύρον.

90. See Henderson 1987, 182, on the variants *alabastos*/*alabastron* and on the uses of *alabastra*.

91. For discussion, see chapter 1. Cf. fig. 21.

92. Cf. Aul. Gell. 17.9.6.

93. For other examples of this epithet for old men, see Henderson 1987, 115. Cf. the use of σορός, "coffin," to describe an old woman (e.g., Machon 300–301 [Gow 1965]).

94. Van Leeuwen (1903) believes the Official's remark is a call to arms (cf. ἀλλ' ἀμυντέον τὸ πρᾶγμ' ὅστις γ' ἐνόρχης ἔστ' ἀνήρ, *Lys.* 661).

95. In Euripides *Andromache*, Peleus upbraids Menelaus for his conduct after the war: "You didn't kill your wife after you had her in your control, but when you saw her breast, throwing away your sword, you received her kiss, fawning over that treacherous bitch, you wretch, weaker than Aphrodite (ἥσσων πεφυκὼς Κύπριδος)," 628–31. The sword and the phallus are both symbols of male aggression and power; Menelaus famously throws the former away in order to focus on the latter. Yet Menelaus is clearly not in a position of power despite his enflamed desire. A similar movement is at work in *Lysistrata.* Lampito remarks, just after Lysistrata describes her sex-strike plan for the first time, "Menelaus, for example, when he saw Helen's bare 'apples,' he threw away, I think, his sword," 155–56. The men of *Lysistrata* find themselves enflamed with desire, and, "weaker than Aphrodite," they throw away their swords and agree to stop the war.

96. Cf. Dover 1972, 150, 160–61; Henderson 1987, 80; Loraux 1993, 124. In *Lysistrata*, only at 1092 is intercourse with Cleisthenes suggested.

97. Loraux 1993, 162.

98. Loraux 1993, 166.

99. Stroup 2004, 41. Cf. Faraone 2006. See also Taaffe (1993), who argues that Lysistrata and her allies play the role of "women," that is, hypostasized versions of femininity.

100. For the proverb, see Zenobius 1.49 (L-S i.19), and see chapter 1 for discussion of the gardens.

101. For the role of gardens of Adonis in Plato's *Phaedrus*, see chapter 4.

102. War devastates crops and is in this way fundamentally incompatible with proper farming.

103. Cf. Henderson 1987, 163.

104. Henderson notes that this is an "unusually specific allusion to the passage of time" (1987, 177).

105. See chapter 1 for a discussion of the season of the Adonia and how the Plutarch passages, along with the *Lysistrata* passage, relate to this problem. Of course there is a certain circularity in marshaling Plutarch as evidence because he was writing so much later, and because we are unsure about his sources. It is certainly possible that Plutarch drew upon Aristophanes's *Lysistrata* for this narrative. He surely was not drawing on Thucydides as the historian makes no mention of an Adonis festival before the Sicilian expedition, nor does he mention Demostratus. Thucydides does describe the mutilation of the Herms, an incident that is mentioned in *Lysistrata* 1093–94.

106. On the Adonis festival as grim backdrop to political events, cf. Ammianus Marcellinus 22.9.14–15, where the mournful cries of the Adonia again make for an unpropitious setting as the emperor Julian enters the city.

107. Cf. Plutarch's use of the verb in *de sera numinis vindicta* 560c, where it appears again in connection with gardens of Adonis. The verb can refer, e.g., to the extinguishing of a flame, a sick body that is desiccated, or a plant that wilts. Cf. Weill 1966, 690–91.

108. Furley 1988. Cf. Keuls (1985, 391, 395), who also connects the Adonia with the mutilation of the Herms.

109. Cf. Ion's solo paean (normally performed by a male chorus) in Euripides's *Ion* (125–27 = 141–43). For discussion of the ways in which Ion's performance reflects his isolation from the larger Athenian community to which he should belong, see Rutherford 1994–1995, 129–31.

110. Other examples: Cinesias laments (οἴμοι τί πάθω; 954); the chorus of old men let out an "*aiai*" in solidarity with Cinesias's plight (κἄγωγ' οἰκτίρω σ'· αἰαῖ, 961). Cf. 1034, 1097.

111. As the divided choruses unify, the men remark, μὴ ὥρασ' ἵκοισθ', a curse usually translated as "may you rot," but which means literally "may you not come in season," 1037. This phrase echoes the Official's earlier imprecation against Demostratus the warmonger (μὴ ὥρασι, "may he rot," 391) and perhaps invokes once more the gardens of Adonis, which are not grown at the proper time (not "in season") but are instead quickly germinated during the summer, the hottest time of the year. See Rogers 1911, 48; and Henderson 1987, 120, on the phrase.

112. On Lysistrata's disappearance as the play draws to a close, see Henderson 1987, 206–7.

113. See, e.g., Homer *Iliad*: ὣς ἔφατο κλαίουσ', ἐπὶ δὲ στενάχοντο γυναῖκες / Πάτροκλον πρόφασιν, σφῶν δ' αὐτῶν κήδε' ἑκάστη, "So she spoke, weeping, and the women groaned in response. They mourned for Patroclus, but also each bemoaned her own sorrows," 19.302–3. Cf. Garland 1989, 4.

114. Foley 2001, 43–44.

115. See Loraux 1986, 45–47; 1990, 35, 82, on the tension between lament and funeral oration. On lament as a counter to dominant ideology, see Alexiou (1974) 2002, 282; Caraveli 1986, 181–82; Holst-Warhaft 1992. See also Ziolkowski 1981, 152–53. Ancient scholars also remark on the inappropriateness of *thrênos* to *epitaphios logos*. See Ziolkowski's (1981, 35–36 and 37) discussion of the two treatises from the Roman Imperial period (the *Ars Rhetorica*, a rhetorical manual falsely attributed to Dionysius of Halicarnassus, and the treatise on funeral speeches by Menander of Laodicea, third century CE).

116. For discussions of the genre, see, e.g., Flashar 1969; Ziolkowski 1981; Clairmont 1983; Macleod 1983, 149–53; Connor 1984, 66–72; Loraux 1986; Thomas 1989; Hornblower 1991–2008, 1:294–96; R. Parker 1996, 131–41; Pelling 1997, 229–32; Todd 2007, 149–64. See also Mills's 1997 chapter, "The Athenian Image of Athens," 43–86.

117. Cf. Aristotle *Rhetoric* 1411a and Plutarch *Pericles* 8.6 (on Pericles's funeral oration). Each of the extant funeral speeches offers some sort of idiosyncrasy marking it as different from the others and emphasizing that it takes the place of traditional mourning (cf. Derderian 2001, 165). For example, Lysias 2 and the fragments of Gorgias's speech could not have been performed by their authors in Athens, inasmuch as Lysias and Gorgias were not citizens. Plato's *Menexenus* is likely a parody of the genre of *epitaphios logos* as a whole, but what exactly that means for our interpretation of the speech is unclear. The authorship of the Demosthenes speech has been called into question. Yet as Loraux (1986) has argued, elements of this distinctively Athenian genre may be traced despite the singularity of the individual orations.

118. Cf. Thucydides's Pericles, who remarks, "I do not lament for the parents of these men" (οὐκ ὀλοφύρομαι, 2.44.1).

119. Bosworth 2000, 2–3. Cf. Lacey (1964), who argues (and Hornblower [1991–2008, 1:314] agrees) that Pericles is emphasizing that women should restrain themselves in their grief. The funerary context is what is at issue with regard to the exhortation to the widows; the words to the widows concern the role of women in mourning. Loraux (1985) argues that Thucydides tends to portray women against a background characterized by turmoil, θόρυβος. Women are generally expected to be disruptive, and their "virtue" in the Thucydides passage consists in their restraint with regard to mourning.

120. Cf. Thucydides 2.34.4 (καὶ γυναῖκες πάρεισιν αἱ προσήκουσαι ἐπὶ τὸν τάφον ὀλοφυρόμεναι), which contains the only other reference to lamentation in Thucydides's description of the state funeral. As Ziolkowski (1981, 166–67) points out, the time indicated by the participle is ambiguous at 2.46.2, and it is thus not clear when the lamentation took place. The passage could mean "since you have lamented (i.e., before the speech), be on your way," but it could also mean "after you have lamented (now), be on your way." Cf. Plato *Menexenus* 249c and Demosthenes 60.37, which also include the conventional *envoi*;

see also Hornblower 1991–2008, 1:315–16. Interestingly, the initial anxiety that the speaker may not succeed in finding words suitable for the occasion that appears in extant funeral oration (e.g., *Menexenus* 236e; Demosthenes 60.1; Thucydides 2.35.2) may be drawn from *thrênos*, where one sees a similar hesitation (e.g., Aeschylus *Agamemnon* 1489–91); see also Alexiou (1974) 2002, 161. So even as *epitaphios logos* attempts to supersede traditional mourning, it may be drawing on conventions appropriate to *thrênos*.

121. Vannicelli (2002) considers points of contact between *Lysistrata* and *epitaphios logos*, especially lines 648–57. Here I draw on several of his arguments, though he does not connect these references to the Adonia. Loraux (1993, 154n22) also suggests parallels between language in *Lysistrata* and language used in *epitaphios logos*. Simms hints at a connection between funeral oration and the Adonia when she remarks, "It is an interesting coincidence that our first literary evidence for the Adonia falls at almost the same time as Pericles' funeral oration for those killed in the first year of the Peloponnesian War" (1997–98, 135). She also describes the Adonia that the Official in *Lysistrata* remembers as "an embryonic political voice" and continues by suggesting that the cult offered "a modest expression of displeasure with those making the political/military decisions. In other words, the women, by exploiting their traditional role as society's lamenters, had discovered a means by which they could make a political comment" (137). She continues, "In the late fifth century, this autonomy, already well established, may have provided a forum in which to express opposition to the current war mentality of the state" (138). Cf. Keuls 1985, 391, 395.

122. Cf. Ziolkowski 1981, 108.

123. Cf. Plato's *Menexenus* 241d.

124. Cf. Demosthenes 60.8; Hyperides 6.5.

125. For the salvation theme in Greek thought more generally, see, e.g., Faraone 1997.

126. For a convincing demonstration that Thucydides's funeral speech was firmly based on tradition, see Ziolkowski 1981 (see especially 133). Early on, it seems, *eranos* referred to a communal meal at which guests contributed by bringing food or took a turn at hosting the meal at another time. Later, the word comes to signify a kind of loan to which friends or relatives contributed. See Millett's discussion of the *eranos* loan (1991, 153–59). Cf. Harris 1992, 311–12. The term can refer to a group, composed of *eranistai*, and such a group can have a religious function (R. Parker 1996, 333).

127. Hornblower concludes, "It is possible that the use by Thucydides and Aristophanes of this metaphor . . . had a common origin in the oratory of the historical Pericles" (1991–2008, 1:312).

128. On Pericles's injunction to become lovers of the *polis*, see Monoson (1994, 260), who underscores the potentially shameful implications of the city as *erômenos* to the citizen-*erastês*. By contrast, Wohl (2002, 63–64n73) suggests that pederasty is not necessarily implied and emphasizes that the city is feminized.

129. Vannicelli concludes that "un ateniese che avesse avuto in mente simili raccomandazioni non avrebbe potuto fare a meno di rilevare l'atteggiamento del tutto opposto delle donne nella *Lisistrata*" (2002, 71).

130. For mention of the gravesite in the speeches, see Derderian 2001, 166. See also, e.g., Thucydides 2.35.1; Demosthenes 60.2, cf. 33; Hyperides 6.1; Lysias 2.1, 66; Plato *Menexenus* 242c.

131. For Athenian militarism perpetuated by means of funeral oration, see, e.g., Hunt 2010, 70. For an early spring or winter date for the state funeral, see, e.g., Thucydides, who indicates that the ceremony took place in winter (2.34.1). Cf. Hyperides's fourth-century funeral oration, which took place in early spring. For some degree of flexibility in the date, see, e.g., Loraux 1986, 37–38; Todd 2007, 149n1. The state funeral tended to be an annual occurrence (Plato *Menexenus* 249b; Isocrates *On the Peace* 87), though it seems there were years when it was not held (καὶ διὰ παντὸς τοῦ πολέμου, ὁπότε ξυμβαίη αὐτοῖς, ἐχρῶντο τῷ νόμῳ, "and during the war, they made use of this custom whenever the occasion arose," Thucydides 2.34.7). Cf. Ziolkowski 1981, 22. For discussion of the summer season of the Adonia, see chapter 1.

132. Loraux 1993, 9. For autochthony, see, e.g., Thucydides 2.36.1; Plato *Menexenus* 237b–c; Demosthenes 60.4–5; Lysias 2.17. See Ziolkowski 1981; Loraux 1986, esp. 148–50; Mills 1997, 62. Loraux comments, "Autochthonous birth does away with the significance of women's maternity, but attributes to Athena (or to the city, in the discourse of the Kerameikos) the roles of nurse, father, and mother" (1993, 8). Most references to Athenian autochthony appear in tragedy and funeral orations (Rosivach 1987, 302). Rosivach suggests that stories about Athenian autochthony were fairly late developments and were tied to fifth-century democracy. Cf. R. Parker 1987.

133. For the Adonia as a ritual that allowed women to lament Adonis as well as their own losses, see Simms 1997–98, 136. Bion's Hellenistic poem on the death of Adonis is called *Adônidos epitaphios* (sc. *logos*). As Reed (1997) points out, it is strange that the poem carries such a title, since *epitaphios logos* refers to the encomiastic prose oration in celebration of the war dead, and Bion's poetic Doric hexameters hardly fit our expectations for prose oration. Although Reed is surely right that the title affixes itself to the poem at a late date, and "Bion's poem is doubtless so called . . . because it concerns the death of an individual (and does . . . use many epicedic tropes)" (1997, 194), perhaps the title may also speak to the connections between the Adonia and *epitaphios logos*, which I have outlined here.

Chapter 4. Philosophy

1. In *Laws* (947b), the Athenian stranger prescribes no mourning at all in his description of an ideal funeral, just hymns. He also suggests that it is blasphemous when a chorus sings sad strains at public sacrifices, expressing disapproval of the words, rhythms, and harmony of the lamenters (*Laws* 800d). In *Republic*, Socrates explains that when something terrible happens to us it is better to be reasonable and take stock of our situation by deliberating and planning instead of wailing and bemoaning our fate (ἐν τῷ βοᾶν διατρίβειν, 604c). Lamentation is, quite simply, a waste of time. The part of us that dwells on lamentation and suffering is irrational, lazy, and a friend of cowardice (τό δὲ πρὸς τὰς ἀναμνήσεις τε τοῦ πάθους

καὶ πρὸς τοὺς ὀδυρμοὺς ἄγον καὶ ἀπλήστως ἔχον αὐτῶν ἆρ' οὐκ ἀλόγιστόν τε φήσομεν εἶναι καὶ ἀργὸν καὶ δειλίας φίλον; 604d).

2. Loraux remarks, "Wailing and beating her breast, Socrates' wife, Xanthippe, has already anticipated the mourning for Socrates, and she has been firmly removed from the group of philosophers right at the beginning of the dialogue. Phaedo, overly faithful to the city's customs, intends to crop his hair in mourning for Socrates. But the philosopher teaches him the uselessness of such funerary rites: at this point all that counts is the *logos*, for it concerns the immortality of the soul" (1995, 148).

3. For a similar opposition between *logos* and writing, and writing as *paidia*, see Alcidamas *Against the Authors of Written Speeches*, 34.

4. E.g., M. Morgan, whose *Platonic Piety* examines ritual language in Plato (especially Plato's use of mystery language), devotes an entire chapter to *Phaedrus*, but only discusses gardens of Adonis in passing (1990, 184, 244n108). Other scholars briefly remark on the Adonia in their treatments of the dialogue (e.g., Nightingale 1995, 166–67; duBois 1985). Detienne ([1972] 1994, see especially 103–4) is less interested than I am in the way in which the metaphor of gardens of Adonis functions in the dialogue *as a whole* and thus interprets the passage as a straightforward pronouncement concerning the fruitlessness of the gardens.

5. Cf. Nightingale 1995, 167. The knowledge of the just, beautiful, and good is analogous to the seeds of the farmer when Socrates remarks, "Do we say that the individual with knowledge of the just and beautiful and good has less sense than the farmer with regard to his seeds?" (τὸν δὲ δικαίων τε καὶ καλῶν καὶ ἀγαθῶν ἐπιστήμας ἔχοντα τοῦ γεωργοῦ φῶμεν ἧττον νοῦν ἔχειν εἰς τὰ ἑαυτοῦ σπέρματα; 276c). Cf. [Plato] *Lovers*, where Socrates offers a similar movement from farmer to philosopher when he mentions, first, the farmer who plants seeds and, then, immediately afterward, the individual who plants "seeds" of learning in souls (134e).

6. Nightingale notes that an objective of *Phaedrus* is to "distinguish the philosopher from all other laborers in the fields of language" (1995, 164).

7. D. Clay 1975, 243 (along with ἄτοπος, "strange").

8. De Vries 1985, 20. Cf. Friedländer on *paidia* (1958, 1:118–25).

9. See K. A. Morgan 2000, 164–79. She remarks, "Plato clearly disapproves of play for the sake of mere amusement and eristic victory. The example of Sokrates, however, has raised the suspicion that philosophers may engage in a very different kind of play, one which merges with seriousness" (173). As the Athenian explains in *Laws*, if one is truly to become wise, one must understand the serious *and* the trivial, "for without *geloia* it is impossible to learn *spoudaia* or any contrary without its opposite if one is to be wise" (ἄνευ γὰρ γελοίων τὰ σπουδαῖα καὶ πάντων τῶν ἐναντίων τὰ ἐναντία μαθεῖν μὲν οὐ δυνατόν, εἰ μέλλει τις φρόνιμος ἔσεσθαι, 816d–e). The point here, however, is to become familiar with the *geloion* in order not to fall prey to it. The close relationship of *spoudê* to play is seen in [Plato's] characterization of *paidia* as "sister of seriousness" (*Epistle* 6.323d).

10. Play as education is underscored repeatedly in Plato's works, especially *Laws*, where play functions as a means of habit formation, which builds character (e.g., *Laws*

643b–c; *Republic* 425a). Cf. S. Morris 1998. On ideological work and games/play, see Kurke 1999, 247–98.

11. The connections between play, education, and philosophy may be glimpsed in a discussion over textual variants in *Gorgias* 485a4. Some editors have Callicles remarking that it is all well and good for one to practice philosophy "for the sake of education" (παιδείας χάριν). Van Heusde and Hartman, however, read παιδιᾶς χάριν (see Dodds 1959, 274). Here, the dispute over two readings points to a connection between the practice of philosophy, education, and play.

12. A "deliberate playfulness" characterizes *Phaedrus*, according to Rowe (1986, 12). "*Phaedrus* is perhaps the most serious and most playful of all Platonic dialogues," claims Lebeck (1972, 289).

13. Cf. *Phaedrus* 265c (ἐμοὶ μὲν φαίνεται τὰ μὲν ἄλλα τῷ ὄντι παιδιᾷ πεπαῖσθαι); 262d (προσπαίζων). In *Euthydemus*, Plato employs nearly the same phrase (ταῦτα μὲν οὖν, ὦ Εὐθύδημέ τε καὶ Διονυσόδωρε, πεπαίσθω τε ὑμῖν, καὶ ἴσως ἱκανῶς ἔχει, 278c–d).

14. For discussion of Plato's incorporation of poetic genres and his creation of the genre of philosophy, see Nightingale (1995), who looks at the appearance of epic, comedy, and tragedy in Plato's works. Cf. Blondell (2002), who outlines the connections between the dialogue form and drama. For Plato's complicated views on poetry, see also Nehamas 1982; G. R. F. Ferrari 1989; Murray 1997, 1–32; Halliwell 2002; Puchner 2010; Destrée and Herrmann 2011.

15. Nightingale 1995, 172.

16. See Nightingale 1995, 186, for a comic chorus in *Protagoras*.

17. Nightingale 1995, 190. Nightingale is interested in the ways in in which Plato is drawing, specifically, on Old Comedy. She remarks: "Although he objected to the comedians' ignorant use of ridicule, Plato was quick to appropriate comedy's 'voice of criticism' for his own dramas" (190). As she points out, Old Comedy gave way to Middle Comedy while Plato was alive. See especially 172–92 for more on Old Comedy's influence on Plato.

18. Olympiodorus *Commentary on Alcibiades I* 2.65–69. See Riginos's discussion, (1976, 176–77). Cf. an epigram attributed to Plato about Aristophanes (14 Diehl).

19. For bibliography on the seriousness of comedy and its relationship to Plato, see Nightingale 1995, 172–92.

20. *Apology* 18c; 19c. Cf. *Phaedo* 70c. In *Symposium* it is the speech of the comic playwright, Aristophanes, that is most memorable.

21. Cf. *Charmides* 155d, where Socrates catches sight of what is under Charmides's cloak.

22. The flirtation in *Phaedrus* gave rise to the belief in antiquity that there was an erotic relationship between Socrates and Phaedrus, or Plato and Phaedrus. Cf. *Anth. Pal.* 7.100.

23. Role reversal is common in Plato's dialogues. As Edmonds points out, "In other dialogues, just as in the *Symposium*, Socrates appears at first to play the role of the ἐραστής, courting the pretty ἐρώμενος, but he soon turns the tables and has the youths pursuing him" (2000, 282). Cf. Halperin 1986; Nussbaum 1986, 216–23, 231–33. As we will see later,

it is erotic *reciprocity* that will be important within the context of *Phaedrus*. In *Phaedrus*, Socrates refers to Lysias as Phaedrus's *paidika* (236b), which would seem to make Phaedrus an *erastês*, not a young *erômenos*. At 278e the implication is that Isocrates is Socrates's beloved. In fact, Phaedrus would have been about forty and Socrates would have been about sixty at the dramatic date of the dialogue—much older than typical *erômenoi*. What is more, historically Phaedrus cannot have been at Athens at the time of the dramatic date of the dialogue, as he was exiled from 415 to 404 for his implication in the mutilation of the Herms and the profanation of the mysteries (Rowe 1986, 13–14). Although it is not uncommon for Plato to be unconcerned about such technicalities (Dodds 1959, 17–18), Nussbaum argues for significance regarding the lack of dramatic date, arguing that *Phaedrus* is "Plato's own Egypt-legend," remarking, "That story wasn't true. You did not get led into disorder and impiety through your appetitive passions, your devotion to *mania*. You did not have to go into exile . . . instead of mutilating the holy statues of Hermes, you were saying a reverent prayer at the shrine of Pan, his son" (1986, 213).

24. On proper *erômenos* behavior see, e.g., Dover 1978; Halperin 1990.

25. Nussbaum describes this moment as "among the most haunting and splendid moments in philosophy" (1986, 211).

26. Nussbaum comments that Socrates "has just caught sight of this impressive young person, whose name means 'Sparkling' and who is clearly radiant with health, good looks, and ability" (1986, 200). By contrast, de Vries emphasizes that Phaedrus could not historically be a *pais* and that "these forms of address only serve to express the inverse coquetry by which an older man often emphasizes the difference in age when addressing a younger man" (1969, 6). And "Phaedrus is not the young, even very young man which he is often supposed to be in the present dialogue" (6). Although historically it is impossible for Phaedrus to be young, he is certainly so figured in *Phaedrus*.

27. For a discussion of the problematic category of foreign cult, see chapter 3. Men could and did become involved in Corybantic *mania* and Bacchic frenzy, but given the loss of *nous* involved, the rituals were associated predominately with women. Cf. Plato's discussion of Corybantic practices in connection with women who calm distressed babies (*Laws* 790c–e). See Scullion 2013 for a recent discussion of male participation in maenadic rituals.

28. In *Lysistrata* a festival for Hecate is described as παίγνια, 700. Cf. Aristophanes *Peace* 817, μετ' ἐμοῦ ξύμπαιζε τὴν ἑορτήν. Aristotle associates *heortai* with play (*Rhetoric* 1380b3). Cf. Thucydides 2.38. And see Mikalson 1982 on the concept of *heortê*. The associations of "good cheer" with *heortê* have led some scholars to exclude ceremonies involving sorrowful activities from the concept *heortê*, but see R. Parker 2005, 159–65, for a more nuanced discussion of the concept of "festival." See Connor 1987 for an analysis of the ideological effects of festival. The Athenians are particularly keen on festal diversions. [Xen.] *Ath. Pol.* 3.2 explains that at Athens they have to hold more festivals (*heortasai heortas*) than any other Greek city. The tremendous importance of *heortê* to Athenian life is expressed in Euripides's *Electra* when Electra complains that she is not only dirty and dressed in rags but also "deprived of festival," 310 (cf. Sophocles *Oedipus Tyrannus* 1490–91; Euripides *Trojan Women* 452).

29. Cf. *Laws* 803d–e, where one should spend time "playing" at sacrificing, singing, and dancing.

30. The festival was most likely the Bendideia (354a); the *thea* referred to is Bendis, not Athena. The torch-race component of the festival is mentioned (328a). See Adam's commentary (1902) ad loc.

31. Cf. Xenophon *Apology* 11, where Socrates defends himself against Meletus's accusation that he does not revere the gods that the *polis* reveres by explaining that everyone has seen him sacrificing at the common festivals and public altars.

32. Plato frequently evokes the notion of the "verbal banquet." *Gorgias* begins with Socrates asking if he has arrived after the "festival" (*heortê*), namely, Gorgias's recent display of *logos* (447a), a formulation that is repeated by Callicles. Similarly, in *Phaedrus*, Socrates inquires if Lysias was "feasting" Phaedrus on *logoi* (τῶν λόγων ὑμᾶς Λυσίας εἱστία, 227b). Cf. Dodds 1959 on Gorgias 447a5. At a feast of words one can dine well or not. At the close of Book 1 of *Republic*, Socrates says that he has not dined well at the feast of Bendis (as we have seen, references to the festival in honor of Bendis open the dialogue); he means that he has not managed to get an answer to the original question that he posed, "what is justice" (354a–c). S. White points out that "the background of large civic events provides a sharp contrast to the personal converse in private gatherings that the dialogues portray" (2000, 158). But the civic festivals that provide background color in Plato's dialogues also provide a *connection* to the private, philosophical discourse, since after all it is the "break" in the festal day that offers the leisure necessary for drawn-out philosophical discussion. Festival is precisely the kind of setting that (potentially) enables truth to come out. In *Phaedrus*, Socrates has σχολή for Phaedrus (227b, 258e), and talking to Phaedrus contributes to "knowing himself." Cf. Lebeck, who remarks that for Socrates "to know Phaedrus is to seek himself" (1972, 282).

33. On historical and poetic nympholepsy, see Connor 1988; Larson 2001; Pache 2011. Archaeological and inscriptional evidence reveals that historical nympholepts cultivated gardens; caves consecrated to nymphs generally have attached gardens. Nymphs are mentioned repeatedly and described by Socrates as having a profound effect on his language.

34. Cf. Xenophon *Memorabilia* 1.1.10, where Socrates is described as spending his time where he can run into the most people.

35. Nehamas and Woodruff 1995, xi. For a similar view see Hackforth, who remarks, "The exaltation of 'divine madness' over rational prudence, and indeed the whole splendid apparatus of the μυθικὸς ὕμνος, are hardly in character with the Socrates whom we know from the 'Socratic' dialogues" (1952, 14). See also Nussbaum 1986 (especially 228 and 203) for the idea that, in *Phaedrus*, Plato reworks his earlier position on madness and eros. The Socrates of *Phaedrus* offers something qualitatively different from what Socrates offers in other dialogues.

36. In *Phaedrus*, Socrates resembles the poet he describes in *Ion* (cf. Demos 1999): "A poet is a light thing and winged and holy; and he is not able to compose until he is possessed by a god and senseless and his *nous* is no longer in him" (κοῦφον γὰρ χρῆμα ποιητής ἐστιν καὶ πτηνὸν καὶ ἱερόν, καὶ οὐ πρότερον οἷός τε ποιεῖν πρὶν ἂν ἔνθεός τε γένηται καὶ ἔκφρων καὶ ὁ νοῦς μηκέτι ἐν αὐτῷ ἐνῇ, 534b).

37. Rowe suggests, "In the *Phaedrus* Plato deliberately and consistently draws our attention to the fact that in putting set speeches into Socrates' mouth he is making him behave in an alien fashion" (1986, 163). Phaedrus remarks that a greater fluency has seized Socrates (παρὰ τὸ εἰωθὸς εὔροιά τίς σε εἴληφεν, 238c).

38. Cf. *Republic* 461e, 540b–c; *Laws* 738b–c, 759c, 828a, 856e, 865b, 914a, 947d.

39. Cf. *Phaedo* 60d, where Socrates is composing a hymn to Apollo while in prison; for Socrates's dedication to Apollo, see *Phaedo* 85b. For many anecdotes relating Plato to Apollo, see Riginos 1976, 9–32.

40. Σωκ. Ἐκ δὴ τούτων ἰδὲ τὸ γελοῖον ἥντινα φύσιν ἔχει.

Π. Λέγε μόνον.

Σ. Ἔστιν δὴ πονηρία μέν τις τὸ κεφάλαιον, ἕξεώς τινος ἐπίκλην λεγομένη· τῆς δ' αὖ πάσης πονηρίας ἐστὶ τοὐναντίον πάθος ἔχον ἢ τὸ λεγόμενον ὑπὸ τῶν ἐν Δελφοῖς γραμμάτων.

Π. Τὸ 'γνῶθι σαυτὸν' λέγεις, ὦ Σώκρατες;

Σ. Ἔγωγε. τοὐναντίον μὴν ἐκείνῳ δῆλον ὅτι τὸ μηδαμῇ γιγνώσκειν αὑτὸν λεγόμενον ὑπὸ τοῦ γράμματος ἂν εἴη.

Soc. Next, consider the "ridiculous"—what its nature is.

P. Please explain.

S. The "ridiculous" is essentially a kind of baseness, giving its name to a way of being. And of the entire category of baseness, the "ridiculous" is that which involves the opposite of what is said by the inscription at Delphi.

P. Do you mean "Know Thyself," Socrates?

S. Yes. And it is clear that the opposite of that—not to know oneself at all—would be what is said by the inscription. (48c–d)

41. On Corybantes in Plato's works, see Linforth (1945 and 1946), who points out that, although the figure of the Corybant appears as early as Alcman, Corybantes rarely appear in classical texts—only about a dozen times—and half of these references are from Plato. For discussions of Corybantes, see Dodds 1964, 77–80; Scullion 1998; Edmonds 2006. For *tympana* in connection with Dionysus, see chapter 3; see also, e.g., Euripides *Bacchae* 58–59; *Heracles* 889–90. For the association of Corybantic ritual with *tympana*, see Euripides *Bacchae* 123–25; Aristophanes *Wasps* 119–20. For a (late) description of Corybantes, see Lucian *Dialogues of the Gods* 20, where the Corybantes run mad through the mountains with *tympana* and cymbals and have the potential to engage in *sparagmos*.

42. As early as Homer, Dionysus is called *mainomenos* (*Iliad* 6.132), an early example of "maenadism as practiced" (Henrichs 1978, 143). See, e.g., Aristophanes *Wasps* 119–20 for the idea that Corybantic rites functioned as a kind of "cure" for madness/sickness. Corybantic rites are one of many ways in which Bdelycleon attempts to cure Philocleon of his addiction to jury service.

43. In a discussion of Corybantic and Bacchic rites in Plato, Scullion concludes that in Plato's works there is a "tendency to treat ecstatic rituals connected with different divinities

under the same general rubric" (1998, 111). For evidence of the syncretism of Couretes, Corybantes, and Dionysus, see e.g., *Bacchae* 120–35. See Gantz 1993, 147–48; Edmonds 2006.

44. ὁ θεὸς αὐτός ἐστιν ὁ λέγων 534d; ὁ θεὸς ἐξαιρούμενος τούτων τὸν νοῦν, 534c; the poet is ἔνθεος and ἔκφρων, 534b; his mind is no longer present, ὁ νοῦς μηκέτι ἐν αὐτῷ ἐνῇ, 534b.

45. Scullion 1998, 112.

46. Cf. Socrates's use of the same verb in *Symposium* (198b), where he has a similar reaction in response to Agathon's speech. See also [Plato] *Lovers* 133a–b, where ἐκπλήττω is used to describe Socrates's response to young, beautiful boys generally.

47. Cf. Euripides's *Bacchae*, where a messenger (employing the same verb) explains, "The entire mountain was possessed" (πᾶν συνεβάκχευ' ὄρος, 726).

48. Cf. *Gorgias*, where Callicles asks Chaerephon if Socrates is being serious or joking (εἰπέ μοι, ὦ Χαιρεφῶν, σπουδάζει ταῦτα Σωκράτης ἢ παίζει; 481b).

49. "I feel shame, Father, looking upon your old age which lacks *nous*" (ἀναίνομαι, πάτερ, / τὸ γῆρας ὑμῶν εἰσορῶν νοῦν οὐκ ἔχον, 251–52). See Foley 1980 for comic elements in *Bacchae*.

50. On the dramatic date of the dialogue, see Nussbaum 1986.

51. For Plato's transformation of traditional hero cult, especially in *Phaedo*, see S. White 2000.

52. For Socrates's *daimonion*, see, e.g., *Republic* 496c. Socrates's *daimonion*, alluded to in other works, actually makes an appearance in *Phaedrus* 242b–c. For Socrates's revolutionary religious messages, see McPherran 2011, especially 111 and 116. Connor explains that "Socrates' religious views were anything but conventional. These beliefs entailed ideas that would profoundly affect the way human beings understood themselves, related to each other, and formed civic organizations. It was, indeed, revolutionary to imagine a community whose common denominator was not the fictions of genealogical ties nor the shared activities of animal sacrifice and religious cult, but a common pursuit of justice and a determination to suffer wrong rather than to do wrong" (1991, 56).

53. For mystery language in Plato's dialogues, see, e.g., Lebeck 1972; de Vries 1973; Riedweg 1987; M. Morgan 1990. See Faraone 2010, 151n14, for bibliography on the representation of Socratic discourse as initiation into mystery cult. Alcibiades begins his speech in *Symposium* by saying that only those initiated into Socrates's rites can listen (218b). Although Aristophanes's portrayal of Socrates in *Clouds* as a leader of a bizarre mystery cult is a caricature, his eccentric "Socrates" must have shared some features with the real Socrates or it would not have resonated with the Athenians. Cf. R. Parker 1996, 203.

54. Some scholars have argued that the charge of religion was used as a pretext, and that, in reality, Socrates was condemned for his politics; but such a rigid separation of spheres, which for the Greeks interpenetrated, is anachronistic. As R. Parker remarks, "It may be that an accusation of impiety was almost never brought before an Athenian court without political anxiety or hatred being present in the background" (1996, 202). See also Gagné 2009.

55. Similarly, in Euripides's *Ion*, Xuthus recalls a night in which he became a participant in maenadic activity (550–54).

56. For *paidia* and the Adonia, see Menander *Samia* 38–49. For the personification *Paidia* associated with Adonis in vase painting, see chapter 2.

57. Phaedrus does invoke central sites of religious activity, vowing to set up statues in honor of Socrates at Delphi and Olympia, if Socrates will only provide him with the *logos* he desires (235d–e and 236a–b). K. A. Morgan (1994) connects statues of Gorgias at Delphi and Olympia with the passage.

58. For the proverb, see chapter 1.

59. Of course, in other dialogues the setting is important, e.g., the (indoor) setting in *Symposium* and *Phaedo*.

60. G. R. F. Ferrari 1987, 3.

61. Pirenne-Delforge argues that Aphrodite took the epithet *en kêpois* because she was worshipped in the area known as "the Gardens" (1994, 65). By contrast, Broneer (1935, 126) argues that *en kêpois* is a cult name and that the goddess gave her name to the district. Cf. Broneer 1932, 53. Aphrodite's epithet was *hierokêpia* on Cyprus (Strabo 14.6.3). Pausanias mentions Aphrodite *en kêpois* twice—once when discussing the area around the Olympieum near the Ilissus (1.19.2) and again in a difficult and much debated passage, when he describes the ritual of the Arrephoroi (1.27.3). Until Broneer discovered the sanctuary of Eros and Aphrodite on the north slope of the Acropolis, it was thought that both Pausanias passages referred to the Ilissus River site. But according to Broneer (1932), these new discoveries were proof that the Athenians had two sanctuaries called Aphrodite *en kêpois*. For bibliography on this site, see also, e.g., Gullini 1944–45; Langlotz 1954. Broneer (1935, 132n2) suggests that the altars and phallic objects found in the excavations of the north slope site might have been used in ways similar to gardens of Adonis, and that the name Aphrodite *en kêpois* could have come from this practice.

62. The references to various shrines in *Phaedrus* have led a number of scholars to attempt to trace the route of Socrates and Phaedrus. Wycherley (1963) and Robin ([1933b] 1966, 10–12) provide accounts of this philosophical hike. Cf. W. H. Thompson 1868; de Vries 1969, 44–45. For more-general maps of the area, see Travlos 1971 and R. Parker 2005, 53 (fig. 4). While Wycherley (1963) argues that the sanctuary to Aphrodite *en kêpois* was a bit farther south, outside the place in which the dialogue is set, by contrast, Motte suggests, "Il s'étendait en effet, estime-t-on généralement, dans cette campagne verdoyante arrosée par l'Ilissus qu'évoque chaleureusement Platon et qui avait été de bonne heure sanctifiée par des cultes rustiques" (1973, 131–32).

63. Pliny the Elder *Natural History* 36.4 reports that a statue of Alcamenes was *extra muros* and called Venus *in kêpois*. Cf. Lucian *Imagines* 4, 6.

64. See R. Parker: "The two most important religious zones in Athens are therefore not acropolis and agora, but rather acropolis and this area around and beyond the Olympieum" (2005, 55). It is noteworthy that the settings of two (extant) Classical Athenian works that mention the Adonia (*Lysistrata* and *Phaedrus*) take place in these two religious zones, thus linking the "marginal" Adonis festival to these "central" areas of religious practice.

65. On the broad semantic range of *kêpos*, see, e.g., Carroll-Spillecke 1989; Brunet 2001. For divinities and *kêpoi*, see e.g., Pindar *Pythian* 5.24 ("garden of Aphrodite," i.e.,

Cyrene), *Pythian* 9.53 ("of Zeus," i.e., Libya); Sophocles fr. 320 Radt ("of Zeus"); Plato *Symposium* 203b ("of Zeus").

66. In Apuleius *Metamorphoses* 1.19, the character Socrates dies near a plane tree (*platanus*) beside a river, a setting very much like that of *Phaedrus*. Cf. Cicero *de orat.* 1.28.

67. The story developed, perhaps because of the passage in *Phaedrus*, that Plato himself swore by a plane tree. See Riginos 1976, anecdote 121.

68. Cf. *Iliad* 2.307; Herodotus 7.31; Theophrastus *HP* 1.4.2, 1.7.1, 4.13.2.

69. Pliny mentions a plane tree that never shed its leaves. This he terms a *vitium* because, as he explains, the point of a plane tree is to ward off the sun in summer and permit it to shine through in winter (*quandoquidem commendatio arboris eius non alia maior est quam soles aestate arcere, hieme admittere, Natural History* 12.5.11).

70. The fact that it is midday (μεσημβρία) is repeated: 242a, 259a, 259d. The "stifling heat" is mentioned (ἐν τῷ πνίγει, 258e). See also 229a.

71. Vergil refers to plane trees as *steriles* in *Georgics* (*steriles platani* 2.70). And Horace *Odes* 2.15.4 refers to the plane tree as *caelebs*. Within the context of the poem, he seems to mean useless and unproductive. Martial calls the plane tree *vidua platanus* (3.58.3).

72. In *Phaedo*, we learn that Socrates had put Aesop into verse while in prison (60d). Cf. 60c. For Aesop's influence on Plato, see Kurke 2011, especially 241–64. Given Socrates's familiarity with Aesop in *Phaedo*, it is possible that Socrates is (implicitly) including a fable of Aesop in *Phaedrus*.

73. Phaedrus is represented as superficial, with his repeated desire for quantity, e.g., insisting that Socrates say *more* words than Lysias (235d, 236b). G. R. F. Ferrari calls Phaedrus an "impresario" (1987, 4–8). Other scholars take Phaedrus more seriously. Nussbaum does not believe Plato would spend so much time on an unworthy interlocutor (1986, 202), and citing Plato's historical relationship with Dion of Syracuse, she sees Phaedrus as standing in for Dion, while Socrates represents Plato (228–33). Rowe (1986, 12) believes that Plato intentionally paints an ambiguous portrait of Phaedrus, and that the dialogue is unclear about whether he is "cured" by Socrates's arguments in the end. The difference of opinion regarding the character of Phaedrus confirms my argument that the results of Socrates's "planting" are uncertain.

74. Phaedrus is called Phaedrus of Myrrhinous by Socrates (244a), and duBois (1985, 101) suggests that the name of Phaedrus's deme, Myrrhinous, recalls Adonis's mother, Myrrha.

75. E.g., the play on Typhon and *atuphia*, 230a; the connections between *mania* and *mantikê*, 244c; the discussion of *eros* whom the gods call *pteros*, 252c. According to some accounts, "Plato" was not the philosopher's original name but a nickname taken because of Plato's broad forehead, chest, or style (Diogenes Laertius 3.4); see Riginos 1976, 35–38, for discussion of this anecdote. We might recall that it is the broad leaves of the *platanos* that make the tree so valuable during the summer months. Also in *Phaedrus* the height of the tree is mentioned twice (229a and 230b), perhaps a suggestion that the tree is closer to the heavenly realm of truth, a further merging of the plane tree and philosopher. Cf. Foley 1998, 45.

76. See *Iliad* 14.346–51; Archilochus fr. 196a W; Sappho frs. 2, 94, 96, 122 V; Ibycus fr. 286 *PMG*. On eroticized meadows and maidens, see Swift, who comments, "being linked to a meadow signifies readiness to marry" (2006, 127). See also Bremer 1975; Foley 1994, 33–34; Calame (1992) 1999, especially 163.

77. The defining activity of nymphs and maidens is play (and dancing), e.g., *Odyssey* 6.105–8. Cf. Anacreon fr. 357 *PMG*; Aristophanes *Birds* 1097–110. For gardens/meadows of nymphs/parthenoi, see, e.g., Ibycus fr. 286 *PMG* and cf. Demetrius *Eloc.* 132 (Sappho T 45 Campbell); Aristophanes's *Clouds*, 271–72.

78. Nussbaum (1986, 207–8) emphasizes Phaedrus's vulnerability.

79. As Edmonds argues, "A reciprocal erotic relationship, in which each partner contributes actively and passionately, serves as the model for Plato's ideal of philosophical learning" (2000, 271). Cf. Halperin, who explains that "sex, as it is represented in classical Athenian documents, is a deeply polarizing experience: constructed according to a model of penetration that interprets 'penetration' as an intrinsically unidirectional act, sex divides its participants into asymmetrical and, ultimately, into hierarchical positions, defining one partner as 'active' and 'dominant,' the other partner as 'passive' and 'submissive.' Sexual roles, moreover, are isomorphic with status and gender roles; 'masculinity' is an aggregate combining the congruent functions of penetration, activity, dominance, and social precedence, whereas 'femininity' signifies penetrability, passivity, submission, and social subordination" (1990, 130).

80. On reciprocity in *Symposium*, see Edmonds 2000.

81. On erotic reciprocity in *Phaedrus*, see duBois 1985.

82. DuBois 1985, 1988.

83. For Diotima, see Halperin's chapter in *One Hundred Years of Homosexuality* (1990, 113–51) titled "Why Is Diotima a Woman?"

84. On the midwife imagery, see Edmonds 2000.

85. Specifically, philosophers are figured as following in the chorus of Zeus in *Phaedrus* (250b). The followers of Zeus receive the most attention in Socrates's second speech—those who are dedicated to Hera and Apollo receive only a brief mention.

86. On Aphrodite's unveiling, see Bergren 1989.

87. The realm of truth described in Socrates's second speech is a meadow (248b–c). The description in Hesiod's *Theogony* (986–91) of Aphrodite's abduction of Phaethon shares similarities with Socrates's relationship with Phaedrus in *Phaedrus*. In Hesiod's account, laughter-loving Aphrodite (φιλομμειδὴς Ἀφροδίτη, 989) snatches up the young (νέον, 988), shining Phaethon (φαίδιμον υἱόν, 986), who is thinking tender/unripe things (ἀταλὰ φρονέοντα, 989), to be her temple keeper. So too laughter-loving (or playful, *geloios*) Socrates seizes the impressionable (shining, *phaidros*) Phaedrus, who is bowled over by Lysias at the beginning of the dialogue, to be one of his philosophic followers.

88. *Apology* 25a, 30b; Favorinus in Diogenes Laertius (2.40). On the charge, see R. Parker 1996, 199–207. Cf. Xenophon *Memorabilia* 1.1.1; *Apology* 10; Plato *Apology* 24c.

89. Cf. Aubriot, who remarks, "Vif et largement répandu était le sentiment que la relation entre hommes et plantes était intime au point que des substitutions réciproque étaient

concevables et qu'on avait affaire, en somme, à une véritable adéquation, entre les uns et les autres" (2001, 57).

90. Schein (1984, 74–75, 96–97, 134, 146) discusses vegetal imagery in *Iliad*, suggesting that such imagery is "characteristically Trojan" except for the case of Achilles. He points out that, in the *Iliad* at least, it serves to reinforce the notion of the hero as mortal because there is no afterlife. Cf. 69–70 for the etymological relationship between *hêrôs* and *hôrê*.

91. For Hesiod, agriculture, the necessity to work for one's food, and the need to sacrifice to the gods to obtain their favor, are punishments that, along with the creation of women, are given by the gods to mortals. Agriculture and human reproduction are thus linked as *punishment*. On agricultural language and human reproduction, see, e.g., duBois 1988.

92. Cf. Hippocrates *Eight Month's Child* 12.

93. See Cole 2004, 146–77, on embryos as plants in the earth. Cole points out that bodies were so conceived of as *land* that certain techniques involving feces were used to promote fertility, in the same way that manure was employed to encourage growth of crops (169–70).

94. Plato describes the human body as housing a soul that, because we are heavenly and not earthly plants, raises us up from earth in the direction of our relatives in heaven (90a); at the same time we are suspended from heaven (90a–b) by our head/root.

95. Cf. *Phaedo* 83e, where the soul is described as a seed that is sown (ὥσπερ σπειρομένη ἐμφύεσθαι).

96. On plant imagery in *Phaedrus*, see Lebeck (1972), who offers an insightful reading of Socrates' second speech.

97. Early on in the dialogue, Phaedrus comments, "It seems that I happen to be barefoot at just the right moment. You always are. So it is most easy for us, going along with our feet in the water and not unpleasantly, given the time of year and the time of day" (εἰς καιρόν, ὡς ἔοικεν, ἀνυπόδητος ὢν ἔτυχον· σὺ μὲν γὰρ δὴ ἀεί. ῥᾷστον οὖν ἡμῖν κατὰ τὸ ὑδάτιον βρέχουσι τοὺς πόδας ἰέναι, καὶ οὐκ ἀηδές, ἄλλως τε καὶ τήνδε τὴν ὥραν τοῦ ἔτους τε καὶ τῆς ἡμέρας, 229a). Barefoot, Socrates and Phaedrus can perhaps be seen to water their feet (roots) in the stream of the Ilissus as, like heavenly plants, their heads reach toward the sky.

98. Cf. "written in the *phrên*," a phrase that Steiner notes is so common as to be almost a cliché for fifth-century poets (1994, 100–101, 107–8).

99. The syntax used to describe both practices is strikingly similar: ὅταν [δὲ] γράφῃ (276d, of the one who writes) and ὅτε καὶ ποιοῖ (276b, of the cultivator of gardens of Adonis). Writing/cultivating gardens of Adonis is not something that one does all the time but is, rather, a "marked" activity, and in both cases the individual looks upon his handiwork and is pleased at the results: πότερα σπουδῇ ἂν θέρους εἰς Ἀδώνιδος κήπους ἀρῶν χαίροι θεωρῶν καλοὺς ἐν ἡμέραισιν ὀκτὼ γιγνομένους (276b, the cultivator of the gardens of Adonis); ἡσθήσεταί τε αὐτοὺς θεωρῶν φυομένους ἁπαλούς (276d, the gardener).

100. For a good summary of this debate, see G. R. F. Ferrari 1987, 204–22. In *Epistle* 7, there is a similar opposition between *geloios* writing and *spoudaios logos* as "Plato" urges the serious man (*spoudaios anêr*) who wishes to deal with truly serious matters not to write

(344c). See Nightingale: "The distinction that Socrates has drawn between spoken and written *logoi* is not sustained throughout the discussion" (1995, 164 [e.g., 259e, 277e]). Cf. Friedländer 1958, 1:108–25; Guthrie 1962, 4:1–3; de Vries 1969; Burger 1980, 101–4; Derrida (1972) 1981; Griswold 1986, 202–29; Steiner 1994, 212–16.

101. Cf. 235d.

102. K. A. Morgan 2000, 175.

103. For discussion of Orpheus and books, see e.g., Steiner 1994, 194–201. I am not concerned here with these rituals as actually practiced. Rather, I am interested in the fact that, in the Greek imagination, certain practices, which were considered "foreign" (including the Adonia), were linked with writing.

104. A bit later, Theseus calls Hippolytus a "chanter of spells and a wizard" (ἆρ' οὐκ ἐπῳδὸς καὶ γόης πέφυχ' ὅδε, 1038). These are the very same terms that Pentheus in *Bacchae* uses to describe Dionysus (λέγουσι δ' ὥς τις εἰσελήλυθε ξένος / γόης ἐπῳδὸς Λυδίας ἀπὸ χθονός, "they say that some foreigner has arrived, a wizard-magician from Lydian lands," 233–34), another divinity whose worship is closely linked with the practice of writing, given the appearance of the gold lamellae throughout the Mediterranean. For a recent discussion of Dionysiac and Orphic gold lamellae, see Graf and Johnston 2007. Socrates, too, is described as an ἐπῳδός (e.g., *Phaedo* 78a) and a γόης (e.g., *Meno* 80b).

105. R. Parker 2005, 121.

106. For writing and Orpheus, cf. Euripides *Alcestis* 962–71.

107. On writing in the Greek imagination, see Steiner 1994. On the possible links between Prometheus and Theuth, see Rowe 1986, 208–9.

108. At least during the fifth century at Athens, writing could be associated with images of foreign despotism. Cf. Steiner 1994, 7.

109. See Chantraine (1968–80, vol. 1) for problems with this derivation.

110. Cf. *Timaeus* 21a–25d. For the export of papyrus from Naucratis in Egypt, see Möller 2000, 211–12.

111. See chapter 1. In *On the Syrian Goddess*, [Lucian] describes a curious ritual that involves the floating of Adonis's "head" down a river. This "head" might be a papyrus head (though Lightfoot [2003] doubts it), and if so might provide an additional connection between the Adonia and technologies of writing. On Adonis's grave, see Σ Lyc. 831 (who reports that it was in Byblos) and Σ Dionysius Periegeta 509; see also chapter 1. Later tradition holds that Adonis's tomb is in Lebanon or Aphaca. Cf. Soyez 1977, 41–43; Lightfoot 2003, 326. The modern name for the Adonis River is Nahr Ibrahim. A river named Phaedrus (the modern name is Ouadi Fedar) runs between the Adonis River and the city of Byblos, another connection between the fifth-century philosophical dialogue and the ancient city of Byblos. Cf. Plutarch *de Iside* 16 and Soyez 1977, 5n8, 72.

112. Cf. D. Clay: "The philosopher is a stranger, or better, a metic in this world. His wealth is his wisdom. He can make off with none of the gold of this world, since it has no value in another" (1979, 353). In *Apology*, Socrates presents himself as a "foreigner" when it comes to matters of law-court speeches (17d).

113. See K. A. Morgan 2000, 159, on the *Gorgias* passage. She remarks, "The most interesting philosophical proposals are likely to seem counter-intuitive to the non-expert, and hesitating between the poles of play and seriousness is an implicit acknowledgement of the marginal status (for ordinary people) of philosophical discussion" (2000, 174). Nightingale explains, "Plato's philosopher is an outsider who is disembedded from the social and political economy of the city" (1995, 191). Other moments when the philosopher is "ridiculous" include *Republic* 516e–517a, where the philosopher, returning from the bright light to the darkness of the cave produces laughter; cf. *Theaetetus* 172c and 174a–d. On these passages, see Nightingale 1995, 178–80.

114. Cf. Dodds 1959, 272.

115. Aeschines 1.173: "Did you kill the sophist Socrates, Athenian men, because he was shown to have educated Critias?" (ἔπειθ' ὑμεῖς, ὦ Ἀθηναῖοι, Σωκράτην μὲν τὸν σοφιστὴν ἀπεκτείνατε, ὅτι Κριτίαν ἐφάνη πεπαιδευκώς). Five of the people convicted in 415 were associated with Socrates. On Phaedrus's connection with the profanation of the mysteries and his period of exile, see Andocides 1.15, and see Hatzfeld 1939; Nails 2002, 232–33. Given Phaedrus's connection with the profanation of the mysteries, it is interesting that, in *Phaedrus*, he is being lectured about philosophical ascent in terms of mystery language; in *Symposium*, Phaedrus (and Alcibiades) listen to Diotima's speech, which is also loaded with references to mystery cult.

116. See Asmis 1986 and Giannopoulou 2010 for discussions of the recurrence of *kalos* and the addresses to the "boy."

117. Asmis 1986. Phaedrus is called *kallipaida* (261a), which Asmis translates as "beautiful boy" (as opposed to "of the beautiful offspring"), commenting: "The juxtaposition of 'beautiful boy' and 'Phaedrus' with the pun παιδ-... Φαιδ-... indicates that Phaedrus is identical with the beautiful 'boy' who has kept reappearing throughout the dialogue" (1986, 165).

118. The son of Hermes, Pan, tends to be accompanied by nymphs and is associated with rustic environs and wild spaces, like the setting of *Phaedrus*. In the *Homeric Hymn to Pan*, among other places, Pan frequents a meadow where grow crocus and hyacinth (a meadow that thus resembles the meadow where young maidens are abducted as well as the landscape of *Phaedrus*). See D. Clay 1979 and Rosenmeyer 1962 on Socrates's prayer to Pan.

119. Cf. 150a–c, 151c–d, 151e, 157d, 160e–161a, 210b.

120. According to Aristophanes (*Birds* 693–97), in the beginning (or soon after) was a wind egg. Far from a merely comedic invention, a variety of cosmogonies involved a cosmic egg as well as some sort of interaction with wind. See West 1994. In some accounts, the egg produces Eros or Pothos (West 1994, 304). In the Aristophanes version, vegetal imagery appears as Eros "sprouts" (ἔβλαστεν).

121. See Reed 1997, 233. Cf. Moschus's *Lament for Bion* 5–7 (a poem that seems to refer to Bion's *Epitaph on Adonis*), where roses, hyacinths, and anemones are commanded to lament.

122. Cf. Pausanias 6.24.7 for the association of myrtle and rose with Aphrodite and with the story of Adonis.

123. For other young men turned into flowers after their death at an early age, see Foley 1994, 34. Pliny *HN* 21.165 links the anemone with wind (and by implication *anemos*): *flos numquam se aperit nisi vento spirante, unde et nomen accepere.* On the anemone and the myth of Adonis, as well as the importance of the odorless nature of the flower, see Detienne (1977) 1979, 49–51. See Lucian *Lex.* 23 for "flowers of speech" (ἀνεμῶναι τῶν λόγων).

Conclusion

1. Cf. Stallybrass and White 1986, 5.

2. For discussions of the reception of Adonis outside the ancient world, see Tuzet 1987; for Adonis in the Italian Renaissance, see Caruso 2013.

3. Cf. Detienne (1972) 1994, 105.

4. Motte points out, "Durant ses séjours à Syracuse, Platon manifeste aussi une prédilection pour les jardins" (1963, 472n68). Cf. *Epistle* 3, 319; 2, 313; 7, 347a. In *Epistle* 7, Plato is banished from the *kêpos* because women need to perform a sacrifice (349d).

5. Cf. Jones 1999.

6. Cf. Motte 1973, 372.

7. Dioscorides: GP 1475–78 = *AP* 5.53, GP 1479–82 = *AP* 5.193, GP 1565–74 = *AP* 7.407.7–8; Glycon: Hephaestion *Ench.* 10.2 = *PMG* Adesp. 1029 (see Reed 1996, 382); Lycophron: *Alex.* 829–31. Euphorion: fr. 43 Powell, preserved by Ptolemy Chennus. For a discussion of the texts associated with Adonis during the Hellenistic period, see Reed 2000, 341–44.

8. Ptolemy IV Philopator *TrGF* 1.119 T 1; Dionysius I of Syracuse *TrGF* 1.76 fr. 1.

9. Callimachus *Iambus* 3, fr. 193 Pfeiffer; fr. 478.

10. Sotades fr. 3 Powell. See Cameron 1995, 18–19, 98.

11. See Glotz 1920; Gow 1952, 262–64; Reed 2000, 340–41. On the (scant) epigraphic evidence for Adonis, see Fraser 1972, 1:198n60, where he discusses a dedication in which Adonis's name (probably) appears along with that of the Dioscuri and Ptolemy Soter, though the stone reads Ἄδωτι (*Sammelbuch* 306 = *SEG* 24.1174). Griffiths (1979, 60–61n26) suggests that the dedication is evidence for a connection in the popular imagination between Ptolemy and the "demigods," like Adonis and the Dioscuri, who move between heaven and earth.

12. Cf. Griffiths 1979, 83; see also Fraser 1972, 1:198, for Adonis's growing popularity in Alexandria. Cf. Reed 2000, 341.

13. As I have argued, Classical Athenian women play the role of Aphrodite. Theocritus's Adonia represents something new: Queen Arsinoë's explicit historical assimilation to Aphrodite. It was frequently the case that when Ptolemaic queens were deified, they were associated with Aphrodite, and *Idyll* 15 makes a strong connection between Arsinoë and the goddess. Glotz comments, "Arsinoé se posait en Aphrodite et préparait son apothéose" (1920, 173). Cf. Gow 1952, 334–35, on *Idyll* 17.50. On Arsinoë in *Idyll* 15, the myths that are referenced within the poem, and their relationship to the court of Arsinoë/Ptolemy, see Griffiths 1979, especially 65–68, 125–26. On Arsinoë generally, see, e.g., Pfeiffer 1926; Longega 1968; Fraser

1972; Hazzard 2000, 81–100. Ample evidence reveals that Arsinoë was assimilated to Aphrodite in cult and worshipped as Ἀφροδίτη Ἀρσινόη. On Aphrodite-Arsinoë, see, e.g., Fraser 1972, 1:239–40; Griffiths 1979, 65–68; Burstein 1982; Pomeroy 1984, 30–38. Arsinoë was also associated with other divinities. In fact, Chaniotis points out that after her death, Arsinoë became "one of the most popular goddesses in Egypt and on Cyprus" (2003, 442). Four poems commemorate a temple to Arsinoë as the Cyprian Aphrodite, two epigrams by Posidippus, one by Hedylus, and one by Callimachus: Posidippus 12 and 13 (GP 3110–19, 3120–25; see Fraser 1972, 1:568–69); Hedylus 4 (GP 1843–52); Callimachus 14 (GP 1109–20). For discussions, see, e.g., Selden 1998 and Gutzwiller 1992.

14. For accounts of Alexandria's foundation, see Diodorus Siculus, *Library of History* 17.52; Q. Curtius Rufus, *Historiae Alexandri Magni* 4.8; Justin, *Historiae Philippicae* 11.11.9; Plutarch, *Alexander* 26.2–6; and Arrian *Anabasis* 3.1.5–2.2.

15. Selden 1998, 290. Scholars have recently shifted their focus to the Egyptian context at Alexandria in an attempt to remedy the tendency to view Alexandrian poetry solely through a Greek lens. Selden (1998), Koenen (1993), and Stephens (2003) all draw attention to the multicultural, bicephalous world that was Alexandria. Koenen titles a section of his 1993 essay "The Janus head of Ptolemaic kingship"; Stephens titles her book *Seeing Double*, in order to emphasize the necessity of keeping two very different worlds in mind simultaneously when thinking about Alexandria. See Reed 2000 for a discussion of the Adonia within an Egyptian context.

16. Selden 1998, 290.

17. Adonis and the Adonia, then, resonate in different ways from what we have seen in Athens. Even the lettuce is differently conceived in Egypt, where it is a symbol of fertility instead of an anti-aphrodisiac. Cf. Reed 2000, 343.

18. Cf. Osborne 1996, 68.

19. Osborne 1996, 68.

Bibliography

Acosta-Hughes, B. 2002. *Polyeideia: The "Iambi" of Callimachus and the Archaic Iambic Tradition.* Berkeley.

Adam, J., ed. 1902. *The Republic of Plato.* 2 vols. Cambridge.

Albright, W. F. 1964. *History, Archaeology, and Christian Humanism.* New York.

Alexiou, M. (1974) 2002. *The Ritual Lament in Greek Tradition.* 2nd ed. Cambridge.

Alexiou, M., and P. Dronke. 1971. "The Lament of Jephtha's Daughter: Themes, Traditions, Originality." *Studi Medievali* 12.2:819–63.

Allan, W. 2004. "Religious Syncretism: The New Gods of Greek Tragedy." *HSPh* 102:113–55.

———. 2008. *Euripides Helen.* Cambridge Greek and Latin Classics. Cambridge.

Amendola, S. 2010. "'I giardini di Adone': Plu. *ser. num.* 560 b–c ed Erasm. *Adag.* I 1 4." In *Paroimiakos: Il proverbio in Grecia e a Roma,* edited by E. Lelli, 123–31. Pisa.

Anagnostou-Laoutides, E., and D. Konstan. 2008. "Daphnis and Aphrodite: A Love Affair in Theocritus *Idyll* 1." *AJP* 129.4:497–527.

Asmis, E. 1986. "*Psychagogia* in Plato's *Phaedrus.*" *Illinois Classical Studies* 11:153–72.

Atallah, W. 1966. *Adonis dans la littérature et l'art grecs.* Paris.

Aubriot, D. 2001. "L'homme-végétale: Métamorphose, symbole, métaphore." In Κῆποι: De la religion à la philosophie; Mélanges offerts à André Motte. *Kernos* supplement 11, edited by E. Delruelle and V. Pirenne-Delforge, 51–62. Liège.

Ault, B. 2005. *The Houses: The Organization and Use of Domestic Space, Excavations at Ancient Halieis.* Vol. 2. Bloomington, IN.

Ault, B., and L. C. Nevett, eds. 2005. *Ancient Greek Houses and Households: Chronological, Regional, and Social Diversity.* Philadelphia.

Aupert, P. 2008. "Hélios, Adonis et magie: Les trésors d'une citerne d'Amathonte." *BCH* 132.1:347–87.

Barrett, J. 2002. *Staged Narrative: Poetics and the Messenger in Greek Tragedy.* Berkeley, CA.

Barrett, W. S., ed. 1964. *Euripides: Hippolytus.* Oxford.

Barringer, J. 1991. "Europa and the Nereids: Wedding or Funeral?" *AJA* 95.4:657–67.

———. 1995. *Divine Escorts: Nereids in Archaic and Classical Greek Art.* Ann Arbor, MI.

Baslez, M.-F. 1986. "Cultes et dévotions des Phéniciens en Grèce: Les divinités marines." In *Religio Phoenicia* (*Studia Phoenicia* IV), edited by C. Bonnet, E. Lipiński, and P. Marchetti, 289–305. Namur.

Bathrellou, E. 2012. "Menander's *Epitrepontes* and the Festival of the Tauropolia." *CA* 31.2:151–92.

Baudissin, W. 1911. *Adonis und Esmun: Eine Untersuchung zur Geschichte des Glaubens an Auferstehungsgötter und an Heilgötter.* Leipzig.

Baudy, G. J. 1986. *Adonisgärten: Studien zur antiken Samensymbolik.* Beiträge zur klassischen Philologie 176. Frankfurt.

Baurain, C. 1980. "Kinyras: La fin de l'Âge du Bronze à Chypre et la tradition antique." *BCH* 104.1:277–308.

Beazley, J. D. 1949. "The World of the Etruscan Mirror." *JHS* 49:1–17.

———. 1950. "Some Inscriptions on Vases: V." *AJA* 54:310–22.

———. 1963. *Attic Red-Figure Vase-Painters.* 2nd ed. 3 vols. Oxford.

Bell, C. 1992. *Ritual Theory, Ritual Practice.* New York.

———. 1997. *Ritual: Perspectives and Dimensions.* Oxford.

Bérard, C., and C. Bron, eds. 1989. *A City of Images: Iconography and Society in Ancient Greece,* Trans. D. Lyons. Princeton, NJ.

Bergren, A. 1989. "The Homeric Hymn to Aphrodite: Tradition and Rhetoric, Praise and Blame." *Classical Antiquity* 8.1:1–41.

Beschi, L. 1967–68. "Contributi di topografia ateniese." *ASAA* 45–46:520–26.

Bierl, A. 2012. "Women on the Acropolis and Mental Mapping: Comic Body-Politics in a City in Crisis, or Ritual and Metaphor in Aristophanes' *Lysistrata.*" In *Crisis on Stage: Tragedy and Comedy in Late Fifth-Century Athens,* edited by A. Markantonatos and B. Zimmermann, 255–90. Berlin.

Blondell, R. 2002. *The Play of Character in Plato's Dialogues.* Cambridge.

Boardman, J., and E. La Rocca. 1978. *Eros in Greece.* New York.

Boedeker, D. 1974. *Aphrodite's Entry into Greek Epic. Mnemosyne* supplement 32. Leiden.

Boehlau, J. 1901. "Ein neuer Erosmythus." *Philologus* 60:321–29.

Böhr, E. 1997. "A Rare Bird on Greek Vases: The Wryneck." In *Athenian Potters and Painters,* edited by J. H. Oakley, W. D. E. Coulson, and O. Palagia, 109–23. Oxford.

Borg, B. E. 2005. "Eunomia or 'Make Love Not War'? Meidian Personifications Reconsidered." In *Personification in the Greek World: From Antiquity to Byzantium,* edited by E. Stafford and J. Herrin, 193–210. Aldershot.

Borgeaud, P. 1988. *The Cult of Pan in Ancient Greece.* Chicago.

Bosworth, A. B. 2000. "The Historical Context of Thucydides' Funeral Oration." *JHS* 120:1–16.

Bowie, A. M. 1993. *Aristophanes: Myth, Ritual, and Comedy.* Cambridge.

Bravo, B. 1997. *"Pannychis" e Simposio: Feste private notturne di donne e uomini.* Pisa.

Bremer, J. 1975. "The Meadow of Love and Two Passages in Euripides' *Hippolytus.*" *Mnemosyne* 28:268–80.

Bremmer, J. N. 1984. "Greek Maenadism Reconsidered." *ZPE* 55:267–86.

———. 1994. *Greek Religion.* Greece & Rome. New Surveys in the Classics. Vol. 24. Oxford.

Brillet-Dubois, P. 2011. "An Erotic Aristeia: The Homeric Hymn to Aphrodite and Its Relation to the Iliadic Tradition." In *The Homeric Hymns: Interpretative Essays,* edited by A. Faulkner, 105–32. Oxford.

Broneer, O. 1932. "Eros and Aphrodite on the North Slope of the Acropolis." *Hesperia* 1:31–55.

———. 1935. "Excavations on the North Slope of the Acropolis in Athens, 1933–34." *Hesperia* 4.2:109–88.

Brouskari, M. 1974. *The Acropolis Museum*. Athens.

Brown, J. P. 1995. *Israel and Hellas*. Vol. 1. Berlin.

Brunet, M. 2001. "Le courtil et le paradis." In *Techniques et sociétés en Méditerranée*, edited by J.-P. Brun and P. Jockey, 157–68. Paris.

Budelmann, F., and T. Power. 2015. "Another Look at Female Choruses in Classical Athens." *CA* 34.2:252–95.

Bulloch, A. W. 1985. *Callimachus: The Fifth Hymn*. Cambridge.

Burger, R. 1980. *Plato's "Phaedrus": A Defense of a Philosophic Art of Writing*. Tuscaloosa, AL.

Burkert, W. 1979. *Structure and History in Greek Mythology and Ritual*. Berkeley, CA.

———. 1983. *Homo Necans: The Anthropology of Ancient Greek Sacrificial Ritual and Myth*. Berkeley, CA.

———. 1985. *Greek Religion*. Cambridge, MA.

———. 1987. *Ancient Mystery Cults*. Cambridge, MA.

Burn, L. 1987. *The Meidias Painter*. Oxford.

Burnett, A. 2012. "Brothels, Boys, and the Athenian Adonia." *Arethusa* 45.2:177–94.

Burstein, S. 1982. "Arsinoe II Philadelphos: A Revisionist View." In *Philip II, Alexander the Great, and the Macedonian Heritage*, edited by W. Adams and E. Borza, 197–212. Washington, DC.

Burton, J. B. 1995. *Theocritus' Urban Mimes: Mobility, Gender, and Patronage*. Berkeley, CA.

———. 1998. "Women's Commensality in the Ancient Greek World." *G&R* 45.2:143–65.

Butler, J. 1990. *Gender Trouble: Feminism and the Subversion of Identity*. New York.

Buxton, R. G. A. 1982. *Persuasion in Greek Tragedy: A Study of Peitho*. Cambridge.

Cahill, N. 2002. *Household and City Organization at Olynthus*. New Haven, CT.

Calame, C. (1977) 2001. *Choruses of Young Women in Ancient Greece: Their Morphology, Religious Role, and Social Functions*. New, rev. ed. Translated by D. Collins and J. Orion. Lanham, MD.

———. (1992) 1999. *The Poetics of Eros in Ancient Greece*. Translated by J. Lloyd. Princeton, NJ.

Cambitoglou, A. 2009. "Three Apulian Vases in the National Museum in Naples Representing Adonis and Persephone." *ASAA* 87:543–55.

Cameron, A. 1995. *Callimachus and His Critics*. Princeton, NJ.

Caraveli, A. 1986. "The Bitter Wounding: The Lament as Social Protest in Rural Greece." In *Gender and Power in Rural Greece*, edited by J. Dubisch, 169–94. Princeton, NJ.

Carpenter, T. 1997. *Dionysian Imagery in Fifth-Century Athens*. Oxford.

Carroll-Spillecke, M. 1989. *Kêpos: Der antike griechische Garten*. Vol. 3. Munich.

Carson, A. 1986. *Eros the Bittersweet*. Princeton, NJ.

Cartledge, P., P. Millett, and S. von Reden, eds. 1998. *Kosmos: Essays in Order, Conflict, and Community in Classical Athens*. Cambridge.

Caruso, C. 2013. *Adonis: The Myth of the Dying God in the Italian Renaissance.* London.

Chaniotis, A. 2003. "The Divinity of Hellenistic Rulers." In *A Companion to the Hellenistic World*, edited by A. Erskine, 431–45. Malden, MA.

Chantraine, P. 1968–80. *Dictionnaire étymologique de la langue grecque.* 4 vols. Paris.

Charbonneaux, J. R., with R. F. Martin and F. Villard. 1972. *Classical Greek Art.* London.

Clairmont, C. 1983. *Patrios Nomos: Public Burial in Athens during the Fifth and Fourth Centuries BC; The Archaeological, Epigraphic-Literary, and Historical Evidence.* Oxford.

Clay, D. 1975. "The Tragic and Comic Poet of the *Symposium.*" *Arion* 2:238–61.

———. 1979. "Socrates' Prayer to Pan." In *Arktouros: Hellenic Studies Presented to Bernard M. W. Knox on the Occasion of His 65th Birthday*, edited by G. Bowersock, W. Burkert, and M. Putnam, 345–53. Berlin.

Clay, J. S. 1989. *The Politics of Olympus: Form and Meaning in the Major Homeric Hymns.* Princeton, NJ.

Cole, S. 2004. *Landscapes, Gender, and Ritual Space: The Ancient Greek Experience.* Berkeley, CA.

Collignon, M. 1894. "Aphrodite Pandémos, relief de miroir en bronze et disque en marbre (Musée du Louvre)." *Monuments et mémoires de la Fondation Eugène Piot* 1.2:143–50.

Connelly, J. 2007. *Portrait of a Priestess: Women and Ritual in Ancient Greece.* Princeton, NJ.

Connor, W. R. 1984. *Thucydides.* Princeton, NJ.

———. 1987. "Tribes, Festivals and Processions: Civic Ceremonial and Political Manipulation in Archaic Greece." *JHS* 107:40–50.

———. 1988. "Seized by the Nymphs: Nympholepsy and Symbolic Expression in Classical Greece." *Classical Antiquity* 7.2:155–89.

———. 1991. "The Other 399: Religion and the Trial of Socrates." *BICS* 58:49–56.

Cook, A. B. 1925. *Zeus: A Study in Ancient Religion.* Vol. 2.1. Cambridge.

Couelle, C. 1989. "Le repos du héros: Images attiques de la fin du Vème siècle av. J.-C." In *Entre Hommes et Dieux*, edited by A.-F. Laurens, 127–43. Annales littéraires de l'Université de Besançon 391. Paris.

Creuzer, F. 1839. *Auswahl unedirter griechischer Thongefässe.* Heidelberg.

Croissant, F., and F. Salviat. 1966. "Aphrodite gardienne des magistrats: Gynéconomes de Thasos et polémarques de Thèbes." *BCH* 90:460–71.

Cumont, F. 1917. "Disques ou miroirs magiques de Tarente." *RA* 5.5:87–107.

———. 1927. "Les Syriens en Espagne et les Adonies à Seville." *Syria* 8:330–41.

———. 1932. "Adonis et Sirius." In *Mélanges Gustave Glotz* 1:257–64.

———. 1935. "Adonies et Canicule." *Syria* 16:46–50.

Dasen, V., and M. Piérart, eds. 2005. Ἰδίᾳ καὶ δημοσίᾳ: *Les cadres "privés" et "publics" de la religion grecque antique; Actes du IXe colloque du CIERGA, tenu à Fribourg du 8 au 10 septembre 2003. Kernos* supplement 15. Liège.

Davidson, J. 2000. "Gnesippuspaigniagraphos: The Comic Poets and the Erotic Mime." In *The Rivals of Aristophanes: Studies in Athenian Old Comedy*, edited by D. Harvey and J. Wilkins, 41–61. London.

Davies, M. 2001. "The Boar-Hunt in Greek Myth." *Prometheus* 27.1:1–3.

de Grummond, N. T. 2004. "For the Mother and for the Daughter: Some Thoughts on Dedications from Etruria and Praeneste." In ΧΑΡΙΣ: Essays in Honor of Sara A. Immerwahr, edited by A. P. Chapin, 351–70. *Hesperia* supplement 33. Princeton, NJ.

Delcor, M. 1978. "Le problème des jardins d'Adonis dans Isaïe 17, 9–11 à la lumière de la civilisation syro-phénicienne." *Syria* 55:371–94.

Delivorrias, A. 1984. *LIMC* 2, s.v. "Aphrodite."

Delneri, F. 2006. *I culti misterici stranieri nei frammenti della comedia attica antica.* Bologna.

Demetriou, D. 2013. *Negotiating Identity in the Ancient Mediterranean: The Archaic and Classical Greek Multiethnic Emporia.* Cambridge.

Demos, M. 1999. *Lyric Quotation in Plato.* Lanham, MD.

de Polignac, F., and P. Schmitt Pantel, eds. 1998. *Public et privé en Grèce ancienne: Lieux conductes, pratiques. Ktèma* 23. Strasbourg.

Derderian, K. 2001. *Leaving Words to Remember: Greek Mourning and the Advent of Literacy.* Leiden.

Derrida, J. (1972) 1981. *Dissemination.* Translated by B. Johnson. Chicago.

Destrée, P., and F. Herman, eds. 2011. *Plato and the Poets.* Leiden.

Detienne, M. (1972) 1994. *The Gardens of Adonis: Spices in Greek Mythology.* 2nd ed. Princeton, NJ.

———. (1977) 1979. *Dionysus Slain.* Baltimore.

Deubner, L. (1932) 1969. *Attische Feste.* Berlin.

de Witte, J. 1846. "Sur les représentations d'Adonis, lettre à M. O. Jahn." *AnnInst* 387–418.

de Vaux, R. 1971. *The Bible and the Ancient Near East.* Garden City, NY.

de Vries, G. J. 1969. *A Commentary on the "Phaedrus" of Plato.* Amsterdam.

———. 1973. "Mystery Terminology in Aristotle and Plato." *Mnemosyne* 26:1–8.

———. 1985. "Laughter in Plato's Writings." *Mnemosyne* 37:378–81.

Diggle, J. 1970. *Euripides: Phaethon.* Cambridge Classical Texts and Commentaries 12. Cambridge.

Dillon, M. 1995. "By Gods, Tongues, and Dogs: The Use of Oaths in Aristophanic Comedy." *G&R* 42.2:135–51.

———. 2002. *Girls and Women in Classical Greek Religion.* London.

———. 2003. "'Woe for Adonis'—But in Spring, not Summer." *Hermes* 131:1–16.

Dimock, G. E., Jr. 1962. "The Name of Odysseus." In *Homer: A Collection of Critical Essays,* edited by G. Steiner and R. Fagles, 106–11. Englewood Cliffs, NJ.

Dodds, E. R. 1940. "Maenadism in the *Bacchae.*" *HThR* 33.3:155–76.

———, ed. 1959. *Plato: Gorgias.* Oxford.

———. 1964. *The Greeks and the Irrational.* Berkeley, CA.

Dontas, G. 1960. "Ἀνασκαφὴ εἰς τοὺς νοτίους πρόποδας τῆς Ἀκροπόλεως καὶ σκέψεις τινὲς περὶ τοῦ ἱεροῦ τῆς Πανδήμου Ἀφροδίτης." *PAAH*: 4–9.

Dover, K. J. 1971, ed. *Theocritus: Select Poems.* London.

———. 1972. *Aristophanic Comedy.* Berkeley, CA.

———. 1978. *Greek Homosexuality*. Cambridge.

Dowden, K. 1989. *Death and the Maiden: Girls' Initiation Rites in Greek Mythology*. London.

duBois, P. 1985. "Phallocentrism and Its Subversion in Plato's *Phaedrus*." *Arethusa* 18.1:91–103.

———. 1988. *Sowing the Body: Psychoanalysis and Ancient Representations of Women*. Chicago.

Dué, C. 2002. *Homeric Variations on a Lament by Briseis*. Lanham, MD.

———. 2006. *The Captive Woman's Lament in Greek Tragedy*. Austin, TX.

Durand, J.-L. 1989. "Greek Animals: Toward a Topology of Edible Bodies." In *The Cuisine of Sacrifice among the Greeks*, edited by M. Detienne and J.-P. Vernant, 87–118. Chicago.

Ebbott, M. 2003. *Imagining Illegitimacy in Classical Greek Literature*. Lanham, MD.

Edmonds, R. 2000. "Socrates the Beautiful: Role Reversal and Midwifery in Plato's *Symposium*." *TAPA* 130:261–85.

———. 2006. "To Sit in Solemn Silence? Thronosis in Ritual, Myth, and Iconography." *AJP* 127:347–66.

Edmunds, L. 1981. "The Cults and Legend of Oedipus." *HSCP* 85:221–38.

Edwards, C. 1984. "Aphrodite on a Ladder." *Hesperia* 53:59–72.

Elderkin, G. W. 1940. "Aphrodite and Athena in the *Lysistrata* of Aristophanes." *CP* 35.4:387–96.

———. 1941. "The Cults of the Erechtheion." *Hesperia* 10:113–24.

Estevez, V. A. 1981. "Ἀπώλετο καλὸς Ἄδωνις: A Description of Bion's Refrain." *Maia* 33:35–42.

Faraone, C. 1993. "The Wheel, the Whip and Other Implements of Torture: Erotic Magic in Pindar *Pythian* 4.213–19." *CJ* 88:1–19.

———. 1997. "Salvation and Female Heroics in the Parodos of Aristophanes' *Lysistrata*." *JHS* 117:38–59.

———. 1999. *Ancient Greek Love Magic*. Cambridge, MA.

———. 2006. "Priestess and Courtesans: The Ambivalence of Female Leadership in Aristophanes' *Lysistrata*." In *Prostitutes and Courtesans in the Ancient World*, edited by C. Faraone and L. McClure, 207–23. Madison, WI.

———. 2010. "A Socratic Leaf-Charm for Headache (*Charmides* 155b–157c), Orphic Gold Leaves and the Ancient Greek Tradition of Leaf Amulets." In *Myths, Martyrs, and Modernity: Studies in the History of Religions in Honour of Jan N. Bremmer*, edited by J. Dijkstra, K. Kroesen, and Y. Kuiper, 145–66. Leiden.

Farnell, L. R. 1907. *The Cults of the Greek States*. Vol. 3. Oxford.

Faulkner, A. 2008. *The Homeric Hymn to Aphrodite: Introduction, Text, and Commentary*. Oxford.

Felson, N. 1983. "Meleager and Odysseus: A Structural and Cultural Study of the Greek Hunting-Maturation Myth." *Arethusa* 16:137–71.

Felson, N., and W. M. Sale. 1984. "Meleager and Narrative Theory." *Arethusa* 17.2:211–22.

Ferrari, F. 2010. *Sappho's Gift: The Poet and Her Community*. Translated by B. Acosta-Hughes and L. Prauscello. Ann Arbor, MI.

Ferrari, G. 2002. *Figures of Speech: Men and Maidens in Ancient Greece*. Chicago.

———. 2003. "Myth and Genre on Athenian Vases." *CA* 22.1:37–54.

———. 2004. "The 'Anodos' of the Bride." In *Greek Ritual Poetics*, edited by D. Yatromanolakis and P. Roilos, 245–60. Cambridge.

———. 2008. *Alcman and the Cosmos of Sparta*. Chicago.

Ferrari, G. R. F. 1987. *Listening to the Cicadas: A Study of Plato's "Phaedrus."* Cambridge.

———. 1989. "Plato and Poetry." In *Cambridge History of Literary Criticism*, edited by G. Kennedy, 1:92–148. Cambridge.

Figueira, T. J., and G. Nagy, eds. 1985. *Theognis of Megara: Poetry and the Polis*. Baltimore.

Flashar, H. 1969. *Der Epitaphios des Perikles: Seine Funktion im Geschichtswerk des Thukydides*. Heidelberg.

Fletcher, J. 1999. "Sacrificial Bodies and the Bodies of the Text in Aristophanes' *Lysistrata*." *Ramus* 28.2:108–25.

———. 2012. *Performing Oaths in Classical Greek Drama*. Cambridge.

Foley, H. 1980. "The Masque of Dionysus." *TAPA* 110:107–33.

———. 1982. "The 'Female Intruder' Reconsidered: Women in Aristophanes' *Lysistrata* and *Ecclesiazusae*." *CP* 77:1–21.

———. 1985. *Ritual Irony: Poetry and Sacrifice in Euripides*. Ithaca, NY.

———. 1994. *The Homeric Hymn to Demeter: Translation, Commentary, and Interpretive Essays*. Princeton, NJ.

———. 1998. "'The Mother of the Argument': *Eros* and the Body in Sappho and Plato's *Phaedrus*." In *Parchments of Gender*, edited by M. Wyke, 39–70. Oxford.

———. 2001. *Female Acts in Greek Tragedy*. Princeton, NJ.

Foucart, P. 1873. *Des associations religieuses chez les Grecs*. Paris.

———. 1879. "Décrets d'un thiase d'Aphrodite." *BCH* 3:510–15.

Fraser, P. M. 1972. *Ptolemaic Alexandria*. 3 vols. Oxford.

Frazer, J. G. 1906. *Adonis, Attis, Osiris: Studies in the History of Oriental Religion*. London.

———. 1922. *The Golden Bough*. 4: *Adonis, Attis, Osiris*. Vol. 1. 3rd ed. London.

Frickenhaus, A. 1912. *Lenäenvasen*. Vol. 72. Berlin.

Friedländer, P. 1958. *Plato: An Introduction*. Bollingen Series 59, no. 1. New York.

Frontisi-Ducroux, F. 1996. "Eros, Desire, and the Gaze." In *Sexuality in Ancient Art: Near East, Egypt, Greece, and Italy*, edited by N. B. Kampen, 81–100. Cambridge.

Frost, F. J. 2002. "Solon *Pornoboskos* and Aphrodite Pandemos." *SyllClass* 13:34–46.

Furley, W. D. 1988. "Die Adonis-Feier in Athen, 415 v. Chr." *Ktema* 13:13–19.

———. 2009. "Drama at the Festival: A Recurrent Motif in Menander." In *The Play of Texts and Fragments: Essays in Honour of Martin Cropp*, edited by J. R. C. Cousland and J. R. Hume, 389–401. Leiden.

Gagné, R. 2009. "Mystery Inquisitors: Performance, Authority, and Sacrilege at Eleusis." *CA* 28.2:211–47.

Gallagher, C., and S. Greenblatt. 2000. *Practicing New Historicism*. Chicago.

Gantz, T. 1993. *Early Greek Myth: A Guide to Literary and Artistic Sources*. Baltimore.

Garland, R. 1985. *The Greek Way of Death*. London.

———. 1989. "The Well-Ordered Corpse: An Investigation into the Motives behind Greek Funerary Legislation." *BICS* 36:1–15.

———. 1992. *Introducing New Gods: The Politics of Athenian Religion.* Ithaca, NY.
———. 2001. *The Piraeus: From the Fifth to the First Century B.C.* 2nd ed. Ithaca, NY.
Gebauer, J. 2002. *Pompe und Thysia: Attische Tieropferdarstellungen auf schwarz- und rotfigurigen Vasen.* EIKON. Beiträge zur antiken Bildersprache 7. Münster.
Giacomelli [Carson], A. 1980. "Aphrodite and After." *Phoenix* 34:1–19.
Giannopoulou, Z. 2010. "Enacting the Other, Being Oneself: The Drama of Rhetoric and Philosophy in Plato's *Phaedrus.*" *CP* 105.2:146–61.
Gilhuly, K. 2009. *The Feminine Matrix of Sex and Gender in Classical Athens.* Cambridge.
Glotz, G. 1920. "Les fêtes d'Adonis sous Ptolémée II." *REG* 33:169–222.
Glowacki, K. 1991. "Topics Concerning the North Slope of the Acropolis at Athens." PhD diss., Bryn Mawr.
Goff, B. 2004. *Citizen Bacchae: Women's Ritual Practice in Ancient Greece.* Berkeley, CA.
Gow, A. S. F. 1952. *Theocritus.* 2 vols. 2nd ed. Cambridge.
———, ed. 1965. *Machon: The Fragments.* Cambridge.
Graf, F., and S. I. Johnston. 2007. *Ritual Texts for the Afterlife: Orpheus and the Bacchic Gold Tablets.* London.
Greene, E., and M. Skinner, eds. 2010. *The New Sappho on Old Age: Textual and Philosophical Issues.* Hellenic Studies Series 38. Washington, DC.
Griffith, M. 1977. *The Authenticity of "Prometheus Bound."* Cambridge.
Griffith, R. D. 1989. "In Praise of the Bride: Sappho fr. 105(a) L–P, Voigt." *TAPA* 119:55–61.
Griffiths, F. T. 1979. *Theocritus at Court. Mnemosyne* supplement 55. Leiden.
———. 1981. "Home before Lunch: The Emancipated Woman in Theocritus." In *Reflections of Women in Antiquity,* edited by H. Foley, 247–73. New York.
Griswold, C. L., 1986. *Self-Knowledge in Plato's "Phaedrus."* New Haven, CT.
———. 1996. *Self-Knowledge in Plato's "Phaedrus."* University Park, PA.
Gullini, G. 1944–45. "Afrodite en Kepois." *RendPontAcc* 21:151–62.
Guthrie, W. K. C. 1962. *History of Greek Philosophy.* Vol. 4. Cambridge.
Gutzwiller, K. J. 1992. "Callimachus' *Lock of Berenice*: Fantasy, Romance, and Propaganda." *AJP* 113:359–85.
———. 2007. *A Guide to Hellenistic Literature.* Malden, MA.
Hackforth, R. 1952. *Plato's "Phaedrus."* Cambridge.
Hague, R. 1983. "Ancient Greek Wedding Songs: The Tradition of Praise." *Journal of Folklore Research* 20:131–43.
Haider, M. 2011–12. "Fragments of an Attic Vase with Procession Scene from the College Site Excavation in Sidon." *Archaeology and History in Lebanon* 34–35:389–98.
Halliwell, S. 2002. *The Aesthetics of Mimesis: Ancient Texts and Modern Problems.* Princeton, NJ.
Halperin, D. 1986. "Plato and Erotic Reciprocity." *CA* 5.1:60–80.
———. 1990. *One Hundred Years of Homosexuality.* New York.
Harris, E. M. 1992. "Women and Lending in Athenian Society: A *Horos* Re-examined." *Phoenix* 46:309–21.
Hatzfeld, J. 1939. "Du nouveau sur Phèdre." *Revue des études anciennes* 41:313–18.

Hauser, F. 1909. "Aristophanes und Vasenbilder." *ÖJh* 12:90–99.

Hazzard, R. A. 2000. *Imagination of a Monarchy: Studies in Ptolemaic Propaganda*. Toronto.

Hedreen, G. 1992. *Silens in Attic Black-figure Vase-painting*. Ann Arbor, MI.

———. 1994. "Silens, Nymphs, and Maenads." *JHS* 114:47–69.

———. 2009. "Ambivalence, Athenian Dionysiac Vase-Imagery, and the Discourse on Human Social Evolution." In *Hermeneutik der Bilder: Beiträge zur Ikonographie und Interpretation griechischer Vasenmalerei*, edited by S. Schmidt and J. H. Oakley, 125–33. Munich.

———. 2014. "The Artificial Sculptural Image of Dionysos in Athenian Vase-Painting and the Mythological Discourse of Early Greek Life." In *Approaching the Ancient Artifact: Representation, Narrative, and Function*, edited by A. Avramidou and D. Demetriou, 267–80. Berlin.

Henderson, J. 1980. "Lysistrate: The Play and Its Themes." *YCS* 26:153–218.

———, ed. 1987. *Aristophanes: Lysistrata*. Oxford.

Henrichs, A. 1972. "Toward a New Edition of Philodemus' Treatise on Piety." *GRBS* 13:67–98.

———. 1978. "Greek Maenadism from Olympias to Messalina." *HSPh* 82:121–60.

———. 1982. "Changing Dionysiac Identities." In *Jewish and Christian Self-Definition*, vol. 3, *Self-Definition in the Graeco-Roman World*, edited by B. F. Meyer and E. P. Sanders, 137–60. London.

———. 1994–95. "'Why Should I Dance?' Choral Self-Referentiality in Greek Tragedy." *Arion* 3.1:56–111.

Henry, A. 2002. "Hookers and Lookers: Prostitution and Soliciting in Late Archaic Thasos." *ABSA* 97:217–21.

Hicks, E. L. 1888. "Inscriptions from Iasos." *JHS* 9:338–42.

Holst-Warhaft, G. 1992. *Dangerous Voices: Women's Lament and Greek Literature*. New York.

Hordern, J. H. 2003. "Gnesippus and the Rivals of Aristophanes." *CQ* 53.2:608–13.

———. 2004. *Sophron's Mimes: Text, Translation, and Commentary*. Oxford.

Hornblower, S. 1991–2008. *A Commentary on Thucydides*. 3 vols. Oxford.

Hugh-Jones, S. 1979. *The Palm and the Pleiades: Initiation and Cosmology in Northwest Amazonia*. Cambridge.

Hulton, A. O. 1972. "The Women on the Acropolis: A Note on the Structure of the *Lysistrata*." *G&R* 19:32–36.

Humphreys, S. C. 1980. "Family Tombs and Tomb Cult in Ancient Athens." *JHS* 100:96–126.

———. 1983. *The Family, Women, and Death*. London.

Hunt, P. 2010. *War, Peace, and Alliance in Demosthenes' Athens*. Cambridge.

Hunter, R. L., ed. 1983. *Eubulus: The Fragments*. Cambridge.

———. 1996a. *Theocritus and the Archaeology of Greek Poetry*. Cambridge.

———. 1996b. "Mime and Mimesis: Theocritus, *Idyll* 15." In *Theocritus*, edited by M. A. Harder, R. F. Regtuit, and G. C. Wakker, 149–69. Hellenistica Groningana 2. Groningen.

———, ed. 1999. *Theocritus: A Selection.* Cambridge Greek and Latin Classics. Cambridge.

Immerwahr, H. 1990. *Attic Script: A Survey.* Oxford.

Inwood, B. 2001. *The Poem of Empedocles: A Text and Translation with an Introduction.* Toronto.

Irigaray, L. 1994. "Sorcerer Love: A Reading of Plato's *Symposium*, Diotima's Speech." In *Feminist Interpretations of Plato*, edited by N. Tuana, 181–95. University Park, PA.

Isler-Kerényi, D. 2007. *Dionysos in Archaic Greece: An Understanding through Images.* Religions in the Greco-Roman World 160. Leiden.

Jahn, O. 1845. "Sur les représentations d'Adonis, letter à M. J. de Witte." *AnnInst* 347–86.

James, S. A. 2010. "The Hellenistic Pottery from the Panayia Field Corinth: Studies in Chronology and Context." PhD diss., University of Texas, Austin.

Jameson, M. H. 1988. "Sacrifice and Animal Husbandry in Classical Greece." In *Pastoral Economies in Classical Antiquity*, edited by C. R. Whittaker, 87–119. Cambridge.

———. 1990. "Domestic Space in the Greek City-State." In *Domestic Architecture and the Use of Space*, edited by S. Kent, 92–113. Cambridge.

———. 1993. "The Asexuality of Dionysus." In *Masks of Dionysus*, edited by T. H. Carpenter and C. A. Faraone, 44–64. Ithaca, NY.

Jeammet, V., and I. Bonora Andujar. 2010. *Tanagras: Figuras para la vida y la eternidad.* Colección del Museo del Louvre. Valencia.

Jenkins, I. 1983. "Is There Life after Marriage? A Study of the Abduction Motif in Vase Paintings of the Athenian Wedding Ceremony." *BICS* 30:137–45.

Johnson, S. E. 1981–84. "The Present State of Sabazios Research." *ANRW* II 17.3:1583–1613.

Johnston, S. 1995. "The Song of the Iynx: Magic and Rhetoric in *Pythian* 4." *TAPA* 125:177–206.

Jones, N. F. 1999. *The Associations of Classical Athens: The Response to Democracy.* New York.

Kaempf-Dimitriadou, S. 1979. *Die Liebe der Götter in der attischen Kunst des 5. Jahrhunderts v. Chr.* Vol. 11. Antike Kunst. Bern.

Kaltsas, N., and A. Shapiro. 2008. *Worshipping Women: Ritual and Reality in Classical Athens.* New York.

Kamen, D. 2013. *Status in Classical Athens.* Princeton, NJ.

Karanika, A. 2008. "Greek Comedy's Parody of Lament." In *Lament: Studies in the Ancient Mediterranean and Beyond*, edited by A. Suter, 181–99. Oxford.

Keuls, E. 1979. "The Apulian 'Xylophone': A Mysterious Musical Instrument Identified." *AJA* 83:476–77.

———. 1985. *Reign of the Phallus: Sexual Politics in Ancient Athens.* New York.

Kindt, J. 2009. "Polis Religion: A Critical Appreciation." *Kernos* 22:9–34.

———. 2012. *Rethinking Greek Religion.* Cambridge.

Kirk, G. S. 1963. "A Fragment of Sappho Reinterpreted." *CQ* 13:51–52.

Kloppenborg, J. S., and R. S. Ascough. 2011. *Greco-Roman Associations: Texts, Translations, and Commentary, I. Attica, Central Greece, Macedonia, Thrace.* Berlin.

Knigge, U. 1982. "ὁ ἀστὴρ τῆς Ἀφροδίτης." *AthMitt* 97:153–70.

———. 1991. *The Athenian Kerameikos.* Athens.

Koenen, L. 1993. "The Ptolemaic King as a Religious Figure." In *Images and Ideologies: Self-Definition in the Hellenistic World*, edited by A. W. Bulloch, E. S. Gruen, A. A. Long, and A. Stewart, 25–115. Berkeley, CA.

Kousser, R. 2004. "The World of Aphrodite in the Late Fifth Century B.C." In *Greek Vases: Images, Contexts and Controversies*, ed. C. Marconi, 97–112. Columbia Studies in the Classical Tradition 25. Leiden.

———. 2011. "The Female Nude in Classical Art: Between Voyeurism and Power." In *Aphrodite and the Gods of Love*, edited by C. Kondoleon with P. C. Segal. Boston: Museum of Fine Arts.

Kowalzig, B. 2004. "Changing Choral Worlds." In *Music and the Muses: The Culture of Mousike in the Classical Athenian City*, edited by P. Murray and P. Wilson, 39–65. Oxford.

———. 2006. "The Aetiology of Empire? Hero-Cult and Athenian Tragedy." In *Greek Drama III: Essays in Honor of Kevin Lee. BICS* supplement, edited by J. Davidson, F. Muecke, and P. Wilson, 87:79–98. London.

———. 2007a. "'And Now All the World Shall Dance!' (Eur. *Bacch.* 114) Dionysus' Choroi between Drama and Ritual." In *The Origins of Theater in Ancient Greece and Beyond*, edited by E. Csapo and M. Miller, 221–51. Cambridge.

———. 2007b. *Singing for the Gods: Performances of Myth and Ritual in Archaic and Classical Greece.* Oxford.

———. 2013. "Broken Rhythms in Plato's *Laws*: Materialising Social Time in the Chorus." In *Performance and Culture in Plato's "Laws,"* edited by A.-E. Peponi, 171–211. Cambridge.

Kretschmer, P. 1915. "Mythische Namen." *Glotta* 7:29–39.

Kurke, L. 1992. "The Politics of ἁβροσύνη in Archaic Greece." *CA* 11.1:91–120.

———. 1999. *Coins, Bodies, Games, and Gold: The Politics of Meaning in Archaic Greece.* Princeton, NJ.

———. 2007. "Visualizing the Choral: Epichoric Poetry, Ritual, and Elite Negotiation in Fifth-Century Thebes." In *Visualizing the Tragic: Drama, Myth, and Ritual in Greek Art and Literature; Essays in Honour of Froma Zeitlin*, edited by C. Kraus, S. Goldhill, H. Foley, and J. Elsner, 63–101. Oxford.

———. 2011. *Aesopic Conversations: Popular Tradition, Cultural Dialogue, and the Invention of Greek Prose.* Princeton, NJ.

Kutzko, D. 2007–8. "All the World's a Page: Imitation of Metatheater in Theocritus 15, Herodas 1, and Virgil *Eclogues* 3." *CJ* 103:141–61.

Lacey, W. K. 1964. "Thucydides II, 45, 2." *PCPS* 10:47–49.

———. 1968. *The Family in Classical Greece.* Ithaca, NY.

Lambert, M. 2001. "Gender and Religion in Theocritus, *Idyll* 15: Prattling Tourists at the *Adonia.*" *Acta Classica* 44:87–103.

Lane, E. J. 1985. *Corpus Cultus Iovis Sabazii.* Vol. 2, *The Other Monuments and Literary Evidence.* Leiden.

———. 1989. *Conclusions.* Vol. 3. Leiden.

Langlotz, E. 1954. *Aphrodite in den Gärten.* Heidelberg.

Lardinois, A. 1994. "Subject and Circumstance in Sappho's Poetry." *TAPA* 124:57–84.

———. 2001. "Keening Sappho: Female Speech Genres in Sappho's Poetry." In *Making Silence Speak: Women's Voices in Greek Literature and Society*, edited by A. Lardinois and L. McClure, 75–92. Princeton, NJ.

Larson, J. 2001. *Greek Nymphs: Myth, Cult, Lore.* Oxford.

———. 2007. *Ancient Greek Cults: A Guide.* New York.

Lattimore, R. 1962. *Themes in Greek and Latin Epitaphs.* Urbana, IL.

Lawler, L. B. 1927. "The Maenads: A Contribution to the Study of the Dance in Ancient Greece." *MAAR* 6:69–112.

Lebeck, A. 1972. "The Central Myth of Plato's *Phaedrus.*" *GRBS* 13:267–90.

Lefkowitz, M. R. 2002. "'Predatory' Goddesses." *Hesperia* 71:325–44.

Levine, D. 1987. "*Lysistrata* and *Bacchae*: Structure, Genre and 'Women on Top.'" *Helios* 54:29–38.

Lewis, D. M. 1955. "Notes on Attic Inscriptions (II), XXIII: Who Was Lysistrata?" *ABSA* 1:1–13.

Lewis, S. 2002. *The Athenian Woman: An Iconographic Handbook.* London.

Lightfoot, J. L. 2003. *Lucian: On the Syrian Goddess.* Oxford.

Linforth, I. M. 1945. "The Corybantic Rites in Plato." *University of California Publications in Classical Philology* 13.5:121–62.

———. 1946. "Telestic Madness in Plato, *Phaedrus* 244de." *University of California Publications in Classical Philology* 13.6:163–72.

Lipiński, E. 1995. *Dieux et déesses de l'univers phénicien et punique.* Orientalia Lovaniensia analecta 64. Leuven.

Lissarrague, F. 1995. "Women, Boxes, Containers: Some Signs and Metaphors." In *Pandora: Women in Classical Greece*, edited by E. Reeder, 91–101. Baltimore.

———. 2012. "Figuring Religious Ritual." In *A Companion to Greek Art*, edited by T. J. Smith and D. Plantzos. Malden, MA.

Lloyd-Jones, H. 1967. "Sappho fr. 111." *CQ* 17:168.

Lombardo, M. 1983. "Habrosyne e habra nel mondo greco arcaico." In *Forme di contatto e processi di trasformazione nella società antiche.* Atti del Convegno di Cortona (24–30 maggio 1981). Pisa.

Longega, G. 1968. *Arsinoe II.* Univ. di Padova Pubbl. Ist. di Storia Antica 6. Rome.

Loraux, N. 1985. "La Cité, l'Historien, les Femmes." *Pallas* 32:7–39.

———. 1986. *The Invention of Athens: The Funeral Oration in the Classical City.* Cambridge, MA.

———. 1987. *Tragic Ways of Killing a Woman.* Cambridge, MA.

———. 1990. *Les mères en deuil.* Paris.

———. 1993. *The Children of Athena: Athenian Ideas about Citizenship and the Division between the Sexes.* Princeton, NJ.

———. 1995. *The Experiences of Tiresias: The Feminine and the Greek Man.* Princeton, NJ.

Lupu, E. 2005. *Greek Sacred Law: A Collection of New Documents.* Vol. 152. Leiden.

Maas, P. 1914. "*Hymenaios*." In *Real-Encyclopädie der classischen Altertumswissenschaft*, edited by W. Kroll, 9:130–34. Stuttgart.

Macé, A., ed. 2012. *Choses privées et chose publique en Grèce ancienne: Genèse et structure d'un système de classification*. Collection HOROS. Grenoble.

Macleod, C. 1983. *Collected Essays*. Oxford.

MacDowell, D. M. 1995. *Aristophanes and Athens: An Introduction to the Plays*. Oxford.

MacLachan, B. 1995. "Love, War, and the Goddess in Fifth-Century Locri." *Ancient World* 26.2:205–23.

Martin, Richard. 1987. "Fire on the Mountain: *Lysistrata* and the Lemnian Women." *CA* 6.1:77–105.

———. 2008. "Keens from the Absent Chorus: Troy to Ulster." In *Lament: Studies in the Ancient Mediterranean and Beyond*, edited by A. Suter, 118–38. Oxford.

Martin, Roland. 1987. "Le palais d'Ulysse et les inscriptions de Délos." In *Architecture et urbanisme*, 221–30. Collection de l'Ecole française de Rome 99. Athens.

Mastronarde, D. J. 1990. "Actors on High: The Skene Roof, the Crane and the Gods in Attic Drama." *CA* 9:247–94.

Matthews, V. J. 1974. "Panyassis of Halikarnassos." *Mnemosyne* supplement 33. Leiden.

———. 1996. "Antimachus of Colophon." *Mnemosyne* supplement 155. Leiden.

McNiven, T. J. 2000. "Fear and Gender in Greek Art." In *Reading the Body: Representations and Remains in the Archaeological Record*, edited by A. E. Rautman, 124–31. Philadelphia.

McPherran, M. 2011. "Socratic Religion." In *Cambridge Companion to Socrates*, edited by D. Morrison, 111–37. Cambridge.

Meritt, B. D. 1935. "Greek Inscriptions." *Hesperia* 4.4:525–85.

Mettinger, T. 2001. *The Riddle of Resurrection: "Dying and Rising Gods" in the Ancient Near East*. Stockholm.

Metzger, H. 1942. "Lébès gamikos à figures rouges du Musée National d'Athènes." *BCH* 66:228–47.

———. 1951. *Les Représentations dans la céramique attique du IVe siècle*. Paris.

Mikalson, J. D. 1982. "The *Heorte* of Heortology." *GRBS* 23.3:213–21.

———. 1983. *Athenian Popular Religion*. Chapel Hill, NC.

Miller, S. 1979. *Two Groups of Thessalian Gold*. Berkeley, CA.

Millett, P. 1991. *Lending and Borrowing in Ancient Athens*. Cambridge.

Mills, S. 1997. *Theseus, Tragedy, and the Athenian Empire*. Oxford.

Mitropoulou, E. 1975. *Aphrodite auf der Ziege*. Athens.

Mitsopoulou, C. 2010. "De Nouveaux *Kernoi* pour *Kernos* . . . Réévaluation et mise à jour de la recherche sur les vases de culte éleusiniens." *Kernos* 23:145–78.

———. 2011. "The Eleusinian Processional Cult Vessel: Iconographic Evidence and Interpretation." In *Current Approaches to Religion in Ancient Greece*, edited by M. Haysom and J. Wallensten, 189–226. Stockholm.

Möller, A. 2000. *Naukratis: Trade in Archaic Greece*. Oxford.

Monoson, S. 1994. "Citizen as Erastes: Erotic Imagery and the Idea of Reciprocity in the Periclean Funeral Oration." *Political Theory* 22.2:253–76.

Monsacré, H. 1984. *Les larmes d'Achille: Le héros, la femme et la souffrance dans la poésie d'Homère.* Paris.

Morgan, J. 2010. *The Classical Greek House.* Exeter.

Morgan, K. A. 1994. "Socrates and Gorgias at Delphi and Olympia: *Phaedrus* 235d6–236b4." *CQ* 44.2:375–86.

———. 2000. *Myth and Philosophy from the Presocratics to Plato.* Cambridge.

Morgan, M. 1990. *Platonic Piety: Philosophy and Ritual in Fourth Century Athens.* New Haven.

———. 1992. "Plato and Greek Religion." In *Cambridge Companion to Plato,* edited by R. Kraut, 227–47. Cambridge.

Morris, I. 1989. *Burial and Ancient Society: The Rise of the Greek City-State.* Cambridge.

Morris, S. 1998. "No Learning by Coercion: Paidia and Paideia in Platonic Philosophy." In *Play from Birth to Twelve and Beyond: Contexts, Perspectives, and Meanings,* edited by D. Fromberg and D. Bergen, 109–18. New York.

Morrow, G. R. 1960. *Plato's Cretan City: A Historical Interpretation of the "Laws."* Princeton, NJ.

Most, G. 1996. "Reflecting Sappho." In *Re-reading Sappho: Reception and Transmission,* edited by E. Greene, 11–35. Berkeley, CA.

Motte, A. 1963. "Le Pré Sacré de Pan et des Nymphes dans le Phèdre de Platon." *L'Antiquité Classique* 32:460–76.

———. 1973. *Prairies et jardins de la Grèce antique: De la religion à la philosophie.* Brussels.

Müller, H.-P. 2004. "Adonis und Adonisgärtchen." *Zeitschrift der Deutschen Morgenländischen Gesellschaft* 154.2:265–84.

Murnaghan, S. 1999. "The Poetics of Loss in Greek Epic." In *Epic Traditions in the Contemporary World: The Poetics of Community,* edited by M. Beissinger, J. Tylus, and S. Wofford, 203–21. Berkeley, CA.

———. 2005. "Women in Groups: Aeschylus's *Suppliants* and the Female Choruses of Greek Tragedy." In *The Soul of Tragedy,* edited by V. Pedrick and S. M. Oberhelman, 183–98. Chicago.

Murray, P. 1997. *Plato on Poetry.* Cambridge Greek and Latin Classics. Cambridge.

Nachmanson, E. 1941 (1969). *Der griechische Buchtitel.* Göteburg.

Nagy, G. 1973. "Phaethon, Sappho's Phaon, and the White Rocks of Leukas." *HSCP* 77:137–77.

———. 1985. "Theognis and Megara: A Poet's Vision of his City." In *Theognis of Megara: Poetry and the Polis,* edited by T. J. Figueira and G. Nagy, 22–81. Baltimore.

———. 1990. *Pindar's Homer: The Lyric Possession of an Epic Past.* Baltimore.

Nails, D. 2002. *The People of Plato: A Prosopography of Plato and Other Socratics.* Indianapolis.

Nehamas, A. 1982. "Plato on Imitation and Poetry in *Republic* 10." In *Plato on Beauty, Wisdom, and the Arts,* edited by J. M. C. Moravcsik and P. Temko, 47–78. Totowa, NJ.

Nehamas, A., and P. Woodruff, eds. 1995. *Plato: Phaedrus.* Indianapolis.

Neils, J. 2008. "Adonia to Thesmophoria: Women and Athenian Festivals." In *Worshipping Women: Ritual and Reality in Classical Athens,* edited by N. Kaltsas and A. Shapiro, 242–49. New York.

Nelson, J. G. 1986. "Xylophones on Gnathia Vases." *BaBesch* 61:30–33.

Neppi Modona, A. 1951–54. "ΑΔΩΝΙΑ e ΑΔΩΝΙΔΟΣ ΚΗΠΟΙ nelle raffigurazioni vascolari attiche." *RendPontAcc* 27:177–87.

Nevett, L. 1999. *House and Society in the Ancient Greek World.* Cambridge.

———. 2010. *Domestic Space in Classical Antiquity.* Cambridge.

Newiger, H. 1980. "War and Peace in the Comedy of Aristophanes." *YCS* 26:219–37.

Nicolaou, K. 1976. *The Historical Topography of Kition.* Göteborg.

Nicole, G. 1908. *Meidias et le style fleuri dans la céramique attique.* Geneva.

Nightingale, A. 1995. *Genres in Dialogue: Plato and the Construct of Philosophy.* Cambridge.

Nock, A. D. (1934) 1986. "Attic Festivals: Review of Deubner, *Gnomon* 10, 1934." In *Essays on Religion and the Ancient World,* vol. 1, ed. Z. Stewart. Oxford.

Noussia Fantuzzi, M. 2010. *Solon the Athenian: The Poetic Fragments.* Leiden.

Nussbaum, M. 1986. *The Fragility of Goodness: Luck and Ethics in Greek Tragedy and Philosophy.* Cambridge.

Oakley, J. 1995. "Nuptial Nuances: Wedding Images in Non-wedding Scenes of Myth." In *Pandora: Women in Classical Greece,* edited by E. Reeder, 63–73. Baltimore.

———. 2004. *Picturing Death in Classical Athens: The Evidence of the White Lekythoi.* Cambridge.

———. 2012. "Birth, Marriage, and Death." In *A Companion to Greek Art,* edited by T. J. Smith and D. Plantzos, 480–97. Oxford.

Oakley, J., and L. Reitzammer. 2005. "A Hellenistic Terracotta and the Gardens of Adonis." *JHS* 125:142–44.

Oakley, J., and R. Sinos. 1993. *The Wedding in Ancient Athens.* Madison, WI.

Oden, R. A. 1977. *Studies in Lucian's "de syria dea."* Missoula, MT.

Oikonomides, A. N. 1964. *The Two Agoras in Ancient Athens.* Chicago.

Olson, S. D. 1992. "Names and Naming in Aristophanic Comedy." *CQ* 42.2:304–19.

———. 2012. *The Homeric Hymn to Aphrodite and Related Texts: Text, Translation, and Commentary.* Berlin.

Osborne, R. 1985. *Demos: The Discovery of Classical Attika.* Cambridge.

———. 1996. "Desiring Women on Athenian Pottery." In *Sexuality and Ancient Art,* edited by N. Kampen, 65–80. Cambridge.

Pache, C. 2011. *A Moment's Ornament: The Poetics of Nympholepsy in Ancient Greece.* Oxford.

Page, D. 1955. *Sappho and Alcaeus: An Introduction to the Study of Ancient Lesbian Poetry.* Oxford.

Pantelia, M. 2002. "Helen and the Last Song for Hector." *TAPA* 132:21–27.

Papadimitriou, I. 1948–49. "Attika 1." *AEph* 86–88:146–53.

Papadopoulou, C. 2010. "Aphrodite and the Fleet in Classical Athens." In *Brill's Companion to Aphrodite,* edited by A. Smith and S. Pickup, 217–33. Leiden.

Parke, H. W. 1977. *Festivals of the Athenians.* Ithaca, NY.

Parker, H. 1999. "Sappho Schoolmistress." In *Re-reading Sappho: Reception and Transmission,* edited by E. Greene, 146–83. Berkeley, CA.

Parker, R. 1987. "Myths of Early Athens." In *Interpretations of Greek Mythology,* edited by J. Bremmer, 187–214. London.

———. 1996. *Athenian Religion: A History*. Oxford.

———. 2005. *Polytheism and Society at Athens*. Oxford.

———. 2011. *On Greek Religion*. Ithaca, NY.

———. 2012. "Epigraphy and Greek Religion." In *Epigraphy and the Historical Sciences*, edited by J. K. Davies and J. Wilkes, 17–30. Oxford.

Patterson, C. 1986. "*Hai Attikai*: The Other Athenians." In *Rescuing Creusa: New Methodological Approaches to Women in Antiquity*, edited by M. Skinner, 49–67. A special issue of *Helios* 13. Lubbock, TX.

Peirce, S. 1998. "Visual Language and Concepts of Cult on the 'Lenaia Vases.'" *CA* 17.1:59–95.

Pelling, C. 1997. "Conclusion." In *Greek Tragedy and the Historian*, edited by C. Pelling, 213–36. Oxford.

Penglase, C. 1994. *Greek Myths and Mesopotamia: Parallels and Influence in the Homeric Hymns and Hesiod*. London.

Petre, Z. 1992–94. "Aphrodite Pandemos." *StudClas* 28–30:5–14.

Pfeiffer, R. 1926. "Arsinoe Philadelphos in der Dichtung." *Die Antike* 2:161–74.

Picard, C. 1953. "Éros, Adonis et la date des Adonies d'Athènes." *RA* 61:200–202.

Piccaluga, G. 1974. "Adonis e i profumi di un certo strutturalismo." *Maia* 26:33–51.

———. 1977. "Adonis, i cacciatori falliti e l'avento dell'agricoltura." In *Il mito Greco*, edited by B. Gentili and G. Paioni, 33–48. Rome.

Pilitsis, G. 1985. "The Gardens of Adonis in Serres Today." *Journal of Modern Greek Studies* 3.2:145–66.

Pirenne-Delforge, V. 1988. "Epithètes cultuelles et interprétation philosophique: À propos d'Aphrodite Ourania et Pandémos à Athènes." *AC* 57:142–57.

———. 1994. *L'Aphrodite grecque: Contribution à l'étude de ses cultes et de sa personnalité dans le pantheon archaïque et classique. Kernos* supplement 4. Athens.

———. 2010a. "'Something to Do with Aphrodite': *Ta Aphrodisia* and the Sacred." In *A Companion to Greek Religion*, edited by D. Ogden, 311–23. Malden, MA.

———. 2010b. "Flourishing Aphrodite: An Overview." In *Brill's Companion to Aphrodite*, edited by A. Smith and S. Pickup, 3–16. Leiden.

Pironti, G. 2007. *Entre ciel et guerre: Figures d'Aphrodite en Grèce ancienne. Kernos* supplement 18. Liège.

———. 2010. "Rethinking Aphrodite as a Goddess at Work." In *Brill's Companion to Aphrodite*, edited by A. Smith and S. Pickup, 113–30. Leiden.

Pollitt, J. 1979. "Kernoi from the Athenian Agora." *Hesperia* 48.3:205–33.

Pomeroy, S. 1984. *Women in Hellenistic Egypt: From Alexander to Cleopatra*. New York.

Porter, J. R. 2003. "Orestes the Ephebe." In *Poetry, Theory, Praxis: The Social Life of Myth, Word, and Image in Ancient Greece*, edited by E. Csapo and M. C. Miller, 146–77. Oxford.

Powell, C. 1979. "Religion and the Sicilian Expedition." *Historia* 28.1:15–31.

Prauscello, L. 2006. "Looking for the 'Other' Gnesippus: Some Notes on Eupolis Fragment 148 K-A." *CP* 101.1:52–66.

Puchner, M. 2010. *The Drama of Ideas: Platonic Provocations in Theater and Philosophy.* New York.

Pütz, B. 2003. *The Symposium and Komos in Aristophanes.* Stuttgart.

Reckford, K. 1972. "Phaethon, Hippolytus, Aphrodite." *TAPA* 103:401–12.

———. 1987. *Aristophanes' Old and New Comedy.* Chapel Hill, NC.

Redfield, J. 1982. "Notes on the Greek Wedding." *Arethusa* 15:181–201.

———. 2003. *The Locrian Maidens: Love and Death in Greek Italy.* Princeton, NJ.

Reed, J. 1995. "The Sexuality of Adonis." *CA* 14.2:317–347.

———. 1996. "Antimachus on Adonis?" *Hermes* 124.3:381–83.

———. 1997. *Bion of Smyrna: The Fragments and the Adonis.* Cambridge Classical Texts and Commentaries 33. Cambridge.

———. 2000. "Arsinoe's Adonis and the Poetics of Ptolemaic Imperialism." *TAPA* 130:319–51.

———. 2002. "At Play with Adonis." In *Vertis in usum: Studies in Honor of Edward Courtney,* edited by J. F. Miller, C. Damon, and K. S. Myers, 219–22. Beiträge zur Altertumskunde 161. Leipzig.

———. 2005. "The Fruits of Adonis." *Philologus* 149:362–64.

———. 2006. "New Verses on Adonis." *ZPE* 158:76–82.

Reeder, E., ed. 1995. *Pandora: Women in Classical Greece.* Baltimore.

Rehm, R. 1994. *Marriage to Death: The Conflation of Wedding and Funeral Rituals in Greek Tragedy.* Princeton, NJ.

Reilly, J. 1989. "Many Brides: 'Mistress and Maid' on Athenian Lekythoi." *Hesperia* 58:411–44.

Reitzammer, L. 2008. "Aristophanes' *Adôniazousai.*" *CA* 27.2:282–333.

———. 2016. "Euripides' *Bacchae* and Athenian Religion." In *The Blackwell Companion to Euripides,* edited by L. McClure.

Revermann, M. 2006. *Comic Business: Theatricality, Dramatic Technique, and Performance Contexts of Aristophanic Comedy.* Oxford.

Rhodes, P. J., and R. Osborne, eds. 2007. *Greek Historical Inscriptions 404–323 BC.* Oxford.

Ribichini, S. 1979. "Per una riconsiderazione di Adonis." *RStudFen* 7:163–74.

———. 1981. *Adonis: Aspetti orientali di un mito greco.* Studi Semitici 55. Rome.

Rice, E. E. 1983. *The Grand Procession of Ptolemy Philadelphus.* Oxford.

Richter, G., and L. Hall. 1936. *Red-Figured Athenian Vases in the Metropolitan Museum of Art.* New Haven, CT.

Riedweg, C. 1987. *Mysterienterminologie bei Platon, Philon, und Klemens von Alexandrien.* Untersuchungen zur antiken Literatur und Geschichte 26. Berlin.

Riginos, A. S. 1976. *Platonica: The Anecdotes concerning the Life and Writings of Plato.* Leiden.

Robertson, N. 1982. "The Ritual Background of the Dying God in Cyprus and Syro-Palestine." *HThR* 75.3:313–59.

Robin, L. 1933a. *La Théorie platonicienne de l'amour.* Paris.

———, ed. (1933b) 1966. *Platon: Phèdre.* Paris.

Robinson, D., and E. Fluck. 1937. *A Study of the Greek Love-Names*. Baltimore.

Rochette, R. 1851. *Mémoire sur les Jardins d'Adonis*. *RA* 8:97–123.

Rogers, B. B. 1911. *The Lysistrata of Aristophanes*. Vol. 4. The Comedies of Aristophanes. London.

Roller, L. 1988. "Foreign Cults in Greek Vase Painting." In *Proceedings of the Third Symposium on Ancient Greek and Related Pottery*, edited by J. Christiansen and T. Melander, 506–15. Copenhagen.

Rose, H. J. 1924. "Anchises and Aphrodite." *CQ* 18:11–16.

Roselli, D. 2002. "Gender and Class in Athenian Material and Theater Culture." PhD diss., University of Toronto.

Rosenmeyer, P. 2004. "Girls at Play in Early Greek Poetry." *AJP* 125.2:163–78.

Rosenmeyer, T. G. 1962. "Plato's Prayer to Pan (*Phaedrus* 279b8–c3)." *Hermes* 90.1:34–44.

Rosenzweig, R. 2004. *Worshipping Aphrodite: Art and Cult in Classical Athens*. Ann Arbor, MI.

Rosivach, V. 1987. "Autochthony and the Athenians." *CQ* 37.2:294–306.

Rowe, C. J., ed. 1986. *Plato: Phaedrus*. Warminster.

Rubensohn, O. 1898. "Kerchnos." *AthMitt* 23:271–306.

Rudhardt, J. 1975. "Quelques notes sur les cultes chypriotes, en particulier sur celui d'Aphrodite." In *Chypre des origines au moyen âge*, edited by D. Van Berchem, 109–54. Geneva.

———. 1999. *Thémis et les Hôrai: Recherches sur les divinités grecques de la justice et de la paix*. Geneva.

Rusten, J. S., ed. 1989. *Thucydides: The Peloponnesian War, Book 2*. Cambridge Greek and Latin Classics. Cambridge.

Rutherford, I. 1994–95. "Apollo in Ivy: The Tragic Paean." *Arion* 3.1:112–35.

Sabetái, V. 1993. "The Washing Painter: A Contribution to the Wedding and Genre Iconography in the Second Half of the Fifth Century." PhD diss., University of Cincinnati.

———. 1997. "Aspects of Nuptial and Genre Imagery in Fifth-Century Athens: Issues of Interpretation and Methodology." In *Athenian Potters and Painters*, edited by J. H. Oakley, W. D. E. Coulsen, and O. Palagiá, 319–35. Oxford.

Salapata, G. 2001. "An Exceptional Pair of Terracotta Arulae from South Italy." In *Studia Varia from the J. Paul Getty Museum*, 25–50. Malibu, CA.

———. 2002. "The Apulian 'Sistrum': Monotone or Melodic?" In *The Archaeology of Sound: Origin and Organisation*, edited by E. Hickmann, A. Kilmer, and R. Eichmann, 415–28. Rahden/Westfalen.

Schaps, D. M. 1977. "The Woman Least Mentioned: Etiquette and Women's Names." *CQ* 27:323–30.

Schein, S. 1984. *The Mortal Hero: An Introduction to Homer's "Iliad."* Berkeley, CA.

———. 2012. "Divine and Human in the Homeric Hymn to Aphrodite." In *Les hymnes de la Grèce antique: Entre littérature et histoire; Maison de l'Orient et de la Méditerranée*, edited by R. Bouchon, P. Brillet-Dubois, and N. Le Meur-Weissman, 295–312. Lyon.

Schibli, H. S. 1990. *Pherekydes of Syros*. Oxford.

Schlesier, R. 1993. "Mixtures of Masks: Maenads as Tragic Models." In *Masks of Dionysus*, edited by T. H. Carpenter and C. A. Faraone, 89–114. Ithaca, NY.

Scullion, S. 1998. "Dionysos and Katharsis in *Antigone*." *CA* 17:96–122.

———. 1999–2000. "Tradition and Invention in Euripidean Aitiology." *Illinois Classical Studies* 24–25:217–33.

———. 2013. "Maenads and Men." Oxford. Available at http://www.classics.ox.ac.uk/tl_files/Downloads/Maenads-and-Men.pdf.

Seaford, R. 1987. "The Tragic Wedding." *JHS* 107:106–30.

———. 1990. "The Imprisonment of Women in Greek Tragedy." *JHS* 110:76–90.

———. 1993. "Dionysus as Destroyer of the Household: Homer, Tragedy, and the *Polis*." In *Masks of Dionysus*, edited by T. H. Carpenter and C. A. Faraone, 115–46. Ithaca, NY.

———. 1994. *Reciprocity and Ritual: Homer and Tragedy in the Developing City-State*. Oxford.

———. 2009. "Aitiologies of Cult in Euripides: A Response to Scott Scullion." In *The Play of Texts and Fragments: Essays in Honour of Martin Cropp*, edited by J. R. C. Cousland and J. R. Hume, 221–34. Leiden.

Segal, C. 1974. "The Homeric Hymn to Aphrodite: A Structuralist Approach." *CW* 67:205–12.

———. 1981. *Poetry and Myth in Ancient Pastoral*. Princeton, NJ.

———. (1982) 1997. *Dionysiac Poetics and Euripides' "Bacchae."* Expanded ed. with a new afterword by the author. Princeton, NJ.

Selden, D. 1998. "Alibis." *CA* 17.2:289–412.

Servais, J. 1984. "La date des Adonies d'Athènes et l'expédition de Sicile." In *Adonis: Relazioni del colloquio in Roma*, edited by S. Ribichini, 83–93. Rome.

Servais-Soyez, B. 1981. *LIMC* 1, s.v. "Adonis."

———. 1983. "Aphrodite Ouranie et le symbolisme de l'échelle: Un message venu d'Orient." In *Le Mythe, son langage et son message: Colloque de Liège et Louvain-la-Neuve 1981*, edited by H. Limet and J. Ries, 191–207.

———. 1984. "Musique et Adonies: Apport archéologique à la connaissance du rituel adonidien." In *Adonis: Relazioni del colloquio in Roma*, edited by S. Ribichini, 61–72. Rome.

Shapiro, H. A. 1985. "Greek Bobbins: A New Interpretation." *Ancient World* 15:115–20.

———. 1986. "The Origins of Allegory in Greek Art." *Boreas* 9:4–23.

———. 1992. "Eros in Love: Pederasty and Pornography in Greece." In *Pornography and Representation in Greece and Rome*, edited by A. Richlin, 53–72. Oxford.

———. 1993. *Personifications in Greek Art: The Representation of Abstract Concepts, 600–400 BC*. Zürich.

Simms, R. 1985. "Foreign Religious Cults in Athens in the Fifth and Fourth Centuries B.C." PhD diss., University of Virginia.

———. 1997. "A Date with Adonis." *Antichthon* 31:45–53.

———. 1997–98. "Mourning and Community at the Athenian Adonia." *CJ* 93.2:121–41.

Simon, E. 1972. "Aphrodite und Adonis—eine neuerworbene Pyxis in Würzburg." *Antike Kunst* 15:20–26.

———. 1983. *Festivals of Attica: An Archaeological Commentary.* Madison, WI.

Simon, E., M. Hirmer, and A. Hirmer. 1981. *Die griechischen Vasen.* 2nd ed. Munich.

Slater, N. W. 1986. "The Lenaean Theatre." *ZPE* 66:255–64.

———. 2002. *Spectator Politics: Metatheatre and Performance in Aristophanes.* Philadelphia.

Smith, A. 2011. *Polis and Personification in Classical Athenian Art.* Leiden.

———. 2012. "Personification: Not Just a Symbolic Mode." In *A Companion to Greek Art,* edited by T. J. Smith and D. Plantzos, 440–55. Oxford.

Smith, J. Z. 1990. *Drudgery Divine: On the Comparison of Early Christianities and the Religions of Late Antiquity.* London.

Smith, M. S. 1998. "The Death of 'Dying and Rising Gods' in the Biblical World: An Update, with Special Reference to Baal in the Baal Cycle." *Scandinavian Journal of the Old Testament* 12.2:257–313.

Sokolowski, F. 1964. "Aphrodite as Guardian of Greek Magistrates." *HThR* 51:1–8.

———. 1969. *Lois Sacrées des cités grecques.* Paris.

Sommerstein, A. 1977. "Aristophanes and the Events of 411." *JHS* 97:122–126.

———. 1980. "The Naming of Women in Greek and Roman Comedy." *QS* 11:393–418.

———, ed. 1989. *Aeschylus: Eumenides.* Cambridge Greek and Latin Classics. Cambridge.

Sourvinou-Inwood, C. 1978. "Persephone and Aphrodite at Locri: A Model for Personality Definitions in Greek Religion." *JHS* 98:101–21.

———. 1987. "A Series of Erotic Pursuits: Images and Meanings." *JHS* 107:131–53.

———. 1991. *"Reading" Greek Culture: Texts and Image, Rituals and Myths.* Oxford.

Soyez, B. 1977. *Byblos et la fête des Adonies.* Leiden.

Stafford, E. 1997. "A Wedding Scene? Notes on Akropolis 6471." *JHS* 117:200–202.

———. 2000. *Worshipping Virtues: Personification and the Divine in Ancient Greece.* Swansea.

Stafford, E., and J. Herrin, eds. 2005. *Personification in the Greek World.* Aldershot.

Stallybrass, P., and A. White. 1986. *The Politics and Poetics of Transgression.* Ithaca, NY.

Stears, K. 1995. "Dead Women's Society: Constructing Female Gender in Classical Athenian Funerary Sculpture." In *Time, Tradition, and Society in Greek Archaeology: Bridging the "Great Divide,"* edited by N. Spencer, 109–31. New York.

———. 1998. "Death Becomes Her: Gender and Athenian Death Ritual." In *The Sacred and the Feminine in Ancient Greece,* edited by S. Blundell and M. Williamson, 89–100. London.

Stehle, E. 1996. "Sappho's Gaze: Fantasies of a Goddess and a Young Man." In *Reading Sappho,* edited by E. Greene, 193–225. Berkeley, CA.

———. 1997. *Performance and Gender in Ancient Greece: Nondramatic Poetry in Its Setting.* Princeton, NJ.

Steiner, D. T. 1994. *The Tyrant's Writ: Myths and Images of Writing in Ancient Greece.* Princeton, NJ.

Stephens, S. 2003. *Seeing Double: Intercultural Poetics in Ptolemaic Alexandria.* Berkeley, CA.

Stewart, A. 1995. "Rape?" In *Pandora: Women in Classical Greece*, edited by E. Reeder, 74–90. Baltimore.

———. 1997. *Art, Desire, and the Body*. Cambridge.

Stroup, S. 2004. "Designing Women: Aristophanes' *Lysistrata* and the 'Hetairization' of the Greek Wife." *Arethusa* 37.1:37–74.

Sulze, H. 1930. "Ἀδώνιδος κῆποι." *Angelos* 3:44–52.

Suter, A., ed. 2008. *Lament: Studies in the Ancient Mediterranean and Beyond*. Oxford.

Sutton, R. 1992. "Pornography and Persuasion on Attic Pottery." In *Pornography and Representation in Greece and Rome*, edited by A. Richlin, 3–35. Oxford.

———. 1997–98. "Nuptial Eros: The Visual Discourse of Marriage in Classical Athens." *Journal of the Walters Art Gallery* 55–56:27–48.

Swift, L. 2006. "Mixed Choruses and Marriage Songs: A New Interpretation of the Third Stasimon of the Hippolytus." *JHS* 126:125–40.

———. 2010. *The Hidden Chorus: Echoes of Genre in Tragic Lyric*. Oxford.

Taaffe, L. 1993. *Aristophanes and Women*. London.

Taplin, O. 1975. "The Title of Prometheus Desmotes." *JHS* 95:184–86.

———. 1977. *The Stagecraft of Aeschylus*. Oxford.

Thomas, R. 1989. *Oral Tradition and Written Record in Classical Athens*. Cambridge.

Thompson, D. W. 1947. *A Glossary of Greek Fishes*. London.

Thompson, W. H. 1868. *The "Phaedrus" of Plato*. London.

Tod, M. N. 1948. *A Selection of Greek Historical Inscriptions*. Oxford.

Todd, S. C. 2007. *A Commentary on Lysias Speeches 1–11*. Oxford.

Topper, K. 2007. "Perseus, the Maiden Medusa, and the Imagery of Abduction." *Hesperia* 76.1:73–105.

———. 2012a. "Approaches to Reading Attic Vases." In *A Companion to Women in the Ancient World*, edited by S. James and S. Dillon, 141–52. Malden, MA.

———. 2012b. *The Imagery of the Athenian Symposium*. Cambridge.

Travlos, J. 1971. *Pictorial Dictionary*. London.

Treister, M. 1999. "Some Classical Subjects on Sarmatian Phalerae." In *Ancient Greeks West and East*, edited by G. R. Tsetskhaldze, 567–605. Leiden.

Tsagalis, C. 2004. *Epic Grief: Personal Laments in Homer's "Iliad."* Berlin.

Tsakmakis, A. 2012. "Persians, Oligarchs, and Festivals: The Date of the *Lysistrata* and *Thesmophoriazusae*." In *Crisis on Stage: Tragedy and Comedy in Late Fifth-Century Athens*, edited by A. Markantonatos and B. Zimmermann, 291–302. Berlin.

Turner, M. 2005. "Aphrodite and Her Birds: The Iconology of Pagenstecher Lekythoi." *BICS* 48:57–96.

Tuzet, H. 1987. *Mort et résurrection d'Adonis: Étude de l'évolution d'un mythe*. Paris.

Van Leeuwen, J. 1903. *Aristophanis Lysistrata*. Leiden.

Van Straten, F. T. 1995. *Hiera Kala: Images of Animal Sacrifice in Archaic and Classical Greece*. Leiden.

Vannicelli, P. 2002. "'Moritur et ridet': Indizi di logos epitaphios nella 'Lisistrata' di Aristofane." *QUCC* 72.3:63–72.

Vérilhac, A. M. 1998. *Le mariage grec. Du VIe siècle av. J. C. à l'époque d'Auguste.*" *BCH* supplement 32. Paris.

Vermaseren, M. J. 1983. *Corpus Cultus Iovis Sabazii.* Vol. 1, *The Hands.* Leiden.

Vermeule, E. 1979. *Aspects of Death in Early Greek Art and Poetry.* Berkeley, CA.

Vernant, J.-P. 1985. "Le Dionysos masqué des *Bacchantes* d'Euripide." *L'homme* 93:31–58 (= Vernant and Vidal-Naquet 1986, 237–70).

———. 1988. *Myth and Society in Ancient Greece.* New York.

Vernant, J.-P., and P. Vidal-Naquet. 1986. *Mythe et tragédie: Deux.* Paris.

Versnel, H. S. 1990. *Inconsistencies in Greek and Roman Religion.* 2 vols. Leiden.

———. 2011. *Coping with the Gods: Wayward Readings in Greek Theology.* Leiden.

Walton, F. R. 1938. "The Date of the Adonia at Athens." *HThR* 31.1:65–72.

Watzinger, C. 1928. "Adonisfest." In *Antike Plastik: Walther Amelung zum sechzigsten Geburtstag,* 261–66. Berlin.

Webster, T. B. L. 1967. *The Tragedies of Euripides.* London.

Wehgartner, I. 1987. "Das Ideal maßvoller Liebe auf einem attischen Vasenbild." *Le Journal des librairies* 102:185–97.

Weill, N. 1966. "Adoniazousai ou les femmes sur le toit." *BCH* 90:664–98.

———. 1970. "La Fête d'Adonis dans la *Samienne* de Ménandre." *BCH* 94:591–93.

West, M. L. 1970. "Burning Sappho." *Maia* 22:307–30.

———, ed. 1978. *Hesiod: Works and Days.* Oxford.

———. 1992. *Ancient Greek Music.* Oxford.

———. 1994. "Ab Ovo." *CQ* 44:289–307.

———. 1997. *The East Face of Helicon: West Asiatic Elements in Greek Poetry and Myth.* Oxford.

———. 2001. "Some Homeric Words." *Glotta* 77:118–35.

———. 2003. *Homeric Hymns, Homeric Apocrypha, Lives of Homer.* London.

———. 2005. "The New Sappho." *ZPE* 151:1–9.

Westlake, H. D. 1980. "The *Lysistrata* and the War." *Phoenix* 34.1:38–54.

White, C. H. 1981. "Theocritus' Adonis Song." *MPhL* 4:191–206.

White, S. 2000. "Socrates at Colonus: A Hero for the Academy." In *Reason and Religion in Socratic Philosophy,* edited by N. D. Smith and P. B. Woodruff, 151–75. Oxford.

Wilamowitz-Moellendorff, U. von. 1919. *Platon.* Vol. 1. Berlin.

———, ed. 1927. *Aristophanes: Lysistrate.* Berlin.

Williamson, M. 1995. *Sappho's Immortal Daughters.* Cambridge.

Wilson, N. G. 1982. "Two Observations on Aristophanes' *Lysistrata.*" *GRBS* 23:157–61.

Wilson, P. 2000. *The Athenian Institution of the "Khoregia": The Chorus, the City, and the Stage.* Cambridge.

Winkler, J. J. 1990. *The Constraints of Desire: The Anthropology of Sex and Gender in Ancient Greece.* New York.

Wohl, V. 2002. *Love among the Ruins: The Erotics of Democracy in Classical Athens.* Princeton, NJ.

Wycherley, R. E. 1963. "The Scene of Plato's *Phaidros.*" *Phoenix* 17.2:88–98.

Yatromanolakis, D. 2001. "Visualizing Poetry: An Early Representation of Sappho." *CP* 96.2:159–167.

Yatromanolakis, D., and P. Roilos, eds. 2004. *Greek Ritual Poetics*. Washington, DC.

Yunis, H., ed. 2011. *Plato: Phaedrus*. Cambridge Greek and Latin Classics. Cambridge.

Zaccagnino, C. 1998. *Il thymiaterion nel mondo Greco: Analisi delle fonti, tipologia, impieghi*. Rome.

Zarkadas, A. P. 1989. "Μία παράσταση των Αδωνίων στη λήκυθο 6471 του Μουσείου της Ακροπόλεως." *Horos* 7:137–43.

Zeitlin, F. 1986. "Configurations of Rape in Greek Myth." In *Rape*, edited by S. Tomaselli and R. Porter, 122–51. Oxford.

———. 1990. "Thebes: Theater of Self and Society in Athenian Drama." In *Nothing to Do with Dionysos: Athenian Drama in Its Social Context*, edited by F. Zeitlin and J. Winkler, 130–67. Princeton, NJ.

———. 1996. *Playing the Other: Gender and Society in Classical Greek Literature*. Chicago.

Zellner, H. 2006. "Sappho's Supra-Superlatives." *CQ* 56:292–97.

Ziolkowski, J. 1981. *Thucydides and the Tradition of Funeral Speeches at Athens*. New York.

Index

Page numbers in italic refer to illustrations.

Index

Index

Index Locorum

WISCONSIN STUDIES IN CLASSICS

Laura McClure, Mark Stansbury-O'Donnell, and Matthew Roller

Series Editors

Romans and Barbarians: The Decline of the Western Empire
E. A. Thompson

A History of Education in Antiquity
H. I. Marrou
Translated from the French by George Lamb

Accountability in Athenian Government
Jennifer Tolbert Roberts

Festivals of Attica: An Archaeological Commentary
Erika Simon

Roman Cities: Les villes romaines
Pierre Grimal
Edited and translated by G. Michael Woloch

Ancient Greek Art and Iconography
Edited by Warren G. Moon

Greek Footwear and the Dating of Sculpture
Katherine Dohan Morrow

The Classical Epic Tradition
John Kevin Newman

Ancient Anatolia: Aspects of Change and Cultural Development
Edited by Jeanny Vorys Canby, Edith Porada, Brunilde Sismondo Ridgway, and Tamara Stech

Euripides and the Tragic Tradition
Ann Norris Michelini

Wit and the Writing of History: The Rhetoric of Historiography in Imperial Rome
Paul Plass

The Archaeology of the Olympics: The Olympics and Other Festivals in Antiquity
Edited by Wendy J. Raschke

Tradition and Innovation in Late Antiquity
Edited by F. M. Clover and R. S. Humphreys

The Hellenistic Aesthetic
Barbara Hughes Fowler

Hellenistic Sculpture I: The Styles of ca. 331–200 B.C.
Brunilde Sismondo Ridgway

Hellenistic Poetry: An Anthology
Selected and translated by Barbara Hughes Fowler

Theocritus' Pastoral Analogies: The Formation of a Genre
Kathryn J. Gutzwiller

Rome and India: The Ancient Sea Trade
Edited by Vimala Begley and Richard Daniel De Puma

Kallimachos: The Alexandrian Library and the Origins of Bibliography
Rudolf Blum
Translated by Hans H. Wellisch

Myth, Ethos, and Actuality: Official Art in Fifth Century B.C. Athens
David Castriota

Archaic Greek Poetry: An Anthology
Selected and translated by Barbara Hughes Fowler

Murlo and the Etruscans: Art and Society in Ancient Etruria
Edited by Richard Daniel De Puma and Jocelyn Penny Small

The Wedding in Ancient Athens
John H. Oakley and Rebecca H. Sinos

The World of Roman Costume
Edited by Judith Lynn Sebesta and Larissa Bonfante

Greek Heroine Cults
Jennifer Larson

Flinders Petrie: A Life in Archaeology
Margaret S. Drower

Polykleitos, the Doryphoros, and Tradition
Edited by Warren G. Moon

The Game of Death in Ancient Rome: Arena Sport and Political Suicide
Paul Plass

Polygnotos and Vase Painting in Classical Athens
Susan B. Matheson

Worshipping Athena: Panathenaia and Parthenon
Edited by Jenifer Neils

Hellenistic Architectural Sculpture: Figural Motifs in Western Anatolia and the Aegean Islands
Pamela A. Webb

Fourth-Century Styles in Greek Sculpture
Brunilde Sismondo Ridgway

Ancient Goddesses: The Myths and the Evidence
Edited by Lucy Goodison and Christine Morris

Displaced Persons: The Literature of Exile from Cicero to Boethius
Jo-Marie Claassen

Hellenistic Sculpture II: The Styles of ca. 200–100 B.C.
Brunilde Sismondo Ridgway

Personal Styles in Early Cycladic Sculpture
Pat Getz-Gentle

The Complete Poetry of Catullus
Catullus
Translated and with commentary by David Mulroy

Hellenistic Sculpture III: The Styles of ca. 100–31 B.C.
Brunilde Sismondo Ridgway

The Iconography of Sculptured Statue Bases in the Archaic and Classical Periods
Angeliki Kosmopoulou

Discs of Splendor: The Relief Mirrors of the Etruscans
Alexandra A. Carpino

Mail and Female: Epistolary Narrative and Desire in Ovid's "Heroides"
Sara H. Lindheim

Modes of Viewing in Hellenistic Poetry and Art
Graham Zanker

Religion in Ancient Etruria
Jean-René Jannot
Translated by Jane K. Whitehead

A Symposion of Praise: Horace Returns to Lyric in "Odes" IV
Timothy Johnson

Satire and the Threat of Speech: Horace's "Satires," Book 1
Catherine M. Schlegel

Prostitutes and Courtesans in the Ancient World
Edited by Christopher A. Faraone and Laura K. McClure

Asinaria: The One about the Asses
Plautus
Translated and with commentary by John Henderson

Ulysses in Black: Ralph Ellison, Classicism, and African American Literature
Patrice D. Rankine

Imperium and Cosmos: Augustus and the Northern Campus Martius
Paul Rehak
Edited by John G. Younger

Ovid before Exile: Art and Punishment in the "Metamorphoses"
Patricia J. Johnson

Pandora's Senses: The Feminine Character of the Ancient Text
Vered Lev Kenaan

Nox Philologiae: Aulus Gellius and the Fantasy of the Roman Library
Erik Gunderson

New Perspectives on Etruria and Early Rome
Edited by Sinclair Bell and Helen Nagy

The Image of the Poet in Ovid's "Metamorphoses"
Barbara Pavlock

Responses to Oliver Stone's "Alexander": Film, History, and Cultural Studies
Edited by Paul Cartledge and Fiona Rose Greenland

The Codrus Painter: Iconography and Reception of Athenian Vases in the Age of Pericles
Amalia Avramidou

The Matter of the Page: Essays in Search of Ancient and Medieval Authors
Shane Butler

Greek Prostitutes in the Ancient Mediterranean, 800 BCE–200 CE
Edited by Allison Glazebrook and Madeleine M. Henry

Sophocles' "Philoctetes" and the Great Soul Robbery
Norman Austin

Oedipus Rex
Sophocles
A verse translation by David Mulroy, with introduction and notes

The Slave in Greece and Rome
John Andreau and Raymond Descat
Translated by Marion Leopold

Perfidy and Passion: Reintroducing the "Iliad"
Mark Buchan

The Gift of Correspondence in Classical Rome: Friendship in Cicero's "Ad Familiares" and Seneca's "Moral Epistles"
Amanda Wilcox

Antigone
Sophocles
A verse translation by David Mulroy, with introduction and notes

Aeschylus's "Suppliant Women": The Tragedy of Immigration
Geoffrey W. Bakewell

Couched in Death: "Klinai" and Identity in Anatolia and Beyond
Elizabeth P. Baughan

Silence in Catullus
Benjamin Eldon Stevens

Odes
Horace
Translated with commentary by David R. Slavitt

Shaping Ceremony: Monumental Steps and Greek Architecture
Mary B. Hollinshead

Selected Epigrams
Martial
Translated with notes by Susan McLean

The Offense of Love: "Ars Amatoria," "Remedia Amoris," and "Tristia" 2
Ovid
A verse translation by Julia Dyson Hejduk, with introduction and notes

Oedipus at Colonus
Sophocles
A verse translation by David Mulroy, with introduction and notes

Women in Roman Republican Drama
Edited by Dorota Dutsch, Sharon L. James, and David Konstan

Dream, Fantasy, and Visual Art in Roman Elegy
Emma Scioli

Agamemnon
Aeschylus
A verse translation by David Mulroy, with introduction and notes

Trojan Women, Helen, Hecuba: Three Plays about Women and the Trojan War
Euripides
Verse translations by Francis Blessington, with introductions and notes

Echoing Hylas: A Study in Hellenistic and Roman Metapoetics
Mark Heerink

Horace between Freedom and Slavery: The First Book of "Epistles"
Stephanie McCarter

The Play of Allusion in the "Historia Augusta"
David Rohrbacher

Repeat Performances: Ovidian Repetition and the "Metamorphoses"
Edited by Laurel Fulkerson and Tim Stover

Virgil and Joyce: Nationalism and Imperialism in the "Aeneid" and "Ulysses"
Randall J. Pogorzelski

The Athenian Adonia in Context: The Adonis Festival as Cultural Practice
Laurialan Reitzammer

www.ingramcontent.com/pod-product-compliance
Lightning Source LLC
LaVergne TN
LVHW010606100826
845148LV00014B/2875

* 9 7 8 0 2 9 9 3 0 8 2 4 7 *